Praise for *Cosmodeism*

"Tsvi Bisk has written a thought-provoking book that turns our theological thinking upside-down. Instead of God creating the universe, he argues the universe is creating God, or at least what to our infant consciousness would appear to be gods. It may seem far out, but it is an idea that converges with many thinkers, past and present. The implications of this worldview for traditional and future religions, as well as society at large, are profound. Perhaps the universe is not meaningless after all and cosmic evolution is leading us somewhere. The arguments are all here in this fascinating and readable book."

—Dr. Steven J. Dick

Former NASA Chief Historian
Former Baruch S. Blumberg NASA/Library of Congress Chair in Astrobiology Author of Astrobiology, Discovery, and Societal Impact (Cambridge University Press, 2018)

COSMODEISM

A Worldview for the Space-Age
How an Evolutionary Cosmos is Creating God

TSVI BISK

Westphalia Press
An Imprint of the Policy Studies Organization
Washington, DC
2024

Westphalia Press
An imprint of Policy Studies Organization
1367 Connecticut Avenue NW
Washington, D.C. 20036
info@ipsonet.org

ISBN: 978-1-63723-648-2

Cover and interior design by Jeffrey Barnes
jbarnesbook.design

Daniel Gutierrez-Sandoval, Executive Director
PSO and Westphalia Press

Updated material and comments on this edition
can be found at the Westphalia Press website:
www.westphaliapress.org

Dedicated to

Mordechai Nessyahu

The Epitome of Unacknowledged Intellectual
Imagination and Courage

Acknowledgements

This book would never have been completed without two very important people. Firstly, my wife, Micaela Ziv, whose infinite patience, sense of humor and unconditional love enabled me to get through the daily frustrations of actually writing the damn thing. A very close second has been the persistent encouragement of my newest friend, Bernard Farkin, who has become a very important part of my life. I must also thank my very good friend Dr. Alon Ben Meir who championed my book to Westphalia Press as well as to Dr. Rahima Schwenkbeck, their Director of Publications, whose patience and good humor helped me limp through the final stages of preparation for final publication.

Table of Contents

Preface

IS THIS ALL THERE IS? This was a question that began to haunt me during puberty, when I began to daydream about what my life would be like when I was an adult. I would be rich, I would be President, I would be a sports hero or a patriot saving the republic and of course I would have a family: children, grandchildren, great grandchildren, AND THEN I WOULD DIE.

My eventual death dawned on me in Middle School when I realized that there was not much of a personal future past one's great grandchildren – AND THEN I WOULD DIE. I couldn't sleep for a week until my *Denial of Death* survival system kicked in and I simply ignored this inevitability in order to function. But ignoring it does not mean it goes away at some subliminal level. In a way it has haunted my entire life. It was difficult to take 11th grade algebra seriously, or getting a "good university education," a "good profession," a "good job" just so you could make enough money to retire comfortably while WAITING TO DIE. I hadn't yet heard of *Pascal's Despair*, written almost 400 years ago, but if I had it would have certainly resonated with me. Pascal wrote:

> When I consider the brief span of my life absorbed into the eternity which precedes and will succeed it ... the small space I occupy and which I see swallowed up in the infinite immensity of spaces of which I know nothing and which know nothing of me, I take fright and am amazed to see myself here rather than there: there is no reason for me to be here rather than there, now rather than then. Who put me here? By whose command and act were this place and time allotted to me?

Consequently, I was an indifferent student in high school and dropped out of two colleges before I was drafted into the American Army in 1965. I was a daydreamer and always in my own head and radiated such an air of melancholy that my own mother nicknamed me *Raskolnikov* (imagine what that can do to your self-image). IS THIS ALL THERE IS was a question that preoccupied my thinking. Or, as I rephrased it when an adult: "If there is no cosmic drama, what's the point?" Because if this is all there is within a meaningless cosmos what, indeed, is the point?

I finished my American army service in March 1967 and one week later I was on a plane to Europe. I wanted to clear my head; 1965 to 1967 had not been a good time to be in the American army. I hitchhiked through France, Spain, Morocco, Algeria, and Tunisia, into Sicily and up to Rome, and finally landed in Israel. This is an entire story, in and of itself, but only relevant here because this is where I met the Israeli thinker Mordechai Nessyahu who provided me with the intellectual foundations for what follows. My North African experience was particularly enlightening. The 1960s were characterized by a general disdain for western civilization (as materialistic, consumerist, mechanical, alienated, and artificial) along with a widespread infatuation with third-world cultures which were presumed to be authentic (i.e., not plastic), more human, and less mechanical. Well, to paraphrase Tolstoy's *bon mot* about the family, I learned that every culture is screwed up in its own way. Morocco was interesting, I won't deny that. But its grinding poverty (caused primarily by government mismanagement and corruption), cruelty to animals, nasty treatment of women and children, and superstition was well described in Orwell's brutally honest essay, *Marrakech*. The lack of toilet paper and modern dentistry provided me with a proper perspective on the benefits of having been born in a western country. Never again was I to be seduced by the clichéd drivel of anti-western "intellectuals." Progress was good, technical progress was good, period—my first comprehension of the spiritual implications of industrial society.

By modern standards, my formal academic qualifications for the following undertaking are few. Of course, by modern academic standards even Spinoza and Voltaire would have been dismissed as amateur dilettantes (modern academe does not much respect non-credentialed polymaths). However, might it not be the case that my wide-ranging, non-specialized learning has enabled me to get to the essence of the issues discussed here better than hyper-specialized academics? Writing the definitive book on neo-Kantianism's impact on 20th century Marxist thought might be good for someone's academic career and intellectual reputation, but what in the world would such an enterprise have to contribute to current day human society and culture as they are experienced on a daily basis? As Henry David Thoreau put it in *Walden*, "Nowadays [we have] professors of philosophy, but not philosophers .... To be a philosopher is to solve some of the problems of life not only theoretically but practically." I also rely on the wisdom of Professor John Lukacs to justify my own non-credentialed conceit. He wrote: "What is absurd and ridiculous is the idea that a historian cannot be a historian unless he has a Ph.D. in history: exactly as absurd as to say that every poet ought to have a Ph.D. in poetry."[1] Likewise, I don't feel the obligation to acquire a specialized Ph.D. to address the issues I am about to address, especially as I have no idea what university department would even entertain the subject of this book or what specialized Ph.D. would better prepare me for this task.

Lukacs was following in the footsteps of the distinguished American philosopher William James, who claimed the advantage of the generalist for himself in *The Varieties of Religious Experience*,[2] in which he disdainfully referred to academic "experts" as *intellectualists* (as opposed to true intellectuals). James did not favor professional experts in narrow fields of study who were so enclosed within the ideas and limitations of their own proficiencies that truly profound thinking was beyond their reach. James's philosophical antipode, Nietzsche, agreed. In *Beyond Good and Evil* he wrote:

> The extent and towering structure of the sciences have increased enormously, and therewith also the probability that the philosopher will grow tired even as a learner, or will attach himself somewhere and "specialize" ... he dreads the temptation to become a dilettante ... but the *genuine* philosopher ... lives "unphilosophically" and "unwisely," above all, *imprudently*, and feels the obligation and burden of a hundred attempts and temptations of life—he risks *himself* constantly, he plays *this* bad game.[3]

Nietzsche wrote "the extent and towering structure of the sciences ..." in the 19th century. What are we to say of the philosophers' dilemma in the 21st century? What risks and bad games must be played to really say something of significance for the human condition today? My conceit, in writing this book, is taking that risk and playing that game.

Notes

1   Lukacs, p. 37.

2   James, 2011, pp. 8-9.

3   Nietzsche, pp. 74-75.

Introduction: How an Evolving Cosmos is Creating God

"Not 'In the beginning God created the heavens and earth'
but in the end the Cosmos will have created God."
—Mordechai Nessyahu

"WHAT DOES IT ALL MEAN?" is the fundamental question of the human condition. This is the implicit question my late friend and mentor, Mordechai Nessyahu, asked throughout his intellectual career. It is the same question that all of humanity has asked since it became self-aware—conscious of its own consciousness, as it were. It is the question that has motivated all religious and philosophical speculation, scientific endeavor, artistic creativity, and entrepreneurial innovation throughout the ages. It is the question that we try to answer in order to rationalize our own existence. It is also the question that has generated the modern concepts of angst and alienation. The modern dilemma is that we are finding it increasingly difficult to rationalize our own existence and the subsequent feeling that it is all purposeless.

Nessyahu's response was to formulate what I now call *The Cosmodeistic Hypothesis* (CH). Einstein called these kinds of endeavors "thought experiments." The CH conjectures the Big Bang that created our Cosmos was a *local* event in an *infinite* Universe—a Universe that contains an infinite number of finite cosmoses. Here Nessyahu anticipated current scientific thinking regarding the multiverse by several decades, using pure deductive reasoning. As we shall see below, over the past several thousand years various philosophers, scientists, and religious thinkers had already come to the same conclusion (within the intellectual limits of their historical periods).

Nessyahu conjectured that our Cosmos is an evolutionary entity, in a perpetual process of ever-growing complexity, which has eventually produced conscious life, not as a negligible accident nor as a product of "creative evolution," but rather as a natural and inevitable product of cosmic evolution, similar to the formation of galaxies and black holes—ever-increasing complexification being the salient characteristic of an evolutionary Cosmos. The stage of this complexification that represents the *border* between non-life and life is still unknown to us, even as our understanding of the complexification of life grows daily by leaps and bounds. Likewise, the stage of this complexification represents the border between non-self-conscious life and self-conscious life; these two borders remain and are likely to remain for some time the two greatest challenges to science.

Nessyahu further conjectured that due to the evolutionary nature of cosmic development now being revealed by the *New Physics* and *New Cosmology*, it is statistically certain that untold numbers of conscious life forms (equivalent in self-awareness to human beings) have arisen throughout the Cosmos. It is as if conscious life has been sown as a cosmic genome throughout the Cosmos by the very process of cosmic evolution. A very small *percentage* (but large in number) of these conscious civilizations have expanded or eventually will expand throughout their own solar systems and eventually achieve interstellar exploratory capabilities. By doing so they will have had to have achieved new levels of consciousness: first, *supra-consciousness*, then *supra-supra consciousness*, then *supra-supra-supra consciousness* until a consciousness will have been created that would have appeared to us as if it were "God"—a universal conscious "being." Most of these pre-*supra*-conscious civilizations (of which we are one) will destroy themselves by failing to meet the challenges of their own nuclear stage of development or by ecological collapse or by a failure of collective will (or a combination of all three). But enough will have survived these challenges or will have developed by different means and thus be able to advance to a *supra-conscious* stage of development.

Nessyahu further postulated that a very, very small *percentage* (but also large in aggregate number, given the vastness of the Cosmos) of these pre-*supra*-conscious life forms will produce individuals who will conclude that they must strive to become part of this *Godding* of the Cosmos. (I have borrowed the term *Godding* from Rabbi David Cooper's book *God is a Verb* to describe this evolutionary progression and will expand on it below.) Nessyahu assumed this as part of what I would call "cosmic humility." He believed that if he had envisioned this concept, it is certain that other individual members of conscious life forms in the Cosmos would also have conceived of it. Nessyahu also assumed that many of these other individuals would be more politically astute than he in convincing their civilizations to pursue this ambition. This assumption is essentially ontological, a variation of the ontological argument for the existence of God. Since one cannot conceive of a concept related to cosmic evolution greater than the Cosmos evolving into a "God" and since the Cosmos is producing ever more complex constructs, most particularly consciousness itself as the salient characteristic inherent in this evolution, it is self-evident that a "God" would be the final stage of cosmic evolution. As we shall see below, numerous thinkers on our own planet throughout the ages have anticipated Nessyahu's conclusions—although without his force and specificity. The fact that so many rational thinkers on this one planet have increasingly become preoccupied with what Nessyahu called "the border between physics and metaphysics" lends credibility to his assumption that this preoccupation must be a general cosmic phenomenon of conscious civilizations on many other planets.

Nessyahu's final conjecture is that amongst those civilizations pursuing this ambition, an infinitesimal percentage (but also great in absolute number) will succeed in using science and technology to transcend their bodies, thus isolating and enhancing the most essential part of their "humanness"— their consciousness. They will in effect have become pure consciousness, or if you will, pure spirit expanding throughout the Cosmos. They will join with other so inclined cosmic civilizations eventually becoming one with the Cosmos. Arthur C. Clarke in *2001 A Space Odyssey* anticipated this with the kind of speculative imagination we should be cultivating in ourselves and in our children:

> ... evolution was driving toward new goals. The first ... had long since come to the limits of flesh and blood; as soon as their machines were better than their bodies it was time to move. First their brains, and then their thoughts alone, they transformed into shining new homes of metal and plastic. In these they roamed the stars. They no longer built spaceships; they were spaceships. But the age of the machine entities swiftly passed. In their ceaseless experimenting they had learned to store knowledge in the structure of space itself, and to preserve their thoughts for eternity in frozen lattices of light. They could become creatures of radiation, free at last from the tyranny of matter. Into pure energy, therefore, they presently transformed themselves ...[1]

The subsequent expansion of this higher consciousness throughout the Cosmos will be unfettered by physical limitations and eventually consciousness will fill the entire Cosmos. Consciousness will have become one with a Cosmos that has dissolved into pure radiation as an inevitable consequence of entropy. Thus, the Cosmos will become *in its entirety* a conscious universal being, i.e., the Cosmos will have become "God." Cosmodeism posits God as the *consequence* of the Cosmos and not as its *cause*. Not *in the beginning God created the Cosmos* but, in the end, *the evolving Cosmos will have created God*. The fateful question that every conscious civilization throughout the Cosmos must eventually address is: will we take part in this cosmic race for survival and strive to survive in the cosmic "End of Days" or will we choose to perish along with the rest of cosmic organization? Will we accept the limitations of our physicality, or will we try to transcend them?

Nessyahu did not see his hypothesis as a deterministic teleology but rather as a *volitional* teleology as it pertained to our human race. His hypothesis was rooted, however, in what one might term a neo-teleological interpretation of cosmic evolution. In other words, he claimed that certain cosmic developments were inevitable based on empirical scientific evidence and deductive logic as applied to that empirical scientific evidence. But it was completely dependent on the volitional decision of the conscious beings on this or any other planet if they wanted to take part in these cosmic developments, thus guaranteeing their "spiritual" survival well past the physical existence of their respective planets. In other words, according to Jewish tradition, "all is determined but human volition is given."[2] This would guarantee the cosmic significance of the billions of years of life on this planet. Failure to do so would degrade the cosmic significance of the entire evolutionary drama of life on this planet to nothing more than a statistical contribution to cosmic probability "striving" to become God. It would be a tragedy in the classical Greek sense of the word.

Theses of God as the consequence rather than the cause of the Cosmos are not novel. The 20th-century British Jewish philosopher Samuel Alexander championed this view in his book *Space, Time and Deity*. The Jesuit theologian/philosopher Teilhard de Chardin presented the idiosyncratic view that God was both the cause and the consequence (the *alpha* and *omega*) of cosmic existence and evolution. He saw the end of human history as pure consciousness becoming one with the *Alpha God* to create the *Omega God*. In his book *Technology and Cosmogenesis*, the Italian architect/philosopher Paolo Soleri, influenced by de Chardin, described how human technology would enable conscience life to evolve into "God." In his review of Dr. Ted Chu's extraordinary book *Human Purpose and Transhuman Potential: A Cosmic Vision for our Future Evolution*, philosophy professor Michael Zimmerman praises Chu's proposal that "humanity is not the pinnacle of evolution, but instead is a crucial phase in all-encompassing cosmic evolution, which can be understood as God in the making." Chu calls this development *The Cosmic Being*, or *CoBe*. Modern German literature and philosophy is rife with human ambition to be Godlike. As Robert Tucker points out in his book *Philosophy and Myth in Karl Marx*, "The movement of thought from Kant to Hegel revolved in a fundamental sense around the idea of man's self-realization as a godlike being, or alternatively as God."[3] History for Hegel was God realizing itself through the vehicle of man. This is the underlying implication of all Enlightenment thought. When we ask, "what will history say about us," we are really substituting history for God. What attracted Marx to Hegel and the use of his philosophy as his own philosophical infrastructure was that "he found in Hegel the idea that man is God."[4] Marx, of course was completely wrong when predicting that solving of the economic problem will make religious thinking superfluous. George Orwell, being closer to humanity as it is, rather than humanity as a Marxist historical abstraction, and despite his general hostility to religion (especially the Catholic variety), realized that solving the economic problem and liberating humanity from daily soul-destroying drudgery would make "religious" questions about the ultimate meaning of life even more acute. Orwell recognized that when people are only a few meals away from starvation they simply don't have the energy to ponder the meaning of life, while satiated people confronting the brute fact of their own existence are more likely to suffer from existential anxieties. It seems obvious to me that the growth of the psychology and self-improvement businesses, as well as numerous cults, parallel the growth in our standard of living.

Carl Becker, in his classic *The Heavenly City of the Eighteenth-Century Philosophers*, argued that the Enlightenment was simply a secularization of the search for the Godhead. Enlightenment thinkers called it "Natural Law" and wanted to base political organization on it. This has been the subtext of all western political theory from Hobbes onward—how to create political cosmos out of political chaos—i.e., to be godlike in terms of our own human society; a secular "hubris" that appalls fundamentalist religions across the globe, but which is essential to the identity of Western Civilization and to the Constitutionalism which has become the West's primary contribution to humankind in general. Nessyahu must be seen as a continuation of this Enlightenment tradition. His contribution was to base his thinking on a solid foundation of the most up-to-date cosmological thinking, framed by rigorous deductive logic and related to the present revolution in the human means of production (i.e., the spiritual potential inherent in modern technology). He was close to Paola Soleri's views even though he was completely unaware of Soleri's work, as he was of de Chardin and Alexander. He would have been exhilarated by Dr. Chu's arguments if he hadn't died 20 years before Dr. Chu published his book.

This book, therefore, presents a *neo-teleological* worldview that reflects the philosophical outlook of *Emergentism*, which is based on evolution as the grand paradigm of all of existence and not only as a descriptive explanation of the development of organic life alone. It reflects mathematician Roger Penrose's intuition "... that the universe has a purpose, it's not somehow just there by chance ..." and tries to fulfill Carl Sagan's wish for the emergence of a science-based religion; something that might be a necessary condition for humanity to build an extraterrestrial civilization as part of its next evolutionary advance. Sagan wrote: "A religion, old or new, that stressed the magnificence of the Universe as revealed by modern science might be able to draw forth reserves of reverence and awe hardly tapped by the conventional faiths."[5]

This book is a dangerous undertaking. I intend to sojourn on roads of inquiry with insufficient evidence because I believe we are at a point in our intellectual history where playing it safe is no longer an option. New audacious hypotheses and educated guesses must be risked. We can deal with the minutia of our present preoccupations without end, but this does not enhance our ability to confront the ultimate questions of the human condition in its confrontation with ultimate reality. In this respect I identify with Ernest Becker when he wrote in the Preface of *The Birth and Death of Meaning*: "This is an ambitious book. In these times there is hardly any point in writing just for the sake of writing: one has to want to do something really important."[6]

Doing something "really important" regarding ultimate questions of the human condition in confrontation with ultimate reality requires a certain amount of intellectual *chutzpah* and recklessness. But this is not a *New Age* book that celebrates the irrational and the mystical, or a science fiction book, the storyline of which violates the known laws of nature. It is a book that reflects an attitude of mind which celebrates the rational, the logical, the coherent, and the scientific. Science is as necessary to this enterprise as oxygen is to life. But science alone, while necessary, is not sufficient. Science cannot progress without informed intuition and educated guesses. I agree with Northrop Frye that we require an *educated imagination*. Pulitzer Prize winning biologist Edward O. Wilson would agree; he writes: "Without the stimulus and guidance of emotion, rational thought slows and disintegrates. The rational mind does not float above the irrational; it cannot free itself to engage in pure reason."[7] In contrast to Wilson I would have substituted *nonrational* for *irrational* and reworded to have said "The rational mind does not float above the *nonrational*, but rather is sustained by it." Emotions (love, friendship, empathy, etc.) might be nonrational but are not irrational. The sources of new ideas (intuition, inkling, insight, etc.) might be nonrational but they are not irrational.

Consequently, this book will deal with the cultural and spiritual implications of the Cosmodeistic Hypothesis as human civilization moves further out into the Cosmos—speculating how Cosmodeism might generate a new cultural energy to overcome the pessimistic malaise of postmodernism and, like Monotheism in the past, transform the course of human history. In short, it will try to envision the preliminary stages that human society must achieve in order to reach the final vision, and see how, by envisioning these preliminary stages, we might address and resolve the essential existential dilemmas of the human race in the 21st century.

The book is divided into two parts. Book One is entitled *Our Age of Discontent* and delineates the various crises of our civilization. Part I deals with *Our Existential Predicaments* and Part II with *Our Intellectual and Material Predicaments*. Book Two is entitled *Evolving Towards Homo Divinitas* and proposes what must be done to mitigate our various crises and provide ultimate meaning to the human condition. Part III, *Reclaiming a Heroic Vision of Human Potential*, presents a grand strategy of what has to be done in order to form the civilizational foundations of the ultimate project of creating God. Part IV is entitled *The Nessyahu Conjectures* (a bare bones summation of his comprehensive thinking) and Parts V and VI are a historical overview of the religious, philosophical, and scientific precursors to the *Cosmodeistic Hypothesis*.

A final word on my writing: I use references and footnotes to clarify, illustrate, and strengthen my own conclusions, not to justify my arguments to some invisible jury of academic peers. My references are just that—references—not authorities. I cherry pick what is amenable to me in any given thinker's worldview and reject what is not. I believe much of academic writing can be likened to a cow having four stomachs: constantly eating and re-gurgitating and eating again and regurgitating again the same material. I, on the other hand, intend to graze into entirely new spiritual and intellectual pastures. I am doing this on my own cognizance, completely unsupervised by the "adults" of the academy. This is essentially a first-person subjective journey that I alone am responsible for. It is my attempt to find a commu-nity of readers that have had or are having a similar existential journey as I have had.

Notes

1   Clark, 2001, p. 245.

2   In Jewish tradition the expression is: *HaKol Tsafui vey HaRashoot Netuna* (all is determined but human volition is given). Modern science has begun to give sanction to this view of reality: genomes are the given determining factor of nature; but epigenetics is the volitional giving factor. Quantum me-chanics claims that the "intention" of the observer also affects reality.

3   Tucker, p. 31.

4   Ibid., p. 75.

5   Sagan, p. 50.

6   Becker, E., 1971, p. vii.

7   Wilson, p. 123.

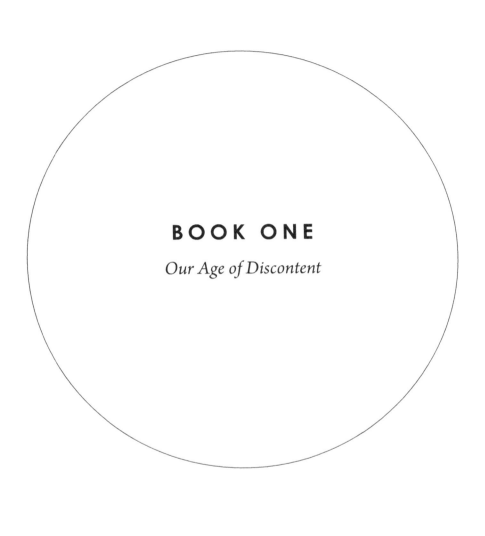

BOOK ONE

Our Age of Discontent

PART I

Existential Predicaments

"A human being is part of the whole called by us universe, a part limited in time and space .... Our task must be to free ourselves ... by widening our circle of compassion to embrace ... the whole of nature in its beauty .... We shall require a substantially new manner of thinking if mankind is to survive." —Albert Einstein

Chapter One: Our Modern Dilemmas

The Universal Dilemma

If there is no ultimate cosmic drama, what's the point? What's the point of our own individual, ephemeral lives on this small planet around a mediocre star in a midsized galaxy of some 300 billion stars whose closest galactic neighbor, *Andromeda* contains one trillion stars, in an "observable universe" that numbers two trillion galaxies (the largest of which contains 100 trillion stars)? Especially since scientists estimate that this "observable universe" is still only a tiny portion of the actual magnitude of the "universe" which may contain 500 trillion galaxies, and which might be an infinitesimal part of a *multiverse* containing trillions upon trillions of "universes."[1] If there really is a supernatural god (a god outside of nature that created nature), does she really care if the Jews on this particular inconsequential planet eat bacon, or Catholics go to confession, or Evangelicals accept Jesus as their personal savior, or Muslims make the Haj? One would think that executive responsibility for such a vast regime would preclude such detail-oriented supervision by the Supreme Being.

Increased awareness of the vastness of existence introduced an angst that humanity has never fully recovered from. *Pascal's Despair* was written in the 17th century. What gloom are we supposed to feel today when we know that "the infinite immensity of spaces" is immensely more immense? Never in history has Pascal's despair about his own insignificance been so relevant. Even within the narrow and cosmically insignificant history of our own planet, what is the real significance of our own lives? Consider that our planet is only 4.5 billion years old and that life on our planet roughly evolved as follows:

- 3.8 billion years ago simple cells appeared
- 3 billion years ago photosynthesis appeared
- 1 billion years ago multi-cellular life appeared
- 600 million years ago simple life forms appeared
- 550 million years ago complex life forms appeared
- 500 million years ago fish and proto amphibians appeared
- 475 million years ago land plants appeared
- 400 million years ago insects and seeds appeared
- 360 million years ago amphibians appeared
- 300 million years ago reptiles appeared
- 200 million years ago mammals appeared
- 150 million years ago birds appeared
- 130 million years ago flowers appeared
- 2.5 million years ago the genus Homo appeared
- 130,000 years ago, modern Homo Sapiens (us) appeared in Africa
- 6,000 years ago, recorded (written) human history began
- 550 years ago, the Renaissance
- 450 years ago, the Scientific Revolution
- 350 years ago, the Enlightenment and advent of Constitutionalism
- 250 years ago, the Industrial Revolution and advent of political movements

Modern human beings presently have an 80 to 90-year lifespan which will probably increase to the Biblical 120 years by the end of this century. What is that in relation to the "eternity" which preceded human civilization on this planet, and which will succeed it? Does the Cosmos really give a damn who is elected President of the United States? Indeed, does the Cosmos even "care" about the 3.8-billion-year history of life on this planet? Would it lament if runaway global warming turned our planet into another Venus? We live as if in the grand scheme of things our lives are significant. We want to "leave our mark." But when contemplating the time scale above, on the background of the vastness of the Universe, it is difficult not to plunge into Pascal's despair.

But what if we envision the *essence* of the Cosmos in an entirely different manner? What if we perceive that *evolution* is the eternal characteristic of our cosmic existence; the "Holy Spirit" of cosmic existence as such, if you will? What if, like Nessyahu, we perceive our Cosmos as a *finite* domain/process; an evolutionary entity created by the natural workings of *infinite* Nature creating ever higher levels of complexification (the inherent characteristic of existence itself); a cosmic "genome" with its own Cosmic Blueprint, in the words of Paul Davis, or its own Cosmic Code, in the words of Heinz Pagels? Consciousness has been a consequence of this evolutionary complexification, of these cosmic codes and blueprints. This is self-evident; after all *we* do exist. Logically, it should be hard to refute the assumption that we Homo Sapiens are not the last stage in the evolution of conscious life; that consciousness itself is constantly evolving and, thus, that it is inevitable that consciousness will *eventually* evolve into supra-consciousness and then into supra-supra consciousness at various places in the Cosmos. This assumes that evolution is as eternal as existence itself; that eternity and existence is one and the same thing: existence/eternity being the definitive space/time. This evolutionary process will continue until a consciousness is created that will appear to us as if it were a god; the *Godding of the Cosmos* being an inherent characteristic of the Cosmos's very evolutionary existence.

The question then becomes: what if we conscious Homo Sapiens perceive that we are an integral and vital part of this cosmic evolution; that what our species does on this planet will contribute to or detract from this process; that what we do as individuals will contribute to or detract from this process; that our own individual lives have cosmic consequence no matter how *infinitesimally* small (much like the butterfly effect of chaos theory)—that the very chaos of our existence is the vital ingredient creating the cosmos (order) of existence as such?

This is to place the emergence of self-reflective consciousness at the center of the cosmic drama, to affirm that while the Cosmos, as such, is not teleological and has no purpose (i.e., that it does not represent a planned *supernatural* religious drama with a specific end), cosmic purpose *has been created* as a consequence of the evolutionary cosmic process. This might be termed a neo-teleological interpretation of existence. The civilizational consequences of a widespread acceptance of this worldview would be as profound as those of Monotheism. Would not such a comprehension be the proper antidote to Pascal's despair? These are the *Nessyahu Conjectures*.

He called his philosophy *Cosmotheism*, which I have renamed *Cosmodeism* for various reasons. Foremost among them that *theism* conjures up an image of a supernatural god (outside of nature and natural laws) while *deism* places the concept within the tradition of natural theology—a theology that presumes to be consistent with science and depends on rigorous logic.

The Academic Dilemma

We live in an era dominated by what William James termed "intellectualists": the credentialed academics who parade accumulated expertise as real thinking, for whom James had little use. In his preface of *The Denial of Death*, Ernest Becker implies that knowing ever more facts is not necessarily a way to true knowledge. I would add that it certainly is not the way to wisdom. Henry Adams agreed: "Nothing in education is so astonishing as the amount of ignorance it accumulates in the form of inert facts".[2] Don't get me wrong—facts can be very important. They can also be very dangerous. Facts can devastate some majestic and enthusiastically embraced theories unreservedly propounded by many of those credentialed intellectualists: from Marxism to trickledown economics. But mountains of facts cannot buy true clarity and insight into what is "really important" to the human condition. As Ernest Becker notes: "The man of knowledge in our time is bowed down under a burden he never imagined he would ever have: the over production of truth that cannot be consumed."[3] I would have substituted the over production of *facts* that cannot be consumed. There can never be an over production of truth, and truth is not necessarily based on facts but rather on imagination. Consider the truths we often glean from literature and poetry and music (and dancing and making love).

It is the *tsunami* of facts that is overwhelming the modern human being—to the point that like a saturated sponge we are unable to absorb anymore, let alone perceive their significance or make use of them. During the Renaissance, a western scholar could have read every book ever written in the western canon during his lifetime. Today "professional experts" (as distinguished from true scholars) cannot possibly have read even one thousandth of one percent of the literature in their particular field by the end of their lives. Indeed, an expert can be defined as someone who learns more and more about less and less until he knows absolutely everything about absolutely nothing of any real significance for human beings trying to make sense out of their own existence.

The manufacture of credentialed experts seems to have become the goal of the university experience. This has not only had a deadly effect on truly creative thought; it has resulted in a degrading of nuanced public discourse. Recognized expertise in ever more specialized fields of inquiry seems to have become a badge of honor amongst too many career academics. To be called a "Renaissance Man" in today's university is really a polite way of calling someone a dilettante. This at a time when *transdisciplinary*[4] thinking has never been more needed. As Ernest Becker writes "The time is right for a synthesis that covers the best thought in many fields, from the human sciences to *religion* (italics mine) ...."[5] I would even dare to include science fiction in Becker's transdisciplinary equation, given that civilization is ripe for the same kind of speculative imagination that characterized the Renaissance. Physicist Freeman Dyson, recommending a creative imagination in science, would probably agree. In his book *Infinite in all Directions* he writes, "Looking to the future, we give up immediately any pretense of being scientifically respectable .... I make no apology for mixing science with science fiction. Science fiction is, after all, nothing more than the exploration of the future using the tools of science."[6]

The internal structures of modern universities are presently divided into ever more specialized disciplines that rarely communicate with one another. Evolutionary theorist Lynn Margulis condemned this as "academic apartheid." Writing about her experiences at Berkeley, she lamented the lack of communication between the department of paleontology ("where evolution was studied") and the department of genetics ("where evolution was barely mentioned"). Since she was interested in "the evolutionary history of cells," she "was shocked by the depth of academic apartheid. Each department seemed oblivious to people and subject matter beyond its borders."[7] The communication gap of this particular example has long since been bridged, but it still serves as an example of the inherent weakness of the classic university structure. A dean of engineering at a rather prestigious university once confided in me that the current separation of engineering faculties into electric, mechanical, robotics, computing etc. has become artificial (robotics being computer, electrical, and mechanical all at once). He averred that this separation is damaging to preparing the engineers of the future and that it only continues because each faculty has its own dean, assistant dean and so on and thus is more amenable to the personal ambitions of faculty members.

I had a similar experience some years ago while coordinating a think tank on social policy, composed of academics and politicians, for the, now deceased, Israeli Labor Party. One particular meeting was to be addressed by an economist about the current macro-economic climate. While calling around to make sure the members of the think tank would attend, one tenured professor, head of the Department of Labor Relations at one of Israel's most prestigious universities, responded: "Economics is not my field; I don't think I will attend." Flabbergasted, my first thought was "How in the hell can you deal with labor relations outside of the economic context?" and my second thought was "Idiot, don't you have a pension plan, and wouldn't you like to know how it might fare in the near future?" My third thought was "How can you be so incurious and still consider yourself an intellectual?"

Such a hyper-specialized situation is fundamentally averse to a comprehensive approach to the human condition. Such specialization might be *initially* beneficial when studying the so-called exact sciences, but it is noxious for creative thinking in the Humanities and Social Sciences, as well as for *really creative* advanced thinking in the exact sciences (as Margulis argued). In the USA, in particular, during the first years of your BA, you study a wide range of introductory courses (not the case in most of the rest of the world). While ostensibly being remedial work to make up for a mediocre high school education, these are usually the most interesting and enriching part of the university experience for those of a curious and imaginative turn of mind. In their junior and senior years American students are forced to major in something which narrows the range of where their curiosity can graze. If they don't restrain their curiosity and end up take too many electives, they will not receive their BA. European and Asian students, blessed with less politically constipated educational systems making remedial study unnecessary, are forced to narrow the range of their curiosity at the outset.

After the BA comes the MA with its thesis (often dictated by one's mentor to coincide with the mentor's own research needs) narrowing the field of inquiry even further. Lastly comes the PhD dissertation (as with the thesis, often dictated by one's mentor's research needs) narrowing the field of inquiry further still. This is sometimes followed by postdoctoral research, which narrows inquiry to the point of an intellectual singularity, written in a language so convoluted and rarified that few other human beings can even understand what is being deliberated (if anything significant at all is being deliberated). Usually this is followed by some pretentious intellectualists pretending they understand and writing pretentious commentary, the "profundity" of which is often in inverse proportion to its ability to be understood.

As the era of hyper-specialization has progressed, we have increasingly lost the ability to be thrilled by true insights. Indeed, the expectation to be thrilled is often treated as indicative of a lack of intellectual sophistication. This is why optimism is often perceived as being naïve and pessimism as being more intellectually sophisticated. This is why academic intellectualists almost always seek to be perceived as sophisticated. Consequently, universities seem to specialize in producing prophets of doom rather than prophets of achievable positive visions. What negative consequence this has had on the psychological health of society can only be imagined. The university sacrament of peer review, with its unconditional stress on "expertise" and facts for facts' sake (rather than informed speculation), only exacerbates this dilemma. The problem is that to have true insight into the human condition, one must graze lightly over multiple fields of human inquiry; one must, as Nietzsche observed, risk being a dilettante in order to become a true philosopher. This is why modern academic intellectualists will never really achieve the status of philosopher; they will never jeopardize their reputations by risking being called a dilettante. The university has become a graveyard for intellectual imagination rather than a bastion of originality.

The Social/Political Dilemma

We are well into the third decade of the 21st century armed with 19th-century ideologies. We are at the dawn of a new age, yet indulge ourselves with the comfort of familiar and agreed upon political bromides. The spiritual and social potential of the space age is ignored or misused even as we worship the idol of its technology. We now have the ability to realize the social vision of the prophets by scientific means, but are diverted by the inertia of prejudice, fear, and custom; not to mention material and psychological vested interests. Oddly, psychological vested interests might be more significant than material ones, given our intense identification with inherited cultural values and assumptions. One's very personhood is assaulted when one's inherited values are being battered by rapid change. This might explain Trump, Brexit, Putin, and other populist phenomena (rightwing and leftwing) now current worldwide. The *increased rate of the rate of change* has overwhelmed our ability to accommodate it. We feel adrift in a stormy sea and grasp wildly at any cultural or political flotsam that is in the leastways familiar to us, no matter how irrelevant.

Creative political thought has historically grown out of the rich soil of social, economic, and technological development. Yet creative political thought for our era has not yet emerged, even though we are in the midst of the most profound social, economic, and technological changes in human history. The increased rate of the rate of change has been so extreme that political thinking has not kept pace, while the quantitative extrapolations of academic social scientists have long ceased to be of any real value. These extrapolations have produced a glut of prophets of doom preaching global catastrophe. Endless research papers showing how climate change, population growth, shortages of water, deforestation, food shortages, and the end of oil are all converging to destroy the planet and modern human civilization as we have known it! Their conclusion is we must stop economic growth in order to "save the planet" and survive as a species!

Some even call for "de-development." James Lovelock (of Gaia fame) has been quoted in the Rolling Stone magazine that "the whole idea of sustainable development is wrongheaded: we should be thinking about sustainable retreat." Environmental activist George Monbiot says that the campaign against climate change "is a campaign not for abundance but for austerity ... not for more freedom but for less ... it is a campaign not just against other people, but against ourselves."[8] In other words, we must forgo our growth fetish and addiction to unfettered consumerism and embrace the "halcyon simplicity of years gone by." Monbiot says this policy must be achieved by "political restraint," i.e., enforced by the police power of the state—in effect, criminalizing innovation and creativity, a kind of *Eco-Stalinism*. Opponents to this dreary outlook do not offer creative alternatives for the human future—*some actually deny these problems even exist!* We are confronted with social/political debate that might be entitled *Dumb and Dumber*.

But history matters! It teaches us that prophets of doom—from Malthus to Ehrlich to "The Club of Rome"—have been proven wrong time after time by what futurist Ramez Naam calls the "infinite resource"—the human mind. But only if we first *acknowledge* the problems! The energy/environment conundrum is the primary grand-strategic challenge for human civilization in the 21st century. But how are we to evaluate the facts while steering clear of fashionable catastrophism? After all, if it is "already too late" and the earth is doomed, why even bother? Anxieties about global warming are so severe, that there are reports of children requiring psychological treatment, and in some areas a sub-specialty of psychology that treats "Global Warming Anxiety Disorder" has arisen. The collective anxiety attacks of the more radical environmentalists do not do anybody any good; they certainly do not solve any problems; they just cloud the issues with hysterical hyperbole.

The Religious Dilemma

> "Institutions are not pretty. Show me a pretty government. Healing is wonderful, but the American Medical Association? Learning is wonderful, but universities? The same is true for religion ... religion is institutionalized spirituality." —Huston Smith in *Mother Jones*, November/December 1997

I am ambivalent about the word "religion." The religion *business*, which is really older, and more indecent, than what is usually termed "the oldest profession in the world," repels me, preying as it often does on fear, ignorance, and superstition. I loathe those who peddle the supernatural. The religious *instinct*, on the other hand: the sense of awe at the very existence of existence, the ambition to know, or intuit, ultimate reality holds endless fascination for me. In that sense I guess my entire intellectual life has been a "religious quest." Whatever mystical dreaminess I sometimes exhibit derives from the wonder I feel that there is anything at all; the wonder I feel when pondering the fact that material existence actually exists. This leads me to reject the false dichotomy between materialism and spiritual enlightenment. I am convinced that the Scientific Revolution and the Industrial Revolution are the two most spiritual events in human history. Together they have provided the means to liberate the human spirit from ignorance and superstition on the one hand, and from soul-destroying drudge work on the other. Without material well-being there can be no real spiritual enlightenment for the greater mass of humankind. As Jewish tradition puts it, "if there is no bread there is no Torah." For Jews, asceticism—the volitional denial of permitted bodily pleasures—is a sin.

I have never met a self-declared religious person (of any organized religion business) who has not made his or her religious practice a dull habit. Ironically, the most interesting "religious" searching seems to come from nonbelievers trying to make some kind of sense out of their own individual existence. In a sense, therefore, this book might, in part, be described as an exercise in speculative *Natural Theology* because it is based on a scientific view of the origins and future of existence that has significant theological implications. A view the internal logic of which I believe is irrefutable and which is necessary to address our present civilizational crises—the crisis of meaning. The biologist E.O. Wilson got it right when he wrote that "people ... yearn to have a purpose larger than themselves. We are obliged by the deepest drives of the human spirit to make ourselves more than animated dust, and we must have a story to tell about where we came from, and why we are here."[9] This yearning is the driving force behind the *Cosmodeistic Hypothesis.* I caution again, that this is not a New Age project. It is, rather, a hybrid of informed scientific speculation, philosophy, and theological ambition; an ambition that attempts to fulfill Carl Sagan's hope for a new religiosity based on science—an ambition anticipated by Albert Einstein when he wrote:

> What is the meaning of human life, or of organic life altogether? To answer this question at all *implies a religion* [italics mine]. Is there any sense then, you ask, in putting it? I answer, the man who regards his own life and that of his fellow-creatures as meaningless is not merely unfortunate but almost disqualified for life.[10]

Thus, I will limit my arguments within the *present* boundaries of scientific knowledge and rules of logic, while allowing that the rules of logic sometimes challenge the self-imposed boundaries of working scientists. I will, therefore, reference the thinking of many religious, philosophical, and scientific thinkers throughout the ages in support of my central conjectures. I will present this thinking primarily through the lens of western intellectual and faith traditions with tangential references to other intellectual and faith traditions when appropriate to the central thesis of the book.

Chapter Two: WHY? The Ultimate Existential Question

Why are we here? What *is* here? Why does existence exist? Why is there anything at all, rather than nothing? Why are we alive? What is life? What is the meaning and purpose of our life? Does life itself have any meaning? Why does this planet have life on it and does the Cosmos even care? If all life were exterminated on this planet or if the planet exploded, would our planetary history have had any cosmic significance whatsoever? These are the gnawing questions that serve as the background music of human *being*. These are the unanswerable questions that have generated a civilizational *zeitgeist* of angst and alienation. By the 20th century, the elemental question for thoughtful people had become: Is life worth living? Camus wrote "There is but one truly philosophical problem and that is suicide ... Whether or not the world has three dimensions, or the mind nine or twelve categories comes afterward."[11] Indeed, why not commit suicide and avoid the tribulations of a meaningless existence. Everything else, all our cultural and scientific product, is marginalia to this ultimate existential question.

The irony is that science, the most sublime creation of the human spirit; the activity that reflects human curiosity and imagination at its highest stage of development, has revealed an existence of such vastness and complexity that it makes our human lives (collective and individual) seem inconsequential. Moreover, science inexorably morphed into "scientism"— an "ism": an *ideology* that posited that things, issues, events or feelings which could not be described according to the canons of reductionist/empirical science were of no concern to the intellectually tough-minded *or did not even exist.*

Thus, behaviorism (the ultimate expression of scientism) eventually claimed that consciousness did not exist—it was simply an arbitrary construct used to explain behaviors. As Jacques Barzun put it, scientists (especially sociologists and psychologists) seemed to take great pleasure in "being able to undeceive one's fellows";[12] to disabuse them of the superstitions of pre-science; the superstitions that love and purpose and concepts of honor and duty, were intrinsic to human existence.[13] The 19th century scientific view that gave birth to Darwin, Marx, and Corporate "Taylorism" "chose to assume that matter was the source of everything in the universe, including life and consciousness."[14] Darwin and Marx had triggered a mental inclination that "made final the separation between man and his soul."[15]

As a result, "the only reality was plain: a premium was put on fact, brute force, valueless existence, and bare survival."[16] As one 19th-century scientist put it, "Neither the moral law nor the law of beauty can be found in nature."[17] This is a view now being challenged by a few scientists— most prominently E. O. Wilson in *Consilience*. I identify with the same camp that intuits that existence, human life, and consciousness *do* have meaning and purpose.

Western angst began with the Copernican Revolution and what followed. Before Copernicus, medieval western man lived in a cozy universe. Earth was the center of God's creation, enveloped in the warm embrace of ever purer crystalline spheres that contained the planets and stars up to the very throne of God. God's full-time job was maintaining this physical order, keeping track of our behavior (for future reference regarding salvation) and, once in a while, interfering in the planet earth's natural order with a miracle here or there. People knew that life on this earth was temporary (temporal) and was actually a test of our moral stamina in facing physical pain and the various distresses of daily human life in order to qualify us for eternal life in the world to come. Temporal life was nothing more than a rite of passage; God's matriculation exam to qualify for heaven. Medieval western man knew that if he obeyed the rules and accepted Jesus as his savior his suffering in this life would be rewarded with eternal bliss in the world to come. Things might be dreadful now, but all his suffering would be eliminated, and confusion would be made clear in a world where all was truth. All this changed with the Copernican Revolution. Copernicus introduced a kind of spiritual agoraphobia by upsetting our coziness and making us aware of the vastness of existence that caused Pascal to despair. Angst and doubt about the meaning of our existence became our constant companion. So why shouldn't we commit suicide? The Viennese psychiatrist and Holocaust survivor Viktor Frankl would ask his depressed patients why they didn't commit suicide. Frankl testified that in rationalizing their reasons for not doing so his patients often discovered purpose and became less depressed.

Actually, very few people (the most interesting ones) ask the great "why" questions and even those few do so only very irregularly—else they would cease to function at all and become catatonic. Yet human beings do not just exist; we are symbolic creatures that require *meaning* to survive. The Darwinian *mechanism* of physical survival is not a sufficient *reason* to survive; it is simply an *explanation*. Indeed, we cannot even rationalize our subjective physical survival without objective meaning. Why *should* we live? The call by existentialist philosophers for individuals to "invent" their own meaning is an intellectualist cop out. Symbols and volitional reason are the primary evolutionary survival mechanism of the human species. Birds fly, deer are swift, lions are powerful—human beings *think,* and they *direct* their thinking (volition) in terms of their symbols, values, and meanings.

Until science revealed the infinite vastness of space and time, most human cultures since the beginning of recorded history lived within a teleological worldview. They assumed that existence, and human life within that existence, had a purpose. "Purpose and design are a part of or are apparent in nature ... that phenomena are guided not only by mechanical forces but that they move toward certain goals of self-realization,"[18] that existence has meaning and value. Humankind has invented religions, myths, and social and cultural devices to express this inherent feature of human nature. Teleological worldviews see the ends of history (what Aristotle called "Final Causes") as directing its course and providing meaning to everything that has happened, happens, or will happen (God's will, God's plan).

The human experience is future-directed; we implicitly assume it is leading to something of significance and this makes sense out of our lives. This is why we do not commit suicide. We, perhaps subliminally, assume that life does have meaning; we assume that our individual lives have meaning. We assume (and recent science supports this assumption) that every individual is unique, that every individual is distinct in the entire Cosmos, that in all of infinite nature nothing is entirely similar to each and every one of us. We are, each and every one, the "one and only." As Dr. Manhattan put it in the graphic novel *The Watchman:*

> ... in each human coupling, a thousand million sperm vie for a single egg. Multiply those odds by countless generations, against the odds of your ancestors being alive; meeting; siring this precise son; that exact daughter .... Until your mother loves a man ... and of that union, of the thousand million children competing for fertilization, it was you, only you, that emerged. To distill so specific a form from that chaos of improbability ... that is the crowning unlikelihood. The thermo-dynamic miracle ...

There is, of course, correspondence and species similarity connecting every human being, and one might assume every self-reflective conscious being, in the Cosmos, by virtue of their consciousness. But our own individuality is a cosmic absolute, as is the uniqueness of every distinctive culture and civilization. Cosmic evolution produced our uniqueness and these particular uniquenesses (individual or cultural) may perhaps be valuable to cosmic evolution. But unlike animals, whether our uniqueness is or is not valuable is entirely up to us. It is a *volitional* evolutionary choice both on the individual and the civilizational level. Individuals and cultures that wallow in inherited resentments and daily trivialities, rejecting the evolutionary obligations of consciousness, betray their divine potential. There is no other creature in the entire Cosmos with *your* specific consciousness and self-awareness. This makes *you* a distinct human being to yourself and to others. Understanding our distinctness and our specialness is a heavy and frightening responsibility. This is why so many run away from the responsibility of their own individuality and try to imitate others (to conform) or to surrender to the will of external authority such as the state, ideology, guru, demagogue, or religion, as well as current political or social fashion—a state of mind that serves as the psychological basis of despotism and religious fanaticism.

Conformism is a spurious symbol of attachment because it is our very individual distinctness that empowers us to be part of human society. Actually, there wouldn't even be a need for society if human beings were completely identical. Distinctiveness is what both obligates and sustains society, because society is the mediator between the distinctiveness of individuals. In fulfilling this role, society completes what is lacking in each and every individual that composes it. This is not only true for human beings it is also true for most advanced animals and perhaps even for the environment at large. Indeed, we might perceive our planet's ecology as a living society sustained by the interaction between the numerous species and individual members of those species without which those species and individual members of those species could not survive. Perhaps this is how we should view the Cosmos at large, as a giant society.

Western civilization in particular, from Monotheism to Marxism, has been teleological. The problems of angst and alienation began when teleology became either pluralistic or invalidated by science. When one was offered a lengthy menu of alternative teleologies to choose from (or no teleology which one found compelling), religions ceased to have a monopoly on the question of meaning. When science became triumphant and secular civilization was born, we were set adrift. Alternative teleologies can be accommodated socially by Constitutionalism but are more difficult for the critical mind to accommodate psychologically. The proliferation of alternative teleologies is partially responsible for the crises of modernism (which gave birth to teleological pluralism on the one hand, while invalidating teleology, in principle, on the other). This eventually gave birth to nihilistic postmodernism, which denied that the very concept of meaning had any meaning, as well as a paleo-conservatism which reembraced premodern teleologies. Postmodernism denies there are objective values and meanings, only social and cultural *constructs*. These constructs, they assert, reflect a false consciousness that alienates human beings from their "true" selves. False consciousness inhibits human development and thus it becomes the primary duty of "intellectuals" to engage in a project of deconstruction; to deconstruct inherited values and "undeceive" human beings in order to "free" them from their preconceptions and their prejudices in order to create a more just society and a healthier culture. The ironic consequence of this postmodernist project has not been to free us from alienation but to deepen our alienation; to deconstruct social solidarity as such and to create "cultural" expressions dedicated not to the transcendent elevation of humanity, but to the awareness of our basic animal nature. Alienation has become a full-time career choice for some.

Chapter Three: The Alienation Racket

Modern alienation theory is an invention. There is no empirical evidence that modern man is more alienated than the generations that preceded the Enlightenment and the Industrial Revolution. The predicament of human angst and alienation has been reduced from its true cosmic dimension to a provincial social and political dimension by intellectual dwarfs. It has been hijacked and manipulated by paleo-conservative and "progressive" cultural agendas, some of which assume a pose of contempt for "materialism"; a pose of "look at me I am so much more sensitive and spiritual than the rest of you." This is often characterized by romantic predispositions towards rural life, that living "close to the soil" is somehow preferable to urbanites "alienated" from the so-called natural order. For such people it is *axiomatic* that the urban individual, living in a consumer society, is alienated. The solution for the left has been to change the economic order to socialist, while the paleo-right peddles pathologies of nostalgia —a return to the eternal verities of faith, family, and community. Both views are infected with "bourgeoisphobia"—feigned disgust for the vulgar busyness of those commercial and professional classes that actually generated the Renaissance, Scientific Revolution, Enlightenment, and Industrial Revolution and physically sustain our present-day civilization. There is something claustrophobic about these versions of alienation that are detached from the cosmic context and reduced to the trivia of earthbound human society. The modern dilemma is certainly a sense of the meaningless of existence. But it is the immensity and fact of existence itself that is the problem, not the consumer society or false consciousness.

A good example is a book I was required to read in university, called *Man Alone: Alienation in Modern Society*. Looking back, I realize it was really an introduction to why college students should feel melancholic if they want to be considered sophisticated. Upon rereading it recently, I was struck by the realization that the contributors just say things and support what they say by citing other people who just say things. The whole theoretical edifice is an intellectual *Potemkin village*. Indeed, one searches in vain for any sign of empirical support for opinions in the entire book. One suspects that what the contributors wrote reflects their own personal pathologies rather than objective empirical reality. It was as if they were trying to prove Nietzsche's observation that philosophies say more about the philosophers who propagate them than they do about reality. (What does this book say about me?) Books like *Man Alone* are rife with puffed-up statements such as "one of the most disturbing phenomena of western culture has been man's sense of estrangement from the world he himself has made or inherited—in a word man's alienation from himself and others."[19] Yet evidence that premodern man was characterized by greater degrees of optimism, hope, and certainty than modern man or that pessimism, despair, and uncertainty are unique to modern man is rarely if ever presented. An entire theoretical edifice has been built on non-evidence; an entire industry of university courses, literary and social theories, and journalistic pseudo-sophistication has been generated based on **NOTHING!**

This lack of evidence has not deterred the disciples of civilizational neurosis. Indeed, the very appeal to empirical evidence would be treated with contempt by many advocates of alienation theory—those who are the progeny of "Critical Theory" and who disdain the brute coarseness of "facts." If one has the audacity to point out that when real human beings living real lives are presented with a choice between rural life and urban life they overwhelmingly choose urban life, this is attributed to the false consciousness of the masses titillated by the artificial hype of the consumer society. But the truth is that the Tin Pan Alley song of WWI "How ya gonna keep 'em down on the farm after they've seen Paree" displayed more sociological wisdom than these learned professors of alienation.

Are we really to believe that human beings living before the great technological and political revolutions of the late 18th century were more optimistic, hopeful, and secure than the generations that followed? Before these revolutions, 70% of children died before the age of five; sudden epidemics decimated entire populations; the vagaries of weather joined to the preindustrial lack of infrastructure caused regional famines from one year to the next when surpluses of food were available less than what today would be a half a day travel. Social violence was the norm (police departments are a 19th-century invention); and the great mass of humanity couldn't even conceive of a better life for their children, let alone hope for it since *The Idea of Progress* not yet taken hold of the popular imagination. How, then, could they be more hopeful or optimistic, or feel secure? Was medieval man spending his entire life looking up the backside of an ox, or making the miniscule metal rings of chainmail *by hand*, in endless repetition, more fulfilled in his individuality than the modern man working on an assembly line? Are Henry David Thoreau's "lives of quiet desperation" really unique to the modern era? And if they are, is it because of the time to think and reflect about the meaning and purpose of one's life afforded by the material prosperity of the industrial era? That gnawing feeling that we are wasting our lives is a consequence of being well fed. People who are one or two meals away from starvation do not have the luxury of feeling alienated.

Ironically the editors of *Man Alone* provide the anti-evidence to their own theory. When referencing Huizinga, they remind us that the Middle Ages were violent, diseased, corrupt, superstitious, and bleak beyond the comprehension of the modern individual. They quote a medieval French poet:

> Why are times so dark?
> Men know each other not at all
> Days dead & gone were more worthwhile,
> Now what holds sway? Deep gloom and boredom,
> Justice and law nowhere to be found
> I know no more where I belong.[20]

The editors themselves call this "the alienated lament of all ages" and admit that "Romantic notions about our own past or about primitive cultures do not help us here."[21] (This admission begs the question as to why they wrote the book.) But this poem was the reflection of a *literate poet* who read and thought. Would an *illiterate serf*, who was in essence a human ox dumbed down by backbreaking, never-ending drudge work and malnutrition, have been so aware of his "alienation?" Such a claim would be analogous to the false claim that the early Industrial Revolution *caused* poverty rather than having made heretofore less discernible rural poverty visible by concentrating it in the cities. Indeed, look again at the words in this poem. Do they not reflect the present-day general resentful mood that produced Brexit and Trump? "Deep gloom and boredom ... I know no more where I belong," could be a description of present day, postindustrial, opioid ridden, small town America.

Quoting Emile Durkheim, the editors strike to the very core of my own intellectual ambitions. Durkheim writes that when man understands "that he is an instrument of a purpose greater than himself, he will see that he is not without significance."[22] The question is what kind of purpose Durkheim and the editors are referring to. This indeed is the real issue; because if it is not a cosmic significance as proposed by *Cosmodeism* but rather a social/

political significance, then it is an invented, provincial, earthbound, soporific significance geared to tricking ourselves out of truly facing up to the ultimate existential question—WHAT DOES IT ALL MEAN? Alienation is not an ailment particular to modern society or even to the West; it is inherent in being human. The wearied pose of never-ending estrangement is an affectation characterizing a certain breed of pretentious intellectuals who have trouble figuring out the meaning of their own lives. Oddly, "regular folks" are not usually beset by angst. "Regular folks" do not think about the meaning of life, they live their lives and find whatever meaning they can in the living. Ironically, they are living the ideal of the alienation theorists— they are "being" in the full sense of the word and not "thinking about being." They are not in the embrace of "that whore reason"[23] the irrationalists so denigrate as desiccating true being by substituting analysis for real life. They are in the embrace of their own lives and their own human "being". It is the alienation theorists that substitute analysis for real life; they are the alienated ones.

Alienation theory is most often promoted by people with an ideological ax to grind. The left—especially Marxists and Critical Theory devotees (the Frankfurt School)—champion the notion that alienation is a disease of capitalism and urbanization and that it can only be "cured" by socialism. Environmentalists of the primitivist persuasion argue that it is a disease of urbanization and consumerism and that the "cure" is a return to a simple lifestyle on the land where we can get back to nature and discover our own authentic selves. Cultural paleo-conservatives, such as T.S. Eliot, who are uneasy with the consequences of the Enlightenment, posit that alienation is a disease of modernity itself, and the frantic unending change it generates, and can only be "cured" by returning to the past's social and theological certainties and the stability of class and church. As Northrop Frye wrote: "T.S. Eliot [will] tell you that to have a flourishing culture we should educate an elite, keep most people living in the same spot, and never disestablish the Church of England." Eliot's anti-Semitism might have stemmed from the fact that, historically, Jews have been radical change agents who subverted, by their persistent dissatisfaction, restlessness and "busyness," the stability and "eternal" verities of premodern societal values that Eliot was so nostalgic for. I offer as evidence the "juiciest" Jew-hating parts of his poems.

What unites all three is the pathology of nostalgia—the "good old days" when people were whole and sure of who they were within the norms of family and community; the assumption always being that in the past family and community were healthier social constructs than today. This, of course, is a most doubtful assumption for anyone with a minimum knowledge of social history. These are all silly escapisms from the true scale of the problem. The Woody Allen movie, *Midnight in Paris*, chronicles the enduring pathology of nostalgia with exquisite irony. But nostalgia has become particularly characteristic of our time because of the very rate of change. As Eric Roll has written:

> It is (during)... rapid and radical changes in the economic and social structure that there can be found those who are distressed ... but who cannot rise to more than an idealization of the past. They want to re-establish a mythical golden age, since they cannot understand the forces which are transforming their own society .... The German Romantics of the nineteenth century urge(d) ... going back to the ... Middle Ages ... many of the suggestions for social reform that are finding adherents today have the same romantic quality.[24]

Because of this, adulation of the past has become the new idol worship of many political leaders and cultural elites. Nothing can be more destructive to human progress. As Peter Gay has noted:

> Nostalgia runs deep in the human psyche; it is almost irresistible, all the more so because it generally masquerades as rational criticism of the present (where there is always much to criticize) and rational praise of the past (where there is always much to praise). But nostalgia drives reasonable criticism and ... praise to unreasonable lengths: it converts healthy dissatisfactions into an atavistic longing for a simpler condition, for a childhood of innocence and happiness remembered in all its crystalline purity precisely because it never existed. Nostalgia is the most sophistic, most deceptive form regression can take.[25]

These quotes describe most politics today. Capitalists yearn for a simpler unregulated past; academic Marxists yearn (ironically) after the romantic spirit of bygone revolutions. Socialists and unionists grow misty over the struggles and alliances of yesteryear, and the sense of community formed in those struggles and alliances (the "Wobblies syndrome"). Third World leaders search for "culturally traditional political forms" (as if such could even begin to be relevant in the Space Age). We are witness to a loss of nerve reminiscent of the fearful quaking medieval man. All shades of the political spectrum deal in scholastic nitpicking, nervously going through source material searching for support for political points which have no real relevance for current political problems.

The minority that is truly alienated is so as a result of the Copernican Revolution revealing the infinite vastness of existence that opened the door to Pascalian despair. It is the human condition on the background of the vast, endless obscurity of space/time that causes alienation and angst—not the city or the assembly line, not the consumer society or mendacious politicians. It is the ability to reflect on this human condition (an ability provided by the material prosperity produced by capitalism and science) that generates angst; it is a real anxiety, not an artificial one caused by the wrong kind of social environment or false consciousness. It is a cosmic alienation not curable by therapy or social revolution, but only by substantive intellectual and spiritual confrontation. Capitalism and the consumerism it produced are consequences of the Scientific Revolution and of the Enlightenment which derived from it—they themselves are effects, not causes. They have not caused alienation they have just made us aware by providing the material ease that allows us to reflect on the human condition and the knowledge to better understand what that condition is. It is the apple of knowledge that is the cause; it is our very humanity that is the cause; it is asking questions that have no answers that is the cause; it is being thrown out of the "Garden of Eden" of our own smug ignorance that is the cause. At best, one can say that our frantic busyness and consumerism are escapes from the cause; they are the effect, not the cause.

The alienation racket gave birth to a negative ideology called postmodernism which aims to deconstruct all social values and to turn objective truths into subjective narratives. This has amplified the very anomie that the alienation theorists criticize in modern society. In other words, alienation theory has been very successful at marketing itself and thus has become a self-fulfilling prophecy. The hidden agenda of left-wing intellectuals is to inculcate the feeling that there really is no objective hierarchy of values. This creates a subsequent moral vacuum that must be filled (preferably by them). The hidden agenda of right-wing intellectuals is to create a paranoiac suspicion of the social and cultural consequences of modernity per se, and thus encourage people to return to the eternal verities of that mythical "traditional" society. One must acknowledge that the right has been more successful in their aims than the left regarding real political power in western societies. Nothing characterizes this more than the ascendance of *alternative facts* as an essential component of right-wing discourse in the era of Trump. There is gorgeous irony in the left caterwauling about the right's use of alternative facts, since leftist postmodernist academics have been denigrating the very notion of objective facticity for decades—advocating the prominence of subjective *narratives* over "so-called" objective reality and historical facticity.

The decline of optimism and belief in *The Idea of Progress* producing better human beings, following WWI, in conjunction with the vast progress of science in describing both the vastness and the minuteness of existence has had profound philosophical and psychological consequences. The obscurities of religious belief and the rise of Darwinism and Freudianism undermined the civilizational self-esteem of western elites. If we are related to monkeys and not to God (as per Darwin) and if we really want to do to our mothers what Freud says we want to do, it is difficult to sustain a transcendent view of human being.

Without comprehensive civilizational myths, how do we even address the mystery of the existence of existence—the fact that there is an 'is'? We range from wonder at our own scientific ability to uncover the mysteries of the "mind of God" to a Pascalian melancholy about the very meaninglessness of life. Alienation and anxiety about our very existence has been dominating our spiritual ecology: nihilism, existentialism, cultural anarchy, and cultural relativism. We hide from this behind a false return to fundamental religions or the self-imposed haze of drugs and shopping.

Chapter Four: The Consequences

Postmodernism, angst, and alienation are poor spiritual fare to feed to the intellects of future generations. One cannot produce robust, self-reliant, intellectually independent, and responsible citizens of the planetary future on such insipid fare. Orthodox religious fundamentalists of all sorts do not have this educational problem, but their ideals and ideas are dysfunctional to a Space Age planetary civilization. The optimistic nonobservant are, therefore, left in the lurch. They are instinctively turned off by the disdainful, self-conscious, posed weariness of pseudo-sophisticated postmodernists, but also appalled by the smug self-satisfied ignorance and lack of critical thinking of the religiously orthodox. The arrogant self-assuredness of both leaves the hopeful nonobservant dissatisfied. Consequently, the number of people without a spiritual homeland in either camp seems to be growing, a kind of spiritual silent majority. This is where the *Cosmodeistic Hypothesis* has an important intermediate role to play. In addition to its philosophic and scientific logic, its message can contribute to moderating alienation by presenting a metaphysical and meta-cosmological vision capable of assuaging much of what ails human society in *this* century.

I am not only polemicizing against postmodernism and alienation theory here. I am also polemicizing against a superficial and shallow secularism; the desiccated secularism revealed in behaviorism and statistical sociology, which equates small 'r' religiosity with big 'R' theological Religion (and dismisses both equally); the secularism that denies the *objective* wondrousness and mystery of existence itself, reducing it to a dead 'isness' that one must simply analyze and explain; the sociological, behavioral secularism that dismisses with an infuriating haughtiness all talk of sublime attributes of existence, reducing such talk to the *subjective feelings* of the interlocutor, who declare with repulsive self-confidence that existence is not sublime it just "is"; that you may have sublime *feelings* about existence but this is simply a symptom of false consciousness. This judgment is often presented with a jarring, self-assured and self-satisfied pedagogical tone of voice; self-satisfied because its transmitter has just fulfilled *his duty* to enlighten you, to "undeceive you" from your naively optimistic benightedness. Cultivating spiritual weariness is the key to intellectual sophistication for this mindset. Existence for such people is not enchanted—science has disenchanted it.

The frame of mind described above has had serious subversive educational effects well described by cultural conservative C.S. Lewis in *The Abolition of Man*. Lewis intimates that unless we reenchant existence (especially our own existence) and dwell on the *objective* wonder of existence and *our own existence*, the human condition will have become so impoverished and enervated that it will endanger civilization itself. While Lewis was himself a big 'R' religious believer (the Anglican Communion) he argued his case from a small 'r' sense of religious awe at the facticity of existence. He did not believe that our ever-growing ability to explain the constituent facts of existence takes away from the wondrous facticity of existence as a whole—that existence per se is sublime. As he put it: "The feelings which make a man call an object sublime are not sublime *feelings* but feelings of veneration."[26]

Here Lewis reveals a profound fundamental truth about the human spirit; the inherent need to venerate something greater than ourselves. Veneration is as universal a human attribute as language. There is not a human culture on the face of the earth that does not have a deeply rooted history of veneration of one form or another. To be truly human it seems that we as a species are driven to venerate something "greater" than ourselves; something outside of ourselves. One might assume that veneration is to the soul what food is to the body. As Martin Buber might say our subjective "I" requires an objective "thou" in order to best realize the "I." Thus, the subjective need for God or the various substitutes for God—i.e., organized religion, patriotism, ideas, cultural icons, etc. These objects of veneration can be positive, inspiring, or even sublime—or they can be nightmarish. Religion can uplift and help, or it can promote intolerance, fanaticism and war; patriotism can turn from a healthy love of the folkways, food and rhythms of one's nation into fascism; ideas can inspire or become the justification for the worst kinds of atrocities; cultural icons can be models for heroic ambitions or turn one into a mindless worshipper of an empty-headed pop star (people actually committed suicide when actor Rudolf Valentino died). Objects of veneration can help us develop concepts of honor and dignity; they can make us noble and aspiring to greatness. But they can also be twisted into something horrific as with Nazism, Fascism, Communism, and Japanese militarism.

One of the negative reactions to horrific venerations, by various fashionable academic ideologies, has been to deny or denigrate the very objectiveness of honor, nobility, and heroism; to claim that that sublimity is invented by our subjective need and has no objective sanction; to deny that all these are nothing more than the delusions of a false consciousness, created and manipulated by "the powers that be;" that to be truly free one must rid oneself of these false ideas. This might be the most decadent human perspective in history. It leaves an empty shell of what superficially looks like a human being but has no human content; what Lewis has called "Men without chests." And yet, the human spirit instinctively yearns for these attributes and if the higher culture, infected as it is by the spirit of postmodern deconstructivism, cannot supply them then comic books and action movies will. Every historical endeavor to do away with inherited modes of veneration has resulted in alternative venerations: ideologies, leaders, causes, even contrariness for its own sake. Being a contrarian today has taken on the characteristics of a profession, second only to the profession of "activist." Some of these alternative venerations in the 20th century caused some of the greatest horrors in human history: Fascism, Nazism, Stalinism, Maoism, Pol Pot, and so on. Nazi Germany, Fascist Italy, Stalinist Russia, and Maoist China were initially successful because they revived a sense of purpose within a totalitarian mechanical and scientific society. As Jacques Barzun has written:

> What has happened [in these countries] can happen wherever the [human] *need* (italics mine) for enthusiasm and action is given a goal. It is easy enough to manufacture slogans out of current superstitions—race, autarky, the Cultural Revolution—and make them seem genuine outlets from the impasse into which a narrow science of nature and human nature has led us.[27]

As an antidote to the totalitarian "solution" for the need for veneration *Cosmodeism* proposes that we venerate existence itself and our own existence within that existence. The fact that existence exists, that it "is," is represented by the biblical metaphor of the burning bush which throughout the ages declares to us (in our own moments of insight) "I am that I am"—I am existence and I exist. The proper translation from Modern Hebrew would be "I will be what I will be"—I (God) am existence and I am never complete. *Yahweh* is a verb not a noun. In Biblical Hebrew it is in the imperfect form. Consider the irony of that; that the so-called "perfect being" is described by an imperfect construct. The implication is that God's perfection is not yet complete but is in an ever-continuing evolutionary process of developing and realizing its, as yet uncompleted divinity—a *perfectioning* if you will.

In Modern Hebrew's future tense this implication becomes more explicit. The ancient Hebrew instinct is that God "itself" is an evolutionary concept. I put "itself" in inverted commas because the God of the Jews is not a thing or being that can be defined in a positivist manner: "it" is *no thing;* "it" *is nothing*—"it" is "it"—ultimate reality as such. That this concept of "godness" has been subverted by various Orthodox Judaic cults to their own particular idolatrous venerations (the "Land of Israel"; the "Rebbe"; the more unattractive portions of the Bible, etc.) has become a more dangerous threat to future Jewish survival than the Iranian bomb. As for the dangerous idolatries of Christian, Muslim, and other faith traditions, I will leave the reader to his or her own analytic and observational devices.

To realize Emil Durkheim's belief that when we serve something greater than ourselves, we uplift ourselves—we must acknowledge that some things, some values, some emotions "*merit* our approval or disapproval, our reverence or our contempt."[28] For this to happen we must acknowledge—against the claims of multiculturalism[29]—that there is a hierarchy of social, political, and cultural values. All ideas are not created equal; all cultures are not equal. This hierarchy changes from one historical epoch to another. There is no question that during the European Dark Ages, the Arab Caliphate was superior in every way to European civilization; but there is also no question that since the Enlightenment, European civilization has been superior to Arab civilization. To deny this is political correctness on steroids. Does this fact make Europeans superior human beings than Arabs? Of course not! Just as the superiority of Arab civilization in the Middle Ages did not make Arab individuals superior to European individuals. But within every civilization, some individuals are superior to others, and some are inferior to others. Human beings might be created equal before the law, but they are in no way born equal in their intellectual, emotional, and spiritual potentialities. Thomas Jefferson knew he was Thomas Jefferson—a superior intellect in every way (as well as a superior hypocrite), and that few human beings on the planet were his equal.

If we don't find the "greater than" in the concept of "God" or *Godding* or some other transcendent ideas, we will find it in rightwing and leftwing fascists (the T-Shirt craze of Che for example), or New Age cults or pop stars. If our need to venerate something "greater than" is not directed towards something affirmative, it will be directed towards something negative. What could be more positive and spiritually satisfying than venerating the *Godding* of the universe and our own part in that *Godding*? But we cannot cultivate such an attitude of mind in an atmosphere dedicated to debunking any sense of the heroic and noble; an atmosphere dedicated to "proving" that such emotions are "contrary to reason and contemptible";[30] an atmosphere that radiates a mindset that concepts of honor and duty are but mere subjective social and cultural constructs (manipulated by "the powers that be") with no objective validity, and not innate in what makes us truly human. If one does not believe that valor, good faith, justice, duty, and honor are real *objective* virtues, intrinsic to our true humanity, then why not answer the question posed by Camus by committing suicide? This human need for the "greater than" has been referred to by thinkers as diverse as Abraham Maslow, Viktor Frankl, and Ernest Becker. It is reflected in the Muslim cry *Allahu Akbar* which, contrary to common belief, does not mean "God is Great," but rather, "God is greater *than* ..." Greater than what? Greater than anything, than everything—greater than the very ability to be described! Its perversion by Islamist Jihadists into a maniacal war cry is a perfect example of how one particular Religion business has twisted an originally profound spiritual insight into a disgusting instrument of manipulation in order to serve the private pathologies of repulsive old men.

Some debunkers are cynical subversives of western civilization, but most are sincere people who view themselves as honest laborers in the cause of Enlightenment, freeing us from the false gods of our inherited culture. They want to "undeceive" us from the idolatry of our own emotions and "invented" values. "They see the world around them swayed by emotional propaganda ...."[31] Given the level of current political and social discourse it is hard to argue with this view. But as Lewis says, "The right defense against false sentiments is to inculcate just sentiments [else] ... we only make [people] easier prey to the propagandist when he comes ... a hard heart is no ... protection against a soft head."[32] In other words, a misguided program of freeing us from "false" values without providing an alternative creates a moral vacuum easily filled by demagogues and charlatans. Witness how many "idealistic" 60s radicals became Jesus freaks, fanatic Orthodox Jews, cultists, Yuppies, or neo-con politruks. The debunkers have thus served the manipulators rather than freeing us from them.

In his book, Lewis uses the *Tao* as the generic word for what he is trying to describe. "... the *Tao* ... is the reality beyond all predicates, the abyss that was *before* (italics mine) the Creator himself."[33] He claims this to be a fundamental concept which expresses itself in different forms in all systems: "Platonic, Aristotelian, Stoic, Christian and Oriental" (and as we shall see, Jewish).[34] He claims: "It is the doctrine of objective value, the belief that certain attitudes are really true and others really false."[35] In other words, there is a real reality and not "your narrative and my narrative." I believe Lewis has chosen *Tao* to describe what he is driving at in order to avoid the charge of being a Christian apologist. He is talking about universal truths that we know viscerally to be truth even though we cannot rationally articulate them. To be a whole human being is to cultivate our visceral intuitions by means of our intellect; not to debunk them by the snooty use of our intellect. "We laugh at honor and are shocked to find traitors in our midst. We castrate and bid the geldings be fruitful."[36] We condescendingly express amusement at those who claim that existence has purpose and shudder at the subsequent social anarchy.

The Scientific Revolution changed the rules of the human condition. It did so because, unlike religion, science does not even presume to put people in touch with ultimate reality. It analyses the various phenomena of reality. It is the absolute necessity and standard of measurement of human progress. But it is in no way *sufficient* to satisfy the spiritual needs of the great majority of humankind. A small elite of humanity might find in the scientific project the kind of religious (small 'r') wonder that historically Religions (big 'R') have presumed to provide. An example would be Albert Einstein, whom I consider one of the most "religious" human beings of the 20th century; in constant awe and wonderment at both the complexity and simplicity of existence itself. But, unlike the Einsteins of the world, this kind of wonder is not accessible to the great mass of humankind for whom Einsteinian and quantum physics are as mystifying as magic. *Cosmodeism* presumes to put people in touch with ultimate reality (or at least get closer to it). Yet *Cosmodeism* is fundamentally different from religion in that it will not base itself on anything that contradicts science; it will be the metaphysical equivalent of the self-correcting system that is science. Let me repeat Carl Sagan's hope that: "[a] religion that stressed the magnificence of the universe as revealed by modern science might be able to draw forth reserves of reverence and awe hardly tapped by traditional faiths. Sooner or later, such a religion will emerge."[37]

28

Notes

1   I put "universes" in inverted commas because I believe it is a misnomer. My assumption is that the Universe is a synonym for all of Existence per se (or all of Nature per se) and that it is infinite in space and time. It is certainly not a synonym for Cosmos which means order. Order must, of necessity, have border, thus it must be finite. Therefore, I suggest we replace Multiverse with Multicosmos—that the infinite Universe is composed of an infinite number of finite cosmoses!

2   Adams, p. 379.

3   Becker, E., 1973, p. xvii.

4   I prefer this term over the more commonly used "interdisciplinary" which actually creates even narrower disciplines.

5   Becker, E., pp. xviii-xix.

6   Dyson, pp.103-104.

7   Margulis, p. 26.

8   Monbiot, p. 215.

9   Wilson, p. 6.

10 Einstein, 1931, p. 3.

11 Camus, p. 3.

12 Barzun, p. 4.

13 Lewis in *The Abolition of Man* eviscerated this attitude of mind.

14 Barzun, p. 9.

15 Ibid., p. 3.

16 Ibid., pg. 5.

17 Ibid., pg. 4.

18 Random House dictionary, p. 1350.

19 Josephson, p. 10.

20 Ibid., p. 17.

21 Ibid., p. 16

22 Durkheim, p. 374.

23 Barrett, p. 121.

24 Roll, p. 19.

25 Gay, p. 92.

26 Lewis, p. 8.

27 Barzun, p. 6.

28 Lewis, p. 14.

29 I differentiate between multiculturalism and multicultural. The first is a noun, an 'ism,' an ideology advocating the moral equality of all cultures; a false ecumenism pilloried in the 1965 Beatles movie *Help* in the delicious scene depicting a theological discussion between a Thugee holy man and a politically correct Anglican priest trying to make a metaphorical analogy between church practices and Thugee human sacrifice. The second is an adjective describing a socio-political fact that must be constitutionally accommodated with optimal mutual respect.

30 Lewis, p. 11.

31 Ibid., p. 13.

32 Ibid.

33 Ibid., p.15.

34 Ibid., p.16.

35 Ibid.

36 Ibid., p. 20.

37 Sagan, p. 50.

PART II

The Crises of Post-Modern Civilization

Chapter Five: The Crisis of Science

Science is currently confronted by four fundamental philosophical problems:

1. Metaphysical: What was *before* the Big Bang

2. Empirical: What are Dark Matter and Dark Energy and do they even exist? (Our mathematics says they must exist because our formulas demand it – but do they really?)

3. Epistemological: Is mathematics a science or just a language? (This question is significant for problems 1 and 2)

4. Methodological: Is the *Law of Parsimony* (LOP) otherwise known as "Occam's Razor" pertinent in all cases or only in special cases (and is it about to be preempted by a *Law of Plenitude*?)

I will discuss these philosophical problems based on three logical axioms:

a) Something cannot come from nothing; whatever caused the Big Bang and the "creation" of our material universe is a "something" not a nothing;

b) We cannot logically conceive of a largeness of which nothing can be larger, or of a smallness of which nothing can be smaller. In other words, existence as such is unbounded, while cosmos (order) is by definition bounded (order has border). So, while existence as such must be infinite (in space and time) *our* Cosmos is, by definition, finite.

c) What was before the Big Bang is a question that empirical science cannot answer (although mathematics and logic can speculate about). When dealing with the ultimate questions of existence we have, therefore, reached a border between physics and metaphysics; between the possibility of empirically detailed observations joined to coherent explanatory mathematical formulae and inadequate but logical metaphysical speculations.

Ancient Greek philosophy searched for "perfect order" (cosmos) in nature. It did so by way of an astounding integration of rational flights of imagination and aesthetic aspirations. In doing so, it revealed several contradictions which could not be solved—first and foremost the question of the finiteness and infiniteness of nature. Modern science has no pretensions to know infinite nature. In contrast to classical science, it doubts the very ability to precisely know even those finite domains of nature which it researches. These doubts stem from Heisenberg's *Uncertainty Principle* in physics and Gödel's *Incompleteness Theorem* in mathematics. Heisenberg exposed the limits of physics by revealing the ambiguities of Quantum Mechanics: i.e., we can measure position and momentum of a quantum particle with precision, but neither position nor momentum can possess precise values simultaneously. Gödel defined the limits of mathematics in the following way: 1) there will always be statements about the natural numbers that are true, but that are unprovable within the system; 2) no mathematical system can demonstrate its own consistency. Evaluating the nature of radiation and using mathematical formulae are the technical means (the very tools) used by scientists to research the large and small scale of nature. The problem is that both limit our ability to realize the ambition of mechanistic science to uncover a unified causal law operating in nature (radiation in practice and mathematics in theory). The primary question, therefore, remains: are we even capable of discovering a cosmic formula—a mathematical equation that accurately explains the *all-inclusive* operations of the *entire* material Cosmos (i.e., a unified causal law, a theory of everything)?

The transition from philosophy to science which ushered in the beginnings of the modern era was dependent upon experimentation liberating itself from the yoke of scholasticism. Scholasticism reflected the logic and creative imagination of ancient times as it was summarized and eventually fossilized by medieval philosophy. It is ironic, therefore, that classical mathematics, which was fashioned at the onset of the modern era as a basic instrument of science, has itself become a gigantic "scholastic" barrier to the continuing progress of science. Classical mathematical formulas have frozen concepts and laws. Only the advent of new concepts and laws (new languages as it were), reflecting current experimentation and aided by logic and creative imagination, will enable the birth of the new formulae required today. The limits of empiricism and of mathematics are the essence of the crises of science.

The Limits of Empiricism

Unless we recognize the limits of empiricism and the validity of reasonable assumptions and logical speculations, science will not be able to progress. The inconvenient truth of "empirical" science is that it has always been based on non-empirical beliefs—certain things that must be assumed in order to engage in science, but which cannot be verified by experience (what Kant might have termed *synthetic a priori*). Broadly, science has been based on *faith* in three overlapping assumptions that cannot be proven empirically:

1. Nature's laws are universally uniform throughout all of natural existence, i.e., the laws of thermodynamics pertain for all of existence.

2. Nature's laws do not evolve, i.e., they are no different today than they were ten billion years ago.

3. Mathematics is the universal language of all of existence: e.g., π (*pi*) is an irrational number *everywhere* in all of existence. (Carl Sagan played with this as a subplot in his sci-fi novel *Contact* when trying to reach a point where *pi* became a rational number.)

When scientists wake up in the morning and begin their work, they have to assume these beliefs are true, else they couldn't do their jobs. But the only way they could actually *prove* them empirically would be to be a supernatural entity outside of nature, capable of looking at all of nature. In other words, they would have to be God. (Some scientists actually adopt a godlike pose as we know, but this is a personal pathology not a datum.) We *reasonably* assume that these beliefs are true because all our experience SO FAR affirms, reaffirms, widens, and deepens their validity. But as Scottish philosopher David Hume noted in *An Enquiry Concerning Human Understanding* over 250 years ago, the SO FAR aspect proves nothing. Because the SO FAR ends the minute you run into the first exception. And this is the paradox of science: something is science (and not religion) only because *it is falsifiable*. In other words, the "bedrock" assumptions that enable science to function are also falsifiable, so cannot, in fact, be bedrock, else they would not be science.

On a more material and less theoretical level, cosmologists cannot prove empirically that the galaxy Andromeda really exists. We can prove it existed 2.5 million years ago, because that is what we see when we look at it: the light of its existence having traveled the 2.5 million light years of distance that separates us. We have no way of knowing whether or not the galaxy blew up a million years ago and no longer exists. If it did (or did not) blow up will be known to us only in another 1.5 million years. This, by definition, is true for the rest of the Cosmos and even large parts of our own galaxy that are tens of thousands of light years away from us. Perhaps, within our own galaxy the star cluster our sun is part of is alone in existence and there is nothing more. We cannot prove otherwise empirically, that's for sure. Do I believe this is the case? Of course not! I reasonably assume that while greatly evolved and altered from the time we see them (sometimes billions of years ago) the Cosmos is well populated by trillions upon trillions of cosmic bodies, even if they are most probably greatly different in present space/time than they were in those past billions of years we are presently observing them. Note that my use of "reasonably assume" and "most probably," while also implicitly assumed by cosmologists in order to do their work, are not terms that usually characterize scientific rigor.

This space/time dilemma also affects our search for intelligent life on other planets. We might discern a planet with an atmosphere we perceive to be amenable to life and analyze that atmosphere to determine by its composition, whether intelligent life has created a complex civilization. The problem is that if we are looking at a planet 50,000 light years away, intelligent creatures might have already developed a sophisticated civilization and already destroyed themselves. Or what we are seeing might be the planet at a stage of development equivalent to our own Neanderthal stage. That would be the same problem if those same intelligent creatures were looking at our planet. Remember our "intelligent" civilization is only 6,000–7,000 years old and what they would be seeing would be before the emergence of modern humans. Just as it would be *reasonable to assume* that Andromeda, and other cosmic bodies, do indeed still exist (else why even engage in science?) I believe it is also *reasonable to assume* that intelligent life exists elsewhere in our Cosmos. Yet, while scientists function on a daily basis according to these assumptions (and could not function otherwise), they would be horrified if asked to acknowledge that the entire scientific enterprise has always been based on certain metaphysical beliefs, even before recent cosmological inquiry has brought us to the very boundaries of physics and metaphysics.

The Limits of Mathematics

Does mathematics have an objective reality that must correlate with the material universe or is it just a language by which we can talk about the material universe with ever-increasing accuracy while never really understanding the *noumenon* (the thing in itself) as Plato and Kant would have it, or ultimate reality, as Einstein would have it? Heisenberg distinguished between scientists who are "pragmatists" (if it works "as if" that is sufficient) and "realists" who strive to understand the *real* reality (the *noumenon*) of a thing. Turing would be the pragmatist (if you cannot tell the difference between a real human being and a computer then for all intents and purposes the computer is a conscious "being"). Einstein would be the realist (no, all it means is that YOU can't tell the difference and is meaningless regarding the essential reality of the computer).

If Gödel is right, we will never understand the *noumenon* by way of mathematics. If the most precise instrument ever created by the human intellect cannot understand "the thing in itself" but only its external *phenomena* (and not even that to the nth degree) then, by definition, we have reached another border between physics and metaphysics. These borders (mathematical and empirical) require *trans-scientific speculation* about the very nature of existence. *Metaphysical speculation must once again become a legitimate avocation of scientific inquiry if science itself is to progress.* Practicing scientists must begin to take *philosophies* of science seriously. Albert Einstein (Gödel's best friend at Princeton) likewise understood the philosophical limitations of mathematics when, in a lecture before the Prussian Academy of Sciences in 1921, he said: "… as far as the laws of Mathematics refer to reality, they are not certain; and as far as they are certain, they do not refer to reality." Centuries earlier, Francis Bacon, in the *Novum Organum,* cautioned against the presumptions of mathematics: "… mathematics … ought only to give definiteness to natural philosophy, not to generate or give it birth." In fact, mathematical proofs only prove the proof of the mathematics, not the proof of the reality it is describing or trying to manipulate.

Nothing demonstrates the limits of mathematics more than the phenomena of life. We have no way to describe life *as such* mathematically. Mathematics can measure some familiar aspects of life (blood pressure, blood sugar, cholesterol, the number of neurons in the brain, the speed at which they interact etc.), but not life itself. What makes something alive, rather than "not alive" is still beyond our comprehension and there is certainly no biological equivalent of $E=MC^2$ (a unified causal law of life that can be described mathematically). We know that life has evolved, and that mathematics can describe the genomic connection of all life on earth. We know mathematically (and empirically) what happens as life becomes more complex. We can talk mathematically about genes, chromosomes, reproduction, and population, but life as such is beyond mathematical description.

Mathematics is a simplified abstraction of a complex reality; it is certainly not reality as such and as polymath Howard Bloom put it: "... abstractions may be indispensable ... [but] they don't accurately reflect reality."[1] Theoretical cosmology and theoretical physics, being essentially mathematical constructs, are rife with abstractions. They help us relate to some of the particulars of reality, but they are never completely identical with reality and thus do not enable us to really *understand* reality. They can describe and measure ever-growing areas of reality but not reality as such. To confuse matters even more, mathematics can also "describe" non-reality. Theoretical (or *pure*) mathematics can deal with non-reality as powerfully as it can with the *phenomena* of reality, but never with reality *as such*: the *noumena* of reality. The mathematically inspired artwork of Maurits Cornelis Escher (made famous in Douglas Hofstadter's book *Gödel, Escher, Bach: An Eternal Golden Braid*) can reflect mathematics but they do not reflect anything in physical reality. The job of mathematics is to explain observed phenomena, not to invent new phenomena in order to justify mathematical theories about the physical universe, or because fictional phenomena can be presented in a precise mathematical grammar. Dark matter and string theory, as explanations trying to save the Big Bang, might turn out to be fictional phenomena invented to address the anomalies of mathematical explanations of the physical universe. Alternatively, they might be the infinitesimal consequence of the fundamental process of the Cosmos, as described (below) by Nessyahu—to wit: the endless splitting of particles into ever smaller particles ad infinitum, with no final smallness. Particles so small they do not reflect light and thus are beyond observable.

Since mathematics can also be the language of "non-realities" it can be mistaken for reality when able to describe even a non-reality coherently within the accepted grammatical rules of mathematical language. This cannot happen in the usual languages of human communications. For example, "the Earth is flat" is a perfectly grammatical sentence; it reflects the logic of grammar and is internally consistent. But just because we can say it grammatically does not mean that the earth is flat. As Kenneth Boulding put it, "Mere internal consistency is not enough, for there may be views of the world which are internally consistent and irrefutably logical, but which are, nevertheless, not true, in the sense that the real world does not conform to them."[2] Social science and political philosophy are rife with such internally, logically consistent examples that have little if any connection to actual human reality as it is actually experienced—Marxism and Behaviorism being the most prominent.

The mathematics of "non-realities" is pertinent to the problematical notions of "Dark Matter" and "Dark Energy." Scientists speculate that these *must* exist, even though we have no empirical proof (only inference), because the mathematical formulae we use to demonstrate the internal consistency of the present standard cosmological model says they must exist. But, 19th-century cosmology's need for internal consistency produced the theory of the *luminiferous ether*. The *luminiferous ether must* exist (even though no one ever saw it). The theory of the *luminiferous ether* became extinct when cosmological theory was revolutionized by Einstein. Perhaps "Dark Matter" and "Dark Energy" are the *luminiferous ether* theory of the 21st century and will no longer be required (mathematically) when cosmological theory itself is once again revolutionized. To say that they must exist because our mathematics says they must, is like saying God must exist because logic says it must (Aristotle's "first mover").

This confusion between reality as such and mathematics as the language of reality has become a real stumbling block to the advance of human knowledge as we approach the border between physics and metaphysics, the border between the empirically accessible finite and the inaccessible infinite. Mathematics has become especially obstructionist if we assume evolution to be the grand narrative of all of ultimate reality (not only the descriptive metaphor for the development of organic reality). Evolution is characterized by *qualitative change*, by the interaction between the internal unfolding and external development of reality. Mathematics can only deal with *quantitative change* and movement: with the measurable externals of ultimate reality, with the *phenomenal* world not with the *noumenal* world. It can deal with the *appearances* of the world not with the *essence* of the world. This is the essential message of Kant's *Critique of Pure Reason*. Kant uses reason or rational (from ratio) in its precise technical sense, referring to the laws of non-contradiction inherent to mathematical ways of thinking. There is a limit to knowledge not available to empirical investigation but only capable of mathematical description (*pure* reason). With this critique Kant sets the stage for Hegel's dialectical way of thinking, a mindset more suited to evolutionary thinking. Nessyahu was within the Kantian tradition when he defined the limits of possible experience by creating a *practical* metaphysics that defined the border between the finite and the infinite. He was clearly within the Hegelian tradition when he identified the essential dialectic inherent in the evolutionary synthesis.

The Non-Mathematical and Non-Empirical are also Real

Reality is much richer than the reductionist experiments we use to apprehend it and the mathematical language we use to describe it. Both tend to shrivel the luxuriant richness of reality. Good examples are economic theories and practices as they relate to the actual reality of human economic activity. Economic theory is as mathematical as quantum physics, and market research tries to be as empirical as any other scientific research. But business is not simply bookkeeping or a mechanical reflection of economic theory or researching consumer trends. It is passion, belief, imagination, falling in love with your own creativity. It is sometimes even a sense of mission, reflecting a sincere desire to change the world for the better. Steve Jobs' disdain for market research and the financial bean counters that hampered his imagination is a perfect example of this. Elon Musk's wild ambitions regarding space and alternative transportation are another. Starting a business is an aesthetic act of creation no less than an artist painting a mural or a composer writing a symphony. This is because human creativity is indivisible; whether used to make a better mousetrap, develop an improved crop, or paint a picture, it stems from the same source: the human desire, unique amongst species, to make sense of itself and its environment and leave its mark on the future. Human creativity is its own justification and needs no other sanction; it is what makes human beings human and thus godlike. God creates and we create. God creates cosmos from chaos, and we create cosmos (paintings, music, sculptures, products, and services) from chaos. The truth is that God did not create us in his image; we created him in our image. God is an induction, not a deduction; an induction from our own human propensity to create order out of chaos.

Economic theory might be useful for the formulation of monetary and fiscal policies, but it is utterly insufficient for understanding what is really happening in society and the economy. As Ronald Coase, Nobel laureate in Economics put it: "Economics as currently presented in textbooks and taught in the classroom does not have much to do with business management, and still less with entrepreneurship. The degree to which economics is isolated from the ordinary business of life is extraordinary and unfortunate."[3] Proof of Professor Coase's reflection is that economists rarely, if ever, succeed in the real economy of products and services. At most, they can serve a useful function in the financial sector. I cannot think of one economist who ever started and ran a new business outside the financial sector, let alone created a whole new sector of economic and business activity. Economists are limited by the "rationality" of their mathematical way of thinking. Since one cannot mathematize imagination or creativity or passion, or gut instinct (the hallmarks of the entrepreneur), not to mention diverse social energies and cultural values, they are stuck in their analytical thinking and thus prevented from entering the world of synthetic thinking intrinsic to the entrepreneur. And yet it is the entrepreneurs that create economies, not economists. Economists analyze economies, businessmen and businesswomen create economies.

Another instructive historical example of the limitations of mathematics would be the mathematical models Secretary of Defense Robert McNamara and the Pentagon initially used to prosecute the war in Vietnam (before the empirical facts on the ground educated them to the deficiencies of their models). These models had nothing to do with the human passion on the ground. McNamara could never mathematize the Vietcong and North Vietnamese *refusal to lose*, or the cultural differences that explained their "willingness" to suffer losses inconceivable to the American mind. This is why the social science pose of intellectuals is very often suspect in the eyes of the common man—too much abstraction, not enough passion and gut feeling. Nonintellectuals care little for learned sociological and anthropological explanations for the source of their patriotism and religious venerations, or why they love their own children more than others or biochemical explanations of why they fall in love. They deeply resent the supercilious condescension implicit in these explanations and are deeply suspicious of the analytical coldness of the explainers—there is something nonhuman about it.

Consider also the nonrational need for literature and poetry and love. Rationality is never more productive than when it sails on the ocean of the nonrational imagination. The daydreaming of Newton and Descartes and others has been the necessary fertilizer for scientific flowering. The unsophisticated imagination of Edison and Ford and others has been the necessary fertilizer for technological and economic progress. Edison never finished grade school (although he was a voracious, endlessly curious, reader). Ford's formal education ended after 8 years. Neither went to high school, let alone college. There is an interesting, probably apocryphal, story about Edison's lack of formal education. Two professors are talking. One says, my God what could Edison have accomplished if he had had formal scientific training. The second responds, are you crazy? With formal training he would have learned what was impossible and not invented half of what he did. The intimation being that formal education and the accumulation of knowledge according to strict rational rules often stifles the creative nonrational imagination. More recently, Steve Jobs and Bill Gates were both college dropouts.

Einstein was hard put to explain the source of his own revolutionary ideas. Jacob Bronowski, in *The Ascent of Man,* cites the three "Bs" as the source of creativity (where flashes of insight occur): the bedroom, the bathroom, and the bus. Regarding the bathroom, my father would judge the intellectual level of a family according to the reading material in arm's reach from the toilet. For him it wasn't the bathroom, it was "the reading room"; the place where real thinking took place. Martin Luther would have certainly agreed with my father. He testified that his great insight, which led to the Reformation, occurred while he was otherwise occupied in the privy (some of his hymns came to him also in that place of sacred bodily release). Reason is not the source of creativity; reason is used to organize nonrational intuitions in a rational manner. It is not the cause of ideas; it is the instrument necessary to turn ideas into effect. It is a tool, a necessary tool, but certainly not one sufficient to explain the human condition within ultimate reality. It is because of this limitation that religions still exist, to the dismay of many dedicated scientists. Because of this, a new natural theology that reflects the new cosmology and the new physics must emerge (apropos Carl Sagan). It is my hope that Cosmodeism might contribute to such a development.

Chapter Six: The Tyranny of the Law of Parsimony

"It is futile to do with more things that which can be done with fewer" —William of Ockham

If science were to have a "religious" dogma it would be the *Law of Parsimony* or LOP (otherwise known as *Occam's Razor*) which inadequately stated means "all things being equal, the simplest explanation is *usually* the correct one." I italicize "usually" because the meaning of the word "usually" is usually forgotten or ignored. The tremendous success of the LOP in advancing human knowledge and human welfare is undisputed. It has been the standard by which physics and its language—mathematics—consistently judges itself. The search for reductionist simplicity and elegance of explanation and theory is the methodological standard of each. But has the *Law of Parsimony* become a tyranny limiting creative imagination, restricting scientific freedom of thought? Has conventional science become a religion and conventional scientific methodology the sacraments of that religion? William James thought so and felt that this threatened civilization itself. He wrote "the law of parsimony ... is nothing but the passion for conceiving the universe in the most labor-saving way" and "will, if made the exclusive law of the mind, end by blighting the development of the intellect itself ..." He continued:

> ... if the religion of exclusive scientism should ever succeed in suffocating all other appetites out of a nation's mind and imbuing a whole race with the persuasion that simplicity and consistency demand a *tabula rasa* to be made of every notion that does not form part of the so-called scientific synthesis, that nation, that race, will just as surely go to ruin, and fall prey to their more richly constituted neighbors ...[4]

The principles of LOP are deeply rooted in the western mindset. The Greek contribution can be traced to *Thales* of Miletus (624–546 BC). He is considered the first to philosophize in a scientific manner about the nature of existence, thereby initiating the sustained transition from mythology to reason. He observed that everything is connected to everything and therefore there must be a single ultimate substance. He concluded that ultimate substance to be water—"all is water" (the first "theory of everything").

All other substances have derived from water (we moderns would say "evolved"). Thales postulates that *water* is the principle of all things; and that God is that Mind which shaped and created all things from water. The Hebrew contribution to LOP is Monotheism. Why have many gods when one will suffice? Indeed, *Occam's Razor* was originally a philosophical/theological argument for one God, before it became a sacrament for scientists. For Occam, other explanations for existence other than one God were superfluous (one God was quite enough, thank you!). Indeed, one could ask if something similar to the LOP could have been possible in pantheistic cultures which advocate multiple causes to explain phenomena (Sun God, River God, Fertility God etc.)? Has Monotheism been a necessary foundation to the emergence of modern science? I am inclined to think so.

Both empiricism and mathematics favor the LOP. Empiricism—because it is easier to test simple explanations than complex ones; and mathematics—because the fewer the assumptions, the sharper the formulae and the more precise the predictions: "A hypothesis with fewer adjustable parameters will automatically have an enhanced posterior probability, due to the fact that the predictions it makes are sharp".[5] The self-evident problem with this approach is that ever-sharper predictions of ever-smaller slices of reality, and easiness of testing, push one further away from the intricate complexities of reality as such. Scientists have no workable theory for what love is, so they reduce this most intense, complex, and inexplicable human emotion to bio-chemical reactions or the microelectronics of brain neurons. Orgasms become analogous to an oil change and the profound poignancy one feels when holding one's first grandchild become equivalent to adjusting the sparkplugs of one's car.

Yet while most scientists and mathematicians implicitly conform to the strictures of the LOP as precisely as Orthodox Jews obey their dietary laws, there have always been philosophic objections to its perceived absolutist methodological presumptions. Leibniz and Kant both objected to it. Leibniz formulated the *Principle of Plenitude*, according to which God created an infinitely varied world. Kant wrote that "the variety of beings should not be rashly diminished."[6] The mathematician Karl Menger (1902–1985) thought that mathematicians were overly parsimonious regarding variables, and formulated the *Law against Miserliness*, to wit: "Entities must not be reduced to the point of inadequacy"[7] and "It is vain to do with fewer what requires more." I personally am sympathetic to Menger's formulations, especially regarding the problems of life and evolution—two areas in which reductionism and mathematics have little, if anything, to say of real value.

I am not hostile in all cases to the LOP. There are many fields of current inquiry in which the principle is unfortunately ignored. Many social scientists, postmodernists and critical theorists would be rendered mute if they followed its strictures (to humanity's universal benefit). The LOP has been most useful in the history of cosmology and physics. The simpler Copernican hypothesis supplanted the ever- growing complexity of the Ptolemaic universe and laid the groundwork for modern cosmology. Einstein's $E=MC^2$ is the epitome of parsimony, erasing the complexities of ether theory (although Einstein was subsequently flummoxed by the complexifications of quantum theory). But the LOP is self-evidently insufficient when it comes to issues related to biology/evolution as well as to anything related to historiosophy and psychology. Nature/evolution is constantly generating endless "solutions" to the challenges of our hostile environment, even when prior solutions worked, and often still work quite well, (sometimes even better). Aquinas, anticipating Occam, wrote: "If a thing can be done adequately by means of one, it is superfluous to do it by means of several, for we observe that nature does not employ two instruments where one suffices." But Aquinas was plainly wrong. Think of how many varieties of animals and birds make their living as scavengers (competing with one another for the carrion), or how many birds, insects, and animals pollinate (complementing one another) or how many different species of trees occupy the same ecosystems (competing with *and* complementing one another). Nature contradicts Aquinas; it favors plenitude over parsimony *in all things*. It is the limited human intellect that favors parsimony for the sake of convenience. Evolution is an ongoing interaction between the "inorganic" world molding the "organic" world and the "organic" world changing the "inorganic" world, creating infinitudes of varieties, sub-varieties and sub-sub varieties competing with and complementing one another in an endless process of change that creates ever-growing plenitude.

Biological evolution is not linear, proceeding in lock step to some "final cause"; it is not always creating ever-more advanced species or advanced versions of species to fill certain niches. It will sometimes produce a species more primitive than ones already extant in order to "test" if it can fill a certain niche more efficiently. Nature is profligate and unselective, not parsimonious and discriminating. Yet it is certainly the case that, at the macro level, evolution tends to ever greater complexity and sentient advancement. The ongoing complexification of existence over cosmic time seems to be self-evident. But the "daily business" of evolution does not concern itself with any greater cosmic "mission." It busies itself with "experimenting" with endless varieties of life to "test" if they will work (i.e., survive and prosper *efficiently* in particular ecological niches). The cosmic inclination of evolution (i.e., evolution on a cosmic scale) is, however, complexification. The planetary proclivity of evolution is endless tinkering: trying out various forms of life that will fit into the unending number of nature's niches. Chaos theory might give us some insight here. Environmental fractals constantly create new niches for new variations of life. The very existence of these fractals function as a *local* final cause drawing/driving evolution to develop new life forms and new versions of similar life forms capable of filling them. These new life forms create new fractals, and their various versions may or may not be more complex than previous versions because local evolution is indifferent to the general trend towards complexification of cosmic evolution. This general trend might be the basis for a scientific neo-teleology.

Darwinism is to evolution what Copernicus was to cosmology and Neo-Darwinism is to evolution what Galileo was to cosmology. In other words, we are still at the dawn of evolutionary theory rather than at its dusk. Genetics proves that evolution is an absolute fact (human beings share 50% of their DNA with bananas). But we have not, as yet produced a comprehensive theoretical account that sufficiently explains it. I mark this down to the desire to reduce the evolutionary phenomena (not phenomenon) to simple terms according to the LOP. Unfortunately, in battling the nonsense of the creationists, many evolutionary biologists have made Neo-Darwinism an absolute dogma, ignoring disagreement with it from scientists such as Lynn Margulies and philosophers of science such as Karl Popper. This brute fact of evolutionary history renders *Occam's Razor* suspect. If there was one elemental cause of natural and social phenomena, the LOP would pertain. But since we observe a multiplicity of solutions, each with its relative advantages, then we must conclude that natural and social phenomena most often have multiple causes.

With regard to the social "sciences"—those intellectual endeavors that deal with human history and society—academes' simplistic, reductionist theories that explain everything (economic, social, political history) are so intellectually impoverished as to be silly. Marxism and behaviorism are the biggest violators. Both oversimplify complex phenomena to the point of absurdity. A small dose of Alfred North Whitehead's skepticism about LOP (*"Seek simplicity, and distrust it"*[8]) would have enriched their research. The instinctive anti-intellectualism of the worldly layman when confronted with these theories is therefore quite healthy. The various schools of history are a case in point. What were the causes of America's Revolutionary and Civil Wars? Any real reading of the facts and events reveals that they were a combination of political ideals, economic interests, cultural differences, accumulated resentments, personal ambitions, greed, racism, and divergent social/political/cultural histories.

Regarding evolution and human society, I would turn Occam on its head and claim that "all things being equal, the most complex explanation is most likely to be closer to the truth". Evolutionary theory should embrace complexity not reductionist simplicity. Meteorology, not physics should probably be the "queen of sciences" for biologists. Weather is caused by a myriad of complex phenomena. Complexity can contain and entertain more nuance and subtlety, more ambiguity and paradox than a parsimonious explanation. Life *per se* is nothing if not nuanced and subtle; human society is nothing if not ambiguous and paradoxical. If evolution is correct, it must perforce contradict the Law of Parsimony. I am not talking about a hesitant, almost apologetic, allowance that some explanations do not conform to the Law of Parsimony. Rather I am advocating the full-throated enthusiastic support for the most complex explanation. I realize that the present and near future generation of scientists will have trouble with this notion because of the sociological inertia of science. Max Planck, recognizing this inertia, wrote "a scientific truth does not triumph by convincing its opponents ... but rather because its opponents eventually die and a new generation grows up that is familiar with it."[9]

If "existence" is infinite in all directions, and *for all time,* then its complexity (as a whole and in all its parts) is also infinite. The LOP only pertains to very small *arbitrarily determined* space/time domains, relating to clearly defined inquiries pertaining to this Cosmos only, but certainly not for infinite Nature. Within this restriction, it has been extremely effective and has advanced civilization more than any other principle in human history. But as we approach a largeness that is the "outer" boundary of our Cosmos and a smallness that is the "inner" boundary of our Cosmos the relevance of the LOP as a guiding principle to our endeavors begins to break down. As with mathematics, it begins to be a "scholastic" barrier to further understanding. Quantum physics has already revealed the ultimate complexity, ambiguity and paradoxicality of reality. As with reductionism, the LOP still has a valuable role to play in furthering our knowledge of clearly defined domains, but whenever we approach the border between physics and metaphysics, its methodological validity begins to dissipate.

The truth is that NOTHING is only one thing or even a multiplicity of things. In fact, even a NOTHING is really a "something." Reductionism only enables enough information to manipulate nature (it never enables one to reach "the thing in itself"). I might have once allowed the LOP dominion in one area—mathematics. Yet even here some philosophers of mathematics would object—e.g., Gödel's theorems and Menger's thinking. The LOP is certainly not suitable for any endeavor that cannot be mathematized. If you can mathematize something then in most cases, for all intents and purposes, it probably pertains. But life, biology, evolution, history, politics, love, friendship, innovation, entrepreneurship cannot be mathematized. In other words, mathematics has little, if anything, to do with what occupies and preoccupies human beings in the overall course of their lives—little to do with what it means to be human. The LOP as applied to the social and evolutionary sciences is an obstacle not an aid. The existence of consciousness indicates that behaviorism, or any reduction of human behavior to chemical interactions, is absurd enough to self-evidently prove the impoverishment of LOP. Consider also that the LOP could be one of the foundations for totalitarianism—ONE logical way to do something— no bourgeoisie messiness—just a simple explanation. Constitutionalism and Democracy are sloppy and disorderly; endlessly multi-dimensional as they are constantly, in real time, reacting to the rational, irrational, and non-rational behavior of the totality of the citizenry. Is the LOP inherent in every dogmatism, including scientism? Is Marxism scientism with an anthropological face?

We must cultivate a post-postmodern civilization that is liberated from the LOP, if it is to optimally fulfill its promise. Indeed, the LOP runs counter to current ecological wisdom and might be one of the subliminal causes of monoculture farming that has caused so much ecological devastation worldwide. If nature functions according to the *Law of Plentitude* and not the *Law of Parsimony*, then a healthy ecology is characterized by ever-growing numbers of species, sub-species and varieties of species and sub-species interacting with one another. A degraded ecology is characterized by an ever-diminishing number of species, sub-species and varieties of species and sub-species; all interactions being "weeded out" in order to produce an elegant order that can be easily manipulated for a specific purpose. I suggest that much of the environmental catastrophe that is presently endangering human civilization is a consequence of "applied LOP."

Yet there is a risk in rejecting the LOP completely. We might fall into the trap of postmodernist gibberish! There is no question that the LOP has been necessary in the history of thought in order to clear away the rubble of superstitious mumbo jumbo we inherited from our esteemed ancestors. Moreover, it is still a valuable tool in detecting and clearing away the rubble of superstitious mumbo jumbo of much of academic writing in general, and that of the postmodernist variety in particular. But once it accomplished its historic task, it left a smooth surface—"elegant" in its reductionist simplicity but meaningless for any effort to describe the complexity of existence. It was so reductionist it reduced to nothing; it became a formal system as in mathematics—internally consistent but irrelevant for the "I/Thou" relationship that individual human beings have with the infinite complexity of the brute fact of their own existence vis-à-vis the brute fact of existence itself. The new science of complexity has come to help us to build a magnificent structure on this smooth surface (prepared for us by the LOP) and dig a deep foundation below. We have been equipped to grow out of our intellectual infancy and advance into our cosmic majority.

Has the LOP run its course? Has it exhausted its great historic task in the cause of human progress; is it now a great barrier preventing significant breakthroughs in human understanding? Is there, similar to mathematics, a historical analogy to scholasticism in that the great medieval synthesis enabled tremendous intellectual progress up to a point (even producing the LOP) and then became a barrier to further intellectual progress—from which the West was only rescued by the Renaissance and subsequent Scientific Revolution? The LOP applied to historical causation has been a major contributor to poor intellectual integrity in the social sciences and even to some degree in cosmology and evolutionary thinking. A Marxist historian will often artificially force the diverse and dissimilar components of human interactions into Marxian theories of history and economy that ignore the particulars of different cultures and different historical epochs. The explanations will be internally logical and thus difficult to refute, but this will be because they will be one-dimensional to a very great degree and thus much easier to deal with. Marxists break out in rashes when confronted with the *sui generis*. Neo-Darwinists and Big Bang cosmologists have similar problems. As Sidney Ratner has written "... even professional scientists and philosophers become so absorbed in defending some vested interest or eloquent idea that they do not welcome truth but seek victory and the dispelling of their own doubts."[10] Ratner's observation must come under the rubric of "nothing new under the sun." Remember it was the Natural Philosophers of the academies (the equivalent of university professors today), whose entire careers and status was based on Aristotelian/Ptolemaic cosmology that were even more hostile to Galileo than some in the Church. The scholars of the academies refused to look into Galileo's telescope to see the proof that refuted their "scholarship." Some Jesuit astronomers, on the other hand, actually confirmed Galileo's observations by way of their own improved telescopes. Galileo's real "crime" was ignoring the Pope's instruction to promote his theory as a hypothesis and not as fact. This was not an unreasonable condition given that there were several scientific issues still outstanding regarding his theory based on his observations. Complaining about this purposeful ignorance of academics, Galileo wrote to Kepler:

> My dear Kepler, I wish that we might laugh at the remarkable stupidity of the common herd. What do you have to say about the principal philosophers of this academy who are filled with the stubbornness of an asp and do not want to look at either the planets, the moon or the telescope, even though I have freely and deliberately offered them the opportunity a thousand times? Truly, just as the asp stops its ears, so do these philosophers shut their eyes to the light of truth.

Perhaps the search for a "theory of everything" is indicative of the tyranny of the LOP. Perhaps there are *"theories of everything"*—that existence *per se* and the evolution of existence *per se* is driven by and created by multiple "gods"—a cosmic polytheism, or by a god with multiple aspects—an *Elohim* (plural) rather than an El (singular); a god with multiple personality disorder: a god of Cosmology and a god of Quantum (who infrequently communicate with one another). Maybe the same is true for biological evolution. Perhaps Neo-Darwinism is but a special case of a much broader and deeper phenomenon; much as we might consider Newtonian gravitation as a special case, subsequently subsumed into and superseded (but not excluded) by Einsteinian gravitation. And maybe Einsteinian gravitation might ultimately be superseded (but not excluded) by a theory that eventually explains the paradox of so-called dark matter and dark energy. I suggest that obstacles to theoretical and practical progress in cosmology and evolution are due to the implicit assumption that one neat theory can explain "everything." I suggest we should be looking for *"theories of everything(s)."*

Chapter Seven: The Crises of Philosophy and Religion

> "Institutions are not pretty. Show me a pretty government. Healing is wonderful, but the American Medical Association? Learning is wonderful, but universities? The same is true for religion ... religion is institutionalized spirituality."
> —Huston Smith in *Mother Jones*, November/December 1997

The atomization of philosophy into the materialistic, idealistic, scientific, and existential is a creation of modern academe. This atomization has made philosophy incompetent to deal with ultimate questions regarding human existence. Individual meaning requires metaphysical meaning, which means cosmic purpose. The artificial partition of philosophy into distinctive academic courses might make it easier to grade students and grant status to professors, but it has distorted the true philosophic vocation and desiccated the inherent qualities of human *being*. The dichotomy between all-inclusive "objective" Hegelian style philosophies and individualist "subjective" existentialist philosophies that relate to the angst of the individual being is a false dichotomy if it is Pascal's universe which is the cause of our angst. This explains the obstinate appeal of religion. Religion combines an all-encompassing cosmology with the individual's place and purpose in that cosmology—it invests existence with meaning. Cosmodeism is admittedly, first and foremost, an objective Hegelian-like enterprise, but it is fundamentally driven by the desire to provide a substantive answer to the very subjective question of the meaning of our own existence, rather than academic hubris striving to create a theoretical construct to be admired by other academics. The irony is that in order to satisfy this personal need, we are driven to undertake such speculations, such conjectures, and such hypotheses. Philosophy has not had such a comprehensive ambition for over a century, while religion has never really been able to transcend its Bronze Age roots despite its various more modernist iterations. Philosophy has adapted to science, religions have not.

By implication, western thought has accepted the Cartesian dichotomy: matter versus mind or materialism versus idealism. But I have always failed to understand this dichotomy. Philosophic materialism refers to all of nature and all that is contained within it. It posits that nature exists objectively, independent of our idea or view of it. This materialist view of existence is axiomatic for me—existence exists, we are not dreaming it. And if we were dreaming it, what is the "we" that would be doing the dreaming? Would not Cartesian logic then conclude "I dream; therefore I am?" The ontological reality of existence is absolute. Yet this does not contradict spirituality or philosophic idealism. Because conscious life, as a product and part of this objective existence (this ontological reality), uses ideas (mind) to change matter (the material universe) and even life. Moreover, the ideas that change objective existence are very often generated by existential angst— the problematic of the meaning of our own existence—the spiritual distress inherent to the human condition.

Recent scientific progress has, in essence, confirmed how our subjective will, formed by our ideals and spiritual wonder, can impact and change objective reality. Current epigenetic research has indicated that our environment, especially our intellectual environment, can actually advantage certain higher level genetic propensities and potentialities *which can be passed on to future generations,* thus impacting the intellectual and spiritual development of future generations: our *subjective* angst driving our *subjective* curiosity to create a new *objective* consciousness reality that will impact certain aspects of the *objective* material universe (as humanity has consistently done throughout the history of our species). Epigeneticists call this *neo-Lamarckism.* Stem cell researchers also use the term *neo-Lamarckism* as the changes acquired by means of stem cells are also passed on to future generations. Directed changes of the environment, as well as the practical application of stem cells, are both consequences of the human mind, human ideas and human idealism impacting and changing objective material reality. Thus, human idealism has the potential, at first indirectly and later directly, to change the future of cosmic history. Where, then, is the dichotomy between the objective and the subjective; between mind and matter; between the spiritual and the material?

Human beings have created religions and philosophies to quiet our anxiety about the meaning and significance of our finite lives within the vastness of existence. Since the Enlightenment, some have attempted to turn science into a worldview—even a religion. But science is neither a worldview nor a religion. It is a proximate methodological tool (a much more reliable proximate tool than religion or philosophy) by which we attempt to reveal the physical secrets of existence and of life. It is and must be the very foundation of all further human inquiry—but it is not enough; it is necessary but not sufficient. We require a much greater religious/philosophical vision of the human condition than science can ever provide, not only to satisfy our own human dispositions, but, perhaps paradoxically, to drive science ever onward, so that the scientific project itself will not degenerate and become smug and arrogant (as it often did in the 19th and 20th centuries).

Our subjective visions of the future are proximate *final causes* for every aspect of human intellection; they focus and concentrate human activity towards a meaningful "predetermined" end (predetermined in the sense that we envision the end we desire, which motivated the activity in the first place). Futuristic envisionings are subjective teleologies. This is most apparent in the arts but, paradoxically, at an even deeper level, in the sciences. We engage in science to find answers to specific questions. We often desire specific answers and just as often are disappointed by those answers when they do not substantiate our original hypotheses (sometimes a fancy name for our prejudices—literally prejudgments). Scientists develop an intriguing hypothesis based on educated guesses relating to various aspects of empirical evidence available to the scientific community. They begin discussing their ideas and earn a bit of notoriety from their colleagues. Full of excitement at the possibility of publishing a breakthrough paper that will establish their scientific prominence, they devise experiments the results of which often show that their original hypothesis was not even close to reality, even though they did everything in their power to bend the results to their will.

In other words, scientific research is intentional and purposeful; it is consumed by purpose even though this is denied because such an attitude is assumed to be anti-scientific. But it is decidedly not anti-scientific. It is the essence of scientific ambition; an ambition that *reflects* our philosophical and religious worldviews as much as it is committed to gaining a better understanding of the world. Science is as purposeful as any political ideology or supernatural religion. The scientific pose of purposelessness was an invention of the 19th century. But the greatest scientific minds in history have often been driven by a "religious" purpose. Copernicus wanted to preserve God's honor by providing a more elegant/rational explanation of the cosmic order than Ptolemy. Newton wanted to discover and read the mind of God. And Einstein was religious (in the true sense of word) to his core. Our task is to reinstate metaphysical purpose to the scientific project because the civilizational price of purposelessness is calamity. We must rid ourselves of supernatural theology, but only in order to invent a more robust natural theology—non-contradictory in every way to science.

Historically, religion gave birth to philosophical thinking while religious and philosophical thinking gave birth to scientific thinking. The original purpose of *Occam's Razor*, for example, was to prove the philosophical validity of Monotheism over Polytheism, but quickly became the holy grail of scientific thinking. I have often wondered if the Scientific Revolution could have occurred in a non-monotheistic civilization, rather than a civilization that had already created a theological law of parsimony: *one* God; *the* One (and *only*)? Perhaps it is time for science to repay its debt to religion and create a philosophy which could create a religion suitable for the human race as it expands outward into the Cosmos? Perhaps it is time to realize Carl Sagan's dream. It is self-evident that the organized "Religion Business," in all its current manifestations, is utterly unqualified to honestly relate to the possibility of a natural theology suitable for the space age. The fundamental crisis of the organized (dogma-ridden) "Religion Business" is that it has become not only irrelevant, but also dysfunctional to the spiritual needs of the 21st century. Some denominations are even hostile to the very idea of the 21st century and thus are dysfunctional to the survival needs of the 21st century. This at a time when an all-encompassing religious vision—celebrating the very fact of existence and of conscious life in that existence—is needed as never before. We live in a spiritual desert and instead of spiritual water, our legacy religions are spreading spiritual vinegar, while at the same time complaining about our stunted spiritual growth. Ever since the Scientific Revolution, our inherited religions have been unable to restore purpose. They could only do so by conversing with a more relevant intellectual partner—with science. As Harvey Cox put it:

> For centuries, theology's principal sparring partner has been philosophy. Augustine argued with the Neoplatonists, Aquinas carried on a lifelong conversation with Aristotle. Nineteenth-century theologians conversed with the philosophical idealists and twentieth-century theologians with the existentialists.[11]

In the 21st century, the crucial conversation theology *and* philosophy must have is with science. Not only by *listening* carefully to what science has to say about *proximate reality*, but also by *talking back* to science, thus enriching scientific inquiry by suggesting informed speculations about *ultimate re-*

ality. This would expand the territory that scientific imagination can apply to *proximate reality* and in doing so increase its scope. Speculations about *proximate reality* must be in complete non-contradiction to the scientific attitude—based on reality as science describes it. But such speculations must not be as limited when it comes to proposing informed conjectures about *ultimate reality*; conjectures that we must concede, *a priori*, can never be proven empirically but which can be useful as working assumptions providing hints and clues for the scientific investigator. Science should not be adverse to this because, as already indicated, it is already working according to assumptions that can never be proven empirically. As Peter Russell puts it, "the image a society has of itself can play a crucial role in the shaping of its future."[12] As with society, so with the scientific project; for example, how did concepts such as *The Great Chain of Being* and *The Idea of Progress* facilitate the development of evolutionary thinking? Ever since we have seen that blue marble of our earth hanging in the total blackness of space, the collective human soul has needed a new self-image and a new all-human vision and project that contains the possibility of quieting Pascal and Camus.

The decline of optimism in the 20th century also weakened the belief in the *Idea of Progress*. This, in conjunction with the enormous progress of science in describing the vastness and the minuteness of existence, has had profound philosophical and psychological consequences. The abstruseness of traditional religious beliefs as well as the rise of Darwinism and Freudianism undermined the self-esteem of western elites. Enlightenment men were usually still believers in God (although often contemptuous of organized religion) and accepted that men were made "in the image of God," by God himself. Newton and Locke were devoutly religious men. Along comes Darwin and demonstrates that man is not created by God but is related to apes and monkeys. Enlightenment thinkers believed that man was a rational being amenable to self-improvement as a consequence of rational social and political policy. Along comes Freud and blasts away this naive psychology and demonstrates the dark and often primitive complexity of the human psyche. We began to ask unanswerable questions. What is the meaning of life? How do we even address the mystery of the existence of existence—the fact that there is an "is?" We range from wonder at our own ability to uncover the mysteries of the "mind of God" to a Pascalian melancholy about the very meaninglessness of what we discover. Alienation and anxiety about our very existence began to dominate our spiritual ecology: nihilism, existentialism, cultural anarchy, and cultural relativism. As previously mentioned, these anxieties often seek relief in the false bromides of fundamentalist religion or in the self-imposed haze of drugs and shopping.

The challenge is to create a logical natural theology, non-contradictory to the scientific attitude, which supplants mystical supernatural theologies. Social "theologies," humanistically commendable in themselves, have not in any way quelled the despair that Pascal expressed centuries ago. Advocating social justice for the wretched of the earth, while admirable, in no way addresses the fundamental question: WHAT DOES IT ALL MEAN? No subsequent theological formulation has ever come close to *honestly* responding to Pascal's honest despair. Unless organized religions cultivate the ambition to undertake this task, they will remain irrelevant (the more liberal religions) or dangerous (the more fundamentalist ones). The crisis of religion will deepen.

Chapter Eight: The Crisis of Psychology

The crisis of psychology is the crisis of meaning. Psychology, since its inception as a modern discipline, has been preoccupied with meaning. Words like angst and alienation recur like a mantra throughout the history of psychology—from Freud, Jung, Adler and Rank, to Maslow, Frankl and Becker. The general explicit or implicit theme of them all is that if we find meaning in our lives, we will find mental health. The problem is that psychology, unlike religion and classic philosophy, does not even presume to provide meaning to human existence; it simply preaches that meaning is meaningful. Indeed, psychologists talk about the need for meaning endlessly. They offer strategies and tactics for individuals to "find" meaning. They often recommend public policies and programs that would enable individuals to find meaning. But they never offer a convincing worldview of their own by which a modern rational person might infer meaning. Psychology satisfies itself with *the search for meaning* but never supplies an answer to the question—"WHAT DOES IT ALL MEAN?"

And this is why, at the end of the day, psychology has failed, and why it may have caused more psychological damage than remedy. Preaching the subjective need for meaning while not providing *objective* meaning tends to increase anxiety, not mitigate it. Methodologies and life strategies that enable us to *pretend* we have meaning might enable us to temporarily escape from our individual and civilizational neurosis—but only temporarily. In this the psychology industry resembles the diet industry. Its long-term economic soundness is based on the fact that it provides no long-term solutions and we become addicted to various therapies much like diet addicts (as in "I tried Freudian; now I'm into Jungian"). I will limit my observations to four major figures who have dealt with meaning in a substantive way: Jung, Frankl, Becker, and Maslow.

Jung

Freudians are preoccupied with "meaning making" as a mental health *project* rather than with meaning as an inherently serious philosophical challenge to the psychological project itself. Jung, on the other hand, seemed to be a little more daring, leading him into speculations that bordered on the religious and even the mystical (a tendency which earned Freud's displeasure). But even Jung—the most "religious" and "mystical" of the founding fathers of psychology—did not come through, and really could not, given the scientific pretensions (and thus self-imposed limitations) of the psychological project. I say scientific pretensions because when you read the writings of Freud you are reminded more of Transcendentalist essays, than scientific papers—except Theroux and Emerson were better writers. William James is a far superior writer, and in my opinion has more subtle psychological insights as to human nature than Freud. I find nothing scientific about Freud or Jung whatsoever.

Jung asserted "Man cannot stand a meaningless life [...] Meaninglessness inhibits fullness of life and is therefore equivalent to illness." He wrote: "That gives peace, when people feel that they are living the symbolic life, that they are *actors* in the *divine drama* (italics mine). That gives the only meaning to human life; everything else is banal and you can dismiss it."[13] But after telling us that we are sick because we don't have meaning in our lives, he coyly avers that "Psychology is concerned with the act of seeing and not with the construction of new religious truths."[14] In other words, life is meaningless without the divine drama, but don't expect me to provide it. I'm just here to tell you how screwed up you are unless you are an actor in one.

Jung is like an erotically provocative person who after teasing his partner, fails to come through when the partner is aroused. He simply increases frustration rather than alleviating it—psychological "blue balls" as it were. He also contradicts himself at a very basic level. He traces our civilizational and individual neuroses to the absolutist (almost totalitarian) triumph of the objective scientific attitude over our civilizational mythologies and subjective individual intimations, dreams, and religious instincts. He initially censors this absolutist scientific attitude but then frees himself from responsibility for ameliorating its consequences with the copout that psychology is itself a science concerned with seeing reality not with providing new religious truths. In this he is not different from Freud. Is this spiritual hypocrisy? Did Jung himself really search for the *divine drama* (what I have called the cosmic drama) or, like Freud, did he see religions as therapeutic—providing an illusion of "meaning" whether they divined ultimate reality or not? Was religious faith good because it revealed ultimate meaning or was it good because it made you feel good (kind of like Prozac) and filled the existential vacuum? Consider that the desire to fill the postmodernist vacuum might be one of the causes of the present mass worldwide return to fundamentalist religions. Such a return occurred once before in the 19th century when the dislocations of the Industrial Revolution resulted in mass religious revivalism, alcoholism, and money grubbing. Today, we also have religious revivalism, with drugs added to alcoholism, and shopping as a mindless, therapeutic distraction, dulling the ache of our existential vacuum. Regarding the psychological function of "shopping" as a recreational pastime, my late dear friend Bill Cohen once commented that if America closed all its shopping centers for one weekend, 30 million Americans would have a nervous breakdown.

Jung also contradicted himself regarding work. On the one hand, he claimed that a sense of mission gives meaning, but on the other hand he indicated that work is an alienated reification. As Mark Vernon put it in an article in the Guardian:

> ... Jung wondered whether modern individuals are (using work) to atone for an ill-defined sense of moral failure (because) we are no longer sure what makes something valuable, bar an arbitrary designation of financial worth, and this transforms the humdrum need for money into a kind of worship of money. (Marx also dwelled on the alienated worship of money.)

My first reaction upon reading this was "such divorced from reality condescension!" Is all overwork a worship of money or is it often driven by that same sense of mission Jung sees as praiseworthy; by that adrenalin our bodies produce when we are in the thralls of the very joy of creating—by the existential meaningfulness that creativity provides? Think of Voltaire, Edison, Picasso, and Steve Jobs—workaholics all. Think of medical students and start-up entrepreneurs who put in 100-hour weeks; or single parents working three jobs to give their children a better life; or athletes who have achieved greatness by being workaholics (Michael Jordan, Larry Bird, Jerry Rice, and any Olympian). There is no question that workaholism is often an escape mechanism from the existential emptiness of one's life. But unless you are capable of providing a *real* (not invented) alternative meaning, it would be best to shut up, lest you exacerbate the alienation you are critiquing. I would agree that it is often the case that for some people having money and all the trappings that money can buy demonstrate that their life is meaningful (Donald Trump is a perfect example of such existential hollowness). However, showing people that overwork is an artificial antidote to the meaninglessness of their own lives without actually providing meaning is simply cruel. On the other hand, I believe Jung was on to something when he stated:

> There exists "an archetype of meaning" that represents one
> of the primary loci of the psyche and, its relentless longing
> to manifest is itself an archetypal quest. We need to con-
> sider however, that as human consciousness has trudged
> along its evolutionary trajectory, subtle, profoundly signif-
> icant changes in the character of this archetypal quest have
> taken place.[15]

I believe the archetypal quest he is referring to represents the same desire
that led Nessyahu to intuit Cosmodeism—that the ultimate meaning of existence is the ongoing divinization of existence to which our own existence
contributes (Jung's divine drama). This archetypal spiritual quest also in-
spires us to contribute to perfecting the "kingdom" (the Kabalistic "Malchut") we are born into (e.g., the 21st-century planet Earth) as a necessary
preparation/first step towards the great cosmic project. Recognition of this
ultimate purpose is what could provide real meaning to our lives and not
made-up meaning and thus perhaps serve as the foundation of an efficient
therapeutic tool. For Jung, meaning is an archetypal component of our psychological existence. He writes: "In the same way the body needs food, and
not just any kind of food but only that which suits it, the psyche needs to
know the meaning of its existence—*not just any meaning* (italics mine), but
the meaning of those images and ideas which reflect its nature and which
originate in the unconscious."[16] I suggest that Cosmodeism might provide
us with an opportunity for submersion into a higher level of consciousness—an amalgamation of hyper-individuality within cosmic collectivi-
ty—not an either/or but rather the "this" by way of the "that" or the "that"
by way of the "this." The individual finding his or her true significance in
the very evolutionary process of the Cosmos is itself a contribution to the
evolutionary process. This would be the ultimate I/Thou relationship.

Victor Frankl and Abraham Maslow

Holocaust survivor Victor Frankl was as much a philosopher as he was a
therapist (perhaps the best therapists are philosophers or religious in the
true sense of the words). He indicated that one must have a concept of what
it actually means to be human before presuming to treat human neuroses;
one must first have "a theory of man." Mental health for him was essentially
spiritual health; finding meaning in one's life was essential to the therapeu-

tic process. Certainly, no one dealt more with the problem of meaning for mental health. Just look at the titles of his books: *Man's Search for Meaning; The Will to Meaning; The Unheard Cry for Meaning; Man's Search for Ultimate Meaning*. His treatment was "logotherapy," which literally means "meaning therapy." Frankl's therapy was to help the patient search for (or find?) meaning. "Logotherapy maintains that psychological problems arise when someone loses their sense of purpose and finds themselves in an existential funk, at which point it is the therapist's duty to help them find it once again."[17] As Dr. Alex Pattakos put it in an article in *Psychology Today*:

> To Dr. Frankl, the problems of aggression, addiction, and depression could be traced, in large part, to an "existential vacuum" or perception that one's life, including one's work life, appeared to be *meaningless*. He observed that the existential vacuum was a widespread phenomenon of the 20th century and underscored that these conditions were not truly understandable, let alone "treatable," *unless the existential vacuum underlying them was recognized* (italics mine).[18]

My problem with Frankl is that, unlike him, I perceive the existential vacuum as an objective fact rather than a subjective pathology. Pathologies are subjective, the vacuum is not —the vacuum is as real as $E=MC^2$. Meaning cannot be invented or found in some biological or cultural cause; it is either inherent to existence or existence is without meaning. If existence *per se* is without meaning, then our individual lives are without meaning and thus neurosis is not only reasonable, it is mandatory (a modern iteration of Pascal's despair). Frankl is one of my favorite thinkers because of his preoccupation with meaningfulness. Yet what substantive objective meaning does he offer? Can there be subjective meaningfulness without objective meaning? Unlike Freud (but like Jung) he relates respectfully to the place of religiousness for psychological wellbeing, especially in his book *The Unconscious God*. Yet in the end all he can offer is that we must change our *attitude* to our existence. In the end that is all that the entire psychological project can offer. For psychologists the problem is attitude, not reality as such. To my mind, that is a self-manipulation—the problem *is* reality as such.

Maslow's *Hierarchy of Values* has become well-known as one of the foundations of modern self-help literature. By concentrating on what makes people spiritually healthy rather than neurotic he might have angered a few

Freudians, but he undoubtedly made a positive contribution to the psychological project as a valuable civilizational tool, in addition to its therapeutic value for the individual. But in the end he, too, missed the point—a view shared by Frankl, who wrote in *Man's Search for Meaning*:

> ... the real aim of human existence cannot be found in what is called self-actualization. Human existence is essentially *self-transcendence* (italics mine) rather than self-actualization. Self-actualization is not a possible aim at all; for the simple reason that the more a [person] would strive for it, the more [they] would miss it. For only to the extent to which [people] commit [themselves] to the fulfillment of [their] life's meaning, to this extent [they] also actualize [themselves]. In other words, self-actualization cannot be attained if it is made an end in itself, but only as a side-effect of self-transcendence.[19]

Frankl's critique of Maslow is right on, but Maslow could have turned the tables and countered: "Alright Viktor, but where is the *actual* self-transcendence in *logotherapy*? Describing the need for self-transcendence is not the same as providing the mechanism for it. All you are doing is generating an unattainable goal for someone who is already neurotic. Won't this exacerbate his neurosis?" Maslow's later thought indicated he realized the limitations of his own hierarchy. If he had lived longer, he might have added a higher pinnacle to his hierarchy of values; following Frankl's suggestion he might have called it transcendent realization—what Jung called the divine drama and I have called the cosmic drama. But as with the fictional rejoinder to Frankl, wouldn't he also have just been creating an unattainable goal?

Ernest Becker

Becker was more a polymath than a trained psychologist, but his writings have great relevance for the crises of psychology. His formal academic credentials are in cultural anthropology, but his creative work references a wide range of thinkers: Freud, Hegel, Kierkegaard, Fromm, Reich, Rank, and Norman Brown, as well as many others from various fields, including religion. In daring to try to formulate a comprehensive "theory of man" rather than promote his own academic status by concentrating on the field in which he was credentialed, Becker wandered far and wide—risking being called a dilettante, following in the intellectual tradition of James and Nietzsche. Given all this, the most honest encounter with the problem of meaning I have encountered is Becker's *The Birth and Death of Meaning*. But even he does not, in the end, provide an empirically objective meaningfulness for the existence of conscious human life—*nor does he even presume to*. I stress human life because there can never be an empirically objective meaning for existence itself; why existence exists; why there is anything at all rather than nothing. This will remain the eternal mystery.

The Scientific Revolution and the subsequent European Enlightenment began to empty life of its invented meaning, creating a civilizational neurosis that bred the individual neuroses that triggered the Freudian revolution. Erich Fromm explained it thus:

> What characterizes medieval in contrast to modern society is its lack of individual freedom .... But altogether a person was not free in the modern sense, neither was he alone and isolated. In having a distinct, unchangeable, and unquestionable place in the social world from the moment of birth, man was rooted in a structuralized whole, and *thus life had a meaning* [italics mine] which left no place, and no need for doubt.[20]

I consider Fromm's comment to be an over-simplification derived from the predeterminations of the modernist ideologies he advocated (Marxism and Freudianism). Both 'isms' have a particular agenda that exceeds the presumed scientific search for "objective" truth. As referenced in my chapter "The Alienation Racket," I believe that alienation has been inherent to the human condition throughout the entire history of the human race. It simply became increasingly difficult to *pretend* it wasn't an inherent part of the human condition once the scientific attitude conquered every aspect of human life.

Becker persuasively argued this very point in his great book, *The Denial of Death*. Yet there is no denying that the rise of the evolutionary paradigm—a product of the Scientific Revolution—exacerbated the dilemma by disabusing us of our inherited/invented creation mythologies. If we have descended from lower animals rather than a higher God (in whose image we were created); if we are more akin to a monkey that to the ruler of the universe, then self-esteem takes a real hit and alienation becomes an existential requisite rather than an object for scientific therapy. Becker justifiably criticizes the social sciences for "...not getting at the knowledge that instantly makes people feel powerful and satisfied, that gives them the sense that they are taming their world, taking command of its mystery and danger ...."[21] The question left hanging is how one can even presume to take command of the mystery of existence *per se*—that there is anything at all rather than nothing? Becker, as with every other commentator on the human condition, limits his critique to the personal, social, and political realms—never daring to venture into the cosmic dilemma that is the existential framework for every single realm of intellectual inquiry. Yet what attracts me to Becker, as well as Frankl, and Maslow is that, although all three are thoroughgoing secular scientists, they are willing to treat the religious instinct with respect rather than with Freudian disdain—especially regarding the problem of meaning. Becker does this in an historical rather than a metaphysical way (as befits the scientist) but by implication reveals the tremendous psychological shortcomings of the secular civilization that arose after the European Enlightenment. Ultimately, Becker also admits that anxiety is inherent to the human condition: "... life (has) a quality of driveness, of underlying desperation, an obsession with the meaning of it and with his own significance as a creature."[22] In other words, the burden of self-aware human beings is a real bitch.

Becker writes "the world of meaning of any animal is created out of the range and subtlety of its own reactivity .... Man himself coins a designation for an object, and then responds to that arbitrary designation."[23] In other words, the human environment is not the jungle or the ocean or the desert; it has become, overwhelmingly, our own spiritual and physical creation. Ironically, our social inventions have resulted in a cultural and psychological evolution which provides us with the freedom that enables us to increasingly choose what to react to (unlike every other beast and plant of the earth that has *no choice* but to react to an explicitly objective environment). Do human beings actually exercise this freedom of choice? I would claim that, with isolated exceptions, we do not do so to any significant degree. More likely we choose not to exercise our freedom but rather to escape from it. Fromm's fine book, *Escape from Freedom*, describes this civilizational cowardice with pitiless precision. As Nietzsche indicated, we are afraid to stare into the abyss of the meaning (or meaninglessness) of our lives. Hence psychology has increasingly come to serve the escape from freedom rather than the pursuit of freedom. It has become the handmaid of advertising, human resource departments, policy think tanks as well as the economic interests of the psychology industry itself.

Every living thing reacts to and *creates* its environment. It reacts to an environment its own organic being has helped mold. The earliest plants created our oxygen rich environment which enabled the future creation of more complex life which further modified the environment. This dialectical interaction reaches its zenith in the human species. The range and subtlety of the human environment we currently interact with on a daily basis is overwhelmingly our own creation: buildings, plumbing, food, roads, traffic, tools, workplaces, etc. I refer not only to the objective physical environment we have created but also to the intellectual and spiritual environment that our own pervasive curiosity and desire to understand have created. The evolutionary story of humankind is its adaptation to an environment increasingly created by human beings. This has had as its consequence the demystification of existence. The more we know about proximate nature the less mysterious it seems. We are increasingly disabused of our own inherited beliefs until, ironically, in many cases we begin to disabuse ourselves of this amazing knowledge and return to pre-enlightenment religious beliefs because we cannot bear to stare into the abyss of the vastness of our own insignificance—hence the worldwide revival of fundamentalist religion. Biologists, chemists, and physicists try to understand nature; psychologists, sociologists, anthropologists, economists, and historians try to understand us—as do marketers, advertisers and politicians. The human environment has increasingly been dominated by abstractions created by human beings: gods, God, values, principles, mathematics, religions, ideologies, dogmas, laws, and relationships. Nature provided water but man created the abstraction H_2O and made it "holy," giving it "special powers that even nature could not give.

With the very significant exception of outer space, the human environment is now totally created by humans and not by "natural" evolution (in other words by humanity's own abstractions). Everything is self-referencing. Objective reality might exist objectively, but we are only capable of relating to it by way of our own abstractions (God, science, ideology); by way of our own constructs—Plato's shadows on the cave walls. In fact, we are now at a point in the planet's history in which every living thing on the planet must adapt to the abstraction-rich planetary environment that we humans have created. The environment must adapt to us as much as we must adapt to the environment that we ourselves have created. We have become a rather conflicted god, capable of destroying through our own predations, yet also intervening to protect and preserve because we fancy ourselves as a compassionate and loving god. We are now "free" to choose what we react to and everything we react to is now to a great degree a creation of our own hands. Even the damage of hurricanes Katrina, Sandy, and Harvey were a creation (of human negligence). In New Orleans, incompetent authorities didn't properly repair the levees that human beings built; in Houston, it was the lack of zoning laws that resulted in development that overwhelmed the land's ability to absorb water; in New Jersey people simply ignored the fact that nature couldn't care less about a great view of the ocean and built where they shouldn't have. But the human project to escape the boundaries of our own planet has changed all this. At once it returns us to wonder and awe and mystery (why there is anything at all) while also forcing us back to a pre-primate evolutionary challenge; forcing us to adapt to an environment that for the time being is 100% objective and material, with no human imprint. Yet even this seemingly objective reality will be related to us by way of our own invented abstractions, such as mathematics and whatever cosmological model is in vogue at the time.

Evolution is the true god of existence—the "Force" (may it be with you) that guides, drives and originates all existence—BUT STILL WHY? The challenge for psychology is whether it can ever offer an objective therapeutic solution to our civilizational and individual neuroses without grounding that therapy on a scientifically reasonable metaphysical foundation. I believe that unless the therapist can convince the patient that their very existence is a necessary and contributing factor to the oneness of existence, their alienation from the meaning of their own existence will not be alleviated. This is *the* crisis of psychology.

Chapter Nine: The Material Crisis

Exacerbating the existential, scientific, philosophic, and psychological crises is the material crisis—exemplified by the energy/environment challenge. Not only have we inherited the post Scientific Revolution anxiety about our place in the Universe, but we are also beginning to suspect we don't even belong to the planet Earth. The material crisis contributes to our sense of angst. We are told we have to change our lifestyles, that in order to survive as a species we have to limit growth and return to a simpler past. But since few are really willing to renounce the benefits of modern science, hygiene and universal literacy and return to the ignorance, filth, and illiteracy of that "simpler past," this is a survival strategy that doesn't have much hope of ever being implemented, especially since the entire population of the planet Earth seems determined to achieve a Euro/American standard of living within the next several decades.

The Middle-Class Revolution

The energy/environment conundrum represents the grand strategic "joint" in the struggle for sustainable human existence in the 21st century. It is being exacerbated by the growing global middle class. According to the Brookings Institute and other sources, the global middle class has been growing by 80 million people a year. By 2015, the number of Asian middle-class consumers was equal to Europe and North America combined. Today Asia's middle-class is significantly larger and is the key to a sustainable global environment. On present trends, there soon could be more than 2 billion Asians in middle-class households. By 2030, China could have 600 million middle-class consumers and India, 500 billion. By 2020, the global middle class had grown to 52 percent of the global population, up from 30 percent in 2008, and heading to 80 percent by 2060.

The energy needs are vast. There is no way that the present energy paradigm can satisfy them. In 2005, China *added* as much electricity generation as Britain produced in a year. In 2006, it *added* as much as France's total supply. By 2018, its electricity generation had doubled over 2005. In 2011, it passed the United States in electricity generation. Yet shortages of electricity and power outages were common, and millions still lack reliable access to electricity. And even though China is the world's leader in solar power installation, its coal-powered generating capacity actually increased to 1300 GW in 2020, from 960 GW in 2016. Coal still constitutes 70%

of China's total energy consumed and 80% of its electricity generation, as opposed to the United States, where coal represents only 11% of total energy consumed and 19% of electricity generation (and continues to decline). And even though India is the third largest electricity producer in the world, a population roughly the size of the United States still doesn't have any electric power. The demand for electricity in India will grow fivefold in the next 25 years. Since 75% of India's electric power is still generated by coal, the negative environmental consequences are second only to China.

The universal middle-class desire for personal transportation and the consequent energy demands are prodigious. The USA has 800 cars for every 1,000 people, while China only has 200 cars per 1,000 people but is already the world's largest car market and already has more cars (300 million) than the United States (275 million). Consider the implications. China's car market is growing by 20% a year. India and the rest of Asia have begun to follow suit. India already has 170 cars per 1,000 people and some projections have India passing China in total car ownership by midcentury, since its population has already surpassed China's. Even if the developed world increases energy productivity and decreases energy consumption, global energy consumption will continue to increase yearly. The energy challenge is, indeed, an existential challenge to the human race.

Sense and Nonsense about Energy

Energy is central to "limits to growth" arguments. Critiques of the present energy paradigm are for the most part correct. Transportation is still overwhelmingly dependent on oil. Moreover, 300,000 products are made of materials whose feedstock is oil or natural gas. 40% of the oil consumed in the world is used to make product (25% in the United States). These include plastics, chemicals, herbicides, pesticides, fertilizers, medicines etc. Petroleum is the most versatile, multipurpose natural resource that Mother Nature has provided us with, yet we burn it to move mass! Future historians will probably look back at us and conclude that human society must have had a collective psychotic breakdown to use this resource in this way. We might as well have burned Louis XIV furniture to move mass.

Nuclear energy is not the answer. It cannot solve the transportation or the product feedstock problem. It only provides electricity, and the United States (and much of Europe) is, for all intents and purposes, already self-sufficient in electricity production. Polls showing 60% of Americans in favor of nuclear power are irrelevant—try building a plant in their back-yard. Inevitable local opposition (NIMBY) will turn any new nuclear plant into a 10 to 20-year project even if approved by national authorities, and the subsequent overruns will double or triple original cost estimates. Even to-day, existing nuclear plants cannot compete pricewise with natural gas and renewables. The nuclear industry also has a demographic problem, as we shall see. Moreover, uranium, like oil and coal, is a finite resource. Uranium supplies available today can only enable us to maintain the current nucle-ar infrastructure with difficulty. There simply isn't enough to add another 40, 50, 100 new nuclear power plants. Given the impending demographic crisis of mining engineers and other nuclear industry professions, the U.S. will have difficulty even maintaining its present nuclear plants (see below).

"Drill, baby, drill" is not a solution. Oil industry "experts" laugh at the "end of oil" prognosticators because a plethora of new technologies, such as fracking, horizontal drilling, and computerized efficiencies, have made vast amounts of previously inaccessible resources economically feasible. This causes temporary market gluts, mollifying the apprehensions of many peo-ple. But, if you think long term, nothing has really changed. In this respect, the West's "A.D.D." puts it at a disadvantage when competing with Asia. In the West, a "quarter" is 3 months; in Asia a "quarter" is 25 years. Technolo-gy can transform ever-growing amounts of hydrocarbon resources (what is in the ground) into reserves (what can be technological and economically extracted), but it can never increase the resources in the ground. Resourc-es are still finite, and even if we could technologically and economically extract the last ton of hydrocarbons from the Earth's crust, the question remains whether we should. What would be the long-term *economic* costs of pollution and climate change? The damage to property, health, and ma-jor sectors of the economy (such as tourism) are never figured into the true costs of hydrocarbon extraction. These costs are always externalized onto tax-paying citizens and small businesses. The most recent example of this is the United States Federal Government planning to spend tens of billions of dollars to cap "orphan wells"—three million wells irresponsibly abandoned by the private sector, emitting as much greenhouse gas as all the cars in the USA, as well as leaking toxic oil into the ground water, yet not producing one gallon of usable fuel.

The 2022 war in Ukraine has shown that the developed world's self-satis-faction at the apparent defanging of OPEC's and Russia's stranglehold on the energy sector was premature and shortsighted. At present, the United States is self-sufficient in and a net exporter of natural gas. It has also expanded its natural gas reserves tremendously because of fracking, but the U.S. Energy Administration reported in 2015 that the U.S. has enough natural gas to last 86 years at present (pre-Ukrainian war) levels of consumption. But even if we assume that unforeseen discoveries, technological breakthroughs, and coal gasification double the amount of natural gas available and economically accessible to last 150 years, maintaining present levels of consumption within the current energy paradigm is highly unlikely, as gas continues to replace coal for electricity generation and liquid natural gas (LNG) is likely to replace Bunker[24] in shipping and Diesel in rail and trucking. Consequently, global demand for natural gas is estimated to grow by more than 50% over the coming years.

Estimating amounts of hydrocarbons still left in the earth's crust is a complex undertaking, but if we are to make rational policy, we must base our decisions on data provided to us by professionals. *Rystad Energy*, a respected oil and gas intelligence data firm, released a report on July 04, 2016, that estimated overall *global* oil reserves at 2,092 billion barrels. This was 70 times the yearly production rate of 30 billion barrels of crude oil at the time. In other words, if consumption flat lines we could continue to consume oil until almost 2100. But since the number of cars in the world is predicted to double from 1 billion to 2 billion by 2050 it is clear that the days of oil-based transportation are even shorter. And that is not even mentioning the oil needed to produce the over 300,000 products (and still counting) we consume for the three billion added members of the global middle class by 2060. There is no question, of course, that technological innovation and increased efficiencies will continue to turn heretofore unusable resources into usable reserves and that oil will probably be available after 2100. The problem is that the more challenging it becomes to turn a resource into a reserve, the more expensive it becomes, not to mention the environmental costs, which are also the indirect economic costs of oil.

The situation is compounded by increased domestic use by the major oil exporters. Before the Ukraine debacle, Russia extracted about 10 million barrels a day and consumed 5 million of those barrels—leaving 5 million for export. Given the exodus of the major oil companies with their advanced technological expertise in tandem with the tremendous brain drain of technological manpower it is difficult to see how they will be able to maintain such production over the medium term. Iran also consumes 50% of the oil it extracts and given the implications of the 2022 uprising and the resultant tumult in their oil industry, it is also doubtful they will be able to maintain let alone increase their current production. Indonesia is an extreme case in point. It was forced to leave OPEC (of which it was a founding member) in 2008 because it had become a net oil importer—a consequence of its growing middle class and growing domestic consumption. Ten years earlier it was exporting a million barrels a day, but has become a net importer for the past almost two decades. Mexico is on the same course and may also become a net oil importer by 2040 if it keeps developing at its current rate. We tend to forget that prior to WWII the United States was the world's largest oil exporter,[25] yet within a decade after WWII it became the world's largest importer. It is imperative that the West begin thinking of a quarter as 25 years, and not 3 months.

Worldwide reserves of coal have also been greatly exaggerated. Until recently, they have been evaluated on the basis of volume rather than energy content. Revised figures indicate that by *energy content* the USA in 2005 had about 120 years of reserves at then current rate of use, not the 250 years that was being cited at the time. (Given the decline of coal use since then, U.S. reserves at current rate of use is probably back up to 250 years). By energy content, China has about 60 years of reserves at current rate of use. The energy content of coal being mined has been in decline as we have moved from bituminous to sub-bituminous and in many areas to lignite. Until recently, the U.S. had been increasing the *volume* of coal mined by 1% a year. By 2010, 15% more coal by volume was being mined than 20 years previously. But the *aggregate energy content* of this coal had declined by 4% since 1998—in other words, the U.S. reached *Peak Coal* (by energy content) in 1998. Since 2010, the volume of coal mined has also decreased—exacerbating the decline in coal's contribution to American energy even more. Liquefaction is only a stop gap: If the USA liquefied *all* the coal it burned for electricity in 2010, it would have produced a little more than 3 million equivalent oil barrels a day of liquid fuel for transportation.

Environmentalist "Alternative Energy" wet dreams are also not the solution. The laws of thermodynamics are not revoked because something is fashionable. Energy generated from wind and tide *use* wind and tidal energy. The amount of wind that exits from the blades of a windmill is *less* than the amount of wind that enters the blades of the windmill. The same is true of tidal energy that enters and exits a tidal turbine. That energy is, of course, preserved in another form (the electricity we use), but it is no longer energy that is part of that natural environment that generates weather. Use of either or both on a large enough scale to significantly affect global energy supply could have major unpredictable impacts on climatic patterns that may be no less catastrophic than those predicted for the CO_2-induced greenhouse effect. Some environmentalists claim that using *only* 1% of the wind blowing across America's Great Plains would be sufficient for all of America's energy needs. But what would be the effect on weather patterns? How would it affect the Gulf Stream? We simply do not know. What we do know is that, environmentally speaking, there is no "free lunch." Winds, tidal and most geothermal sources may be "alternative," but they are not renewable (as is solar) —when you use them, they are used. I am reminded of an article I read in *Popular Science* magazine around 45 years ago (during the height of the 1970s oil crises) discussing the possibility of using the Gulf Stream as a major alternative source of power. One of the contrarian views cited in the article was that using *only* 1% of the energy of the warm Gulf Stream would turn Great Britain into a gigantic ice cube.

Giant windmills also have environmental issues. Environmentalists opposed to them usually cite their danger to birds and bats, their noise, their unsightliness, and the damage they do to the environment when built on land: the need for access roads, removal of natural cover and so on. None, to my knowledge, use the potential climate change arguments I have cited above. And few mention the huge consumption of concrete and other minerals needed for the foundation and structure of these monsters. It takes 5-10 times more concrete to produce a watt of energy from a windmill than from a nuclear reactor. Giant windmills require 800-1,000 tons of concrete for their foundations. Cement is the major component of concrete, and its production is one of the most energy intensive of all industrial manufacturing processes and one of the most significant sources of manmade CO_2 (7%—more than twice that of aviation). It also releases numerous particulates and toxic materials into the environment. Moreover, we don't know the additional aggregate energy costs over the lifetime of a windmill. Given their tremendous torque, how much will be invested in maintaining them—replacing parts, moving repair teams by sea or land and so on; all of this requires energy. Think of the aggregate energy used by smartphones. While charging is energy negligible, its overall yearly energy consumption, by accessing data processing centers, is greater than the yearly energy consumption of your refrigerator. Windmills also require various minerals that must be mined, processed, and transported to the site. The energy used for this and the particulates this releases into the atmosphere not only are harmful to health and property, they also contribute to climate change. It takes solar panels three years to repay their energy debt (the amount of energy consumed to produce them) and more than twenty times over during its working life of 30 years. The question of how long it takes windmills to pay back its full life cycle energy debt is still being debated.

The Demographics of the Problem

This material crisis is exacerbated by demographics. Two billion people are still without clean water, not mention their dreams of a middle-class lifestyle. Ten billion people are projected to inhabit the planet by 2060.[26] There are not enough mineral resources on the planet to satisfy the needs of 10 billion people with a middle-class lifestyle given the present means of production. For example, to satisfy the food needs of an additional 2 billion we would have to add farmland equivalent to the size of Brazil—even using the most developed farming methods. Moreover, people are voting with their feet in search of the middle-class way of life. In 2008, more than half the world's population, 3.3 billion people, was living in urban areas. By 2030, this will reach 5 billion.[27] By 2060, 8 billion people will live in cities—80% of the human race. How will these people be fed if 80% of the land that can be used to grow crops is *already* in use and 15% of that is already deteriorated? Global communications have turned everyone into "city dwellers." People may live in rural/small-town areas, but they are no longer culturally rural and often find small town life oppressively boring. Some theorize that this boredom is a major contributor to the current opioid crisis in rural and small-town America.[28]

America's 2022 agricultural census revealed that that the average age of farmers was 58 (7 years from retirement age) while the age of farmers lower than 35 was only 9%. Almost 40% of farmers are already over 65. Given the capriciousness of weather and markets, most farmers are reluctant to see their children become farmers and their children even more reluctant.[29] It is estimated that family farmland valued at 2 trillion dollars has been and will be coming onto the market in recent years and years to come. Since, according to the U.S. Department of Agriculture, family farms still constitute 95% of the farming population in the United States, control 84% of agricultural land and produce 87% of the food, this is tremendously significant.

Especially since only 43% of farms had positive net cash farm income in 2022 and well over 50% of farmers had to make a living working other jobs. This, plus age, explains the decline of 7% in number of farms since 2017 and the decline of acreage under cultivation of over 2%. Within 5 years America's farming population declined by 7%.

The situation elsewhere is not better. In Great Britain, the average age of farmers is 59. A third of European farmers are older than 65. In Japan, the *average* age of farmers is already over 70. Dissatisfaction with farming life is not limited to the developed world. In Thailand (one of the world's largest rice exporting countries; to rice what the Ukraine is to wheat), the proportion of the agricultural workforce less than 40 years of age fell by almost 20% between 1985 and 2003 and the proportion of farmers over 60 doubled. In China, the average age of farmers is already over 50. Indonesia is struggling to keep young people working in the rice paddies with little success. In Zimbabwe and Mozambique, the average age of farmers is over 45 with many over 60. In Côte d'Ivoire, where the median age of the population is 19, the average age of a cocoa farmer is 50. In Malawi, the average age of farmers is 65. In Kenya, the average age of farmers is almost 60.

The nuclear industry also has a demographic problem. There is a worldwide shortage of master welders[30] as well as of mining and civil engineers. A master welder is defined as having 10 years' experience and "perfect every time" welding ability. In the United States, there are 13 universities issuing mining engineering degrees, down from 20 programs in the 1980s. The U.S. has graduated less than 10,000 mining engineers since 1975, many of whom no longer work in mining. The peak years were the early 1980s when 600-700 were graduating a year. In the first decade of the 21st century, this had declined to about 100 graduates a year. Given environmental concerns, it has become a decidedly unfashionable profession. Current statistics indicate that out of a total of 5,900 mining and geological engineers presently in service, 90% are over 50 years of age: 52% between 50 and 55, 28% between 55 and 60, and 10% over 60. The average yearly retirement numbers projected by the industry in coming years is as follows: about 300 will retire at the age of 62 every year; about 230 at 65; and 170 at 70. One doesn't have to be an expert in statistics to realize that the United States' mining industry is heading for a severe shortfall of mining engineers, especially since only 40% of these engineers actually work in mining (the rest in government agencies, engineering consulting firms and academia). Who is going to mine the uranium needed for 100 new reactors?

The shortage of master welders is particularly distressing. Catastrophes related to poor welding include the Bhopal gas leak, and Chernobyl. The U.S. Nuclear Regulatory Commission has an entire web entry entitled "Reactor Coolant System Weld Issues." Welding has been a significant factor in almost every nuclear accident since the advent of nuclear power. It should be a moral imperative to have nuclear reactor welding done by master welders, not by apprentice level welders. Master welders are in such demand that they can earn up to one million dollars a year. There certainly are not enough of them to build another 100 reactors safely, as the American advocates of nuclear propose.

There is also a universal shortage of civil engineers in countries as diverse as the USA, India, England, South Africa, New Zealand, Australia, and Canada. The causes differ from country to country. In the United States it has been caused by decades' long lack of state investment in infrastructure and subsequent decline of enrollment in civil engineering degree programs (your market mechanism at work). In India it is being caused by huge state investments in much needed infrastructure at a time when many civil engineers are leaving the profession for better paid computer programming jobs (once again your market mechanism at work). Since "Civil engineering has an important part to play at every stage of the nuclear fuel cycle," according to R. Dexter-Smith, editor of *Civil Engineering in the Nuclear Industry*,[31] building another 100 nuclear plants without them might come under the heading of "criminal negligence." Additionally, 35% of the American nuclear energy workforce is close to retirement age while 25% are *already* past retirement age. Less than 8% are younger than 32.[32] Few people today are studying nuclear engineering and nuclear energy specific skills. The American Nuclear Society (the industry's professional organization) reports that 700 nuclear engineers need to graduate each year to satisfy *present* demand, but only 250 are presently doing so. The oil industry likewise has a demographic problem related to universal changes in cultural attitudes. According to the World Petroleum Council, 50% of the global oil workforce will retire within the next 10 years; the average age of skilled oil workers is already now over 50 and in certain areas there is a 38% shortage of workers. These chronic shortages of skilled human resources in the mining, nuclear and oil industries reflect a revolution in values. We ignore this "cultural revolution" at our own risk. Mining and petroleum are no longer subjects that are fashionable to study. More and more people are consuming not only on the basis of price and quality but also on the basis of values; this includes the consumption of education and choosing one's profession. Thinking conventionally and simply extrapolating from our present methods of doing things, the material crisis is inevitable and real. But there are different ways of doing things already in the pipeline that can forestall the crisis and enable us to expand the prosperity of the entire human race to American levels while reducing the strain on the environment. I will discuss these in a subsequent chapter.

Conclusion to Book One

"Every great idea is met with violent opposition from meager minds" —Albert Einstein

The material well-being, scientific knowledge, and technological ability of the human race have reached such a level that we could bring about a messianic age if we could only mobilize the will. Yet we flounder around rudderless, in a society and culture we ourselves have created, because we have no realistic, unifying, inspiring vision of our human and *supra*-human evolutionary future. This lack of vision exacerbates Pascal's despair. As Proverbs 20:18 puts it: "Where there is no vision, the people perish." Nothing is more necessary for rational decision making than having a vision. Without comprehensive visions of desirable futures how can one be rational? Every day we make yes and no decisions—yes to this, no to that. How do we do that unless we are clear as to where we want to go? Visions are practical tools as much as mathematics. In order to resolve the various aspects of the human dilemma, we require an integrated worldview. The crises are related and interrelated; they are interwoven into such a complex Gordian knot that we need the sword of a clear vision to cut through it. As Pete Williams referring to Jung's *Modern Man in Search of a Soul* writes on the Jung Society of Atlanta website:

> The modern man is a newly formed human being ... he has a present-day consciousness ... he has become "unhistorical" in the deepest sense and has estranged himself from the masses who live within the bounds of tradition. He has come to the very edge of the world, leaving behind all that has been discarded and outgrown. A higher level of consciousness is like a burden of guilt.

Isn't it self-evident that those of us who have reached a higher level of consciousness require a higher level of meaning, from a mundane preoccupation with our earthly needs to a cosmic preoccupation with our cosmic destiny? Yet isn't it also self-evident that this will not be possible unless and until we satisfy all our mundane material earthly requirements. Maslow specified that individuals must satisfy lower-level needs before achieving higher-level growth targets. Every human being is capable of progression towards self-actualization, and ultimately to self-transcendence. This applies to entire civilizations not only individuals. But it is doubtful this can be achieved without a vision of human *being* that is part and parcel of a cosmic drama. Unfortunately, progress towards enunciating such a cosmic drama is disrupted by our failure to meet the lower-level needs of humanity at large. Unless we deal satisfactorily with the material and constitutionalist needs of real human beings, we will not be able to address our ultimate cosmic purpose. "If there is no bread there is no Torah" is not an either/or—only the transcendent or only the material. Indeed, I would claim that Maslow's progression is not as linear as he implied. I believe that a transcendent vision of our ultimate purpose as conscious beings can generate a titanic energy that will enable us to attain the lower rungs of Maslow's hierarchy faster. I believe such a transcendent vision can increase the pace of human prosperity and constitutionalist rights.

Book Two will enunciate in greater detail the cultural, intellectual, and material resources already extant in human civilization that will enable us to formulate a transcendent vision that is accessible to and compelling for the greater part of the human race.

Notes

1   Bloom, p. 28.

2   Boulding, p. 146.

3   Coase, p. 2.

4   James, 1956), p. 132.

5   Jeffreys, Berger, & James, pp. 64-72.

6   Kant, *p. 92.*

7   Menger, p. 104.

8   Whitehead, p. 143.

9   Kuhn & Hacking, p. 150.

10   Ratner, p. 411.

11   Cox, *Religion in the Secular City,* p. 216.

12   Russell, p. 10.

13　Quotes from Jungian Center for Spiritual Sciences.

14　Jung, *Psychology and Alchemy*, p. 13.

15　From Jung Society website.

16　Jung, *Alchemical Studies* (Vol.13), p. 346.

17　Sinicki.

18　Pattakos.

19　Frankl, 1977, p. 175.

20　Fromm, 1941, pp. 41-42.

21　Becker, E. 1971, p. vii.

22　Ibid., p. x.

23　Ibid., p. 6.

24　Bunker is a high-viscosity residual oil. The low-grade bunker fuel used by the world's 90,000 cargo ships contains up to 2,000 times the amount of sulfur compared to diesel fuel used in automobiles and is responsible for 35% of particulate pollution worldwide.

25　The oil boycott the USA imposed on Japan as a consequence of its atrocities in China probably triggered Pearl Harbor, which in Japan's mind was protecting its flank as it conquered the oil resources of Southeast Asia.

26　The United Nations Population fund.

27　Ibid.

28　Iso-Ahola & Crowley, p. 260.

29　Astyk.

30　The American Welding Society notes that more than half of the existing 500,000 strong welder workforce is approaching retirement and that demand for skilled welders currently outstrips supply by 200,000.

31　Dexter-Smith.

32　This data is based on Nuclear Energy Institute's 2010 Work Force Report.

BOOK TWO

Evolving Towards Homo Divinitas

PART III

Reclaiming a Heroic Vision of Human Being

Chapter Ten: No Limits to Growth

Calling for the end of growth is a sanctimonious self-indulgence of those privileged enough to have been born into a consumer society. Much of this anti-consumerist affectation is clothed in a dreamy pose of spirituality—a rejection of vulgar materialism. Jewish tradition, in contrast, would find this attitude to be absurd and self-contradictory. Unlike Christianity, Judaism does not advocate depriving the body in order to reach a higher level of spirituality. Quite the opposite, it believes in satisfying all of one's bodily needs in order to reach a higher level of spirituality. Suffering has no intrinsic spiritual value for the Jew. The Jewish Sabbath is an excellent example of spiritual sublimity being dependent on bodily satisfaction. Fridays, in preparation for the Sabbath, observant Jews go to the *Mikvah*—the ritual baths that provide not only spiritual purification in preparation for the Sabbath, but also bodily refreshment and a physical feeling of well-being. (Keep in mind that before the second half of the 20th century people not only did not bathe every day, they often didn't even have a bathroom at home.) Friday evening, they put on their best clothes before going to synagogue in order to welcome and be welcomed by "Queen Sabbath." Following services, they partook of their best meal of the week; usually traditional Jewish comfort food that increased their sense of well-being. Upon retiring they engaged in sex (provided it was the proper time of the month for the woman). The following morning, they ate a traditional comfort food breakfast before synagogue. In the afternoon after services, they engaged in sex again. In other words, observant Jews satisfied all their physical needs in order to enable then to devote their complete attention to the spiritual requirements of the Sabbath. Taking the Sabbath as our model, I suggest that the spiritual quest of all humanity must inspire us to contribute to perfecting our physical realm (our *Malchut*—kingdom) —the 21st-century planet Earth—as a necessary preparation and first step towards the great cosmic project. This necessitates reembracing of the *Idea of Progress*—and by this, I mean the material progress required to free humanity from soul destroying drudge work and unremitting worry. Having lived and traveled in pre-consumerist societies I can attest to how aesthetically barren and harsh the life of the vast majority of people in these societies is. The collapse of Communism and the failed Arab Spring reflect the collective scream for escape from such a barren environment.

The consumer society is not the problem; the production system is the problem. The production methods *presently* used by manufacturing, mining and agriculture are what are destroying our planet's ecosystem, not ostentatious consumerism. The revolutions presently taking place in material science, water engineering, and energy and food production are the solution. The message of this chapter is the counterintuitive notion that the world economy can continue to grow *indefinitely* at 4-5% a year while our negative footprint on the planet simultaneously declines; that by the end of this century the planet will be able to carry a population of 12 billion people with a Euro/American standard of living with little or no negative human environmental impact. America's traditional pre-postmodern infectious "can do" attitude towards problem solving must triumph over the "can't do" or "mustn't do" pessimism of the fashionable chattering classes. As Thomas Jefferson once wrote in a letter to his daughter: "It is wonderful how much can be done if we are always doing."

My Environmental Due Diligence

I believe that every sane and rational human being is inherently an environmentalist. Who wants to breathe, eat or drink filth? Yet we all relate through a filter of our own values, perspectives, and life experience. The tradition of rational humanism is my personal standard—rational in that our judgments are based on rigorous scientific standards; humanist in that we place human welfare at the center of our concerns. This standard has been the foundation of Western Civilization from the Renaissance to the Scientific Revolution to the Enlightenment; it is the foundational idea of the United States.

Let us first define some terms with precision. *Ecology* is a science; *environmentalism* is an 'ism,' i.e., an ideology, a set of beliefs of how human beings should live in their environs. *Ecology* literally means *knowledge* of our house (our house in this instance being nature itself); as economy means *management* of our house (our house in this instance being commercial human society). *Environmentalism* is a value-laden philosophy and social movement concerned with how human beings treat their environs (natural and social). The ideology of environmentalism can either be based on the science of ecology (i.e., facts) or it can stray into theology (a dogmatic belief system). Environmentalists, therefore, can be divided into two major categories:

1. *Human Centered (anthropocentric)* – a point of view which centers on the value of human beings and advocates for a clean environment because it is good for human beings. This is my viewpoint, which I call *humanistic environmentalism.*

2. *Nature Centered (biocentric)* – A point of view which centers on the value of non-human species, processes and ecosystems, the proponents of which sometimes denigrate policies based on a primary concern for human beings. I call this *pagan environmentalism*—a latter-day version of nature worship.

While there is often some overlap between these two categories in real flesh and blood human beings, I believe *anthropocentric* environmentalism trumps *biocentric* environmentalism from a strategic PR point of view, because, in democracies, arguments for quality environmental policies relating to the health of one's children are most effective. While no one wants their children to eat, drink or breathe pollutants, few are willing to forgo their standard of living to save some obscure rodent. Thus, the more human-centered arguments usually win the day, and indirectly result in policies that also benefit the obscure rodent.

More significantly, these categories often reflect dissimilar attitudes to life: whether one believes in the human capacity for innovation and imagination to solve problems (the *cornucopian attitude*) or one is skeptical (the *catastrophic attitude*). The *cornucopian attitude* embraces the theme of futurist Ramez Naam's book *The Infinite Resource* (referring to human imagination), of which Ray Kurzweil wrote "Naam shows that innovation is the only force equal to the global challenges that face us, and that we can prosper if we harness it." The *catastrophic attitude* expresses itself in prophecies of doom that see humanity headed for global catastrophe due to climate change, population growth, water shortages, deforestation, etc.—all converging to destroy the planet and human civilization as we have known it. As I have written previously, some even advocate using the police powers of the state to end economic growth in order to "save the planet" and survive as a species! I loathe such attitudes. I am a *cornucopian*—I believe we are capable of designing a development paradigm that *enhances* the natural environment as we provide material plenitude to ever-growing numbers of the human race. I believe that calls to de-develop will result in a subsistence economy that will actually degrade the environment, as deforestation in the developing world attests. Interestingly, forests and green cover are *expanding* in the "consumerist" developed world and are shrinking in the poorest parts of the world. Development, unlike stagnation, can enhance the environment. Underdevelopment is the main cause for human suffering and consequent environmental degradation. Women and children in Africa spend up to 80% of their time gathering wood and fetching water. This colossal waste of human energy not only denudes the world's forests and jungles, it is also the primary cause of chronic poverty and the inferior status of women, as well as a massive form of child abuse.

History matters! It teaches us that since the emergence of the three self-correcting and interconnected systems of science, constitutionalism, and capitalism, prophets of doom have been proven wrong time after time by that "infinite resource"—the human mind. I challenge the assumption that catastrophe is inevitable unless we forgo industry and reject our middle-class lifestyles; that problems caused by human beings cannot be corrected by human ingenuity; that we cannot maintain our lifestyles while, at the same time, *enhancing* the environment. This is because growth in *value* is not synonymous with growth in the *volume* of raw materials. We can grow value while using less of our natural resources; the "wealth of nations" can increase as the human burden on the carrying capacity of the planet decreases. I assert that by "imagineering" alternative futures—based on solid science and technology—we can create a situation in which there are "no limits to growth."

Consumerist capitalism is not the cause of environmental degradation. To advocate this is to ignore the environmental devastation left behind by the former Soviet Union,[1] which was several times greater than the capitalist West, without the saving grace of having delivered a quality standard of living. It also ignores the historical fact that environmentalism as a major social movement actually emerged from western middle-class consumerism—the bourgeois realization that we all are "consumers" of our environment and thus want that environment to be of the highest quality. It has been bourgeois civil society that has taken the lead in this development, not the so-called working class, which is often hostile to environmentalists who they see as threatening their traditional ways of making a living and way of life.

Climate change has become the central concern of policy makers (although not, in my opinion, the most compelling for the average citizen). I have two axioms by which I relate to global warming, based on the *science* of ecology:

1. Global warming has been a natural phenomenon for the past 20,000 years. 20,000 years ago, New York City was covered by a mile thick sheet of ice and ocean levels were 60 meters lower than today. The Great Lakes, formed by the melting ice of the last ice age, are less than 30,000 years old.

2. Human activity since the industrial revolution has increased the pace of global warming beyond what natural cycles can account for and might trigger a cascading effect that could be dangerous for organized human society.

Since it is a natural phenomenon, I believe that "stopping global warming" and "saving the planet" are unscientific catchphrases. The globe will warm or cool as it pleases (we are in for another "ice age" in about 1,500 years no matter what we do,[2] and the planet will be here for billions of years after the human race has disappeared and will eventually be destroyed by our expanding sun. More accurate but less sexy slogans would be to "minimize and mitigate the human contribution to any natural cycle of global warming in order to slow its rate, give the eco-system time to adapt, and save ourselves." Or, if you are one of those outliers who rejects the very concept of global warming, then "minimize and mitigate humanity's devastation of our forests, oceans, rivers and soil in order to save ourselves." It is not the planet that needs saving or even life on this planet—it is us, the human race, that needs saving. The planetary ecosystem has survived mass extinctions in the past (95% of species wiped out; 65% of species wiped out etc.).[3] Evolution will certainly overcome the human species' puny efforts to lay waste the ecosystem. But the real question is, will the human race survive its own criminal abuses of the environment which have little to do with global warming. I refer to our pollution of our atmosphere, our water, and our soil; our decimation of plant and animal diversity; our transformation of the planet's beauty into an ugliness which attacks our senses and our mental health. We must radically reduce the human burden on the environment for our own physical *and mental* well-being.

The view that reducing the human burden on the environment would be a crushing burden on our economy is silly. If history is any judge, the opposite will be the case. It will create a more robust economic foundation of human civilization and greater economic opportunity for more individuals. The potential positive economic potential of environmentalism is tremendous. The space program could serve as an analogy. When Kennedy declared the aim of landing a man on the moon, no economist would have recommended it on purely economic grounds. Its great expense was considered justified for security and political reasons alone. Yet our entire modern economy has derived from it. "No other government program can match the economic impact of space program spin-offs that include applications in medicine, computer technology, communications, public safety, food, power generation and transportation."[4] Near space has already become a part of humanity's *natural* environment as much as our rivers and forests. If our presence in near space, as embodied by our communications satellites, would somehow disappear overnight human civilization would collapse. Yet the greatest benefits of space are still before us. Given a smidgen of political will and imagination, near space could provide significant solutions to our present environmental challenges. By the end of this century, OR SOONER, various space-based technologies could provide most of our energy needs and significant amounts of our raw materials. Earth based power plants and mining operations could all but disappear. Planet Earth could become the bedroom community of human civilization.

Might we not expect that a massive national or international project to completely liberate the planet from dependence on fossil fuels by 2050 to have much the same results as the space program? We would create economic sectors and products (and thus economic opportunity and growth) that we cannot even imagine. There is a rich history of how other proactive national projects instituted for non-economic reasons have revolutionized the economy; they include America's interstate highway system and the Internet (both initiated for national security reasons). Consider, also, the expense of the United States policing the Persian Gulf to secure the flow of oil—between $50 billion a year according to the Hudson Institute, and $90 billion a year according to the Rand Corporation. The United States might have spent $6.8 trillion between 1980 and 2007 to keep oil flowing from the Gulf (*not including* the expense of the two wars America prosecuted in the Gulf). What could have been done with that money for alternative energy, energy conservation, super-efficient public transport etc.? One of the arguments against solar and wind had been its need to be subsidized (no longer the case). I believe the temporary direct subsidies to alternative energy pale in comparison to the monstrous indirect subsidies to the oil industry that have been embedded in America's defense budgets.

Defining the Dilemmas

Human beings require three things to survive: water, food, and energy. Modern civilization requires three additional things in order to survive and flourish: waste disposal (sewage, garbage, trash, and industrial refuse), education, and health maintenance. Present methods of production and distribution of the first three are *the* major threat to public health and the environment. For example, the *Intergovernmental Panel on Climate Change* (IPCC) attests that agriculture generates 20% of anthropogenic greenhouse effects (more than all the world's vehicles), as well as numerous harmful particulates. Two billion people lack clean drinking water, a consequence of inadequate sewage and garbage disposal. The four bottlenecks to environmentally sound development are therefore food, water, energy, and waste disposal. Addressing these creatively can revolutionize human civilization quicker than presently imagined.

Immediate Steps

The United States is in a unique position to set the tone and regain its place as a moral force in the world by making moves that would have an immediate positive impact on the world's environment. The President of the United States has the power to issue executive orders such as:

1. Ban the import of wood and paper byproducts sourced from forests that aren't certified as sustainably managed by the *Forest Stewardship Council* or comparable organizations. Current forensic science enables easy identification of the forestry sources of paper, cardboard, and wood products. Such a policy would also have positive geopolitical ramifications for the West. It would highlight the environmentally criminal negligence of Russia regarding how it manages its forests as well as China's rape of African, Asian, and South America forests to supply its furniture industry. Russian wood, cardboard and paper products from their ravaged Siberian forests are a major Russian export after oil and such a policy would constitute another major sanction against Putin's imperialism. Such a policy would earn the support of America's logging, paper, and furniture industries.

2. Ban the import of all fish and seafood products from sources not certified for good practices by organizations approved by the *Marine Stewardship Council* (for fishing) or the *Aquaculture Steward-*

ship Council (for farmed fish and seafood). This would earn the support of the fishing industry.

3. Enforce all *current* environmental laws that can be reasonably applied to maritime shipping. This includes, but is not limited to, the *International Maritime Organization* (IMO) 2020 low-sulfur fuel regulation. This, in effect, forces the maritime industry to cease using bunker fuel, which is 100 times more polluting than marine diesel and 1,000 times more polluting than automobile diesel. This would require ships entering and leaving American ports to use the equivalent of automobile diesel or preferably LNG. In addition, refuse access to American ports for ships whose ports of egress do not robustly enforce the IMO low-sulfur fuel regulation. Refuse access to American ports to cruise ships that dispose of their solid waste in the high seas—which is responsible for up to 25% of ocean waste. Vigorously enforce all environmental laws that can be legitimately applied to water pollution from discharge of ballast and bilge water as well as general waste disposal when at anchor in American ports. If such a policy were universally enforced worldwide it would lower the maritime contribution to global warming from 4% to less than 1%, as well as significantly clean up the oceans.

4. These steps can be constitutionally justified, before any challenge in the courts, under a national security rubric (the President being Commander and Chief) by alluding to policy papers from various segments of the American intelligence community (specifically the CIA and Military Intelligence) citing the security dangers of climate change and environmental devastation. This argument can further be augmented by citing the two Gulf wars and the blood and treasure spent protecting oil supplies. Also, how droughts and environmental devastation in the Middle East and Africa have served as the background to ISIS (in Syria especially) and other radical Islamist terrorist groups as well as the massive refugee problem in Europe and elsewhere. Stressing the security aspects rather than "goody-two-shoes," "save the planet" arguments would also be appealing to a much broader and less sophisticated audience.

5. The massive yearly federal purchasing power of $500 billion can also be applied to improving the environment. Retrofitting Federal buildings by way of existing maintenance budgets and favoring the purchase of hybrid and electric vehicles are only two examples. The

President, as chief executive (CEO) of the Republic, can issue an order to favor *green suppliers*—e.g., companies certified by *Green Seal* or similar organizations. The President could also encourage big Democrat controlled states like California (the 5ᵗʰ largest economy in the world—larger than India, Great Britain, France, and Italy) and New York (the 12ᵗʰ largest economy in the world—larger than Canada, Russia, South Korea, and Mexico) to do the same.

ALL of this can be done by executive fiat and enable the President to assume global leadership in calling for environmental criteria for WTO and OECD rules as well as other trade agreements. The moral pressure on the rest of the developed world—the EU, Japan, Korea, and most of Australasia—to adopt similar policies would be irresistible.

What Not To Do

Self-righteous environmentalism doesn't work. Ignoring reality does not make you an idealist, and self-righteousness in the name of a just cause is not a virtue. The present campaigns against aviation and meat are examples of idealistic and self-righteous environmentalists ignoring reality. Aviation generates 2.5% of anthropogenic greenhouse gas but is the backbone of the hospitality industry, which employs, directly and indirectly,313 million people (10% of the global workforce) and depends on a billion cross-border travelers a year. Aviation-dependent tourism and agricultural exports are significant development levers for undeveloped countries. Aviation carries 30% of world trade value but only 1% of volume. Using this calculus, aviation is already the "greenest" sector of the world economy per unit of value. Limiting aviation to the extent that environmentalists would like could trigger a global depression. A more rational approach would be to impose a 1% surcharge on plane tickets, dedicated to reforestation. Eight billion dollars yearly would be generated; equal to the *total* cost of the *Green Belt Project* intended to reverse the desertification of the sub-Saharan Sahel region. This would completely mitigate emissions from aviation (perhaps even making the industry a net CO_2 sink).

As for meat, do we really expect Brazilians, Argentineans, Texans, and Australians to stop eating steaks, Germans pork, or the English beef? Will 1.5 billion Muslims forego lamb? Will Hindu India cull its 150 million cattle? Will the Maasai and other African peoples, for whom cattle are a vital part of their culture, stop raising millions of cattle? What about the 400 million people living in extreme poverty that are pastoralists and smallholders and rely on livestock for food and livelihoods? Actually, eating English grown beef in London causes less greenhouse gas than eating avocados grown in Chile and flown to London. "Eat local" is a far more environment-friendly rallying cry than "let's all go veggie."

Smart environmentalism would target easier objectives, for example, shipping. As noted above, the universal fuel of shipping is "bunker," which is 1,000 times more polluting than truck diesel, generates 4% of climate change emissions and up to 35% of toxic airborne particulates, killing tens of thousands of people a year globally. One giant oil tanker emits the same amount of cancer and asthma-causing chemicals as 50 million automobiles (as well as polluting the oceans when it flushes out its bilge water). The resultant global health costs are over $300 billion a year. Eliminating seaborne oil by favoring the domestic oil industry (with a $5 per barrel tariff on imported seaborne oil) would generate an *immediate* significant net environmental benefit—equal to eliminating the pollution from the entire American automobile fleet. The 2017 *Lancet Commission on Pollution and Health* reported the global cost of pollution as "$4.6 trillion per year – 6.2% of global economic output." Steve Cohen of The Earth Institute at Columbia University claims, "Between 1970 and 2017 the U.S. invested about $65 billion in air pollution control and received about $1.5 trillion in benefits." According to futurist Ramez Naam, "every dollar spent on increased efficiency of buildings saves three dollars in energy bills ... efficiency investments could cut energy use in half ... with a net savings of $400 billion per year." Environmentalists should be selling the *economic benefits* of environmentalism and stop preaching *sacrifice*, constantly bragging about their veganism. It is precisely this kind of shallow virtue signaling, which completely ignores economic, cultural, and social realities, which alienates potential allies.

Water

There is no shortage of water; there is only a shortage of intelligence in managing and allocating water. "Waste not, want not" is always good advice. Eliminating Non-Revenue Water (NRW) is the easiest and most economical efficient way to increase the water supply. NRW is defined as water produced then lost during the water cycle from leaking water mains, service line pipes and connections, as well as primitive irrigation methods, leaky kitchen and bathroom faucets, malfunctioning toilets etc. The United States wastes 7 billion gallons of water a day (over one trillion gallons a year) needlessly contributing 13.5 million kg of CO_2 to the atmosphere daily. Los Angeles loses 50 % of its water due to leakage; Israel only 6-7%. According to the World Bank, the average water loss in the developing world is 40-50% (60% in some water systems). Leak detection technologies *already* exist that can prevent this waste. Efficiency represents a huge new global water resource. Israel recycles 87% of its sewage water constituting 40% of its agricultural water source. Recycling and eliminating NRW represent additional, presently underexploited, global water resources. These technologies *already* exist and could rapidly be applied universally.

According to the OECD, "Farming accounts for around 70% of water used in the world today and also contributes to water pollution from excess nutrients, pesticides and other pollutants." Primitive irrigation methods in the developing world (and in California) waste an enormous amount of water. Agricultural efficiencies are a major underutilized global water resource. Again, technologies *already* exist and likewise could be universally applied quickly. Globally, we are capable of doubling our food production while using half the water with *existing* technologies. Moreover, by abandoning open field agriculture and adopting urban agriculture (see below) we could cut agricultural water use by 90%, thus increasing the global availability of drinkable water by 60%.

Seawater desalination is still more expensive and energy-intensive than *local* natural fresh water. It is, however, equivalent in financial and energy costs to fresh water pumped from significant distances. The problem has been various environmental issues regarding the leftover toxic brine when dumped back into the sea as well as desalination's high energy requirements. But innovations are already in the pipeline designed to reduce energy requirements, lower costs, and mitigate the brine issue. For example, scientists at MIT have developed a process which can extract useful chemicals from the brine. These include sodium hydroxide (caustic soda) and hydrochloric acid (as well as others), not only alleviating the environmental impact but also creating another income stream. German scientists have developed a new method of desalinization called capacitive deionization (CDI)—supplanting the current energy-hungry reverse osmosis process. According to scientists at the *Leibnitz Institute for New Materials*, this not only removes salts and heavy metals, but also *generates* electricity from emissions present in the water as ions (as well as from waste heat). Even the reverse osmosis process can be made more energy efficient by replacing the membranes currently used with graphene. Buying "wasted" (and cheaper) electricity off the grid during low consumption periods, as is common in Israel's desalinization plants, is another energy saver. Alternatively, thermal desalinization methods can exploit the waste heat from power plants and industrial installations. In other words, every environmental and cost objection to desalinization is already being addressed and well on its way to resolution.

Despite current philosophic (not scientific) objections to it, genetic engineering offers many interesting opportunities. The ability to irrigate food crops from seawater would alleviate two problems: hunger and water shortage. We could, for example, exploit the existing evolutionary adaptation of mangrove trees by grafting mangrove genes onto salt-sensitive plants, or by engrafting mangrove trees with productive fruit producing plants.

Energy

Once again "waste not, want not!" Energy *not used* is the cheapest, most plentiful, and most environmentally beneficial. *Negawatts* is a term coined by environmentalist Amory Lovins. Megawatts are what we produce; negawatts are what we stop producing by more prudent consumption—literally negating watts. For example, we can significantly lessen the energy consumption of buildings with economically viable technology *already in existence*. The energy potential of the developed world through exploitation of negawatts is tremendous. In 2009 McKinsey & Company conducted research showing that:

> ... the U.S. economy has the potential to reduce annual non-transportation energy consumption by roughly 23 percent by 2020 [a date we have obviously missed due to inferior political leadership] ... eliminating more than $1.2 trillion in waste—well beyond the $520 billion upfront investment ... required. The reduction in energy use would also result in the abatement of 1.1 gigatons of greenhouse-gas emissions annually ... the equivalent of taking the entire U.S. fleet of passenger vehicles and light trucks off the roads.

According to the report, the energy efficiency revolution has been under-way for some time: "Since 1980, energy consumption per unit of floor space had (by 2009) decreased 11 percent in residential and 21 percent in commercial sectors, while industrial energy consumption per real dollar of GDP output had decreased 41 percent." Energy produced onsite, locally, or regionally is the second most environmentally beneficial and econom-ically viable, after non-use. We are already capable of implementing com-binations of garbage and sewage *depolymerization*, solar and small-scale wind installations, passive geothermal and other technologies that cut the household importation of energy (electricity and cooking gas) significant-ly. Household electricity storage systems for intermittent energy sources are presently being developed and marketed. First adopters are even now making these technologies fashionable. So, given historical precedent, it won't be long before they become economically viable for mass consump-tion. By 2030 home electricity storage systems could be as ubiquitous as home air conditioners.

Buildings consume 39% of America's energy and 68% of its electricity (these numbers are similar in Europe). They emit 38% of the carbon di-oxide, 49% of the sulfur dioxide, and 25% of the nitrogen oxides in our air. Instituting a policy of government-backed mortgages to *Retrofit America, Retrofit Europe, Retrofit Japan and Korea* (using the negawatt principle and abovementioned technologies) would have greater environmental impact than eliminating aviation, meat and maritime pollution combined while benefitting national economies, home owners, the commercial real estate industry and the construction and home improvements industries, as well as the various financial institutions that would have to create an entire slew of new mortgage products. Consider also the high-paying jobs this would create, gathering support from labor. Retrofits raise property market value by 2% to 5% with energy savings actually paying for the retrofit mortgage. The Empire State Building retrofit lowered energy bills by 40% and paid for itself in less than 10 years. The Sears Tower retrofit cut energy for heating by 50% and electricity by 80%. This kind of environmentalism would sell prosperity rather than austerity. Puritanical, self-righteous environmental-ists alienate the very people who would otherwise benefit the most from a rational environmental policy. When environmental billionaires begin to get the same kind of media attention as Silicon Valley billionaires, we will know environmentalism has triumphed over the purposeful ignorance of the climate deniers. Not puritanical sacrifice, but rather the general enrichment of humanity is the message environmentalists should be selling.

Waste-to-energy technologies, for example, can augment our energy mix while saving a great deal of money. Garbage, sewage, organic trash, agricultural and food processing waste are essentially hydrocarbons that can be transformed into ethanol, methanol, bio-butanol, or biodiesel. These can be used for transportation, electricity generation or as feedstock for plastics and other materials. Waste-to-energy represents the recycling of existing CO_2 rather than the introduction of additional fossil CO_2 into the environment. Extensive application of waste-to-energy technologies would eliminate methane emissions (18% of anthropogenic greenhouse gas) from organic waste in landfills. This is less than CO_2, which constitutes 72% of anthropogenic greenhouse gas, but still emits as much greenhouse gas as all the vehicles in the world. Numerous prototypes of a variety of waste-to-energy technologies are already in place. As their costs decline, they will become commercialized and, if history is any judge, will replace fossil fuels very quickly—just as coal replaced wood in a matter of decades and petroleum replaced whale oil in a matter of years. Waste to energy should gain wide grassroots support because it would benefit taxpayers and businesses and would not endanger livelihoods. For example, present sewage treatment, garbage disposal and fuel costs represent a huge portion of municipal budgets. Consider, also, the costs of waste disposal and fuel costs in stockyards, on poultry farms, throughout the food processing industry and in restaurants. Turning waste into energy by various means would be a huge cost saver and value generator, in addition to being a blessing to the environment.

The U.S. army has developed a portable field apparatus that turns a combat unit's human waste and garbage into biodiesel to fuel their vehicles and generators. It is called TGER—the Tactical Garbage to Energy Refinery. It eliminates the need to transport fuel to the field thus saving lives, time, and equipment expenses. The cost per barrel must still be very high. However, the history of military technology being civilianized and revolutionizing accepted norms is long. We might expect that within 5-10 years, economically competitive units using similar technologies will appear in restaurants, on farms and perhaps even in individual households—turning organic waste into usable, economic fuel. We might conjecture that by the second half of the century, centralized sewage disposal and garbage collection will be things of the past and that even the centralized electricity grids (unchanged for over one hundred years) will be deconstructed into a Lego-like system of mini-grids.

Material Science

The embryonic revolution in material science will become a major factor in a "no limits to growth" civilization. I refer to "smart" and superlight materials. Smart materials "are materials that have one or more properties that can be significantly changed in a controlled fashion by external stimuli."[5] They can produce energy by exploiting differences in temperature (thermoelectric materials) or by being stressed (piezoelectric materials). Other smart materials save energy in the manufacturing process by changing shape or repairing themselves as a consequence of various external stimuli. These materials have all passed the "proof of concept" phase (i.e., are scientifically sound) and many are in the prototype phase. Some are already commercialized and penetrating the market. R&D in "structural batteries" (or "zero mass batteries") is quite extensive and has every chance of becoming quite common by mid century. We are talking about batteries that can double as part of the very structure they are supplying energy to. For example, they can constitute the chassis of an electric car obviating the need for very heavy specialized batteries (thus zero mass). The surface of the car can be photovoltaic material producing electricity that can be stored immediately in the interior walls and frames.

Researchers at *Chalmers University of Technology* in Sweden are working on a cement-based rechargeable battery that can constitute the walls of buildings enabling the surface of the buildings to be coated with photovoltaic material producing electricity that can be stored immediately in the supportive walls of the building. *Saule Technologies* of Poland makes sheets of solar panels using a unique inkjet printing procedure that can serve as cladding for almost any existing building. Thermoelectric materials transforming waste heat from manufacturing alone in the United States would provide an additional 65,000 megawatts; "enough for 50 million homes."[6] Smart glass is already commercialized and can save significant energy in heating, air-conditioning, and lighting.

But it is super-light/super-strong materials that have the greatest potential to transform civilization. I refer to carbon nanotubes—alternatively called graphene sheets or Buckypaper. Carbon nanotubes are between $1/10,000^{th}$ and $1/50,000^{th}$ the width of a human hair. They can be as flexible as rubber and as strong as steel. They are 100-500 times stronger than steel per unit of weight (depending on the quality grade). Composites containing this material are already being used in dozens of applications from golf clubs to bicycles to airplanes. Airplanes being produced today are already 35% lighter than they were only several years ago, and as the price of these composites declines, will become ever lighter. Imagine the energy savings if planes, cars, trucks, trains, elevators were made predominately from this material and weighed $1/100^{th}$ what they weigh now. Imagine the types of alternative energy that would become practical. Carbon nanotube composites could eventually replace many common industrial materials. For example, replacing concrete would eliminate up to 10% of *lifecycle* anthropogenic greenhouse emissions. Replacing steel would eliminate another 10%. Further development might enable us to move our industrial and energy infrastructures into near space. Arthur Clarke's "Space Elevator" might become a reality, enabling the economically feasible mining of asteroids and the moon for various minerals. Increasing the photovoltaic efficiency of graphene might enable super-light solar space installations capable of generating solar energy 365 24-hour days a year. The extreme cold of outer space would make them considerably more efficient than earthbound "sun-belt" solar installations (heat being a major inhibitor of photovoltaic efficiency).

Carbon nanotubes are still quite expensive, but keep in mind that cotton was more expensive than silk until the cotton gin was invented, and aluminum was once more expensive than gold or platinum.[7] When Napoleon III held a banquet his most honored guests were provided with aluminum plates. Less distinguished guests made do with gold plates. When the Washington Monument was completed in 1884 it was fitted with an aluminum cap, to show respect for George Washington. It weighed 2,850 grams. Aluminum at the time cost $1 a gram. A typical day laborer working on the monument was paid $1 for a 10–12-hour day. Today's aluminum soft-drink container weighs 14 grams and would have bought 14 ten-hour days of labor in 1884. Using labor and the present American minimum wage of $15.00 an hour as a measure of value, a soft drink container would cost $2,250 today, if not for the *Hall-Héroult Process* which turned aluminum into one of the world's cheapest commodities just *two years after* the Washington Monument was completed. The would-be $2,250 soft drink container now costs less than half a cent.

96

Today the *average* cost of the various grades of nanotubes is already 15 times cheaper in *real* cost than aluminum was in 1884. The cheapest carbon nanotube grades cost $100-200 per kilogram. Production methods are being developed that will drive costs down even more. Cambridge University researchers have been working on a new electrochemical production method they reckon could produce nanotubes for around $10 a kilogram. Researchers from Vanderbilt University are developing an electrochemical process that will suck CO_2 from the air as the feedstock for constructing carbon nanotubes cheaply—a win-win environmental/production strategy. Developments like these will do for carbon nanotubes what the *Hall-Héroult process* did for aluminum. Nanotubes could become the universal raw material of choice—displacing concrete, steel, aluminum, copper, and other metals and materials, eventually all but eliminating the ecological devastation of mining for these resources. Given that mining, processing, and preparing resources for use account for 53% of the world's carbon emissions, this alone would be a complete game-changer.

History has shown that extraordinary things can be achieved in short periods of time if they do not violate the laws of nature. The atomic bomb took 4 years; the man on the moon 8 years. It is reasonable to conjecture that by 2030, a low-cost process for producing carbon nanotubes will have been developed; a major step to solving our energy, raw materials, and environmental problems.

Food Production and the Environment

Our present food supply system is a major producer of greenhouse gases. Massive amounts of oil and gas are needed to manufacture fertilizers, herbicides, and pesticides. Every stage of present food production is dependent on oil: planting, irrigation, feeding, harvesting, processing, and distribution. Enter the "Urban Vertical Farm," representing a new paradigm for producing food. It is a concept first popularized by Prof. Dickson Despommier of Columbia University. He has demonstrated that a 30-story urban vertical farm located on 5 square acres could yield food for 50,000 people. These are high tech installations that multiply productivity by a factor of 480: 4 growing seasons, times twice the density of crops, times 2 growing levels on each floor, times 30 floors = 480. This means that five acres of land could produce the equivalent of 2,600 acres of conventionally planted and tended crops. Just 160 such buildings occupying only 800 acres could theoretically feed the entire city of New York. Given this calculus, an area the size of Denmark could feed the entire human race. Present technology could theoretically enable the entire population of the planet Earth to fit comfortably into an area the size of Texas and be food, water, and energy self-sufficient. Of course, 30 story farms might not be optimal value for money given construction costs, so this is just an example of what can be done technically. Optimal value for money might be less costly 2-4 story installations built over what I call urban deserts—parking lots, roads and highways, rooftops and so on. For example, two story installations built in the airspace over the United States interstate highway system alone could feed the entire United States.

Vertical farms would be self-sustaining. They would have glass walls that produce solar energy. Located contiguous to or inside urban centers, they could also contribute to urban renewal, while reducing the food deserts that characterize so many inner-city areas resulting in catastrophic health consequences such as pathological obesity, diabetes, and other associated afflictions. They would be urban lungs, improving the air quality of cities. They would produce a varied food supply year-round. They would use 90% less water. Since agriculture consumes two-thirds of the water worldwide, mass adoption of this technology would in effect solve humanity's water problem by itself. Food would no longer need to be transported to market; it would be produced at the market, in the market, and would not require use of petroleum intensive agricultural equipment. This, along with lessened use of pesticides, herbicides, and fertilizers, would not only be better for the environment, but would eliminate agriculture's dependence on petroleum and significantly reduce petroleum demand. At present, 13% of farm expenses are petroleum based (fuel, fertilizer, pesticides etc.). Farm expenses increase when the price of oil goes up, which of course increases the cost of food.[8] Not subject to the vagaries of nature and petroleum politics, food prices would become less volatile.

Many of the world's damaged ecosystems would be repaired by the consequent abandonment of farmland. A "rewilding" of our planet would take place. Forests, jungles, and savannas would reconquer nature, increasing habitat and becoming giant CO_2 "sinks," sucking up the excess CO_2 that the industrial revolution has pumped into the atmosphere. Countries already investigating and implementing the adoption of vertical farms include Abu

Dhabi, Saudi Arabia, South Korea, and China; countries that are water starved or densely populated. Singapore, with 50% the population density of the Gaza Strip, hopes to eventually produce 80% of its food using these technologies. As of 2018, there were 34 vertical farms in Singapore (compared to 12 in 2016) growing vegetables and fruits as well as fish such as seabass, giant trevally, species of grouper, crabs, and shrimp. Including other systems, such as rooftop farms, in 2020 this had grown to 238 licensed high-tech urban farms as part of the 30 by 30 project, dedicated to providing 30% of its food needs by 2030 with the percentage increasing every year until the desired 80%. Urban agriculture already produces up to 10% of the global output of pulses (lentils and beans) and vegetables. Hong Kong grows 40% of its vegetables within city limits.

Wide-ranging building of vertical farms *within the boundaries* of the markets they serve, not having to ship foodstuffs long distances, would help decrease the shameful food waste characteristic of modern society. In 2012, the American *National Resources Defense Council* published a report indicating that 36% of all fruits and vegetables are lost in the supply chain before reaching the consumer. In the developing world, statistics are much worse due to poor logistics infrastructure. Food wasted includes production losses (planting and harvesting), post-harvest handling and storage losses, processing and packaging losses, distribution, and retail losses. An additional 28% are thrown out in the household (statistics in Europe are similar). It is estimated that the average American household tosses out $1,500 worth of food a year. The United Nations reports that:

> Getting food from farm to fork [consumes] 10 percent of the total U.S. energy budget, uses 50 percent of U.S. land, and swallows 80 percent of all freshwater consumed in the United States. Yet, 40 percent of food in the United States goes uneaten ... rotting in landfills as the single largest component of municipal solid waste where it accounts for a large portion of U.S. methane emissions.

The Promise of the Electric Car

EVs are not, as some claim, a problematic challenge for the underperforming electrical grid; they are the means to rationalize the most inefficient industry in the world. According to the *USA Energy Information Administration,*

Demand levels rise throughout the day and tend to be highest during a block of hours referred to as "on-peak," which usually occurs between 7:00 a.m. and 10:00 p.m. on weekdays. Demand levels are generally lowest between 10 p.m. and 7 a.m. and on weekends. This is usually referred to as "off-peak."

On-peak periods also have differential demand. New Jersey, for example, has 18,000 megawatts of total capacity. This capacity is required for less than 200 hours out of a 3,600-hour year; usually during the summer months in late afternoon and early evening when workplace use is still high and optimal home use begins to kick in as people return from work. During the year, sometimes as little as 8,000 megawatts are required. In other words, this extremely expensive capital investment generates optimal value less than 90% of the time—a level of inefficiency unmatched by any other economic endeavor. Different regions have different peak times, of course, but on-peak times are when blackouts occur and off-peak times when energy waste is highest.

Actually, an EV fleet would not necessarily increase net electric draw because, using the American example, it takes the equivalent of 6 kWh of power to refine a gallon of gasoline while a *Tesla Roadster* can travel 20 miles on that same 6 kWh of power. But even if this were not the case, EVs have the potential to mitigate the colossal inefficiency of the present grid. Let's assume America's 275 million cars are all EVs equipped with 75 kWh batteries. Each kWh takes an EV about three miles —a 225-mile range for a 75-kWh battery. The average American drives about 1,100 miles a month. In theory this would increase demand by 970 billion kWh per year, which would be an additional 23% of the current total U.S. production of 4.2 trillion kWh per year. But this increased demand would not entail building hundreds of additional power stations because staggered billing would enable an on-board "app" to buy electricity when it is cheap and sell it back to the grid when it is expensive. The EV fleet, in aggregate, would be functioning as a gigantic battery. If a blackout were imminent, electricity companies could offer a premium to car owners to pump energy back into the grid for that crucial period. Two-way charging outlets, on streets and in parking lots, could eventually become as ubiquitous as parking meters once were. This potential for energy rationalization would be greatly enhanced when home batteries become as ubiquitous as air conditioners and, along with the vehicle fleet, dwellings evolve into a second gigantic battery. These developments would greatly increase the feasibility of intermittent energy sources such as wind and solar. Consider that energy from classic electricity grids is still being produced, and thus wasted, during off-peak periods; it is simply not being used (analogous to idling at traffic lights). These two gigantic batteries (vehicles and homes) would enable a grid to function in fuel-efficient cruise mode rather than the "stop and go" of peak and low demand.

The environmental impact of a mostly electric fleet would be profound. According to the U.S. *Department of Energy*, a kWh produced by a coal-fired power plant creates two pounds of CO_2 while burning one gallon of gasoline (8.4 pounds) produces 20 pounds of CO_2. In 2019, the United States consumed 3.4 billion barrels of gasoline, creating 3 trillion pounds of CO_2. If the entire fleet was electric, CO_2 emissions would be cut to 1.2 trillion pounds even if *all* electricity were produced by coal. But since coal in 2023 produced less than 17% of U.S. electricity (down from 34% in 2014 and still declining), the universal adoption of EVs would cut America's automobile related emissions up to 80%. This equation doesn't even reflect the energy presently expended and emissions produced by:

1. Exploring, locating, testing, and surveying oil fields.
2. Getting the equipment in place to extract the oil.
3. Manufacturing the equipment.
4. Pumping the oil out of the ground.
5. Transporting the oil to a refinery.
6. Transporting the refined fuel to regional storage facilities.
7. Transporting the refined fuel to filling stations.
8. Filling the vehicle's tank.
9. Maintaining and cleaning filling stations.
10. Transporting employees to and from work for all of the above.
11. The energy required to manufacture and build this entire logistical infrastructure.

Other Mitigators

Reforesting only 12% of global semi-arid areas would offset the annual CO_2 output of one thousand 500-megawatt coal plants (a gigaton a year).[9]

Reforesting 60% of the world's semi-arid areas would offset five thousand 500-megawatt coal plants (five gigatons a year). According to the *World Resources Institute*, humanity is presently pumping 40 gigatons of CO_2 into the atmosphere annually. Thus, while afforestation is not the silver bullet some claim it to be, it does have a significant contributory role to play in reducing greenhouse emissions, within the multi-faceted strategy described above. Since large swathes of semi-arid areas contain or border on some of the world's poorest populations, we could put millions to work in forestation and ancillary occupations, thus accomplishing two positives: fighting poverty and the environmental degradation contributing to the refugee flood now destabilizing much of Europe. The EU might consider financing the greening of the semi-arid Sahel region of the southern Sahara, thus creating an economic situation that reduces the incentive to join the refugee flood, a cheaper and more humane alternative to present policies. Reforestation also mitigates water and food challenges. Food security is dependent on water security and water security is dependent on forests. Forests are vital to our water supply. They influence how and where rain falls. They filter and clean our water. By protecting the world's forests, we are also protecting the clean water that we depend upon for our survival.

Various methods of *artificial photosynthesis*, now being developed, will be able to suck CO_2 out of the air with increasing efficiency. This CO_2 could then be combined with hydrogen to create the hydrocarbons we need for product: plastics, fertilizers, chemicals, etc. (as well as for manufacturing carbon nanotubes). Hemp and other fast-growing plants can eventually replace wood for making paper (thus relieving the pressure on our forests and jungles). Beef should gradually give way to other forms of animal protein that do not impact the environment as much. For example, pork emits one-fourth the life cycle emissions as beef and poultry one-fifth. Norway is leading the way in demonstrating how fish farms can provide a major share of our non-vegetable protein needs with less environmental damage than at present. Eating local is another mitigator; as already mentioned, eating British beef in London in the winter results in fewer lifecycle emissions than eating avocado imported from Chile.

Biofuels produced from algae could eventually provide a substantial portion of our transportation fuel. Algae has a much higher productivity potential than crop-based biofuels because it grows faster, uses less land, and requires only sun and CO_2 plus nutrients that can be provided from gray sewage water. It is a primo CO_2 sequesterer because it works for free (by way of photosynthesis), and in doing so can be a feedstock for producing biodiesel and ethanol in much higher volumes per acre than corn or other crops. "The biggest challenge is how to slash the cost of production, which by one Defense Department estimate now runs to more than $20 a gallon."[10] But once commercialized in industrial scale facilities, production cost could go as low as $2 a gallon (the equivalent of $88 per barrel of oil) according to Jennifer Holmgren, director of renewable fuels at an energy subsidiary of Honeywell International.[11] Given that the very production of algae uses wastewater, thus to a great degree eliminating the cost of water purification, would make $88 a barrel already economically feasible. Add in the fact that CO_2 is its primary feedstock, its use to produce transportation fuel or feedstock for product would actually improve the environment; a win-win-win situation.

What is Growth—Really?

But there is a much bigger philosophical challenge. We must reevaluate the philosophical underpinnings of the very concept of growth. What, for example, is meant by GDP (Gross Domestic Product) and how do politicians, economists, and corporate interests manipulate our ignorance to our detriment. Does growth in GDP really mean growth in real economic/social value? Consider the precise technical definition of GDP:

> **GDP** = private consumption + gross investment + government investment + government spending + (exports – imports). For the gross domestic product, "gross" means that the **GDP** measures production regardless of the various uses to which the product can be put.

In other words, GDP is the aggregate of *every* transaction that takes place in the economy *no matter what its purpose*. Quantitative economic activity *per se* is all that counts. GDP treats everything as an economic positive. *All* transactions are added to the GDP and thus treated as growth. This is what the sentence "regardless of the various uses to which the product can be put" actually means (product includes services). What does this really mean in practice? Consider:

1. A terrible traffic accident occurs: two people killed, three injured. The cost of the ambulances that remove the people is *added* to the GDP; the cost of the wrecking crew that removes the cars is *added* to the GDP; the cost of the funerals is *added* to the GDP; the cost

of the hospitalization, treatment and rehabilitation of the injured is *added* to the GDP; the costs of the various insurance claims paid out (including purchase of new cars) is *added* to the GDP. In other words, traffic accidents are good for the GDP and thus the economy in any given year.

2. Various innovations cause a drop in energy consumed per capita by 25%. People spend less to fill up their cars and light, heat and air-condition their homes. As a consequence, the energy sector shrinks. This is *subtracted* from the GDP. There is less damage to property and health from pollution; so, the home improvements sector shrinks and people spend less on health care. Both savings are *subtracted* from the GDP. In other words, energy innovation is bad for the GDP and bad for the economy in any given year.

3. A huge tax cut is implemented and as a result there is a trillion-dollar windfall for corporate America. Most of this money is used for stock buybacks. These buyback transactions are *added* to the GDP. The price of the stock goes up which is *added* to the GDP. As a consequence, the officers of the corporation get bigger bonuses at the end of the year which is *added* to the GDP. As a consequence, the country's budget deficit and debt increase, and the government has to spend more money on servicing the debt which is *added* to the GDP. In other words, the tax cut was good for the GDP (and the economy) in the year implemented, even though there were few new capital investments or investments in R&D, or new production facilities or products or services. How has the average citizen benefited from this? Will not the increased national debt require some future cut in services that will have a negative impact primarily on the middle class?

4. The American Department of Defense spends over 100 billion dollars a year policing the Persian Gulf and the salaries and cost of equipment of this operation are *added* to the GDP. The cost of military funerals is *added* to the GDP. The cost of VA hospitals is *added* to the GDP. Lowering military casualty rates detracts from the GDP. In other words, war is good for the economy.

But even if we overlook the weaknesses of the very concept of GDP as an indicator of economic health, the growth in *value* (of GDP) is still not synonymous with growth in the *volume* of raw materials (as the "limits to growth" prophets claim). In reality, we are capable of growing value while shrinking our exploitation of natural resources. The "wealth of nations" can increase as the human burden on the carrying capacity of the planet decreases. A good example, as we have already mentioned above, is aviation. Furthermore, when one factors in the growth of the proportion of GDP of personal and non-personal services, the picture becomes even less foreboding. According to the IMF, services and commerce have become the major drivers of global economic growth. They constitute over 63% of global GDP and well over 70% of the GDP of the developed world, and the proportion is increasing. And while services such as translation, consulting, planning, accounting, massage therapy, legal advice, financial planning, gerontology, and so on, also consume a certain amount of our natural resources, the quantity is infinitesimal in relation to the economic value produced. For example, if I translate a 100,000-word book for $10,000 I have consumed the electricity and wear and tear on my computer and the electricity used to send the translation as an email attachment and nothing else that is even measurable. If I manufacture actual goods for $10,000, I have consumed a huge quantity of natural resources and energy in comparison.

Mark Twain famously once said there are three kinds of lies: lies, damn lies, and statistics. He was referring to how statistics, divorced from the reality of real life, are manipulated and sold to the uninformed to distract them from what is really important. The question is never how much the economy grew in terms of GDP. The question is how the economy has impacted the standard of living and quality of life of real human individuals and communities. Americans brag that US economic growth (GDP) is greater than the EU and Japan and this proves that the welfare state is a burden on the economy resulting in a lower standard of living. The truth is that the economic growth of both the EU and Japan *per capita* is equal to the U.S. since their populations are static or shrinking. Considering Japan's and Europe's superior health care, lower rates of poverty, higher life expectancy and smaller income gap (with all that entails regarding health, education, and social morale), we can justifiably conclude that the EU and Japanese economies are doing a better job for their citizens than the U.S. economy. For example, the Kaiser Foundation has found that about one million Americans a year have declared bankruptcy because of medical expenses—a phenomenon almost unheard of anywhere else in the world. Referencing Mark Twain, it is clear that we require an entirely new vocabulary of social/economic/political measurements.

Population Explosion or Population Implosion

One constant refrain of anti-growth advocates is that we are heading towards 12 billion people by the end of the century, that this is unsustainable, and thus that we must proactively reduce the human population to 3-4 billion in order to "save the planet" and human civilization from catastrophe. But recent data indicates that a *demographic winter* will begin to overtake humanity by the middle of this century. Over 60 countries (containing over half the world's population) already do not have replacement birth rates of 2.1 children per woman. This includes the entire EU, China, Russia, and half a dozen Muslim countries, including Turkey, Algeria and Iran—as well as the United States. If present trends continue, India, Mexico and Indonesia will join this group before 2030. The human population will probably peak at around 10 billion by 2060, after which, for the first time since the Black Death, it will begin to shrink. By the end of the century, the human population might be as low as 6-7 billion. The real danger is not a population explosion; but the economic, social and cultural consequences of the impending population implosion.[12] This demographic process is not being driven by famine or disease as has been the case in all previous history. Instead, it is being driven by the greatest Cultural Revolution in the history of the human race: the liberation and empowerment of women. The fact is that even with present technology, we would still be able to sustain a global population of 12 billion by the end of century if needed. The evidence for this is cited above.

Summing Up

The current crisis of human civilization is not a consequence of the consumer society or of hyper-industrialization or of the spread of vulgar Americanization. It is a consequence of the incompetence and dearth of imagination of our politicians and intellectuals coupled with the inertia of outmoded ideas. The "limits to growth" advocates are right in that if we continue to run our societies and economies as we have been doing, we are headed for environmental and civilizational catastrophe. But there is no reason to continue to run our societies and our economies as we have. Nor is there any reason to deprive ourselves and our progeny of the material comforts that the industrial revolution has provided in the name of "saving the planet." Instead, we can envision and then construct a planetary civilization totally committed to enabling the self-actualization of every single human being on the planet; a civilization that will have banished want and hunger for all time; a civilization dedicated to realizing the god-like potential of the human spirit. And in that day, we will finally be free. Amen!

Chapter Eleven: From Postmodernism to Neomodernism

"Where there is no vision, the people (nation) perish ..."
—Proverbs 29:18

"Where there is no vision the people (nation) cast off restraint ..." —Proverbs 29:18

These are two accepted translations (from the Hebrew) of Proverbs 29:18. The first may be interpreted in two ways: without vision the people *literally* die; or conversely, they lose all social coherence and cease to exist as a people—become a mixed multitude, an undifferentiated mass without civilization, which would mean that organized society (the "nation"), will have died. The second version can be seen as implying the second alternative of the first translation. Everybody "doing their own thing" destroys social coherence, which leads to people becoming an undifferentiated mass without civilization. My view is that *without vision, the soul of humankind dies.*

Utopianist thinking is the human construction of future visions—the human construction of final causes. It is a modern iteration of the teleological predisposition of western civilization—a predisposition which has been fundamental to its civilizational health. This is because human beings are value creating creatures, not only materially but also spiritually, and without vision we cannot create value and our inner being (our "souls") begin to decay. The hollowness, angst and alienation that has come to dominate intellectual discourse in the late 20th and early 21st centuries might be seen as a symptom of this decay, preventing us from realizing the messianic potential of modern science and technology. The cure for this decay is a return to utopianist *thinking*. I differentiate between utopianist thinking and utopianisms, which are 'isms' that advocate particular and specific solutions to the human condition. Historically, most 'isms' have degenerated into secular fundamentalist "religions." They become spiritually and psychologically oppressive to the most sensitive and intellectually imaginative members of the community who are the first to "escape," foretelling the ultimate dismemberment of the community. The only secular utopianist communities that have lasted more than one generation have been the *Kibbutzim*—but for very specific *sui generis* national reasons. At the national and transnational level, utopianisms (such as Marxism in actual practice) have produced horrific totalitarian monsters that ended up killing more human beings than Nazism and Fascism combined.

Modern utopianism and the development of utopian thought were coeval with the advent of "modernism" and the *Idea of Progress*. Thomas More's *Utopia* (literally in Greek "nowhere") was inspired by the possibilities of *The Age of Discovery*; the so-called "discovery" of new territories (especially America) which would enable the creation of new societies without the baggage of the past. *Utopia* was an anticipation of that "Enlightenment experiment" called the United States. It projected a vision which has characterized American culture since its inception, and which is reflected in that vague concept called the "American Dream"; every wave of immigration being composed of people desiring to build a future different than their past. Francis Bacon's *New Atlantis* complemented *Utopia*; it envisaged possibilities of the development of rational, organized, intentional scientific society. Indeed, unlike the "knowledge for its own sake" approach, which had characterized Greek inquiry, Bacon was a radical advocate for investigating nature in order to gain knowledge and techniques that would benefit humankind. His technocratic utopianism has affected literature and politics ever since. Much of science fiction as well as Fabian Socialism, and the literary optimism this movement spawned in the persons of H. G. Wells and George Bernard Shaw are genetic descendants of Bacon's basic sense of life and the possibilities of human society framed by science and technology. Capitalism, Marxism, Americanism, consumerism, and reformism are all spiritual descendants of Bacon's fundamental attitude towards life.

The critical thinking of the Renaissance birthed the *Scientific Revolution*, which, in turn, birthed the *Enlightenment* and what came to be called the *Science of Man*. Enlightenment thinkers, such as Locke and Adam Smith in England and Condorcet (and the rest of the Encyclopedists) in France, perceived that just as reason and scientific method could be applied to nature and in the words of Bacon "to wrest her secrets from her," they could also be applied to human society to make it better and more just. This was when the *Idea of Progress* and the belief in the possibility of progress, as a consequence of the directed and focused actions of rational human beings, became the Zeitgeist of western thinkers. The assumption that material progress and the rational organization of society would make better human beings, that there is identity between material progress and moral progress (with its consequent spiritual uplifting) became what we now call *Modernism*. The realization that material progress does not automatically lead to moral progress, that rational and just social institutions do not resolve the problem of human evil has given birth to that anti-ideology which we call *Postmodernism*.

Belief in human progress characterized the founding fathers of the United States, the first polity in history to be rationally conceived and designed for the sole benefit of its constituents (at the time only white men): "We hold these truths to be self-evident, that ... men ... are endowed ... with certain unalienable Rights, that ... to secure these rights, Governments are instituted among Men." In other words, there is no purpose to organized society other than to benefit the human beings that compose it. We have become so used to these words that we have forgotten how truly revolutionary they were at the time and how the United States exploded onto the stage of history, forever changing the course of human events. The United States is the quintessential Enlightenment project and might be called practical, applied utopianism. For Americans (until recently), the "American Dream" was never a dream—it was their reality, and eventually came to include Blacks, Native Americans, and women (and most recently, homosexuals). Karl Marx's "Scientific Socialism" also reflected the same Enlightenment confidence about the possibilities of creating rational and just societies. Recent history, of course, has clearly demonstrated Constitutionalism's superiority to Marxism in making progress towards this end.

Modernity and modernism are not synonyms. Modernity refers to the advent of our technical civilization dedicated to the comfort and convenience of human beings. Modernism, on the other hand, is an 'ism'; an *ideology* that reflects the Enlightenment belief that moral and ethical progress would follow scientific and technical progress and the rational organization of society around scientific principles (thus the Social "Sciences"). Progress for the advocates of modernism was an all-encompassing whole predicated on the assumption that technical and material progress would also raise the moral level of humanity. But this concept of progress ran into trouble right at the outset. Naysayers such as Blake and Rousseau (whom we might classify, in hindsight, as proto postmodernists) excoriated the spiritual impoverishment of a humanity governed by technical reason alone. Ernest Becker, in *The Structure of Evil*, brilliantly describes the ideological debate that raged during the Enlightenment. Thinkers as diverse as Hume, Diderot and St. Pierre (anticipating the future obscenity of a dehumanized *Scientism*) protested against "a science divorced from human affairs" and "a science which would take the universe and not man as the center."[13] They felt that what would follow would be the organization of society according to a scientific approach that celebrated "valuelessness" as the way to avoid value-laden "prejudice" (literally pre-judgment) in order to achieve "objectivity." Given the infinitude of the Universe, what would it even mean to place the Universe at the center of our interest? Why should human beings even care? And if they cared what possible vision could be formulated that would prevent them from falling into the same despairing mood as Pascal?

Accordingly, as science and industry (the very heart of the modernist belief) progressed, they both laid the groundwork for the eventual postmodernist critique, which harkened back to the healthy instincts of these early Enlightenment skeptics. Science became *Scientism*; not a tool of human inquiry into areas amenable to scientific methods, but an almost totalitarian belief system, which denigrated and even negated concepts not accessible to quantitative, measurable, scientific methodology. As noted above, William James was prominent in criticizing this approach. Rather than saying we have discovered magnificent methods for inquiring into phenomena amenable to quantitative measurement, devotees of scientism condescendingly presumed that phenomena not amenable to quantitative measurement were not worthy of being addressed or could not be said to even exist. This intellectual tendency achieved its most grotesque extreme in the *Behaviorist Psychology* of John B. Watson and B.F. Skinner, who essentially denied the very existence of volitional human consciousness because it could not be observed or measured. Mind and soul for them were meaningless words because they could not be quantifiably described. Behavior on the other hand could be observed, described, and statistically measured. Science, the first humanity (science being the basis of Renaissance and Enlightenment Humanism) was now transformed into "scientism," which denied the very humanity of humanity (that is if we accept that what separates the human from the animal is the volitional reasoning mind). This became grist for the mill of postmodernists, who denied that reason was a universal objective human characteristic but rather an ideological "construct" of western culture. They denied that reason had any intrinsic objective value and avowed that non-rational, irrational, and even anti-rational ways of relating to reality should be treated with equal respect (what today might be called "alternative facts"). Postmodernism retreated back into the premodern and put the unsubstantiated metaphysical on the same plane as the empirical physical. Thus, postmodern Marxists (an oxymoron if there ever was one) were able to justify positions that in essence said "Marx is right, it is the facts that are wrong" when continuing to advocate socio/economic/ political structures that had already failed dozens of times.

Multiculturalism was born; medicine men became equivalent to medical men. Pretensions to hierarchies of values became politically incorrect if they were coeval with cultural origin. Even advocating particular values became a symptom of innate racism. Science itself was described as a subjective "construct" of dead European white men; not an empirically based coherent description of objective reality (reality itself, in the eyes of the postmodern multiculturists, being nothing more than a chaotic aggregate of subjective narratives). Objective rational discourse based upon a universally accepted language of meaning became almost impossible in the social sciences and the humanities. New Age affirmations went unchallenged because there was no way one could challenge them other than by applying one's critical reasoning mind—an effort preempted by the inherently anti-western canons of postmodernism. If one attempted to apply critical reason (the glory of western civilization) one became open to accusations of cultural jingoism. Anything went. Analytical and critical questioning became a sign of poor taste and cultural intolerance. The human mind was turned into an uncritical dysfunctional sieve which enabled all kinds of meaningless mush to enter. This was ideal for advertisers and politicians but disastrous for our civilization. Reason created science, science created scientism, scientism created anti-reason. The foundations were laid for a political culture of "alternative facts." It is somewhat amusing to watch the hysterical reactions of the academic left to the rise of the rightwing alternative fact universe when they have been teaching alternative fact attitudes (your narrative and my narrative) for several generations and are as guilty for laying the intellectual and emotional foundations for Trumpism as any other factor.

There is a big difference between multicultural and multiculturism. Multicultural is an objective sociological and anthropological fact while multiculturalism is an 'ism,' an ideology that denies there are hierarchies of cultural and social values and claims all cultures are equally moral and that any claim to the contrary is racism. Taken to its extreme, some even claim that the *Universal Declaration of Human Rights* is cultural imperialism because it is based on European Enlightenment values.

Science had to destroy teleology: the philosophy of purposefulness. In order to do its business, science had to assume that existence has no purpose. Existence just "is" and the job of science is to investigate the brute "isness" of existence. The proper question for a scientist to ask is not *why* (a value- laden question) but *how* (a valueless question). There can be no scientific answer to the question *why* but there can be scientific answers to the question *how.* Richard Feynman in *The Character of Physical Law* relates that when Newton was challenged about his theory: "But it doesn't mean anything—it doesn't tell us anything," Newton responded: "It tells you *how* it moves. That should be enough. I have told you *how* it moves, not *why*."[14] It was just this type of cold mechanistic approach that the early Enlightenment skeptics were afraid of.

When science became scientism and conquered philosophy and academia (and even art) it became a sign of déclassé philistinism to even ask the question *why* (or in the case of modern art, *what*). This approach created the existential dilemma of modern times. If existence has no purpose, then human existence has no purpose. Thus, the spiritual groundwork for twentieth-century nihilism was laid out. The social sciences, like a male dog with its nose up the behind of the in-heat female dog of the physical sciences, quickly followed suit, cutting itself off from its historical roots of a value-laden *Science of Man.* Scientism desiccated the radical humanism of the Enlightenment. Utopian thinking—the vision making enterprise of humanity—could not exist in such a barren spiritual environment.

In addition to scientism, the straightforward course of nineteenth-century science also contributed to the decline of the heroic humanism of the early modernist attitude. The Enlightenment had inherited a godlike image of man from the Renaissance. Enlightenment men were usually still believers in God (although often contemptuous of organized religion) and accepted that men were made "in the image of God" by God himself. Newton and Locke were devoutly religious men. Along comes Darwin and demonstrates that man is not created by God but is related to apes. Enlightenment thinkers believed that man was a rational being amenable to self-improvement as a consequence of rational social and political policy. Along comes Freud and blasts away this naive psychology and demonstrates the dark and often primitive complexity of the human psyche. Both these developments dealt a severe blow to traditional human self-esteem and hence to the self-confidence which lay at the base of the modernist ideology—especially since the "problem of evil" still prevailed despite our material progress.

Ironically, it was the historical misuse of the modernist progress of industry and technology that helped set the stage for twentieth-century post-modernism. The naive belief that rational technical progress would create a more just and enlightened society, and as a consequence, the moral level of humanity would also increase, was a foundational assumption of the *Idea of Progress* and the backbone of Modernism. This assumption was soon destroyed by events. Men did not become better; they became better at killing one another. The American Civil War was humanity's first industrial war. Tens of thousands of men were slaughtered in single battles fought with industrial means. Europe stood appalled and judgmental at this American barbarism, not realizing that the Civil War was but a dress rehearsal for the barbarism of World War I, during which hundreds of thousands of men were slaughtered in single battles. WWI spelt the end of Victorian optimism and blind belief in the inherent goodness of man and the inevitability of progress. The problem of evil was reborn and nihilistic, pessimistic existentialism dominated the European spirit after World War I (until this very day to a very great extent, to the detriment of European civilization).

But the *coup de grace* for naive optimism and belief in the idea of progress as an all-inclusive whole occurred in World War II. Here the most developed nation in the history of the planet (industrially, scientifically, philosophically, and culturally) committed the most heinous crime in human annals *and could not have committed the crime if it had not been so developed*. If the Civil War represented the first case of industrial warfare, then the Nazi Holocaust represented the first case of industrial murder. Auschwitz and the other camps were giant factories dedicated to the production of death. This is the uniqueness of the Holocaust when compared to other mass murders in history (such as that of the Armenians in World War I or the Tutsis more recently). Auschwitz could not have been built by a pre-technological (i.e., pre-modern) society. That it was perpetrated by such a developed society is one of the reasons it is so horrific; not only did it kill millions (nothing unusual in that in human history) it destroyed our most sacred beliefs about ourselves as *modern* human beings. The eventual failure of and consequent intellectual disappointment with the various Marxist-Leninist experiments may be seen as an epilogue to the "Death of Modernism"—Marxism being the quintessential modernist ideology before the postmodernists got ahold of it.

All told, it has been estimated that governments and societies holding the modernist creed as their foundational societal axiom killed over 160 million people in the twentieth century. World War I, World War II, the Holocaust, Stalin's purges and the intentional famine that killed up to 6 million Ukrainians, Mao's Great Leap Forward and Cultural Revolution, Indian Independence and other modern phenomena have piled up bodies in numbers inconceivable to Genghis Khan, Attila the Hun, and Ivan the Terrible. The dismal record of the twentieth century made utopian thinking unfashionable. It seemed silly and infantile. You were not a serious social scientist if you engaged in such frivolity. Ice cold, valueless, statistical social science became *de rigueur*. Some interesting exceptions like C. Wright Mills and Ernest Becker were around, but always on the margins of "serious" social science. If you wanted to get ahead in academia you talked statistics, not values. Statistics are certainly useful analytical tools, but they are not fertile soil for nurturing visionary thought or anything approaching a true "Science of Man." The concrete examples of various twentieth-century utopian pretensions, such as collectivization in the Soviet Union and China, the pathetic self-indulgent communes of the sixties and seventies dropouts, or bizarre religious communes such as Jonestown and Branch Davidians have done little to improve the reputation of utopian speculations and experiments.

The distress of Israel's Kibbutz movement might have been the final nail in the coffin of illusions about human nature. This had been the one twentieth-century utopian experiment given sanction by "serious" social science. Indeed, the Kibbutzniks themselves were fond of joking that more books had been written about the Kibbutz (by anthropologists, sociologists, psychologists, and educators) than there were Kibbutzniks. Given the self-induced economic crises of the Kibbutzim, idealization of the Kibbutz is no longer fashionable. The vast majority of kibbutzim have been privatized to some degree or another in order to survive. The Kibbutz Movement only survived at all because of a 6-billion-shekel bailout by the Israeli government. This caused tremendous resentment amongst Israeli taxpayers, and for the first time in the history of the Zionist project, the general population came to view Kibbutzniks as being part of the problem and not part of the solution. The self-esteem of individual Kibbutzniks, used to seeing themselves as the archetypal Israelis, plummeted. Social disintegration followed and a reverse Darwinist process took place. Instead of the best and the brightest coming to the Kibbutz (the historical precedent), the best and brightest began leaving the Kibbutz.

Second and third generation Kibbutzniks had already radically changed the internal structure of the Kibbutz. Those raised in communal children's houses had painful memories of their experience and refused to raise their own children in the same way and simply brought them home. Recently, a spate of anecdotal articles as well as research has burst the bubble of the halcyon myth of the "children's house," revealing physical, sexual, and psychological abuse which today would be prosecuted. One young former Kibbutznik has sued his Kibbutz for performing a social experiment on him that he claims has left him an emotional cripple. The demise of the "children's house" did not reflect a diminishing of collective values as some dogmatic socialists argued; it reflected the concern of loving parents not willing to make their children suffer what they had suffered in the name of a poorly thought-out ideological abstraction. The demise of the "children's house" and the consequent necessity to expand family dwellings resulted in tremendous expense, which was a major contributor to the financial problems of the Kibbutz. The lesson is that idealistic and axiomatic wishful thinking based upon grand sounding slogans (and little else) can produce mediocre social structures which result in irrational economic organization, which eventually cause economic difficulties, which result in social disintegration and the loss of individual self-esteem for members of the community.

This has been the greatest failure of utopian thought: to understand the connection between economics and ideals; that no matter how lofty the ideal, if it does not rest upon the bedrock of practical, efficient, rational economic behavior, it is doomed to fail. The history of the Soviet Union and Chinese collectivization are other, much more extreme, examples of this truism. If there is to be a "neo-utopianism" it must base itself on this self-evident historical lesson: economic efficiency matters; no moral society can be built on an inefficient economic system. A society might be efficient and immoral, and put its efficiency to the service of immorality, but no society can be both inefficient and moral. Why preoccupy ourselves with utopianism at all, given this sad record? Because, quite simply, we require concrete visions of our possible future in order to live as human beings on this earth—without such visions we shall perish. As the early Enlightenment modernists so rightly understood, what separates the human from the animal is the rational mind. The rational, volitional mind is the chief survival tool of the human species. When we use it, we prosper, when we fail to use it, we endanger our own survival. War and the human suffering it causes are irrational; peace and the human fulfillment it makes possible are rational. A polluted environment is irrational; a clean environment is rational.

Is it even possible to have a rational social science that is not based on a social philosophy embedded with a coherent vision of the innate possibilities of human being? How can we have a rational social science (a true *Science of Man*) without social values, and what would the metaphysical foundations of these values look like? Just as the physical sciences must be valueless in order to be scientific, so the social sciences must be value laden in order to be scientific. Science is a rational, volitional, intentional activity that must say yes or no to the data it gathers. The physical sciences make the decision based upon the quantitative coherence of the data itself after experiment and translation into mathematical language. If the social sciences are to be relevant to the survival of humanity (i.e., rational) they must base their yes or no on *non-quantifiable* values. Values cannot be perceived by way of statistics; they can be perceived by way of pictures or visions or scenarios. Indeed, scenarios are kinds of mini-utopias. Futurist methodologies might become the basic functional tool by which we could construct the metaphysical foundations of a space-age value system. This is because human society cannot conduct itself rationally without a clear idea of where it wants to go. Clear *ideas* (or alternative visions) would be a better term because future visions should be pluralistic in order to avoid the totalitarian "know-it-all" temptation that doomed utopian experiments in the past.

The horrific consequences of a single-minded (as opposed to an open-minded) utopian instinct are well documented in Yaakov Talmon's classic work *Totalitarian Democracy*. Whatever the case, we must have a vision of the kind of future we want, in order to make rational decisions on a daily basis. Having a vision and being a *realistic* visionary are absolute necessities for functioning as a rational human being. This is contrary to prevalent preconceptions, which equate visionary with unrealistic fantasy, but it is nonetheless self-evidently true (without vision we *will* perish). Human beings make practical judgments and value judgments every day of their lives. We must do this in order to survive, as the primary human survival tool is not instinct but the reasoning mind evaluating the human environment. Human beings better at this usually have much more successful lives. Societies and cultures that encourage this kind of thinking are usually much more developed. The question is on the basis of what do we make our judgments? If we do not have a clear vision, or several alternative visions then how do we make rational decisions? If we do not know where we want to go, if we do not have a future ideal of the kind of life we want, how can we judge the practicality or the value of any judgment we must make in the course of our daily lives? A plurality of visions might be a *practical* necessity in such a rapidly changing world, and not only to avoid the totalitarian temptation. Utopianism must avoid becoming a finalistic one-dimensional picture. It must reflect a "new view of the Cosmos (and) be progressively evolutionary, infinite in its capacity and comprehensible, both qualitatively and quantitatively" as Eric J. Lerner wrote in his provocative book *The Big Bang Never Happened.*[15] Or as Stephen Jay Gould, commenting on the ramifications of the human genome project in the New York Times, has written, "only humility (and a *plurality* of strategies for explanation) can locate the Holy Grail ...." (Gould went on to hint at the infinite human potentialities offered by a post-reductionist view of human life.)

Might a new value-laden "Science of Man" find its justification in philosophical insights drawn from new developments in evolutionary theory, genetic research, neuroscience, and our ever-increasing knowledge about life itself? Edward O. Wilson has made a heroic attempt at a synthesis which reintroduces objectivity and meaning into the discussion in his book *Consilience*. Wilson also distinguishes between reductionism as the proper methodology for science while, indirectly acknowledging that it is an insufficient worldview. This, I believe, is the proper distinction—a reductionist methodology within a holistic metaphysical worldview.

There is a socio-psychological price to be paid for the present lack of a civilizational vision. Observe the number of people in the modern world who seem to float through life rudderless, without a clear view of their own value as human beings. They are so confused about the complexities of modern life that they have shut off their rational cognitive faculties; trying to fill the subsequent spiritual vacuum by endless scrolling on their smartphones, getting involved in cults, fundamentalist religions, New Age fads, or becoming "activists" in endless social causes. The inability to construct rational, realistic alternative future visions leads people to create fantastic ones such as benevolent aliens will come in their spaceships to take us away to eternal bliss and in preparation we must first castrate ourselves and then commit collective suicide. This intellectual hollowness has, I believe, been the mental framework upon which the obvious misrepresentations of Trumpism and Brexit have been built.

Human beings are the only species that can conceive of the future, the only species truly cognizant of its own mortality. The resultant angst leads us into the future-conceiving business. Religions had a monopoly on this business for the longest time (the end of days, the coming of the Messiah, eternal life, eventual human salvation, life after death, reincarnation etc.). Science began to replace religion in areas amenable to quantitative measurement. The vocation of *Futurism* has attempted to make this process more comprehensive and as rational and connected to reality (including qualitative reality) as possible. Utopianism was one of the foundational building blocks upon which Futurism was built. Now Futurism must serve as one of the foundational building blocks of a neo-utopianism. Modern utopianism coincided with the secularizing process of the Renaissance. People were beginning to shed the surety about the future provided by Religion. This lack of surety was reflected in the plays of Shakespeare, the first truly modern writer who anticipated the angst of modern man as well as Camus' question regarding suicide. "To be or not to be, that *is* the question!" Utopian speculations, in all likelihood responding to this incipient angst, offered secularized versions of a possible end of days as it pertained to human society on this earth—thus Marxism, the quintessential secular "end of days" worldview.

One of the admirable aims of the postmodernist project was to challenge human certitude (moral, scientific, or political) as insufferable hubris. While this project has performed a valuable service in critiquing some of the arrogance of modernist ideology, it is essentially nihilistic. It offers no coherent alternative to modernism. Indeed, it might even view the very search for coherence as a modernist pretension. But if humanity is to survive and have a meaningful existence, then the intellectual project of the twenty-first century must be to move from postmodernism to neomodernism. We must reinstate the Enlightenment ambition to create a *Science of Man*. We must become neo-Modernists.

Chapter Twelve: Reinventing Social Policy

All social policy is based explicitly or implicitly on ideology. We are all ruled by ideology, whether we admit it or not or are aware of it or not. Ideology is defined by the Random House Dictionary of the English Language as: 1) the body of doctrine, myth and symbol of a social movement, institution, class or large group (nation, people, etc.) 2) such a body of doctrine, myth etc. with reference to some political and cultural plan, along with the devices for putting it into operation.[16] Ideology, thus defined, was loathed by Karl Marx, even though Marxism, as manifested by Lenin, Stalin and Mao, reflected this definition as much as Fascism and Nazism. In communist countries Marxism became a secular religion composed of several denominations, each with its accepted dogmas enforced by cruel and ruthless inquisitions. These denominations had their saints (St. Stalin, St. Trotsky, St. Fidel, St. Che etc.) and their high priests (Lenin and Mao). Marx's declared ambition was to create a scientific instrument—an intellectual tool—by which he could analyze the historical epoch in which he found himself. He claimed he wanted to create a science of society rather than an ideology. Yet in actuality, ideology is exactly what he created; an ideology which, upon gaining state power, has killed more people than any other belief system in history (an example of what happens when ideology becomes theology).

Prior to Marx, Adam Smith, in *Wealth of Nations*, also attempted to create an intellectual tool in order to analyze the economic life of human society—in his case to identify the declining relevance and dysfunctionality of the guiding principles of Mercantilism and to suggest alternative ways of thinking about economic life. He deduced an inherent logic and a manifestation of natural law in a nascent economic order we now call Capitalism (a term neither Smith nor Marx ever used). He aimed to formulate a rational-empirical (i.e., scientific) method for making coherent economic and social policy. Regrettably, the latter-day expressions of both Smithism and Marxism have turned into bodies of ideological doctrine. Their works have become catechisms of dogma to be unthinkingly croaked out in response to social-economic developments far removed from those particular conditions which they analyzed. Adherents of both schools, in their various iterations, came to resemble those religious fundamentalists who search for esoteric interpretations of sacred texts in order to explain current political events. The inertia of such debased thinking still infects current political discourse—even though the various interlocutors (left and right) would fervently deny that their social opinions have anything to do with either gentleman. Current use of the term "ideology" is a confusing mixture of the dictionary definition with pretensions to scientific precision. I offer my own apophatic definition as a preface to my own arguments: i.e., *what ideology is not!* Ideology is *not* theology; it is *not* a religion that one must believe in in order to be "saved." It is an intellectual tool. One does not *believe* in tools; one *uses* tools.

Similarly, scientists do not *believe* in scientific theories but rather *use* theoretical paradigms as working bases for their inquiries. As Israel Scheffler in *Science and Subjectivity* notes, it is impossible to approach data without some kind of theoretical preconception. It would become a jumble of undifferentiated and meaningless facts proffering no real useful information let alone knowledge. Therefore, scientists approach data by means of preexisting paradigms. This allows them to work with the data and make it coherent, but it also prejudices them against new facts that do not fit into their research paradigm. When the anomalies of an increasing amount of data cannot be made to fit and thus begin to paralyze the research tradition of a particular paradigm, great scientific revolutionaries make the leap from one mode of discourse to a new mode of discourse. As Kuhn points out in *The Structure of Scientific Revolutions*, they make a paradigm shift. They step sideways out of their particular research tradition and invent a new research tradition, a new paradigm, oftentimes in the face of great opposition from their own so-called "scientific" colleagues who have vested intellectual, emotional, and professional interests in the old paradigm and dogmatically defend these interests. Dogmatism is a universal human failing and is as common amongst scientists, social scientists, and political theoreticians as amongst theologians. Ironically, Galileo's biggest enemies were the university men (not the Church), whose entire careers and persona depended on an Aristotelian universe. All paradigms—ideological, political, and scientific, must eventually adapt themselves to reality if they are to have any meaningful impact. Interestingly, politicians and scientists do a much better job of adapting to changing facts on the ground than the academic gurus of political ideologies that have been debunked scores of times by historical experience. That anybody can still preach Trickledown Economics or Marxism is simply beyond my understanding, given the appalling failures of both.

C. Wright Mills was, therefore, correct in deriding so-called "objective valueless social science." He recognized that all of us bring our values, beliefs, and prejudices into play when approaching social data; that we all have our own cultural paradigm through which we sift our observations and draw our conclusions; that we all belong to one or another or a combination of several extant research traditions. It is better to recognize this at the outset, state clearly what your axioms are, and where you are trying to go with your research. This is not to say that there is no objectivity in the pursuit of knowledge. When our ideology, our paradigm, becomes so overloaded with anomalies that it can no longer work as a tool for creative inquiry and becomes, instead, a catechism for political "schoolmen," we must have the courage to make that Gestalt switch, to step sideways out of our social paradigm, our ideological research tradition, and create a new language of discourse more suitable for evaluating the new data. If this is difficult for scientists working in the so-called hard or natural sciences, how much more so for those in the social sciences, possessed of ideologies which have become more than intellectual tools and often an entire way of life that incorporates one's entire sense of self.

Loyalty to obsolete ideologies most often stems from confusing ideology with ideals; and thus, confusing the discarding of an ideological position with incipient cynicism, or a feeling of having wasted your life. The sadness that often emanated from some political refugees from the Soviet Union was palpable. They had devoted their entire lives to a "God that Failed." From total body and soul commitment to something that turned out to be dishonest, they were now emotionally adrift—they had become "Hollow Men." But ideology and ideals are not synonymous. Some examples of ideals would be justice, peace, equality, freedom etc. These ideals are not the private property of any given ideology—socialists, liberals, conservatives, and religions have all claimed them for their own. Moreover, ideals are not necessarily positive. Hitler was an idealist (he idealized racism and militarism). Some ideals are intrinsically neutral, such as nationalism, which can be expressed negatively (Mussolini) or positively (Mazzini). But even these concepts of positive and negative are subjective. Pretense to objectivity in these areas is high arrogance. *To be truly objective one must state one's subjective values at the outset.* Objectivity pertains to how one uses the data to make one's argument: i.e., is the data genuine, are you using it in an honest way, or are you making it up?

Given our individual predispositions about how society should be structured, conclusions about social, economic, and political policy cannot be objective at the metaphysical level (as perhaps physics and cosmology can). This was Marx's fatal error; his belief that his historiosophy was an objective absolute rather than a reflection of his own intellectual and emotional propensities. This was the reason why every variation of applied Marxism (Marxist-Leninism in the Soviet Union; Maoism in China) produced deadly regimes that in aggregate killed more people, directly and indirectly, than Nazism and Fascism. As I am an advocate of consequentialist ethics and reject deontological ethics, the objection that Marxists did not *intend* these results (as did Nazism and Fascism) makes no impression on me. The Marxist paradigm enabled and even facilitated the ascendency of sociopaths, sadists, and criminals, in much the same way as the Inquisition did, and in ways that are structurally difficult, if not impossible, in civilizations governed by the rules and attitudes of mind of Constitutionalism.

My Axioms

The standards by which I judge a political system are: 1) Will it contribute to the survival of the human race (and of life itself); 2) Will it rapidly increase humanity's standard of living without destroying the environment; 3) Will it honor and magnify the autonomy and dignity of the individual; 4) Will it release the creative energies of humanity as a consequence of this respect for the individual; 5) Will it tend to lessen the sense of alienation of the individual vis-à-vis society; 6) Will it tend to lessen inequality and increase formal parliamentary democracy. (I define formal democracy as a system that has a free press, independent judiciary, multi-party system, and constitutional protections for individuals and minorities.) As a consequence of all this, will a political system lessen the chances of war. It is clear that points 3), 4) and 6) place me firmly within the Western tradition. My prejudices and predispositions are for the democratic West (even as I strenuously criticize its betrayal of its own values and standards of behavior). I am not a postmodern cultural relativist.

This brings us to a critical question—what are rights and what are values? Are values and rights the same thing? For example, are education and healthcare rights or values? I would like to propose that there are three levels of rights/values.

1. Primary Rights. These are rights enumerated in most democratic constitutions and those, which while not specifically enumerated, can be inferred (such as freedom of movement, which one infers

from freedom of assembly), or which are assumed to be retained by a free people (such as the right to privacy). These rights are absolute and can only be limited by due process of law for very specific reasons. Even an idiot has the right to free speech and equality before the law, as long as he does not hurt the person or property or rights of another.

2. Secondary Rights. I would class education, healthcare, and a decent standard of living under this rubric. These are rights that reasonable people would feel are necessary to guarantee equal access to primary rights (is a homeless person really equal before the law to a millionaire?). But these rights should be conditional on citizens making a good effort to take care of their own health and to perform the tasks necessary to acquire that education which would enable them to achieve a decent standard of living. This includes civilized citizenship in the school. Not making the effort to study or creating disturbance in classrooms, by definition, removes one from becoming educated. Neglecting one's own body, by definition, eliminates one from the ability to be healthy. An idiot may have the absolute right to free speech, but a self-indulgent jerk should not have an absolute right to education or healthcare—these should be conditional on the degree of personal responsibility assumed by the individual.

3. Tertiary Rights. The right to make an honest living—the right to a job. This is super-conditional. An idiot might have the absolute freedom of speech but an incompetent, lazy slob does not have the absolute right to a job. However, in relation to our primary rights, everyone has the absolute equal right to apply for and compete for jobs *without any consideration of race, religion, gender, or whatever-gender.*

Relative income equality is a special case and is quite problematic. On the one hand we know that there is no real equality before the law between the rich and the poor—hence my advocacy for "Social Democracy." O.J. Simpson employed a battery of the finest lawyers in the United States who devoted all their time and energy to his case. An unemployed factory worker has to depend on an overworked public defender—equality before the law ... really? Tremendous gaps have emerged in the ability to access and enjoy one's primary rights, thus resulting in a breakdown of the social fabric—the sense that the system is rigged against you (Trump shamelessly exploited this feeling of unfairness in order to actually *increase* the general unfairness of organized society). There is certainly no equality of access to constitutionalist protections, which, by definition, limits equality of opportunity. On the other hand, how can we regulate this reality without infringing on the freedoms and rights of competent individuals? How might governmental limitations on income, for example, affect innovation, ambition, and the general dynamism of the economy? This is a philosophical and practical conundrum that every generation will have to resolve within the context of the constraints of their particular historical period. I confess I have no definitive suggestions to make regarding this conundrum and harbor deep suspicions of those who, with absolute surety, advocate finalistic solutions; those that are absolutely sure that their solutions are correct and that the rest of us are idiots for not agreeing with them.

If ideology is not theology, there can be no dogma other than the principles of Constitutionalism that must be presumed in order to be considered a virtuous person. Thus, the adjectives "reactionary" and "radical" used as pejoratives are devoid of moral and intellectual content. They are dismissive terms used by the ideological priesthoods of the left and the right in order to declare one's loyalty or test the loyalty of another to the political theology of one's own political "church." Such an attitude of mind cannot be fertile soil out of which imaginative social and political thought can grow. As noted earlier, when intellectual tools or paradigms become so overloaded with anomalies that they are no longer useful it becomes perfectly natural and honest to trade them in for more useful models. This is not a betrayal of one's ideals; it is a rejection of irrelevant analysis based on an outdated ideological paradigm. It betrays nothing except the stupidity of stubbornly holding onto an outdated, useless view of the world.

"Ideologues" of the present era, whether capitalist or socialist, liberal, or conservative, Democrat or Republican, have become priests quoting dogma, or schoolmen debating which dogma; there is little creative, original thought in any camp. Because of this, the distance between reality as it is and programs based on reality as it was, has become is so wide as to be grotesque. The inertia of anachronistic ideology which does not answer the living needs of people results in hypocrisy, stupidity and even cruelty. It becomes an inquisitorial dogma standing in judgment of people rather than a method of serving them.

The Crisis of Class Theory

According to Marx, industrial workers and what he called "the bourgeoisie" (he never used the word capitalism or capitalist) were the two great classes which dominated society after the Industrial Revolution, particularly in the 19th century. The evolution of society since has been so far-reaching as to make both classes unrecognizable in their traditional forms. I would even argue that this Marxist definition of classes was grossly inadequate at the very outset. The advocate of evolutionary socialism, Eduard Bernstein, recognized the poverty of this class dichotomy already in the late 19th century and earned the wrath of Marx. His ideological descendants were sent to Stalinist Gulags and Maoist "Reeducation Camps". Today the very dividing lines have been muddied. In many modern factories the so-called "workers," have post high school educations, push buttons in computerized control rooms, take home good salaries, own stocks, have nice homes, two cars and go on vacations. The "blue-collar" workers in Intel's microchip factories are usually engineers. Factories not reflective of this description have closed down and first moved to China and then other cheap labor countries. Today a factory "worker" in the developed world is very often a technician in a white coat operating computers that operate robots.

What is the essential difference between the modern "worker" and his "bourgeois" manager other than the type of responsibility? Indeed, the manager may be more of a social and cultural progressive than the worker. With the postindustrial age increasingly upon us, workers, and bourgeoisie in the traditional sense of the terms are an increasingly smaller minority of the populace. By 2018, less than 9% of the U.S. and UK workforce was in manufacturing. Despite periodic upticks, the general historical trend is a continued decline in the percentage of people working in manufacturing. Even China, Japan, and South Korea have less than 17% of the total workforce in manufacturing. Poland is the only country in the world that still has more than 20% of the workforce in manufacturing.[17] And in *every* country the percentage of industrial workers is declining.

This workforce model characterizes the entire developed and developing world. The assertion by some that the developing world has become the industrial proletariat of the developed world is dogmatic hyperbole not based on the facts. Only a small proportion of the workforce of the developing world has become the proletariat (in the classical sense) of the developed world, and even those are striving to become part of the postindustrial age. There is simply no genuine need for a large industrial prole-tariat,[18] whether as an indigenous class within the industrial West or as an offshore class in the developing world. A new global class structure is being created. Current research reveals that the "future of making a living" will clearly favor some version of self-employment, which could become a societal majority within the next 50-60 years.[19] The postindustrial self-em-ployed *petit bourgeoisie* will inherit the Earth not, as Marx predicted, the industrial proletariat.

The demise of smokestack industries is the most dramatic symptom of the almost Darwinian extinction of the industrial working class. The so-cial question today is the fate of the remaining manufacturing workers and the social dilemmas inherent in transitioning them into the postindustri-al reality. The fate of the industrial working class has been decided: we are witnessing its ongoing expiration as an historical force.[20] Marxism has been stood on its head. The new manufacturing "proletariats" are the sci-entists, engineers, technicians, computer, and robotics experts. The new proletarians are self-employed freelancers. According to Forbes magazine, an estimated 57 million Americans made part or all of their living as free-lancers in 2017 and "[i]f freelancing continues to grow at its current rate, the *majority* (italics mine) of U.S. workers will be freelancing by 2027, ac-cording to projections in the "Freelancing in America Survey."[21] Freelanc-ing in Europe is not as extensive as in the USA, but according to the Eu-ropean Forum of Independent Professionals (EFIP), "... freelancers [are] the fastest growing segment in the entire labor market ... [European] em-ployment rates have gone up by 3 % since the end of the recession in 2008. But the number of independent professionals has increased by 17%."[22] In most developed countries these citizens have no social welfare rights: no paid vacation time, no sick leave, and no unemployment insurance. This is the new class that needs social justice, not blue-collar workers, a declining demographic by any measure. According to the *U.S. Bureau of Labor Statis-tics*, the self-employed and freelancers comprise around 40% of the Amer-ican workforce as opposed to less than 20% for manufacturing, farming, mining, and construction combined. Granted, many self-employed also work in physical jobs and "shower at the end of the day" (Bernie Sanders people): plumbers, electricians, mechanics etc., but they behave econom-ically and politically as bourgeoisie not as revolutionaries. In any case, no American political party addresses the needs of this new class of people of which "72% said they'd be open to crossing party lines if a candidate said he or she supported freelancers' interests." (Election strategists take note). In Europe the trends are several years behind the United States, but on the same course.

Thus, the present enthusiasm for the return of manufacturing jobs to the United States is exaggerated. Paradoxically, an extreme redomestication of manufacturing might result in a *net loss of jobs*: the customs and logistics personnel needed to process imports; stevedores and port maintenance people; truckers who move the goods from ports; translators and multi-lingual business correspondence people; retail workers that have their jobs because imported goods are cheap. Walmart alone employs more people than the automobile, steel, and coal industries combined, and its salaries are equal to domestic textile and other low-tech industries. These are jobs that exist because of global trade but are not included in the balance of trade statistics. If we tallied the total income generated and jobs created because of Chinese imports and added it to U.S. export statistics to China, the trade gap with China would shrink appreciably. I would class balance of trade with GDP as a misleading statistic regarding the true socio-economic health of a country. What is really important in the dispute with China is their theft of intellectual property, which is much more serious than balance of trade statistics. Consider, also, what the cost of living would be if cheap imports did not exist.

Paradoxically, the redomestication of manufacturing will not only not solve the unemployment problem but will likely exacerbate the labor shortage of skilled human resources. Even when the USA was suffering chronic and debilitating unemployment (over 12%), it was experiencing a severe shortage of civil and mining engineers, skilled welders, and nurses as well as a myriad of other professions. Over three million good paying skilled blue-collar jobs are presently unfilled in the United States because there are not enough skilled workers to fill them. Even countries with much better vocational training systems, such as Holland and Germany, are also experiencing shortfalls of skilled workers. Many traditional workers continue to depend on their legacy skills as the dynamic postmodern economy is destroying the need for those skills and then complaining about the inconvenience of it all. A new underclass is being created because unfortunately, many traditional workers do not encourage their children to respect education. In fact, they often cultivate a kind of reverse snobbism which denigrates people with degrees—the "elites" who try to tell us how to live our lives. An attitude encouraged by certain politicians hoping to gain tactical electoral advantage instead of strategic national improvement. This situation is a rebuke to leftwing romanticism regarding the inherent virtues of "the working class," as well as the rightwing quasi-religious faith that the market will solve everything, and that the government should keep out of the economy (a good example of the stupidity of holding onto outmoded ideological ways of thinking).

This all-too-common working class cultural attitude has had consequences in the labor market. According to the *Bureau of Labor Statistics* in 2020, high school dropouts had a 11.7% unemployment rate, high school graduates a 9% unemployment rate, some college but no degree an 8.7% rate, associate degree 7.1%, bachelor's degree 5.5%, master's degree 4.1%, doctoral degree 2.5%, and professional degree (physicians, nurses, engineers, etc.) 3.1% unemployment rate. In other words, those with no degree at all have a higher rate of unemployment than the national rate and those with some degree less than the national rate. Those with a full degree have less than 5%, which is considered a shortage of labor and explains why even with high unemployment, there is a severe shortage of labor in the highest paying jobs.

A new social contract must be conceived that obligates individual responsibility: taking the initiative in exploiting existing government programs; moving from low employment opportunity areas to higher employment opportunity areas; being proactive citizens in demanding local schools teach critical thinking, fundamental math and communication skills (being able to speak, read and write in one's mother tongue as well as competent standard American English—the global language of commerce and science). In other words, it is up to individuals, not only governments, to be flexible and adaptive to the real time changes inherent in 21st-century civilization.

Reinventing the Welfare State: Non-Altruistic Social Policies

Within another generation or two, there will be no such thing as unskilled labor. Moreover, the increased rate of the rate of change requires a super-flexible workforce amenable to relentless abrupt changes. In democracies, when change is perceived as threatening one's livelihood, it is resisted and the overall efficiency of the economy is stunted; this inevitably stunts the moral progress of society. Witness the resentment residents of coal areas in the USA feel for environmental policies that would actually benefit the health and welfare of their own children and the subsequent opioid crisis resulting from a sense of hopelessness that derives from the feeling they are not in control of their lives. The social and *economic* costs of this sense of alienation are monstrous and impede the changes democracies must make in order to create a truly space-age economy.

The problem, therefore, is no longer the classic ideological dispute between free market advocates and welfare state advocates. The real-time rate of change requires both a super-flexible free-market economy in tandem with a super-robust welfare system that enables economic super-flexibility to be embraced by every segment of society. No-one's ambitions should be constrained by endless committees, procedures, and petty regulations; but at the same time, no one must be left behind for reasons having nothing to do with his or her inherent ability or character. Ironically, it is the huge corporations that benefit most from petty regulations because these make it harder for the small entrepreneur to change the very character of the market dominated by huge corporations.

My father had such an experience. In the late 60s he developed a plastic shoetree which he began assembling in our basement in Philadelphia (by the time he died, my brother had expanded the business into a 20,000 square foot factory). A chemist (working at home in his garage) proposed that he infuse the plastic with anti-fungal elements. They began doing so (still in basement and garage) with some significant marketing success—a first order from the American Army. Very quickly they received a "cease and desist" letter from the FDA and were "invited" down to Washington, D.C. to meet with officials. They were told that since some Americans don't wear socks and these sockless souls might also buy these shoetrees they would have to conduct "triple-blind research" proving that the sockless of the earth would not be injured in anyway by this product. (NO, I am not making this up). They were presented with a pile of forms that would have required a U-Haul to take home to begin the multi-year, multi-million-dollar research. The chemist in a fit of rage actually drank a bottle of the material in front of his interlocutors to demonstrate how safe it was, but this make do impression on the placid dullness of the bureaucratic banalities sitting before them. "Would you like the forms?" they asked. My father, of course, demurred and naively asked how the FDA had even heard about his "enormous" industrial basement facility. The answer: a congressman representing the concerns of one of his constituents. Upon leaving the FDA offices my father commented, "How do the big companies put up with this bullshit?" The chemist, looking at him in wonderment, responded, "Max (my dad's name), they love this petty shit—it keeps small guys like us out of their backyard. And in any case, they have scores of lawyers on tax deductible retainer to scare the crap out of these bureaucrats who then take it out on us small guys." Later, they learned it had been a complaint by a major American company particularly known for its anti-fungal powders that prevent athletes' foot (hint: the first name of the company was Dr.). My father's innovation would have placed them in jeopardy.

If we are to reinvent the welfare state—making it suitable for a space-age economy rather than an industrial era economy—we must confront and revise our inherited bureaucratic practices as well as our ideological assumptions. The current disappointments of the welfare state are actually failures of our creative imaginations: imaginations warped by trying to fit the square pegs of industrialism into the round holes of high-tech and consumerism.

Healthcare or Diseasecare

Nowhere is the requirement for a renewed stress on individual responsibility, or the need to revise our inherited assumptions, more apparent than in the so-called healthcare system. The truth is that it is really the disease-care system—a system that cares for our diseases not our health. It is the job of responsible citizens to take care of their health, not the state. It is the job of the state to take care of our diseases. According to the Harvard University School of Public Health's Lifestyle and Health web page, "Starting in the mid-20th century, the primary causes of death worldwide shifted from infections to chronic conditions, such as heart disease and cancer." The vast majority of these chronic conditions are self-inflicted by self-indulgent eating, smoking, lack of exercise, persistent overweight and general neglect. "Among U.S. adults, more than 90 percent of type-II diabetes, 80 percent of coronary artery disease, 70 percent of stroke, and 70 percent of colon cancer are potentially preventable by a combination of nonsmoking, avoidance of overweight, moderate physical activity, healthy diet, and moderate alcohol consumption."[23] Anecdotally, I once attended a lecture from a hospital nutritionist who claimed, "that 80% of the people hospitalized are there because of their lifestyles." In other words, 80% of us are responsible for our own health deficits and over 80% of the healthcare budget. These statistics require us to fundamentally reevaluate the policies of countries with national health systems. At present, these policies are both immoral and financially unsustainable. They are immoral because they are rewarding and thus incentivizing bad behavior, while indirectly punishing good behavior. They are unsustainable for the same reason; given the demographic dynamics of ever-increasing lifespans and ever more sophisticated treatments, expenses will continue to increase to a point where even the wealthiest, most well-meaning countries will not be able to finance them.

I will use my adopted country, Israel, as a case in point. Every year the health budget is reviewed and reapproved. The budget includes what is called "the basket," which refers to the set of drugs and treatments provided by the health service. Most naturally, the approved basket is geared to the needs of the largest groups of conditions and the sicknesses that derive from them. These conditions and sicknesses are for the most part those that are self-inflicted by poor life choice decisions, i.e., by irresponsibility. Many times, individuals that contract much rarer conditions or diseases find that they are not covered under the basket and must fund their own treatment. Let's take an individual who has literally never been seriously ill a day in his life because he has taken care of himself; has not been a drain on the system which he has been paying into his entire life and thus has a positive balance of payments vis-à-vis the health system. If he contracts a rare sickness not covered under the basket he is out in the cold, left to his own means without any financial aid from the social disease system. While other individuals, who smoke, drink, don't exercise, and who are afflicted with colon cancer, Type II diabetes, or heart disease and thus have a large negative balance of payments with the system, receive ever more money from the system. Can this be called moral or just by any stretch of the imagination?

Today, we have inexpensive genome testing that can tell one's future propensity for certain ailments; providing time to adapt one's lifestyle accordingly. More recently, scientists at Israel's Weizmann Institute have discovered that the gut microbiome (the trillions of microbes in our gut) is different for *every single human being on earth*; that everybody reacts to different foods differently and thus every individual could have his or her own custom designed diet. In other words, the combination of genome and microbiome testing will soon enable everyone who has reached 18 years of age to adopt a lifestyle geared to optimal health. Given this, we can adopt a staggered policy whereby people who exercise and eat properly pay less into the system. Both self-inflicted and inherent conditions (such as asthma etc.) are often exacerbated by filthy environmental conditions. Here we must demand even more forceful governmental interference in economy and society. In other words, neither a pure socialized welfare system, nor a pure libertarian system, but rather a hybrid suitable to the real-time changes of our postindustrial reality. I foresee the development of new kinds of blood and urine tests to supervise observance of proper lifestyle choices. On the other hand, those that neglect themselves would pay more into the system. For example, lose weight or pay full price for weight-related conditions, such as Type II diabetes. People should be rewarded for maintaining their own health. This would take the form of a yearly refund into a discretionary health account to serve as a backup insurance to cover future conditions not covered under the basket (a policy implemented by many private insurance companies who realize that prevention is cheaper than rectification). They could use this refund themselves or to help family or friends to pay for their treatment. This would be part of their estate and could be left to beneficiaries in their will.

But it is the reality of death that must be dealt with in a realistic way; the fact of being born in the first place is 100% fatal. No matter how much progress we make in prolonging life, we are eventually all going to die. Modern civilizations' denial of death puts the greatest moral and financial strain on the disease system than any other factor. Throughout history, even following the great breakthroughs of modern medicine, when people got sick with a terminal disease, they suffered for a period and then they died. Today they get sick with a terminal disease and they suffer, and suffer, and suffer etc. etc. etc. until they finally die. An animal suffering like that would be put down for humanitarian reasons; a human being, begging to die, cannot, in most countries, opt for assisted suicide because the people helping him would be accused of murder. In the battle against death, the state—under pressure from the self-righteous "personal relationship with God" self-entitled Religion Business—compels state sanctioned torture, which if committed in any other context, would be termed a war crime or a crime against humanity necessitating an extensive prison sentence. While living wills and other workarounds have mitigated this situation to a degree in recent years, they are still insufficient. You might have a *living will* but if you are hooked up to life support systems *before* a hospital is aware you have a living will, it is very difficult most times to get unhooked legally. A bureaucratic decision has been made for you, depriving you of your human agency —the State (with the approval and blessings of the Religion Business) has decided you must continue to be tortured.

In addition to this moral obscenity, this life-at-any-cost obsession has significant budgetary implications, which also have moral consequences. In the United States, for example, it is estimated that 25% of total disease-care expenditures occur in the last year of a person's life; 60% of that in the last month of a person's life (when they are often begging to be set free from their suffering). This moral obscenity extends into every area of the disease-care system: monies fighting the grim reaper could be better used in treating and researching pediatric oncology; or in expanding certain preventive services such as colonoscopies; or expanding and intensifying rehabilitation services; or in building subsidized gyms to keep people in shape in the first place; or expanding services for those elderly not yet terminal, and otherwise capable of enjoying the pleasures of life, so they might lead a dignified life. The healthcare system (excuse me the disease-care system) requires a total reevaluation of values and practices if it is to be made suitable for the space age and not bankrupt organized society.

"Handicapped" Liberation

The technological revolution gives us an opportunity to view questions of social justice differently. One example pertains to people with physical disabilities. We now see them as needy unfortunates; objects of social and humanitarian concern rather than autonomous subjects with agency, capable of managing their own lives—at best a paternalistic attitude reminiscent of attitudes towards women not so long ago. These people have become a kind of societal moral test—demonstrating how compassionate or how callous *we* are. The public discussion is about *our* moral egos ("look at me; I'm concerned, so I am better than you") rather than about *their* real social needs ("look at me; I am a complete human being with agency, enable me to realize my full human potential"). Is it the task of a truly enlightened society to show how good *we* are by helping "needy unfortunates" or to provide them with the means and infrastructure which would enable them to become independent and autonomous taxpaying citizens like the rest of us?

In reality, this is a dispute between two worldviews regarding the nature of being human and the functions of society—between social dependence as the basis of so-called solidarity and economic independence as the basis of citizenship. The technological revolution provides us with the practical means to make the latter the truly enlightened choice. Apart from a very small minority of cases, *in the new technological economy there is no such thing as being physically disabled; there are only people with different infrastructure needs.* The new economy doesn't give a bonus to muscle power. It rewards brain power and reliability. This transformation constituted one of the foundational pillars of women's liberation in the 20th century. It can now provide one of the foundational pillars of liberation for the physically disabled in the 21st century. Professor Steven Hawking was not a welfare case, but a self-supporting individual. He did not have to solicit the government or the welfare system to get the services he needed. He hired and fired his caretakers as and when he needed them without having to appear before an evaluation committee to prove how pathetic he was or wait two weeks for a meeting with a tired, overworked, and resentful social worker, who in any case didn't have the budget to help him and who would have gotten annoyed when he requested a different caretaker. He didn't have to demonstrate in front of the Parliament or lobby them in a self-demeaning way. He didn't have to cater to a patronizing media. In short, he didn't have to endure endless humiliation. Why? Because modern technology enabled him to work and to become financially independent!

A truly enlightened policy would provide the severely physically disabled with a telecommuting infrastructure in their homes. This would constitute a virtual freedom of movement to be seen as an unalienable human right, similar to the actual freedom of movement of the non-disabled. Because just as governments see their responsibility to facilitate the constitutional right of freedom of movement for the non-disabled by building roads and railways (thereby also contributing to the economic vigor of society) so must they see their responsibility to facilitate virtual (in addition to actual) freedom of movement for the physically disabled by building information highways that would nullify physical limitations, enabling them to contribute to the economic vigor of society.

Governments must take the lead in implementing this new paradigm. Fifty percent of new government hiring or contracted labor should be amongst the homebound or semi-homebound. Working on spreadsheets, processing computer submitted forms, responding to inquiries, translating and editing, research, writing manuals, purchasing, reviewing tax and voter rolls, etc. are all tasks that do not require a physical presence in a government building. Indeed, the government could begin to save a great deal of money by not having to build, maintain, clean, and insure office space. In other words, liberation for the physically disabled could become a triple boon to present-day taxpayers by eliminating many welfare and administrative expenses as well as widening the taxpayer base. The government could also offer a small remuneration to manpower companies that find telecommuting jobs for these citizens in the global economy; the long-term return on investment would be tremendous.

Since we do not want to make telecommuting a de facto prison for the handicapped, a substantial portion of their taxes should be dedicated, by statute, to making public buildings and byways more accessible. This would be similar to a certain percentage of car licensing and petrol taxes being dedicated, by statute, to the building and improvement of roads. And since the taxes of the physically disabled would be funding much of these improvements, they wouldn't be beholden to anyone. This would be one example of a new *non-altruistic* welfare policy dedicated to transforming net consumers of value into net producers of value by turning them into taxpayers. In other words, no one would be doing anyone any favors.

Creating a Space-Age Economy

The creation of a space-age economy must be the inevitable consequence of humanity's first tentative steps into space. This, of necessity, must result in a complete reevaluation of the concept of work since *all* material "work" (not only drudge work) will be done by the most sophisticated scientific and technological means. Completely automated remote-controlled robots will function in the hostile environs of the various planets, moons, and asteroid belts of our solar system. Technology will be the cosmic proletariat; technology will become Aristotle's slave class, enabling every human being on the planet (not only a minuscule minority) to enjoy a gracious and dignified life; to contemplate the mystery of one's own existence and to take joy in the sensual, intellectual, and spiritual opportunities available to having come into existence as a self-reflective conscious being.

As Professor David Macarov has written in *Quitting Time*, full unemployment might, therefore, become a *positive* societal goal. Full employment is neither achievable nor is it a worthwhile social or political aim. The attempt to achieve it is dysfunctional to both the efficient working of the conventional economy and the achieving of the space-age economy. It is also undemocratic. The social inequality generated by the division of labor (a social pathology first perceived by Adam Smith well before Marx) can only be overcome by the development of a space-age economy. Full unemployment will be essentially different than today's persistent under-employment. Underemployment defined, in this context, as the vast majority of humanity having to engage in work that inhibits or prevents optimal self-actualization. This breeds a permanent, immature adolescence in the underemployed intelligentsia and amongst the so-called working class a morbid, restless infatuation with mass events and their own frustrating resentments about the dissatisfactions of their lives, which results in an inclination to follow the slogans of demagogues and conmen. In a word, it produces the cultural crisis we are now experiencing.

We can halt the deleterious effects of unemployment by ceasing to view it as a curse and begin to view it as an opportunity to build a new civilization giving full rein to the human spirit. Full unemployment is a natural and necessary corollary to the cosmic economy and robotized means of production. Almost a century ago, John Maynard Keynes foresaw the resolving of the "economic problem" in his essay "The Future"; he wrote:

> ... in the long run ... mankind is solving its economic problem .... Thus, for the first time since his creation man will be faced with his real, his permanent problem—how to use his freedom from pressing economic cares, how to occupy the leisure, which science and compound interest will have won for him, to live wisely and agreeably and well.[24]

Keynes' prophecy is exactly how the great medieval rabbi Maimonides perceived the coming of the Messianic age.

Full unemployment will turn underemployment on its head. It will not be a reflection of a statistical reality but the backbone of a cultural revolution of historic proportions. It will mean the separation of *making a living* from work. It will decommoditize the human being and in doing so decommercialize human society. Work will still be sacred but as a concrete manifestation of humanity's spiritual growth; not forced drudgery to keep body and soul together. Human beings will become living human persons rather than abstract economic concepts such as "labor"—a lifeless component of economic cost. Work is only dignified when it is not related to survival. Having to work for a living; having one's survival dependent on one's ability to work is essentially inhumane and anti-human. It drags humanity down to the level of animals. Romantic philosophies about the ennobling qualities of physical work are usually promoted by people who haven't done it or didn't have to do it to survive (Montaigne, Jefferson, and Tolstoy). True, if we have to do it, we invest it with dignity, pride, creativity, and fellowship, i.e., we give it our own humanity, thereby making it more human. But most of the work that humans do to survive or to make a living is inherently degrading to our humanity. Having worked as a field-hand in agriculture, a yard-boy in hotels, a busboy, a waiter and a floor-boy in textile, plastic, and carton factories, I can personally attest to this—I have never met a happy unskilled or semi-skilled worker.

The necessary corollary to full unemployment as a consequence of the space-age economy, and the universal availability of instantaneous information, is to create a society based on creativity: in arts, sciences, innovation, managerial techniques, etc. Drudge work will be eliminated; money grubbing rejected. Education, wisdom, culture, innovation, and inventiveness will become the measure of people. This is the only way to overcome the *ennui*; the cultural and psychological crisis which is now manifesting itself in the latest stages of consumer society. Boredom, emptiness, and violence are the inevitable result of turning human beings into commodities called consumers. Commercializing our means of spiritual rejuvenation by religious hucksterism best characterized by television megachurches or endless varieties of psychological fads and self-help "seminars" might be the obscenest expressions of what I am driving at.

It must become the primary task of space-age political theory to turn men and women into individual creators, optimally exploiting their talents and potentialities with all the tools that space-age society has placed at their disposal. Consumerism must evolve from a compulsive obsession, manipulated by all the tools that modern psychology can bring to bear, into the material complement of the dignified gracious living of life that should be the birthright of every human being. In the post-drudgework era, institutes, research facilities, cultural centers, and entrepreneurial opportunities of every conceivable sort will populate our society in ever-greater variety. I reiterate, creativity of *every* kind is its own justification and needs no other sanction. Therefore, "businesses" will continue to exist in order to enable people with entrepreneurial talent to test their creativity as well as to create the necessary wealth needed to empower every other member of society— but most of all, to continue to fulfill its historical role as the very engine of technological, cultural and spiritual progress. For despite the smug condescension of many on the intellectual left, it is self-evident that it is the managerial and entrepreneurial classes which provide all of us with the societal wealth that enables us to live lives of security and reflection. No business = no universities; no business = no opera; no business = no civilized level of food, clothing, or shelter. Once again, I rely on Keynes:

> When the accumulation of wealth is no longer of high social importance, there will be great changes in our code of morals .... The love of money as a possession—*as distinguished from love of money as a means to the enjoyments and realities of life* (italics mine)—will be recognized for what it is, a somewhat disgusting morbidity, one of those semi-criminal, semi-pathological propensities which one hands over with a shudder to the specialists in mental disease. All kinds of social customs and economic practices, affecting the distribution of wealth and of economic rewards and penalties, which we now maintain at all costs, however distasteful and unjust they may be in themselves, because they are tremendously useful in promoting the accumulation of capital, we shall then be free, at last, to discard.[25]

This is a humanistic declaration, by one of the great prophets of modern capitalism, that surpasses anything that Marx ever wrote or said, regarding how the inner laws of motion of capitalism will eventually drive the evolution of capitalism into a more transcendent reality of humanity's economic life; how it will make the very pursuit of the economic life as a necessity to keep body and soul together superfluous. Economic life *per se* will have become a self-sustaining infrastructure of a space-age civilization and will be a free choice of creativity rather than a brutal necessity.

Chapter Thirteen: The Triumph of Constitutionalism

The human race cannot realize its cosmic potential half slave and half free; half living in dictatorships or theocracies and half in societies governed by constitutionalist protections with optimal democratic access to those protections. It must become enlightened humanity's grand strategy to constitutionalize the entire planet. This must be done in ways that do not lead us into endless wars that not only make vast numbers of global citizens hostile to the democratic West, but also erode the constitutionalist protections of democracies in the name of security. (Think of how the *Patriot Act* has eroded the principle of *habeas corpus* in the United States!) Let us begin with an overview of what exactly we are talking about when we discuss Constitutionalism.

Defining Our Terms

Constitutionalism is an 'ism'; an ideology that acknowledges that human persons have certain unalienable rights that cannot be obviated by monarch or dictator *or majority*. Constitutionalism means the limitation of the power of the sovereign vis-à-vis unalienable rights. The sovereign in England is the monarch—thus the term "constitutional monarchy." The sovereign in America is the people (the *demos*)—thus the term "constitutional democracy." When Americans use the term democracy, they are actually referring to constitutional democracy, of which most Americans have absolutely no understanding, and which is distinct from majoritarian democracy. Majoritarian democracy often leads to what the founding fathers of the United States called "the tyranny of the majority"; meaning that the majority decides everything, including the rights of minorities and individuals. Professor Jacob Talmon, in *The Origins of Totalitarian Democracy*, demonstrated how, in the 20th century, majoritarian democracy, in the form of communism, became totalitarian. At the other end of the spectrum Adolph Hitler was elected democratically in a fair election. He formed his coalition according to democratic norms and ended democracy in a democratic way. And despite the modern mystic faith that "all human beings desire freedom" there can be little doubt that even in fair elections, Stalin, Mao, and Castro would have been elected democratically by the residents of their respective countries, just as Hitler was. Erich Fromm's *Escape from Freedom* should disabuse us of the popular idolatry of the "human spirit yearning to be free." So should experience. Recent polling indicates that up to 30% of adult Russians would *still* vote for Stalin despite his well-documented atrocities. Mikhail Khodorkovsky, one of Putin's severest critics and victim of his megalomania, has admitted that Putin is actually more liberal than 70% of his fellow Russians. And in the United States, large segments of the population view constitutionalist objections to the *Patriot Act* as un-American, even treasonous. Human and civil rights have always been the concern of a minority and it has been the job of the non-democratic courts to preserve and protect these rights against the fears, passions, and prejudices of the majority.

Constitutionality and *constitutionalism* are not synonymous. Constitutionality refers to what is legitimate according to a constitution. Constitutions *per se* do not have to reflect the principles of Constitutionalism. If the Constitution of Nazi Germany stated it was permissible (even a duty) to kill Jews, then killing Jews was in conformance with constitutionality and was by definition constitutional. In the United States, slavery was constitutional until it wasn't. But slavery was never *constitutionalist* in that it was in obscene juxtaposition to the principles of Constitutionalism. In common usage in the West, *constitutional* refers to the prerogatives and powers of governments, the rights and behaviors of individuals, and the laws of society that are in conformance with the principles of Constitutionalism.

Democracy is only a positive cultural value when it expands constitutional protections; it has no value in and of itself. Fair elections are only positive when they take place within a democratic tradition dedicated to expanding constitutional protections; they have no value in and of themselves. "Fair elections" do not obligate us to respect "the will of the people" if the consequences are the reduction of constitutional protections. In the Gaza Strip, Hamas was elected in fair, democratic elections. The consequences were the lessening of constitutionalist protections for women, religious minorities, and political minorities as well as the end of fair elections. Must we really "respect" these results? Should we have respected the will of the German people in electing Hitler? A majoritarian strain in American history respected Jim Crow because it was "the will of the (majority of) people."

History has shown that majorities can be as vicious, ruthless, and indifferent to human suffering as any psychopathic dictator. The founding fathers of the United States understood this; they were afraid of three things: the tyranny of the majority, mass enthusiasms, and the abuse of power. The constitutional, structural, and political character of the American government is geared to neutralizing all three. Consequently, I would claim that the true moral chronicle of human civilization is the ongoing *democratization of constitutionalist protections* as they are afforded to an ever-widening range of human populations. This has been the past history of Western civilization and I believe must also be the future history of all of human civilization if we are to prepare ourselves for the ultimate cosmic project. Whatever impedes the march of constitutionalist protections, whether by dictator or by democratic majority, is iniquitous.

A Brief History of Constitutionalism

The Stoics and the Hebrews created the first constitutionalist genomes, which have mutated and evolved over the centuries. The natural law doctrines of the Stoics propounded universal ideas of individual worth and brotherhood. The Hebrew Bible claimed that every human being is a descendent of Adam and Eve—a clear insinuation that we are all part of the same family. During the English Peasants Revolt in the 14th century, this was cited as evidence that all humans were brothers and sisters and thus none should be more privileged than another. The biblical concept that we are all created in the image of God implies that we are all equal in the eyes of God and consequently, we should certainly all be equal in the eyes of human law. These Stoic and Hebrew antecedents became self-evident truths in the American Declaration of Independence—"... all men are created equal [before the law] and endowed with certain unalienable rights."

The Stoic/Hebrew legacy became the cultural property of Western civilization—modifying, developing, and evolving over the centuries. The Catholic Church democratized sanctity by combining the Stoic and Hebrew traditions. Every human being had a sacred soul—even Jews and Indians— and this made them human. The immediate expression of this conviction had horrific consequences. It became the moral duty of the Church to "save souls" from hell—thus their rationalizations for the Inquisition and imperialism and their assorted tortures and slaughters: "We will cause you terrible but temporary physical pain in this temporal world in order to save your soul from even more ghastly eternal pain in the eternal world to come." But the antidote for these atrocities was also implicit in their causes. For the Church, unlike pagan religions and even Greek civilization at its peak, was forced to recognize the humanness of the "other" by virtue of their sacred soul. For most Greeks (Plato and Aristotle included), the "other" was less than human. Thus, we might say that while the Greeks "invented" the framework of constitutionalism and democracy, it was the Hebrews who "invented" the content. Consider the examples of constitutionalist and universal rights in the Hebrew Bible:

1. Exodus 22:20 – "You shall not wrong or oppress a resident alien; for you were aliens in the land of Egypt." (i.e., Every human person, by virtue of his or her personhood, has rights—not only "citizens" of your particular tribe.)

2. Exodus 23:2 – "You shall not follow a multitude to do evil; nor shall you bear witness in a suit turning aside after a multitude so as to pervert justice." (i.e., A stricture against Majoritarianism and lynch mobs—Socrates would not have been put to death in an ethical regime governed by this principle).

3. Exodus 23:9 – "You shall not oppress a stranger; you know the heart of a stranger, for you were strangers in the land of Egypt." (i.e., We are all human beings, recognize that and never set yourself apart as being special by virtue of your tribe, or the travails your tribe might have suffered in the past.)

4. Leviticus 24:22 – "Ye shall have one manner of law, as well for the stranger, as for the home-born ...." (i.e., Equality before the law for every human person, *citizen or not.*)

5. Leviticus 19:33 – "And if a stranger sojourn with thee in your land, ye shall not do him wrong." (i.e., The law protects everyone not only the members of your tribe or your neighbors.)

6. Leviticus 19:34 – "The stranger that sojourneth with you shall be unto you as the home-born among you, and thou shalt love him as thyself; for ye were strangers in the land of Egypt ...." (i.e., Treating people humanely is a moral requirement that is indifferent to citizenship.)

7. Numbers 15:15 – "... there shall be one statute both for you and for the stranger that sojourneth with you ..." (i.e., Equality before the law for every human person.)

8. Numbers 15:16 – "One law and one ordinance shall be both for you and for the stranger that sojourneth with you." (i.e., Equality before the law for every human person.)

9. Deuteronomy 1:16 – "Give the members of your community a

fair hearing, and judge rightly between one person and another, whether citizen or resident alien." (i.e., Equality before the law for every human person.)

10. Deuteronomy 24:14 – "You shall not withhold the wages of poor and needy laborers, whether other Israelites or aliens who reside in your land..." (i.e., Social justice for every human person, whether a member of your tribe or not.)

11. Deuteronomy 24:17 – "You shall not deprive a resident alien ... of justice." (i.e., Universal rights.)

12. Deuteronomy 27:19 – "Cursed be he that perverts the justice due to the stranger, fatherless, and widow." (i.e., Universal justice.)

13. Jeremiah 7:6-7 – "[I]f ye oppress not the stranger, the fatherless, and the widow, and shed not innocent blood in this place, ... then will I cause you to dwell in this place, in the land that I gave to your fathers, for ever and ever." (i.e., You have rights *only* if you recognize the rights of others.)

14. Jeremiah 22:3+5 – "Execute ye justice and righteousness ... and do no wrong, do no violence, to the stranger, the fatherless, nor the widow, neither shed innocent blood in this place ... if ye will not hear these words, I swear by Myself, says the LORD, that this house shall become a desolation." (i.e., Injustice and racism are not only morally wrong—they are stupid and self-destructive.)

15. Zechariah 7:10 – "... oppress not the widow, nor the fatherless, the stranger, nor the poor; and let none of you devise evil against his brother in your heart ..." (i.e., Equality before the law.)

16. Malachi 3:5 – "And I will come near to you to judgment; and I will be a swift witness ... against those that oppress the hireling in his wages, the widow, and the fatherless, and that turn aside the stranger from his right ..." (i.e., Injustice and racism are not only morally wrong – they are stupid and self-destructive.)

As the Catholic Church democratized sanctity, so the Protestant Reformation democratized belief by advocating a personal relationship with God unmediated by an institutionalized church. Protestants obligated the individual to read the Bible while the Catholics forbade reading it except under aegis of a priest. This set the historical stage for eventual democratic access to constitutionalist protections. Because if all believers had an unmediated connection with God with no need for the intercession of an aristocracy of Church theologians or priest practitioners, then all persons would eventually have unmediated and equal access to constitutionalist protections construed by human beings. This became a major driver in the development of Western individualism. The individual had to find his or her way to God. Everyone had to read the Bible. The printing press and cheap mass-produced Bibles made this possible. This marks the beginning of universal literacy. But by the very nature of the human mind, people understood the Bible in different ways. People of like mind began to form their own churches and thus the plethora of Protestant denominations. This had several consequences of constitutionalist significance. Religious pluralism and the dogmatism inherent in religious belief resulted in the *Wars of Religion*, which in some areas of Europe took as many lives as the Black Plague. The reaction to these horrors was the (secular) Enlightenment ideology of tolerance, as well as the objective need for Europe to develop constitutionalism in order to *institutionalize tolerance* and assure internal social stability.

The Commercial Revolution

A concomitant driver of Constitutionalism was the rise of the Protestant commercial state, first in Holland and then in Tudor England. As Weber and Tawney have demonstrated, Protestantism was more amenable to commerce because of its individualist character. Commercial interests often caused Protestant businessmen to subsume their religious inclinations and prejudices to their economic interests. Commerce is inherently tolerant for the simple reason that it is bad for business to kill your customers or your suppliers because they are of another faith or other tribe. Commerce became one of the major drivers for the democratization of constitutionalist protections. The Jews of New Amsterdam were protected from the anti-Semitism of Peter Stuyvesant by the intervention of the Dutch East India Company. Holland had become a haven for Iberian Jews fleeing the Inquisition despite the protestations of the Calvinist Church. The good Calvinist burghers (who went to church every Sunday) thought the Jews were good for business and that the Church should mind its own business. The Puritans stopped hanging Quakers when trade between Massachusetts and Pennsylvania became an economic mainstay.

The Reformation also gave birth to Anabaptism which had direct and indirect effect on other Protestant denominations. Anabaptism is constitutionalist in its theology. For Anabaptists, baptism only has salvation value if it is made of one's free will—thus their advocacy for adult baptism. Free will evolved into freedom of conscience. It was meaningless to force someone to practice a faith he or she did not freely choose. Of the 13 colonies, two—Rhode Island and Pennsylvania—were founded on the principle of freedom of conscience by individuals who themselves were not Anabaptists. Roger Williams, a refugee from Puritan intolerance in Massachusetts and the founder of Rhode Island, famously said "forced prayer stinks in God's nostrils," and Quaker William Penn established his proprietary colony on the principles of religious pluralism and tolerance at the very outset. Rhode Island welcomed Quakers, Jews and Catholics and Pennsylvania welcomed anyone who worked hard and obeyed the law.

That racism is also stupid in addition to being immoral is self-evident. The Inquisition and expulsion of Jews and Arabs transformed Spain from the richest country in Europe to the poorest, and Holland into the richest. The expulsion of the Huguenots retarded the economic development of France and stimulated the economic development of England. Idi Amin's expulsion of its Indian minority impoverished Uganda and enriched England. The slower economic development of the American South in comparison to the Northern states is in part attributed to the fact that because of slavery and Jim Crow they not only absorbed fewer immigrants, but also did not invest in the education of their unlanded white residents while impeding the potential contributions of its Blacks. Thus, constitutionalism becomes an economic and not only a moral value. Throughout history, economic *interests* have opposed the impulses of cultural purity and furthered the march of constitutionalism. What part, then, might globalization play in the future of constitutionalism? This question has to do with a peaceful strategy to constitutionalize.

The Enlightenment

If the Catholic Church democratized sanctity and the Reformation democratized belief, then the Renaissance, Scientific Revolution and Enlightenment democratized (and secularized) knowledge. The democratization of knowledge depends on its being secularized (taken out of the hands of doctrinal authority) and might be the greatest constitutionalist development in history. The enabling of knowledge eventually enables the perception of one's rights. The immediate drivers of modern constitutionalism were the principles of the Enlightenment, which enabled the secularization of many of the biblical principles cited above. The founding fathers of the United States were all Enlightenment men. (Indeed, sometimes the United States is called "the great Enlightenment experiment.") Almost all were Deists and would have been amused to discover that they had founded the Republic on so-called *Judeo-Christian* values, a concept that came into existence after WWII and an oxymoron in itself. Some were indifferent to these values (Hamilton), others were contemptuous (John Adams and Tom Paine) and some (like Jefferson) had contempt for the clergy, but shrewdly kept their opinions to themselves. It is secularism that enables Constitutionalism; Constitutionalism is secular. Freedom of conscience (which includes freedom of religion as well as the freedom not to believe) can only exist within a secular framework—it cannot exist within a religious framework. The recent disingenuous claim that "we are guaranteed freedom *of* religion not freedom *from* religion" is historically and logically absurd. You cannot be free unless you also have the choice to be free from.

The English-Speaking World

England and the United States are central to the history of Constitutionalism. The *Magna Carta* is the first written document limiting the power of the sovereign, compelling him to recognize that he is bound by the "Common Law" like every other Englishman. This is neither a democratic document nor a modern one, but it does lay the foundations for the constitutionalist notions of limitations of power and natural rights. It is a reaffirmation of the feudal rights and prerogatives of the English nobility vis-à-vis the King, thus limiting his absolutist power. It is a reaffirmation of the social contract of feudal society and became a foundational document that immunized England to a great degree from the absolutist tendencies of "divine right" that became dominant in continental Europe. In conjunction with the special character of the English Reformation and the transformation of England into a commercial state under the Tudors, it became a keystone in the development of Parliamentarianism and Constitutionalism in England.

The English Reformation reinforced the Common Law/Magna Carta tradition. Anticlericalism in England had been rife for centuries before Martin Luther; the venal corruption of Church institutions and clergy being all too obvious. The great reformer, John Wycliffe (1320–1384), not only translated the Bible into vernacular English over a century before Luther translated it into vernacular German, despite the prohibition of the Church against doing so, he also sent out teams of literate priests to teach the general populace how to read. Pre-dating Luther, he taught that the Church was the community of the faithful, not the institutions of the Church of Rome. His disciple, Jan Hus (1372–1415) in Bohemia was burned at the stake for similar beliefs. The reason a general reformation did not take off with Wycliffe/Hus was because they had no printing press to mass produce inexpensive Bibles, and they worked in a weak commercial context with no powerful potential allies. Luther, of course, was more fortunate, having the printing press and a rising bourgeoisie and regional aristocracy increasingly resentful of Rome for draining wealth out of their areas. Today we might ponder how cheap mass-produced computers and the rapid spread of globalization might facilitate both the development and the constitutionalization of the developing world in the future.

Wycliffe's followers (the Lollards) produced a document called *The Twelve Conclusions of the Lollards* (1395). Two have constitutionalist significance. The first rejects the accumulation of temporal wealth by the Church, a reality that alienated masses of peasants from the Church. Years later, when Henry VIII confiscated the monasteries in England, much of the population supported him. The sixth conclusion calls for separation of Church and State. In 1381, Lollard Priest John Ball—a leader of the Peasants' Revolt (1381)—said that we are all descendants of Adam and Eve and are brothers and sisters and thus none should have more privileges than another. The translation of the Bible into vernacular, and teaching believers how to actually read it was social dynamite: if all were created in the image of God, then all are equal in the eyes of God and should be equal in the eyes of man's law.

The Lollards were forerunners of the Levelers who, during the English Civil War, supported constitutionalist principles such as popular sovereignty and equality before the law. This in a way represented a democratization of the Magna Carta tradition. When Constitutionalism and an expectation of its democratization have become internalized into the very soul of a nation, when they become cultural assets of that nation and not only external political scaffolding, then they have triumphed. This is key when looking to the future. The Weimer Constitution failed not because it was poorly written but because it had no resonance in the history and culture of Germany. Russia has retreated from its early attempts to be a constitutionalist state because its 1,000-year history contains nothing that could have been referred to. What then are the cultural assets and traditions of various nations and religions that can be appealed to in order to further the march of Constitutionalism in the future?

The confiscation and sale of the monasteries in England helped create a substantial class of free land holders (yeomen). By weakening the Church of Rome, Henry the VIII inadvertently strengthened the growth of middle-class freeholders and merchants, who were the taxpaying backbone of England, and who dominated Parliament and thus eventually neutered the political power of the English monarchy, turning it into the figurehead it is today. Charles I was beheaded because he betrayed every element of English tradition. His absolutist tendencies violated the principle of limitation of power in the Magna Carta, as well as natural rights deriving from the Bible. Because of this he was forced by Parliament to accept the *Petition of Right* (1628), which among other things, confirmed the principles that taxes can only be levied by Parliament (which represented the taxpayers), that martial law and quartering of troops may not be imposed in time of peace, and that due process (trial by jury) and habeas corpus are to be respected. When George III and Parliament ignored these restrictions with respect to the 13 colonies in the 1770s, they ran into a bit of trouble. The way American history is taught, most Americans don't realize that even after Lexington and Concord, "Americans" were not fighting for independence but rather for their "Rights as Englishmen." America is really England 2.0 and I put "Americans" in the previous sentence in inverted commas because at the time the colonists did not refer to themselves as such, but as Virginians, New Yorkers, Pennsylvanians, etc. and for the British the term "American" was actually a contemptuous pejorative—similar to terms such as "Jewboys," "greasers," or "beaners."

Even the Restoration of the Crown following Cromwell's dictatorial rule did not "restore" everything. Charles II, wiser than his father, kept his head by deferring to Parliament. But his successor, James II, had absolutist tendencies and was deposed in a relatively bloodless coup in 1688 called *The Glorious Revolution* (glorious because it was mostly nonviolent). He was replaced by William and Mary at the invitation of Parliament on condition that they sign a *Bill of Rights* (1689) which affirmed, with greater specificity, the principles of the *Petition of Right*: trial by jury, due process of law (probable cause and rules of evidence), no cruel punishments (torture), no excessive bail or fines, the right to bear arms, the right to petition government (lobbyists), and no taxation without Parliamentary approval (no taxation without representation), etc. This was accompanied by the *Act of Toleration* (1689), which granted limited freedom of religion and ironically (given the American self-image of fighting for religious freedom), shattered Puritan theocracy in New England and weakened the Anglican Establishment in Virginia. This marks the beginning of England's Constitutional Monarchy which, as the American experience progressed, laid the foundations for Constitutional Democracy.

In 1689, John Locke wrote his famous *Two Treatises of Government*, the second of which was a *post facto* philosophical justification for the overthrow of unjust government (i.e., for the *Glorious Revolution*). Locke's intellectual character represented an intersection of three modes of thought: the English (*Magna Carta;* Common Law), the Puritan (individual relationship with God), and the Scientific (Empiricism—just the facts please). His Enlightenment concepts of natural rights deriving from natural law were greatly influenced by his close friend, Isaac Newton (they were both members of the Royal Society). It is claimed that Jefferson had Locke's essays on his desk when he was drafting the Declaration of Independence—certainly not the Bible. The USA is a product of a combination of the English constitutionalist tradition, Enlightenment values, Reformation individualism and the commercial experience of the colonial period. The colonies had been 13 schools of self-government, with Virginia and Massachusetts (the primary protagonists of the Revolution) governing themselves for a longer period of time by 1776 than has elapsed from the Civil War until today. These states had for some time expanded constitutionalist concepts beyond what even England considered "Rights as Englishmen." They were also more democratic in that a much higher percentage of men were eligible to vote. Perhaps even more important, they had achieved 60% literacy—the highest in the world at the time. This is a significant statistic when considering that over 300,000 copies of Thomas Paine's *Common Sense* (calling for complete independence from Britain) were sold to a population of a little over 3 million. One may assume that these copies were passed from hand to hand, and that well over one million colonists read and were enflamed by it.

Despite all this, the United States has had many majoritarian moments. Before the American Civil War, the term "popular sovereignty" meant that the white residents of U.S. territories should decide by majority vote whether slavery would be allowed in the territory; that the white majority would decide the human rights of Black people. Majoritarianism was reflected in certain aspects of the Progressive Movement, especially in regard to Jim Crow. The Progressives said if the white majority wants it, then democratic principles require it. Woodrow Wilson, the great "progressive," introduced Jim Crow into the American civil service on the basis of this principle. But on the whole, the history of the United States has reflected the ongoing democratization of constitutionalist protections; beginning with white man owning property, to *universal* white men suffrage, to black men suffrage (at least in principle), to women's suffrage, to the end of Jim Crow. Suffrage, the right to vote and decide who sits in government, is the vital power given to individuals and minorities to protect their rights. (The Jim Crow 2.0 voter suppression now current in the United States represents a serious backsliding of a sacred American tradition.) Following WWII and up until the present Jim Crow 2.0 Supreme Court, the court had been active rather than reactive in expanding and deepening the constitutional protections of an ever-growing list of minorities and of rights themselves. How might domestic and international judiciaries further the cause of Constitutionalism in the future?

Continental Europe has been essentially majoritarian, (usually placing the state over the individual), throughout its history. However, the evolution of Enlightenment values and the inherent contrarianism of Western European culture have persistently driven Continental Europe towards Constitutionalism and subsumed its majoritarian instincts—especially following the majoritarian outrages of 20th-century European history. Latin America, unfortunately, has not been as lucky regarding its political cultural heritage. There are no "my rights as a Spaniard" or "my rights as a Portuguese" as there are "my rights as an Englishman" (the actual trigger to the American Revolution). There is no constitutionalist tradition in any of these countries. Furthermore, the Inquisition not only destroyed Spain's and Portugal's commercial, intellectual, and agricultural classes (the Jews and Arabs), it, as a consequence, inhibited the growth of a freeholder yeomen class. Spain had no real Renaissance and certainly no Reformation. Moreover, it was anti-Enlightenment and had a low level of literacy. The Spanish colonies had no experience of de-facto self-governing commercial republics for over a century. When trying to formulate a constitutionalist strategy for the future, we must keep in mind that both historical memory and cultural inertia matter.

The March of Constitutionalism in the 20th Century

Constitutionalism defeated the three great totalitarian movements of the 20th century: Fascism, Soviet Communism, and Nazism. I predict it will also prevail over Jihadism and that oxymoron we still call Chinese Communism in the 21st century. Let us review the record since WWII. In 60 years, the United States has gone from lynchings to a Black President. In the 1950s, if someone had suggested there would be Black quarterbacks in the NFL, they would have been committed to a mental hospital. Well, we have had a Black President (and lots of Black quarterbacks). We are not only talking about a formal political development. We are talking about the cultural and sociological progress of America's constitutionalist spirit; we are talking about the ongoing (albeit fragile) democratization of the American soul; and I say this with full understanding of current Jim Crow 2.0 regression in these matters. In these matters I am Asian—a quarter for me is 25 years, not the American 3 months.

We must also note the subversive quality of popular culture and consumerism and their contribution to the democratization of Constitutionalism and the expansion of constitutional protections across the globe. It wasn't for nothing that Nazis, Communists, Fascists, and now Jihadists, pilloried American popular culture. They have all recognized its subversive nature as regards authority. Technology and constitutionalist progress also go hand in hand. For example, the media (movies, radio, TV) driving popular culture and mass sports created black icons, in effect, humanizing Blacks. Could there have been a Martin Luther King without a Jesse Owens, Joe Louis, or Jackie Robinson? Could there have been a Barack Obama without Bill Cosby and Oprah Winfrey? How would the civil rights movement of the 50s have fared without the television images of dogs and fire hoses being used on innocent Black women and children, and the instinctive disgust this engendered? Television and satellite dishes also contributed to the end of Communism in Eastern Europe. When East Germany's and Poland's "workers' paradises" saw how workers actually lived in West Germany, it became increasingly difficult to swallow the lies of official propaganda. Today's social media, however, seems to have removed all moral, intellectual and cultural filters to public discourse, at the same time as they have served as the medium for grassroots rebellion against authoritarian regimes. It remains to be seen what the balance of its negative and positive effects will be—empirical history will be its final judge. The list of other constitutionalist victories since WWII includes:

- The transformation of Japan and Germany from militarist to constitutionalist states

- The growing rights of women deriving from political action in the West and the education of women elsewhere.

- The constitutionalist European Union first absorbing formerly fascist Spain, Greece, and Portugal and then most of the former Soviet satellites and several republics.

- The end of Apartheid in South Africa

- The eclipse of rule by military dictatorships in most of Latin American

- South Korea and Taiwan evolving into parliamentary democracies from their fascistic origins

- The growth of institutions of regional and international governance such as the WTO, OECD, EU, and NAFTA. (Joining such organizations requires different elements of internal constitutional reform—"if you want to join our club, there are rules.")

- The spread of property rights to Communist China. Rights are viral and infectious. It took several centuries in Europe, but property rights for the commercial classes soon evolved into political rights for the bourgeoisie. As the middle classes grew, so did the scope of rights. The skilled working men produced by the Industrial Revolution used their indispensability to the system to gain their rights and trigger the labor movement fighting for rights for the working man. Women after the two world wars did the same. Thus, despite Xi's current relapse into Maoist totalitarianism, he soon will, like Putin, learn that you cannot unscramble eggs.

- The growing number of global nomads due to globalization helps spread the infection of Constitutionalism. The multitude of Chinese students who have studied at American universities helped spread the virus of Democracy when they returned home. People cannot unlearn what they have learned and while China still only has a slight case of democratic sniffles, its recent backward-looking steps, such as its brutal behavior in Hong Kong, indicate that the communist leadership recognizes that this democratic virus is virulent and can still develop into a raging influenza of demand for democratic change.

- Cross-border issues such as water and environment have also helped to develop constitutionalist frameworks of international governance. Water, more than oil, might trigger wars in the 21st century. Avoiding this requires recognizing the "constitutionalist" rights of individual nations as international persons.

- The increased speed of change and innovation requires the decentralization of authority and a culture of people thinking for themselves. This has worldwide constitutionalist implications. China, for example, cannot hope to continue to have it both ways—stifling freedom while encouraging innovation. It simply won't work in the long run. Witness the high tech 21st-century brain drain from Russia following their 19th-century imperialistic invasion of Ukraine and the complete elimination of all democratic rights and norms. Hundreds of thousands of the cream of Russian society are leaving (in addition to the two million who have already emigrated since Putin took power), setting Russia back decades, if not more. As for China, according to the *Migration Policy Institute's Transatlantic Council on Migration*:

  ... high-skilled and high-value emigration from China is rising fast, while low-skilled and unskilled emigration is stagnant—a divergence that has been widening since the late 2000s. The emigration rate of China's highly educated population is now five times as high as the country's overall rate. China's wealthy elites and growing middle class are increasingly pursuing educational and work opportunities overseas for themselves and their families, facilitated by their rising incomes.[26]

Since 350,000 Chinese a year emigrate, this means that 280,000 of them are the scientific and entrepreneurial elite. China will never pass the USA given these stats.

Constitutionalism's Ideological Antipodes—Marxism, Utopianism and Utilitarianism

Constitutionalism works because it doesn't have any illusions about human nature or the moral and ethical limitations of real flesh and blood human beings. Although it was not articulated, anyone reading between the lines of the mentality of the Founding Fathers understands that they realized that their challenge was how to create a fairly well-run society out of inferior raw materials: i.e., human beings. Or as Mark Twain once commented, when challenged by an anti-Semite about his relatively positive opinion of the Jews: "I think they are human; anything *worse* I can say about them?" Constitutionalism makes its peace with human weakness; it is a self-correcting system that abjures perfection and consistently tries to make things "a little bit better." Over historical time, this consistent "a little bit better" has resulted in a civilizational "lot better"—certainly a lot better than the perfectionist ideologies that often carped, in a patronizing manner, at its bourgeoisie compromising.

Categorical certainty and the definite article (*the* problem, *the* solution) are the biggest enemies of clear thinking and civilized discourse, which are the necessary elements of a society characterized by Constitutionalism. Dogmatic certainties are the underpinning of every form of religious and political authoritarianism. The problem is that Constitutionalism appears wimpy (middle-class, middle-aged, and boring) when confronting perfectionist ideologies and their exciting visions of the future, such as Marxism and various utopian programs (as well as religion). But history shows that Marxism or utopianism, or any form of religious or secular perfectionism, will inevitably lead to totalitarianism. Marxism and utopianism are essentially majoritarian. Neither is psychologically amenable to the slow, self-correcting, ongoing, improvement mechanism of Constitutionalism, which they disparage as compromise and "selling out." Historically, utopianism has had a "my way or the highway" element about it. The advocates of a particular utopia often adopt a bullying mode of discourse that might be termed intellectual and moral intimidation. In this respect, utopians—right or left—are little different than Marxists in their temperament and contempt for those who cannot see the "truth" of their vision. Today's so-called "progressives" are a perfect example of this preachy niche of humanity. Utopianism is not the same as utopian thinking which is simply imagining possible better futures and how to get there. Utopian thinking is much more reflective of Constitutionalism. Utilitarianism also opens the door to majoritarianism. Jeremy Bentham's concept of "the greatest good for the greatest number" (an anti-constitutionalist concept if there ever was one) could have been cited by Hitler to justify his policy of exterminating anyone with a physical or mental disability to eliminate their economic and social burden on society. This would have been the greatest good for the greatest number.

The pretensions of Marxism to represent the concrete logic of history, in opposition to the abstractions of formal legal rights, became, at its pinnacle of political power, a show of dialectic hairsplitting which would have embarrassed medieval scholastics. Constitutionalism, on the other hand—always condemned by Marxists as a bourgeoisie abstraction defining abstract rights—has been inherently able to attune itself to the ever-changing human condition and thus has become the most manifest expression of concrete logic in human history. It is an infantile Marxist argument to dismiss Constitutionalism because it was created by the bourgeoisie for the bourgeoisie. While this is historically true, workers, women, different races, and religions, have used this bourgeoisie invention of Constitutionalism to advance and enhance their own humanity. Should we say that since the zero was invented by brown-skinned Hindus and given to Europe by Arab Muslims (both of whom used it for religious reasons) that white-skinned secular Europeans should not use it? Just as the zero is a universal contribution of a particular culture to all of human civilization, so too is Constitutionalism a universal contribution of a particular culture to all of human civilization. It was Thurgood Marshall, I believe, who once said, "We know that the constitution wasn't written for us [Blacks], but we intend to make it ours and make it work for us." Marshall's constitutionalist judicial grand-strategy is perhaps the most underappreciated component of the civil rights struggle.

Marxism ultimately failed in its confrontation with Constitutionalism because it was inflexible in its internal logic and did not recognize that history is analogous to Heraclitus's river and is ever-changing. Basing his entire "scientific" socialism on the internal laws of motion of the Newtonian determinist physics still prevailing in the 19th century, Marx had no way of knowing about quantum theory or chaos theory or indeterminacy theory. Because of this he was scornful of the idea that human will and idealism could significantly alter the internal laws of motion of historical forces. His "scientific" socialism simply analyzed the facts of history and predicted the inevitable proletarian revolution. Of course, he never set foot in a factory or communicated with real workers in an unmediated fashion but related to "*the* workers" as an historical abstraction. Now, of course, we understand that nothing is inevitable except the eventual end of the solar system (in addition to death and taxes). Constitutionalism, on the other hand, is the great modifier of ongoing and constant change; the thermostat that enables real human beings (not that abstraction called humanity) to modify their behavior; to first adapt and then to mold the course of changing conditions. It is a necessity for real-time social and cultural evolution.

Marxists such as Herbert Marcuse (1898–1979) were greatly distressed by the very essence of Constitutionalism; its ability to accommodate and adapt itself to new forces, interests, and groups. He condemned this as cooption. In his 1965 essay "Repressive Tolerance," Marcuse argued that ideas contrary to his concept of progress should not be tolerated and people espousing those ideas should be suppressed. He called liberal ideals of tolerance such as freedom of expression repressive because they give people a false idea that they are really free. In other words, for Marcuse and his ilk, the fact that relative justice can be achieved bloodlessly is evil because it averts revolution which is the only way to achieve absolute justice. Instead of social *evolution* in pursuit of justice, he called for the suppression of relative justice to set the stage for *violent revolution*. That those actually living under the protections of Constitutionalism had no trouble shrugging off this silly proposition is no surprise.

The Future of Constitutionalism

Philosophy, religion, greed, history, culture, and technology as well as natural, positive and historical law have converged to generate a general constitutionalist trend in history. How might these forces be used to assure the global triumph of Constitutionalism in the 21st century? Is international governance to be majoritarian or constitutionalist? This is a serious question. Are countries with small populations and minority cultures to be considered as "international persons" with unalienable rights, or will their rights be violated by an undifferentiated mass of "voters," voting directly for a world government? Will the "tyranny of the majority" in the UN General Assembly continue its practice of voting *Bills of Attainder*[27] for unpopular countries and causes or will some kind of global constitutionalist framework be formed? On the one hand, the dynamic rate of current technological and economic change compels the decentralization of authority and power. Not for ideological reasons but for survival reasons. On the other hand, humanity also requires ever-increasing cooperation between these decentralized centers of power—also for survival reasons. The recent covid pandemic certainly reinforces this view. This requires global institutions that establish universal rules to which all are accountable; with the caveat that these institutions must be limited by constitutionalist principles in order to enable the various centers to thrive.

There are different paths to Constitutionalism that must reflect the history, temperament, and intellectual imagination of each individual culture. For example, the United States is structurally secular, ideologically neutral, and sociologically has, until recently, been one of the most religious countries in the world. Britain on the other hand is structurally theocratic (the British monarch is both head of State and head of the State Church), ideologically neutral and sociologically mostly post-Christian. France is ideologically secular (as the formal state ideology), sociologically mostly post-Christian, and structurally mixed (unlike the United States, it subsidizes religious institutions). These examples reflect a particular history which cannot be ignored. But Constitutionalism can survive and flourish in these and other political traditions as well.

Education can be a great driver of Constitutionalism. This is no guarantee of course. The behavior of professors, scientists, philosophers, lawyers, and engineers under the Nazi regime is not exactly a good poster child for the civilizing attributes of education. But, in general, over the course of history, literacy and education have been major drivers for the progress of Constitutionalism. Education is the key to creating a global middle and professional class as well as achieving the worldwide equalization of rights and status of women. The middle class has been the primary driver of Constitutionalism in the past. I suggest that the rights of women will be its primary driver in the 21st century. Indeed, in another context I have called the 21st century "The Women's Century." In the non-Western world the advancement of women is the key to the development of a middle class. This is certainly true in Africa and the Muslim world.

The media glare of negative public relations and world opinion also cannot be underestimated. Sometimes, of course, external pressure can boomerang when applied crudely in a discriminatory fashion, but on the whole, media glare has played a positive role for human rights. Some are of the opinion that the Iraqi Kurds might have been victims of Saddam Hussein's genocide but for CNN broadcasting their plight. Some go as far as to say that if there had been television during WWII, there could not have been a Holocaust.

Privacy might be the most vital component of a constitutionalist society. Without acknowledging that a private sphere is a categorical necessity of human freedom and a basic self-evident right, it would be impossible to sustain a constitutional democracy. For some Americans to argue otherwise because the Constitution does not *specifically* cite privacy as a right is disingenuous. This disingenuous argument shows the genius of the Ninth

Amendment, which was James Madison's antidote to the fear of unmentioned rights not being recognized. The private sphere is the very foundation upon which life is made worthwhile, liberty made possible, the pursuit of happiness facilitated. Orwell's 1984 is a vision of society without the right to privacy. This has become a major issue given the Snowden revelations regarding the NSA, as well as how big tech mines our data and knows more about us than Big Brother in 1984, and how slipshod big tech has been in protecting our data against hackers. Louis D. Brandeis's famous *Harvard Law Review* essay "The Right to Privacy" (with Samuel D. Warren) has become the standard reference for privacy debates as well as the need to constantly enumerate new rights as society progresses.

Bureaucracy

Bureaucracy generates significant justifiable constitutionalist disquiet. It is a universal phenomenon, and no complex human activity (public or private) can be accomplished without it. The problem is that it has no formal constitutionalist standing, yet it impacts our daily lives more than the three constitutionally anchored branches of government. Its place in Constitutionalism is dualistic. On the one hand, it is a stabilizing constitutionalist force by being the bridge between old and new governments in democracies. On the other hand, it is a prominent violator of individual rights. "You can't fight City Hall" is an expression that encapsulates this. In other words, you cannot fight the bureaucratic jungle so you might as well give up. What is required is some kind of instrumentality that enables real-time responses to bureaucratic infringements on individual liberties, rights, and prerogatives of the individual citizen so that you *can* fight City Hall.

Because bureaucratic infringements are fundamentally trivial in comparison to the life-and-death struggles for foundational human rights, they are unlikely to get human rights activists excited. Bureaucratic problems having to do with business licenses, improving your property or home, overcharging on taxes and so on are not likely to make the evening news. But they can be likened to termites nibbling away at the foundations of everyday individual autonomy. Ironically, this may be as equally dangerous in the long run as the bunker-buster bombs of outright civil rights abuses and are often used as multipliers of outright civil rights abuses. The voter suppression initiatives now current in the United States are all centered around making the registration and voting processes as bureaucratically difficult and timewasting as possible in order to discourage certain ethnic groups from voting. These bureaucratic termites tend to make citizens fearful of their government and officialdom in general and inhibit the willingness to express one's opinion for fear that the bureaucracy will take revenge. I was once advised by my accountant not to challenge a wrongful tax estimate for fear I would succeed, earning the resentment of the bureaucrats and as a consequence be audited every other year, with all the time-consuming nonsense that entails. This kind of fear is intensified in the developing world, where it often takes hundreds of days (sometimes years) to get the simplest license legally. This incentivizes the rampant corruption in these countries and makes a mockery of good governance and constitutionalist rights. It is a significant impediment to economic development and the alleviation of poverty.

The tiny country of Estonia might have already developed a Baltic "light unto the nations" solution regarding how the administrative and service frameworks of the modern state can be revolutionized by taking advantage of the possibilities and potentialities of modern technology. This country of 1.3 million people is making government administration completely digital in order to reduce bureaucracy, increase transparency and boost economic growth. Almost everything is online; there are no lines of annoyed citizens at City Hall, the Ministry of Interior, or the Department of Motor Vehicles! There is one integrated digital platform that supports electronic authentication and digital signatures to enable paperless communications across both the private and public sectors. Estonia's goal is a government that supports its citizens *while staying out of their way* (oh, how I wish Israel would follow suit!). They have already demonstrated that increased efficiency builds trust, improves governance, and saves taxpayer money. "Since the administration of the state works extremely well and efficiently, people trust the system" and don't feel put upon by the powers that be.

Estonia has already realized enormous economic savings from the most mundane of services such as digital signatures. These savings are enormous compared to "old school" signing with pen and paper—(up to 2% of GDP). Other positives include:

- 800 years of working time are saved *annually* thanks to data exchange
- Registering a business takes 18 minutes
- 98% of companies are established online

- 99% of banking transactions are online
- 95% of tax declarations are filed online—it takes only 3 minutes!
- 97% of patients have countrywide accessible digital records
- 97% of prescriptions are digital
- 500,000 queries by doctors and 300,000 queries by patients every year
- 99% of public services online *with 24/7 access*
- No system downtime since 2001
- Police work has become 50 times more effective thanks to IT solutions: e-Police system available in police cars unites over 15 databases, including those of Schengen and Interpol.

All this is making Estonia more competitive in the world market. Investors are attracted to places with non-intrusive, efficient governmental administration, and this has made Estonia the most economically successful former communist country. A serious caveat is whether Estonia's system can be applied in larger countries with heterogeneous ethnic populations and educational levels. My instinct is not as is, but certainly the principles of efficiency, ease of access and not driving your citizens crazy with endless forms, can be adapted to the idiosyncratic needs of all countries. Countries as ethnically and socially diverse as Israel and the United States might require a system of walk-in, *one-stop* storefront outlets that would assist citizens to make their way through the complicated and often contradictory requirements of local, regional, and national bureaucracies, liberating citizens from the endless maze of conflicting and overlapping demands. Other steps to be taken might include:

1. Laws and regulations not written at an 11th grade reading level to be considered null and void.

2. When laws and regulations contradict one another, both are to be considered null and void.

3. Applications not approved or denied within 3 months will be assumed to have been legally approved. If denied there must be a *detailed* explanation why, according to the laws and regulations *in place at the time* of the application. The practice of moving regulatory goal posts in the middle of application processes must end.

Governments are servants of the people; the people are not the retainers of the government. The concept "Civil Servant" must begin to be taken literally: government employees must be *civil* when dealing with citizens and they must *serve* the citizens. The test of a Democracy should be how much of a human being's life must be wasted dealing with a government. Some Russian intellectuals have claimed that the long lines characteristic of the former Soviet Union were not only due to the inherent inefficiency of the communist system but were purposeful; a means of exhausting the general public so they wouldn't have the energy to organize and protest.

How might Constitutionalism Progress in Non-Western Cultures?

As already hinted at, it is always best to progress on the basis of indigenous cultural assets—values and customs that are familiar and comfortable. For example, the American Founding Fathers were fighting for their centuries' old rights as Englishmen as they found common expression in Enlightenment philosophies and Reformation individualism. This mixed cultural heritage created a general attitude of mind that framed their deliberations, their policies, their strategies, and how they "marketed" their ideas to a public infused with the same general attitudes. This is why their cause resonated so much with the English-speaking colonists as well as with the thinking elites of Great Britain and the European continent. The close to 30% of the non-English speaking white settlers (mostly German) took almost no part in this Anglo-Saxon revolution (even though, ironically, the Declaration of Independence was printed first in a German language newspaper in Philadelphia and only appeared one day later in English).

On the other hand, for a civilization with cultural self-confidence, there is no shame in borrowing the values and ideas of another culture. Every great culture has been a borrower. There would have been no European Renaissance or Scientific Revolution without the Arab philosophical, mathematical, and scientific contribution. The Arabs themselves had borrowed from the Hindus, the Byzantines, the Persians, and the Chinese—in fact the Caliphate might be termed the greatest cultural entrepôt in history. Openness to other cultures is itself an indigenous cultural asset. The ability to discern analogies with other cultures is also useful. For example, India has been a Constitutional Democracy since its inception and has been trying to reform its caste system, educate its people and provide women with equal rights and opportunities, even though none of this is rooted in their cultural traditions. Modi's recent backtracking from the essential liberalism of the founders cannot completely reverse this, just as Mrs. Gandhi's dictatorial emergency laws could not do so in the past. India's religious pluralism, like Europe in the 17th and 18th centuries, requires it to constitutionalize even further in order to guarantee social stability which is fundamental to economic prosperity. Its integration into the global economic system over the past several decades as well as its large diaspora has generated more favorable concerns for human rights and Constitutionalism amongst the growing educated classes. Latin America, with some obvious exceptions, has been increasingly internalizing the Enlightenment heritage of Europe and becoming part of the global economic system. It is also an ethnically diverse continent. It seems to me that the constitutionalist process is irreversible.

Constitutionalizing the Muslim World

Islam is the great wild card in speculations about the possibilities of constitutionalization. But one can be cautiously optimistic, because Islam is part of the monotheistic inheritance that has given us two fundamental constitutionalist concepts. We are all made "in the image of God" and we are all descendants of Adam and Eve. Equality before God is inherent in Islam. Its most radical expression is the *Haj* to Mecca where all pilgrims must dress alike to avoid differentiation between class, race, or nation. The *Haj*, joined with certain Islamic traditions that define the inherent (unalienable) rights of the individual human being (probably derived from Stoic concepts about natural rights), as well as the proper function of leadership being to serve the people, indicates that being optimistic about the possibilities of the development of constitutionalism in the Muslim world is not naive, despite the current dreadful level of cultural and political discourse and abysmal levels of governance. Remember, Mohammed is the only founder of a major religion who was a businessman. He would have found nothing anti-Islamic about globalization. Indeed, the "Golden Age" of Islam was one of unprecedented cosmopolitan globalization brought about and dominated by Islam and the Andalusian polymath, Ibn Rushd (Averroes), has even been called the founding father of European secular thought.

The self-criticism (a fundamental component of the constitutionalist temperament) coming out of the Muslim world in recent years is encouraging. It derives from the tradition of *Ijtihad* which is the attempt of Muslims to arrive at a solution to a problem through the exertion of independent, critical reasoning. It literally means conducting a Jihad with your own conscience, intellect, and inherited beliefs. *Ijtihad* has been the key terminology through which reformist Muslims have articulated their visions for over a thousand years. Some of the most trenchant self-criticism of Islamic society has been coming from Muslim women who are asserting their inherent value as persons not conditional on the approval of men. Women with high school diplomas and college degrees who are increasingly involved in the modern economy will not for long accept an inferior status. In Israel 20% of Muslim women over 30 are still single (as opposed to less than 10% in the Jewish sector). These women are for the most part well-educated and are, in effect, telling their male co-religionists that "if you want to get married you better change your attitude towards women." In the extension branches of American universities in the Gulf States, women outnumber men by 2 to 1. One could also consider the impact of American Islam on the global Muslim community; how Americanization affects the self-image of American Muslims. Consider, by analogy, how American Catholics have affected policy decisions of the Vatican. The rebellion of Catholic laypersons in Boston regarding pedophile priests has resonated in other Catholic communities around the globe. Also consider how the views of American Jews have impacted other Jews around the world, including Israel.

The Sudanese-born American Islamic scholar Abdullahi Ahmed An-Na'im (1946) is a contemporary example of how the American experience might impact the future of Islamic thinking. In his various writings, he has contended that a secular state built on constitutionalism, human rights and full citizenship is more consistent with Islam than present visions of an Islamic state. The underlying proposition of his worldview is that

> ... [a] state cannot be Islamic not only since the state as
> such cannot think, feel, or believe, but also because there is
> no agreed and humanly verifiable quality of being "Islam-
> ic" that can be attributed to any institution. The post-colo-
> nial notion of an Islamic state to enforce Sharia as state law
> is conceptually incoherent, historically unprecedented,
> and practically untenable today.[28]

This is not to say that his American experience was formative of his views, but only that it is implausible to me that his views have not been impacted by that experience. He was a devotee of the Sudanese religious thinker (and engineer) Mahmoud Mohammed Taha (1909–1985), who was executed for apostasy by the regime of Gaafar Nimeiry. His crime? Propounding a worldview which distinguished between the foundational Meccan Surahs (chapters of the Quran) and the "subsidiary" Medinan surahs. He viewed the Meccan verses as "suffused with a spirit of freedom and equality" representing Islam in its *perfect* form.[29] In contrast, the Medinan verses are "full of rules, coercion, and threats, including the orders for jihad." Taha believed that they were an adaptation to the reality of life in the backward society of the 7th century, but irrelevant for the 20th century because they violated the values of equality, religious freedom and human dignity.[30] For Taha, Shariah law had the ability "to evolve, assimilate the capabilities of individual and society, and guide such life up the ladder of continuous development."[31] He believed foundational Islam advocated equal status to women and men, Muslim and non-Muslim; that the Sudanese constitution should be reformed to reconcile freedom with social justice and that Islam is compatible with democracy and socialism. He called his movement the "Republican Brothers" (with an auxiliary "Republican Sisters") in which women participated in all their prayers and other religious rituals and composed many hymns and poems. Imagine if the "Republican Brothers" had become as dominant in the Muslim World as the Muslim Brotherhood—how modern history would have been altered.

Preceding Taha, the Egyptian Grand Mufti and social reformer Muḥammad Abduh (1849–1905), believed in educating children in the sciences, fought corruption, and criticized superstition. He studied French law, engaged with western scholars at Cambridge and Oxford as well as in Vienna and Berlin and famously said "I went to the West and saw Islam, but no Muslims; I got back to the East and saw Muslims, but not Islam" indicating that modern European civilization was closer to the principles of Islam than the so-called Muslim countries; that obliviousness to the world and hostility to the sciences because their findings contradicted certain medieval interpretations of Islam did not make you more devout but rather ignorant of the deeper meanings of Islam, i.e., non-Islamic. He stressed that Muslims needed to use reason to keep up with changing times; that in Islam, man was not created to be haltered and led but was given intelligence to that he guide himself by knowledge. A teacher's role was to encourage study not to indoctrinate. Similar to the medieval Rabbi Bahya Ibn Paquda, Abduh frowned on the slavish imitation of traditions that stemmed from a more primitive and backward period of history. For him, independence of will and independence of thought and opinion were essential teachings of Islam and that Europe, not the Islamic world, had gained supremacy by applying these Islamic principles. He rejected nostalgia for the "glorious past" and insisted that Muslims must direct their thinking to the future. He was against polygamy, racial discrimination, and slavery. And similar to the negative views of Maimonides about the Rabbinate, he wanted to abolish the *Ulama* monopoly on interpretations of Holy Scripture; the *Ulama* being composed of men who took pride in their ignorance of the modern world and who thought such ignorance made them more devout—somewhat similar to the present-day Chief Rabbinate of Israel and various other rabbis of ultra-orthodox sects.

Unfortunately, contemporary Islam has been only marginally influenced by this kind of Islamic Modernism. The Wikipedia article on Islamic modernism describes it as follows:

> Islamic Modernism is a "movement" (inverted commas mine) that has been described as "the first Muslim ideological response to the Western cultural challenge" attempting to reconcile the Islamic faith with modern values such as democracy, civil rights, rationality, equality, and progress. It featured a "critical reexamination of the classical conceptions and methods of jurisprudence" and a new approach to Islamic theology and Quranic exegesis (*Tafsir*). A contemporary definition describes it as an "effort to re-read Islam's fundamental sources—the Qur'an and the Sunna (the practice of the Prophet)—by placing them in their historical context, and then reinterpreting them, non-literally, in the light of the modern context."

I put "movement" in inverted commas because it has manifested as more a collection of circumstantial individuals and occurrences rather than an historical force comparable to the European Renaissance or Enlightenment. It hasn't produced an American or French Revolution or coherent ideological phenomena such as Marxism (or even Fascism for that matter). It might be best compared to Teilhardism, but unlike Teilhardism, it is not a singularly coherent intellectual movement with a coherent alternative worldview. It is rather a collection of sincere individuals and groups, dismayed by the second-rate standing of 19th and 20th century Muslim society, who have devoted themselves to reforming Islam socially, culturally, economical, and especially intellectually. In a way it resembles 19th -and early 20th- century Zionism in that it primarily therapeutic; it wanted to cure Muslim individuals and societies of the pathologies they had accumulated since the collapse of the Golden Age in the same way that Zionism wanted to cure the Jews of their ghetto habits and attitudes. Since the late 19th century, at different times and places, various individuals and cultural phenomena have appeared that do allow for a degree of optimism about the ability of Islamic civilization to become an innovative civilizational factor once again, rather than the kitsch imitation of modernity of the Gulf States.

The fundamental problem and reason for modern Islam's relative failure, it seems to me, is that as progressive and modern as these individuals and groups are, they are still advocating religious context and content, even while seemingly promoting a sociologically secular state. Can the framework of a state, in fact, be secular if the content is religious? I don't see any evidence of this worldwide, in spite of many Americans claiming that the United States was founded on Judeo-Christian values, which of course is simply nonsense on stilts, when one investigates the facts and the beliefs of the Founding Fathers. The irony is that America is the most sociologically religious country in the developed world because it is structurally the most secular. Christendom secularized its political frameworks and societal laws after the Enlightenment; it constitutionalized. Can Islam do the same? I remain hopeful.

Constitutionalizing Africa and China

Every African culture is its own civilization. Unlike Christendom, Islam, India, or China, Africa has not inherited a unifying meta-civilization. This might be one of the reasons Pan-Africanism failed. Given the extreme pluralism of Africa (around 3,000 of the world's 6,500 languages are spoken in sub-Saharan Africa) Constitutionalism itself might become the meta-civilization of Africa. Are the European wars of religion analogous to current ethnic strife in Africa and do they require the same constitutionalist medicine? Time will tell. Here I believe that a futurist vision of a constitutionalist Africa could play a very valuable part.

China's awesome economic progress over the past 40 years has turned it into a commercial state de facto. Its present stage of development might be compared to Tudor England—a powerful and growing economic class struggling with a powerful and authoritarian monarch (the communist party). Joining the WTO has already forced the Chinese state to adopt policies that favor the expanding economic class. Recently, shortages of labor (especially skilled labor) have appeared in certain sectors of the Chinese economy. This will empower the working class. The growth of the economic class and the empowerment of the working class are the primary building blocks of Constitutionalism. Given China's recent retrograde behavior regarding human rights, many people in the West have become more pessimistic regarding the future of China. I believe this reflects western *Attention Deficit Disorder* rather than rational thinking. As previously mentioned, in the West, a quarter is 3 months; in the East a quarter is 25 years. Let's see what happens by the end of this century when entire generations that knew not hunger and privation inherit this great civilization and wish as individuals to achieve optimal self-actualization, i.e., when they perceive the pinnacle of Maslow's pyramid.

Reclaiming Natural Law

The deconstruction of Thomas Jefferson's "self-evident truths" has become characteristic of a certain kind of academic snootiness. It goes like this: "This means they are true because we say they are true." Yet Jefferson might have been prescient in anticipating the never-ending intellectual twisting and turning of the worst aspects of postmodernism by affirming that certain truths must be "self-evident"—that to be civilized human beings we must *a priori* recognize the validity of certain first principles based on natural rights that derive from natural law. Even if we believe it empirically impossible to prove natural rights; that rights do not exist in nature but are created by human institutions, we are compelled to act "*as if*" rights are natural and self-evident. If rights are decided only by human institutions (whether constituted by a majority or a minority) then no rights are inalienable and there is no objective standard of morality. If X says lynching black people is immoral Y can say "says who," and then democratically elected institutions can act as if there really are two legitimate positions on the subject of lynching (his narrative and her narrative).

It is one of the paradoxes of modern thought that present advocates of Natural Law are thought to be reactionary, Catholic, conservative. But consider the progressive causes that have been dependent on this "*as if.*" They include opposition to slavery, equal rights for women, and the Nuremberg war trials, all of which are dependent on the assumption of universal *natural* justice. If Constitutionalism is to triumph in the 21st century, then natural rights based on natural law must also be reclaimed by those on the left. Political discourse between left and right, based on the common philosophical legacy of natural law/natural rights/constitutionalism, might become more coherent and more civil. As noted previously, even science has certain axiomatic beliefs that cannot be proven empirically but without which there cannot be any science. So too must *political* science assume that natural rights based on natural law are true.

It may very well be that we may have to redefine the underlying philosophy of natural law/natural rights. Instead of biblical justification or natural law based on the physics of the 18th century, we might resort to a new theory of natural rights based on evolutionary concepts. Evolutionary research attempts, among other things, to discern the primary survival mechanisms of every species. Some species produce millions of offspring at one time in order that three or four might survive. Others use a survival strategy of herds or flocks of birds or schools of fish so that even when dozens or hundreds or thousands of individuals perish the herds survive. Some animals hunt in packs, some alone, some fly, some are swift, some are powerful and so on. The two major survival instruments of human beings are the individual reasoning brain and organized society. The society that enables optimal freedom to individual human reason without threatening the stability of that society is the one that is most robust in the long-term. The reasoning brain requires freedom of thought, freedom of thought requires freedom of speech, freedom of speech requires freedom of the press, and of assembly, freedom of assembly requires freedom of movement, and all of this requires a great degree of privacy (thinking being a very private undertaking). Consequently, we can reintroduce natural law/natural rights back into the fundamental discourse of Constitutionalism, thus making it the basis of the universal discourse of the entire human race—conservative or liberal.

Chapter Fourteen: Debunking the Non-Overlapping Magisteria Thesis

"All religions, arts and sciences are branches of the same tree. All these aspirations are directed toward ennobling man's life, lifting it from the sphere of mere physical existence and leading the individual towards freedom."
— Albert Einstein

If we, as a species, are to reclaim a heroic and optimistic vision of the future, we must renew the intellectual tradition that encourages and celebrates transdisciplinary thinking. In order to do this, we must reject evolutionary biologist Stephen Jay Gould's proposition of non-overlapping magisteria— that science and religion represent distinct, mutually exclusive domains. He presented this questionable (and rather condescending) proposition in a well written and well-argued essay in 1997. To my mind, this was his way of extricating himself from the intellectual burden of dealing with religious/ philosophical speculations about the essence of ultimate reality. It was not only condescending (other "magisteria" can deal with their trivial nonsense, leave us scientists to deal with the really important matters), it made an unfortunate contribution to the ongoing desiccation of the intellectual imagination that began in the 19th century. Presuming that one can compartmentalize one's various intuitions, hunches and speculative imaginings into distinct mutually exclusive domains is historically unsound. I assert that religion, science, and philosophy (as well as art, literature and poetry) are, at their core, complementary parts of the same spiritual project; trying to find out why we are here and what is here. I would also claim that technological innovation and socio/economic entrepreneurial initiatives are tributary manifestations of the same great human project. The Cosmodeistic project, as presented here, is obviously an affront to the non-overlapping magisteria thesis because it proposes that this compartmentalization presents a survival danger to the human race by shriveling the intellectual imagination.

History matters, and the history of ideas, especially, matters. The ontological assumptions of modern science are direct descendants of the archetypal principles of the ancient Greeks. The iconic *Law of Parsimony* (Occam's Razor) ultimately derives from this Greek propensity to construct cosmos from chaos. The ancient Greeks saw "... the cosmos as an ordered expression of certain primordial essences or transcendent first principles, variously conceived as forms, ideas, universals, changes absolutes, immortal deities, divine *archai*, and archetypes." This propensity characterized Greek civilization from Homer, Hesiod, Aeschylus, and Sophocles, up until Pythagoras, Socrates, Plato, Aristotle, and Plotinus.[32] This propensity favored absolute concepts of reality which was reflected in their preference for math, deductive logic, and moral values. The ancient Hebrews also had a propensity towards ultimate, absolute reality (God) and morals from this divine absolute. And with all due respect to the Greeks, the fact is that Occam advanced his law of parsimony in order to prove the validity of Monotheism (to wit you only need *one* God to explain reality) rather than as the vital tool of science which it eventually became. For the Jews, something is good because it adheres to objective absolutes as they relate to individual and societal needs; it is empirical. For the Greeks, something is good because it is logical and coherent; it is rational. This Greco/Hebrew inheritance has dominated Western thought for millennia and is foundational to *The Idea of Progress.* The development of Western thought reflects an interaction of religion and philosophy which eventually gave birth to science. For the early Greeks, nature and divinity were intertwined. To make sense out of nature was to know the gods. Pythagoras formed a religion based on the "dogma" of mathematics. Pindar felt that developing human abilities brought one closer to God.

According to Professor Peter Harrison, "religion" and "science emerged as distinct concepts in Europe *after* the Scientific Revolution and the Enlightenment."[33] (Isaac Newton certainly did not distinguish, as he wrote more extensively on the Book of Daniel than on Optics.) "Religion" became a distinct concept only in the 17th century when the European colonization enterprise made contact with organizing principles of life and society other than what the Europeans were used to. "Science" became a distinct concept in the 19th century in order to create new professional specializations. Until then, "science" had simply been a sub-branch of philosophy called natural philosophy. The term *scientist* was coined by the naturalist-theologian William Whewell only in 1834.

In the Hebrew Bible, the words "Judaism" and "religion" do not even appear. (The Koran also has no word for religion as we moderns understand it.) The Jews have never really distinguished between religious, national, or ethnic identities.[34] Some of the greatest *self-identified* Jews of modernity have been complete non-believers. The Jewish worldview is primarily one of personal conduct and societal duties, not of belief and faith. Orthodox Jews will rarely ask a Jew "do you believe in God"; more common would be "are you *shomrei mitzvot*" (literally, do you observe the practical commandments?). It deals with *Halacha* (literally "the way" you conduct your life). In this it is similar to the word *dharma*.

Hindu hostility to Muslims initially derived from viewing them not as a competitive "religion" but as foreign invaders and occupiers imposing alien cultural values. Japan also had no word for "religion" until Commodore Perry imposed on their self-inflicted isolation in 1853 and forced the Japanese government to sign treaties that included demands for freedom of religion. Japanese hostility to Catholic missionaries previously was not religious but rather cultural and national—these were aliens imposing their foreign views and ways of life. Even the anti-Catholicism of Tudor England has been attributed to the Church behaving as a political faction. The very terms "Buddhism," "Hinduism", "Taoism," and "Confucianism" were invented (by Europeans) in the 19th century. They really had no idea that they were one of the "World Religions" (another term invented by 19th-century Europeans).

Even within a religious worldview of history, the artificial distinction between reason and "revelation" is simply unhistorical. Dr. Yoram Hazony, in his book *The Philosophy of Hebrew Scripture*, cites numerous historical examples demonstrating the superficiality of such distinctions. Using the very words of the Greeks he demonstrates that, like the Jews, they were also coming to their conclusions at the inspiration of the gods. Parmenides (515–440 BCE), called by Plato "father" [of philosophy], describes:

> ... the experience of climbing into the night sky on a horse drawn chariot tended by the "daughters of the sun," which ultimately enters the palace of an unnamed goddess who takes his hand and promises to inform him of "everything." [so] *everything* we have of Parmenides consists of the words of this goddess ... and of the divinity who governs all things ..."

This knowledge of reality was "revealed" as godly commands rather than drawn from his personal deductive logic. Empedocles (490–430) also depended on godly revelations (the goddess Calliopia) for his philosophical insights. Heraclitus (535–475) wrote that "a god is wise in comparison with a man, as a man is with a child." Plato depicts Socrates "as receiving revelations and commands and dreams from gods that gave form and content to his life and work … [that] the philosophy that Socrates pursues is itself the result of a series of divine commands." Hazony's fundamental thesis (supported by strict adherence to the very words of these thinkers) is that "During the two hundred years between Jeremiah and Plato there flourished a philosophical tradition … in which the ability to conduct philosophical inquiry was frequently seen as partially or wholly dependent on revelation or some other form of assistance from a god." The intimation being that there is no essential difference between Hebrew biblical reasoning and Greek "philosophical" reasoning; that if read properly, the Bible provides a political philosophy, an ethical philosophy, an epistemology, ontology, and metaphysics (as well as a more general philosophy of ideas).

At this point in my reading, I began looking for some reference to Julian Jaynes' monumental work *The Origin of Consciousness in the Breakdown of the Bicameral Mind,* but in vain. This was surprising, given that Hazony's research provided so much evidence for Jaynes' fundamental thesis which is "that until late in the second millennium B.C. men … were … obeying the voices of gods … that human consciousness … is a *learned* process brought into being out of an earlier hallucinatory mentality … *and still developing* (italics mine)." Or in other words, when a human being had an idea, insight or understanding he did not realize it was himself having that idea or insight but felt that it was knowledge or understanding being provided to him by some outside force—a god, or "God." I have no idea if Hazony is aware of Jaynes' theory or not, only that he provides much supporting evidence. Bruno Snell published his classic *The Discovery of the Mind in Greek Philosophy and Literature* 30 years before Jaynes, in which he anticipated much of Jaynes' work. Anticipating both Jaynes and Hazony, Snell writes that "Homer's man does not regard himself as the source of his own decisions"[35] but rather as a consequence of the gods talking to him.

The discoveries of science, in turn, have transformed both philosophy and theology. Deism and Natural Theology are the religious offspring of science's impact on religion; scientific philosophy is the philosophical offspring. For a certain historical period, the artificial separation of the three was, no doubt, indispensable for the furtherance of intellectual clarity and precision. But now that separation is responsible for the intellectual and spiritual impasse at the root of current civilizational neuroses. Could the *Idea of Progress* or theories of evolution, which doubtless derives from the *Idea of Progress*, have arisen in a civilization that did not contain Plato's notion of becoming?[36] Plato's concepts of being and becoming (of Idea and Form) might be compared to Jewish perceptions of God. The *Idea* of the being of God is an absolute, while the phenomenon (the *form*) of God is a becoming. As Rabbi David Cooper notes, the Hebrew word for God is a verb; it is in effect a platonic *form* in the process of becoming. Judaism requires us to be partners with the *Idea* of God in order to facilitate the *Becoming* of God. In ethics, one could legitimately conclude that everyone should live their lives as if it might eventually be revealed that he or she might be the Messiah.

Forms are not immortal, but ideas are. Ideas endure even though the form these ideas take evolve and change. The idea of God is the preeminent example of this. God is the ultimate archetypal ideal; indeed, it is *the* ideal. Has Plato become relevant again? Is Plato's theory of ideas the ultimate source of the law of parsimony? $E=MC^2$, as well as other scientific theories, are prime examples of those platonic "deeper and timeless order of absolutes" that clarify "the surface confusion and randomness of the temporal world." This is why Plato preferred mathematics which is an absolutist language.[37] Pagan gods are a pre-Plato intimation of transcendent ideas: god of the river, etc. For the Greeks, gods were simply those platonic archetypal ideas which warranted that contemplation which was the highest form of human endeavor. Was the original concept of the Hebrew God a similar intimation? One of the deep roots of the *Law of Parsimony* comes from ancient Greece—the *arche*,[38] which is the fundamental principle that governs all of nature (one principal, one God—not many principles, not many gods). Thales saw evolving existence as divine; Homer saw all of nature as divine[39] (was Homer a precursor to pantheism—to Spinoza?). Thales represented "a distinct overlap of the mythic and scientific modes" when he said, "All is water and the world is full of gods."[40]

Mythologies produced literature (Homer and Sophocles), which produced tragedy. Tragedy is a reflection of the human condition; how self-reflective consciousness interacts with objective existence, i.e., those objects (human and non-human) other than one's own self-reflective consciousness. What is the meaning and purpose of my own existence? How should I act in relation to existence per se (human and non-human)? Great myths are invented to explain why there is "anything at all rather than nothing." Religions grow out of these creation myths. These religious explanations generate dilemmas and questions which require theologies, which eventually evolve into philosophies and finally science. But despite the pretensions of science to be intellectually autonomous, the working scientist, as a real living human being in organized society, is a product of the social/cultural milieu she is born into and therefore greatly influenced by the legacy of the civilization she is born into. The *Scientific Revolution* is a product of the Greco/Hebrew inheritance—the desire to discover the absolute. Plato juxtaposed "primordial mythic deities with ... mathematical and rational forms ... many gods ... with the single God ... (and) the religious significance of scientific research ..." This was a unified, speculative imagination that did not refuse to entertain any approach to access understanding because "it's not my field," as today's fastidious and fussy academics might remonstrate. I have no doubt that if Plato were alive today, he might also have enlisted the speculative imagination of what we now call science fiction in his quest for ultimate understanding (as the Dominican friar Giordano Bruno did two millennia later with speculations about existence that might legitimately be termed proto-Science Fiction). The Hebrews and the Greeks had many analogous myths, such as Odysseus seduced by knowledge and Eve seduced by a curiosity for knowledge. Our knowledge is the root of tragedy. Tragedy is the artistic expression of Pascal's despair. We are the only species that knows it is going to die and wonders why it lives; why we are here, and what is here. This is the poisoned fruit of the human condition; the inevitable dilemma of the Greco/Hebrew inheritance—knowledge of our own finiteness.

Even psychology cannot be seen as a separate and distinct magisterium, since it is the essence of the observer who is always subjectively involved in one way or another with what is observed.[41] Jung's universal archetypes are nothing more than the modern iteration of platonic forms.[42] The proposition of non-overlapping magisteria is a psychological defense mechanism. It is simply an intellectual device to make life easier for academics that prefer intellectual safety within the feudalistic walls of their own clearly defined "fields" of study (a field being an area with precisely defined borders). It is really a reflection of intellectual cowardice of people afraid to venture outside the comforts of their own expertise. It is not designed for greater precision in discussing ultimate reality; it is a convenience, not a serious intellectual proposition. To continue with the feudalistic analogy, the Western intellectual tradition must recreate an "intellectual commons" in which people from different "fields" can graze and intermix without fear of being chastised by the editor of some peer reviewed journal that he or she has not provided a footnote for this or that particular transdisciplinary speculation.

Until the 19th century, when universities quarantined thinking into academic departments, it would have been difficult to differentiate between the philosophical, religious, artistic, and scientific mindset. As already mentioned, the very word scientist was coined in 1833 by an Anglican priest, William Whewell, who was also a historian of science and a philosopher—a non-compartmentalized thinker if there was ever one. If you had called Newton a scientist, he would not have known what you were talking about. Newton was a "natural philosopher" who wrote at least two and a half million words on theology. He "did science" in order to discover the "Mind of God." In modern terms, Leonardo Da Vinci was an engineer, scientist, and artist. But if you had asked him to define himself "professionally," he would not have understood the question. Da Vinci represented a fusion of technology, science, and art; each permeating and enriching the other. He could not have been the artist he was without his technological genius, which was suffused with the same aesthetic instinct that characterized his art. Even today, despite artificial compartmentalizations, scientists will talk about the "elegance" of a theory and engineers the "beauty" of a design.

To a significant extent, *The Scientific Revolution* derived from the religious thinking of the late Middle Ages, especially the sophisticated thinking of Aristotelian scholastics exemplified by Thomas Aquinas (1225–1274). As Professor Emmet Kennedy has written, "Aquinas is essential to a history of secularism, primarily because he drew a famous distinction between what is known by reason and what is known by revelation, concerning the natural and the supernatural worlds."[43] This intellectual space was necessary for the secular thinking which eventually created science, as well as economic theory (Lord Acton called Aquinas the first Whig). Aquinas embraced two articles of Catholic faith: first, that God was a God of reason who ordered the world rationally; and second, while he is the first cause, he operates in the world by way of the secondary causes he created. This permits us to explain natural phenomena and the interaction of nature's constituents by things *secondary* to God's *direct* intrusion. This doctrine enabled the Roman Catholic Church to accept evolution (a secondary cause created by God) without abandoning *creatio ex nihilo*. As with Laplace, modern scientists have had no need for the God hypothesis to explain natural events; not realizing the theological roots (secondary causes) of that very mindset, just as most scientists do not know the religious motivation of the Law of Parsimony that they live by. Aquinas' genius is diminished when subjected to non-overlapping magisteria compartmentalization. As Michael Novak noted:

> Aquinas has come down to most American students as a philosopher, rather than a theologian. Most read only what is of interest to the philosophy professors ... (but) when you rip Aquinas from the whole sweep of his theology ... you get a much thinner Aquinas than the great intellectual figure that he actually is. And you open him to charges from theologians, who dismiss him as "just another Aristotle."[44]

While Aristotelian scholasticism created much of the intellectual space that enabled subsequent scientific inquiry it also left in its wake a great deal of intellectual rubble that would have hindered the progress of science if not cleared away. Subsequent Church thought removed much of this intellectual rubble. In 1277, Bishop Stephen Tempier headed "a council in Paris [which] condemned [many] Aristotelian theses [including] ... the view that even God could not create a void, or an infinite universe of a plurality of worlds."[45] Tempier felt that God being God could do whatever he wished. This purely theological decision provided science with the freedom to speculate about the nature of existence without any *a priori* dogmatic conclusions, such as those Aristotelian deductions eventually proven to be nonsense by the progress of science.

Occam's Razor is the quintessential example of the overlap between the philosophical, the religious and the scientific. William of Ockham (Occam in Latin) (c. 1287–1347) was an English Franciscan friar, scholastic philosopher, and theologian. His philosophical intent was to substantiate the validity of Monotheism. But *Occam's Razor* (the Law of Parsimony), as we know, eventually became the holy grail of scientific research. Ockham's religious motivation made a major contribution to the scientific mindset. This raises the question—could the Scientific Revolution have occurred in a non-monotheistic civilization—a civilization that had already created a theological law of parsimony: *one* God; *the* One (and *only*)? The cleric Jean Buridan (c.1300–c.1358), anticipating Galileo, developed the *Theory of Impetus*, demonstrating that there is no *need* for either Aristotle's "First Mover" or Plato's "souls," which are not found in the Bible and which by implication limit God's omnipotence to design the world as he pleases. Here we see the strictures of Christian faith enabling the emergence of a mechanical cosmos by eliminating the need for "intelligences" to explain the movement of celestial spheres. Bishop Nicolas d'Oresme (c.1320–1382) anticipated Copernicus when writing that scripture can be accommodated even if we concede the possibility that the earth moves and is not the center of existence. These conclusions, in aggregate, anticipate the clockwork universe of Descartes as well as Deism. When referring to Buridan's impetus theory, d'Oresme observed, 400 years before the Deists, that "God might have started off the universe as a kind of clock and left it to run by itself."[46] The implication again being that God, being God, can do whatever he pleases (or, as I would put it, "cosmic evolution, being cosmic evolution, can do whatever it pleases"). Butterfield noted that this was "a case of a consistent body of teaching [which] developed as a tradition" that was "still being taught in Paris at the beginning of the 16th century" and influenced Leonardo da Vinci and Galileo.[47] Galileo's theory of inertia reflected Buridan's view that "God might have given these things their initial impetus, and their motion could be imagined as continuing forever" (the fundamental hypothesis of Deism).[48] Kepler believed that "... the Copernican hypothesis ... would directly reflect God's glory."[49]

Preceding Galileo, Copernicus was motivated to simplify the complexities of the Ptolemaic system which, he felt, insulted the omnipotent intelligence of God. If God is the God of reason, who possesses omnipotent intelligence, he certainly would have created a more sensible universe, rather than the "Rube Goldberg"[50] like Ptolemaic contraption. Copernicus was applying the law of parsimony inherent in monotheism and finding Ptolemy wanting. His motivation was to defend the honor of God's unconditional power. When theological imperatives continually generate alternative theories more fitting to the modern scientific mindset, the non-overlapping magisteria concept must be seen as arbitrary and capricious. Especially since science, as noted previously, is also based on *faith* in several overlapping assumptions which cannot be proven empirically. Following the same logic of magisteria that do overlap, I believe that one must never distinguish between material progress and spiritual enlightenment if one is to truly understand social and cultural evolution.

Science, philosophy, and religion are part of the *same* spiritual project—to understand our place and purpose in the Universe. The difference is that religion strives to be a comprehensive worldview (presuming to provide answers for the meaning and purpose of life); philosophy is more preoccupied with attempting to clarify various aspects of human existence; science satisfies itself with being a method for inquiry into the workings of existence. Science restricts itself to the "what and the how" of existence, not the "why" of existence which preoccupies the religious instinct. Philosophy is more about how we might relate to existence. A key difference is that science—unlike philosophy and religion—has a generally accepted universal language and methodology—mathematics and experimentation, which are subject to constant criticism and challenge. And even though we have already mentioned the limitations of both mathematics and experimentation in relating to ultimate reality and intellectual innovation, these tools are precise and have withstood the test of time.

Religion, on the other, hand has no objective stringency of language or methodology. Even the question "Do you believe in God?" automatically invites the epistemological challenge, "What do *you* mean by belief and what do *you* mean by God?" Philosophy, of course, has a generally accepted vocabulary but numerous languages and grammars that advocate different nuances and interpretations when dealing with both the objective and the subjective. Not only are there distinct philosophical kingdoms, such as epistemology, ontology, phenomenology and existentialism, etc., but also a myriad of species and subspecies within each of these kingdoms. There are no standard religious models or standard philosophical models as there are standard scientific models. That being said, scientists are also human (as shocking as that may seem) and subject to the same societal and cultural constraints as anybody else, despite their pretensions otherwise. The religious worldview of a particular society, as well as individual philosophic predispositions, move and effect the individual scientist (as a human being living in one's own civilization) more than most would suspect. The Jesuit priest Lemaitre intuiting "The Big Bang" was certainly cultivated by a mental attitude nourished by the biblical story of creation. Even individual political predispositions have profoundly influenced the history of science. The Quaker scientist Eddington was motivated to prove Einstein's General Theory correct because Einstein was a pacifist like himself. Copernicus exemplified the LOP's relationship to monotheism. How could the Supreme Being—the absolute intelligence of existence—have designed such a sloppy and complicated universe?

The slovenly Ptolemaic universe was actually an insult to God's rationality and Copernicus set out to salvage God's honor with his much more elegant hypothesis.

Religion, while much less intellectually stringent than science or philosophy, is more amenable to human imagination and speculation about the ultimate meanings of existence and life and thus both psychologically *and intellectually* still necessary as a creative survival tool of the human race. It is time for science to repay its debt to religion and generate a philosophy which could produce a religion suitable for the human race as it expands outward into the Cosmos. It is time for a reunification of the human spiritual instinct, whether religious, scientific or philosophical; to realize Carl Sagan's vision that: "A religion, old or new, that stressed the magnificence of the Universe as revealed by modern science might be able to draw forth reserves of reverence and awe hardly tapped by the conventional faiths."[51] It is in this spirit that I would like to present the rough outlines of the Cosmodeistic hypothesis: an iteration of Pandeism—not God becoming the Universe but rather the Cosmos becoming God; not "in the beginning God created the heavens and the earth," but, rather, "in the end an evolutionary cosmos will have created God."

Notes

1   Peterson.

2   Macdougall.

3   Hallam & Wignall.

4   Kraft & Spencer.

5   Bullinger & Behlau, p. 433.

6   Steiner, pp. 230-31.

7   Polmear, pp. 15-16.

8   Sands & Westcott.

9   Senor & Singer, pg. 112.

10 Whisenand.

11 Ibid.

12 Pearce.

13 Becker, E. 1968, p. 10.

14 Feynman, p. 37.

15 Lerner, 1991, p. 327.

16 Random House Dictionary, p. 659.

17 West & Lansang.

18 Reinecke, Logsdon, Caplan, and Cornish all demonstrated *over 25 years ago* how conventional attitudes towards employment must change.

19 Pink.

20 *The End of Work* as we know it has been predicted by Keynes, Michael Harrington, and David Macarov.

21 Pofeldt.

22 Anders.

23 Willett, pp. 695-98.

24 Keynes, p. 198.

25 Ibid., p. 199.

26 Biao.

27 *Bills of Attainder* are laws **especially designed to impose legal sanctions or disabilities on a particular individual or class of people.** They have been unconstitutional in the Anglo-Saxon legal tradition for centuries and are specifically banned in the English Bill of Rights and in the American Constitution.

28 An-Na'im.

29 Packer.

30 Lichtenthaler.

31 Taha, p. 39.

32 Tarnas, p. 3.

33   Harrison, p. 171.

34   Edelheit.

35   Snell, p. 31.

36   Tarnas, p, 9.

37   Ibid., p, 11.

38   Ibid., p, 19.

39   Ibid., p. 19.

40   Ibid., p. 19.

41   Ibid., p. 423.

42   Ibid., p. 424.

43   Kennedy, p. 23.

44   Novak.

45   Butterfield, p. 21.

46   Ibid., p. 20.

47   Ibid.

48   Ibid., p. 25.

49   Ibid., p. 256.

50   Rube Goldberg was an American cartoonist, sculptor, author, engineer, and inventor known for popular cartoons depicting complicated gadgets that perform simple tasks in indirect, convoluted ways.

51   Sagan, p. 50.

PART IV

The Nessyahu Conjectures in Light of Present Science

Introduction: The Bio-Cosmic Challenge of Human Survival

I am including in this part of the book as many of Nessyahu's own words as is practical. I have paraphrased, condensed, and expanded on much of his writing, in order to provide the reader with the intellectual foundations upon which I have built my various theses and arguments. I say "expanded on" because Nessyahu wrote like a Japanese Haiku poet, or rather like a Kabbalist searching for the ultimate *TsimTsum* (reduction? minimalism?) in his thinking. Reading him in the actual style in which he wrote would have left the reader gasping for oxygen. I have rewritten him in a more expansive style, allowing the reader to breathe. I have also injected many of my own conclusions based on his original insights and scientific progress since he died. I will indicate where I have done that by highlighting in *italics* my own observations. And while I have rigorously edited most of what follows, some of it will seem repetitive to what I have already written. But this is a redundancy I believe necessary to elaborate and clarify the basic message of the book. Some of what follows might even appear outdated considering political and social developments as well as scientific progress over the past 20 years, but that takes nothing away from the general thrust of his thought. This part of the book is highly technical, and the reader can be excused if he or she skips over it, proceeds to Part V and chooses to return to it later (if at all). In any case, the bare essence of his thinking has already been described above. However, the understanding of the reader will definitely be enriched by delving more deeply into his conjectures. To fully appreciate Nessyahu's thinking, one would do well to embrace the following definition of the very term *Cosmology* as: "A comprehensive view of all reality, attending to both the nature of the whole and also to the place of all parts within the whole. The origin, order, meaning, and destiny of all that exists are key issues in a cosmological system, as is also the question of what this 'reality' in fact embraces."[1]

Chapter Fifteen: The Cosmos as Matter and Radiation

Science is continually discovering a distinctive interdependence between occurrences in the large and small scale. This distinctive interdependence enables us to delineate a finite domain, thus suggesting an otherness beyond the finite which we humans have named the "infinite." We may then differentiate between the Cosmos (a definable unified organization of reality) as a finite domain within an infinite, non-definable, reality in both its large and small scales. This infinite reality, which we will call Nature, or the Universe, or existence as such, almost certainly contains an infinite number of cosmoses (definable unified organizations of reality) containing an infinite number of systems and particles—including "particles" of life. *As Carl Sagan has noted, "Some scientists think the Universe may be one of a vast number—perhaps an infinite number—of other closed-off universes." Nessyahu first deduced the existence of what is now termed the "multiverse" several decades before it was even speculated upon within the scientific community; much the same way that Kant deduced the existence of galaxies almost 200 years before science actually discovered them. I prefer to call them cosmoses: finite bounded organizations of reality within infinite nature. Precise semantics is important: Cosmos and Universe/Nature/Existence as such are not synonyms. Cosmos means order which implies bounded lawfulness. Assuming the Universe is infinite, it is, by definition, not bounded and may therefore contain an infinite number of different cosmic lawfulnesses. I will use Nature and Universe interchangeably when I am discussing existence as such.*

Astrophysical inquiry into the large scale has brought us so close to the infinite large that we have no choice but to search for any arbitrary border of a finite large-scale domain. Microphysical inquiry into the small scale has brought us so close to the infinite small that we have no choice but to search for any arbitrary border of a finite small-scale domain. Experiment and theory (as well as common sense) confirm that the large and small scales are a unified reality. There is no large without a small and no small without a large; every large contains a small and every small is part of a large. *For example, the largeness of our bodies is determined by the number, activities and interactivities of the biological particles and subsystems that our bodies contain and exist because of these particles and subsystems.* The search, then, is for one, and not two, separate borders: in other words, a unified finite domain of a definitive largeness and smallness. Without this unity of the large and small, it is impossible to differentiate between the finite and the infinite; to delineate a finite domain (cosmos/order) within infinite Nature. In striving for an all-inclusive law of the large and small scale, we must take into account the following:

1. We cannot investigate infinite Nature, neither in the large scale nor in the small scale. We are only capable of investigating a finite organized part of Nature—a cosmos.

2. Nature is characterized by particles in the small scale. (As modern quantum physics has shown, these particles also express themselves as waves.) We are looking for finite particles which are not the static atoms of classical Greek philosophy, but dynamic ever-changing particles that are unendingly dividing into ever smaller particles.

3. Nature is characterized by systems in the large scale (cosmoses as systems of galaxies and galaxies as systems of star-systems). Regarding our Cosmos we are looking for a system which includes all the galaxies within a definable finite domain.

4. There are various combinations of particles, but only three basic varieties: matter, radiation, and electricity as an intermediate.

5. The galaxies differ according to their size, place, and time in our expanding Cosmos. Other than that, they share a basic similarity.

6. Large and small-scale occurrences have a basic connectivity. The transformation of hydrogen atoms into helium atoms taking place within the Sun is a small-scale process which makes the large-scale Sun a star. The Sun is a finite bounded entity characterized by its volume in the large scale, which is a consequence of the process of hydrogen transforming into helium in the small scale. This boundedness makes it a clearly defined entity, relatively autonomous from its proximate environment while interacting with it, much as individuals are relatively autonomous bounded entities interacting with their environment.

7. Nature is not only characterized by the external movement of its particles and bodies. The internal change of the dividing particles is really Nature's fundamental phenomenon, as it is what propels the external movement of particles and bodies. I refer to the division of particles, and their reciprocal interactions, which result in the subsequent organization and disorganization of smaller scale particles and larger scale bodies. In the large scale, for example, or-

ganization would refer to the creation of the stars and galaxies and disorganization would refer to supernovas (and entropy in general). In the small scale, the same supernovas would be creating the atoms of the heavier elements (out of the simplest elements: hydrogen and helium) necessary for the ongoing complexification of the Cosmos, including the eventual emergence of life itself. As for life based on sexual reproduction, two cells join to begin a process of creating a very complex living organization; death disorganizes this complex living organization back into its much simpler component parts.

8. The Second Law of Thermodynamics postulates that the characteristic process of closed systems (and in speaking about the Cosmos we are speaking about a *closed* system) is the increase of entropy: the diffusion of energy on the way to thermodynamic equilibrium.

9. The cosmic limits (or boundedness) of movement are inert mass on the one hand, and the energy of movement at the speed of light on the other, (the speed of light being the absolute, maximal speed of radiation within our Cosmos). Movement, therefore, is a finite phenomenon with clearly defined boundaries.

10. We must assume (as axiomatic) the existence of a certain domain (the Cosmos) possessed of an utmost unity. This unity is basic to the change and multiplication/proliferation taking place within the domain. This domain is unified in the large and the small scales and is part of infinite, undifferentiated Nature. Without this assumption science cannot function.

The question becomes: does a large-scale system which includes all the galaxies exist? Is that large-scale system characterized by small-scale particles whose reciprocal activity actuates the large-scale system? All the considerations we have discussed indicate that the Cosmos is that system whose expansion is the result of the dividing-multiplication process of the sum total of particles which compose it. The Cosmos, then, is a finite expanding domain of a finite ongoing process, identified as an expanding system of dividing particles. If there is unity within this largeness and smallness and between the large and the small, we may anticipate a maximum possible unity of the Cosmos.

Diversity within the Cosmos is represented by the particles which constitute it. Change is represented by the dividing (and reciprocal action) of particles into new types of particles. Unity lies in the identity of the dividing particles in the small scale with the expansion of the system in the large scale as a result of a constant process of change. This constant process of change is the fundamental process of the Cosmos. It causes all occurrences in the Cosmos. It does so by way of the reciprocal action between the two types of particles. We arrive at this hypothesis by way of several internal speculations regarding the Cosmos. But because this conception posits that the Cosmos is a finite domain within infinite Nature, we must complete the picture by way of several external speculations regarding Nature (or the Universe) as such:

1. Nature is infinite in both the large and the small.

2. Infinite Nature is identical with infinite space.

3. Infinite change is identical with infinite time.

4. Infinite Nature is undergoing infinite change in both the large and the small.

5. There is a correspondence between the infinite large and the infinite small, as well as between infinite space and infinite time.

6. We assume that Nature is infinite in every way even though we cannot prove it. This is because, logically, there is no largeness that we cannot imagine something larger and no smallness that we cannot imagine something smaller. Likewise, there is no beginning that we cannot imagine something before and no end that we cannot imagine something after. Nature then, is a process of infinite change which is identical with infinite time.

7. If we speak about space in terms of a system on the large scale and particles on the small scale, and about time in terms of expansion on the large scale and division on the small scale, then we may assume the infinite expansion of an infinite number of expanding systems identical to the infinite divisions of an infinite number of dividing particles.

8. *Speculating on Nessyahu's logical deductions I suggest that this never-ending dividing of particles into ever smaller particles might be what is responsible for producing the so-called "dark energy" and "dark matter." Particles which are "dark" because they are so infinitesimally small they do not reflect light; particles which being so small have no individual measurable mass but which, in aggregate, may have become the greater*

part of matter in the Cosmos. The "dark" energy driving the expansion of the Cosmos being nothing more than the energy produced by this constant splitting of particles—a reflection of Newton's Third Law: "For every action, there is an equal and opposite reaction." (I assume complete responsibility for this particular speculation)

9. We cannot assume the existence of an infinite number of cosmoses *similar* to our Cosmos. We can, however, assume the existence of *many* cosmoses similar to our own (within an infinite number of dissimilar systems in the universe) as part of larger systems composed of smaller particles—*ad infinitum.*

10. Our Cosmos, then, is a finite expanding domain of a finite continuous process, the large and small scales of which are an integrated whole. It is one of an infinite number of finite cosmoses in infinite Nature.

11. Our Cosmos is a closed system which evolves itself, after it has been created out of the fundamental process of infinite Nature (the very process that created the initial singularity *or singularities* that created our Cosmos in the Big Bang, or perhaps several Big Bangs). Existence itself seems to have a self-organizing propensity which we have named evolution. This self-organizing propensity gave birth to the Cosmos and is the driver of cosmic evolution and ultimately of the emergence and evolution of life, which eventually produced consciousness.

12. We have no need to assume interaction between our cosmic order and infinite nature (subsequent to the emergence of our cosmic order) in order to understand the development of the Cosmos, even though there may be such interaction as yet to be discovered.

13. The radiation particles radiated from the matter particles do not create the ordered system as such. Most of them dissipate into disorder and contribute directly to the general expansion of the cosmic system (*this being the dark energy I have already alluded to*). Some of them, however, enter into reciprocal activity with other matter particles, which generate the processes of organization and disorganization within the cosmic system. Two variations of our cosmic system do not exist—there is one integrated cosmic system. But there are two distinct variations of cosmic particles within the one cosmic system. There are matter particles possessed of

maximum mass and minimum speed, and radiation particles possessed of minimum mass and maximum speed.

14. The Cosmos does have a beginning. It is a system of a certain size composed of a certain number of particles "compressed" within itself, in a presumed state of equilibrium when presumably at rest. This is nothing more than the beginning of the Cosmos as such; as a finite process-domain within infinite Nature. The process inherent to this domain—that fundamental process of the interaction between radiation, matter, and electricity – are what "produce" the clumpiness and clusters (stars, galaxies, etc.) which constitute what we call "the observable universe."

15. Our finite Cosmos will have an end. It will be an inestimably larger system composed of an inestimably larger number of inestimably smaller particles which are dispersed throughout the system in a state of equilibrium (maximum entropy). This is nothing more than the end of the Cosmos as such, as a finite process-domain within infinite Nature.

16. The continuous finite process, from its *beginning* as a *compressed* domain (the singularity) to its *end* as a *dispersed* domain, is a process of dividing *primary* particles which radiate, and the creation of *end* particles which have been radiated. That is to say it is the process of the all-encompassing expansion of the system. If we view these *primary* particles as particles of matter possessed of inert mass, and the *end* particles as particles of radiation possessed of energy-movement at the speed of light, then *the fundamental process of the Cosmos is the process of the transformation of matter particles into radiation particles.* (THIS IS THE THEORY OF EVERYTHING).

Does this cosmic conception explain what exists and occurs within the Cosmos? If it were possible to calculate what necessarily derives from the process of radiation particles radiated from matter particles within the framework of the expanding system of dividing particles, would we, at a certain point, get a picture of the Cosmos which is familiar to us? We may depict, in broad lines, the following development:

1. First, the quantitative relationship between the particles of matter and the particles of radiation are described by Einstein's formula $E=MC^2$: what the particles of matter *lose* in mass, the particles of

radiation *gain* in energy. The ever-increasing number of radiation particles is, therefore, the dynamic and dominant factor in the Cosmos. *I repeat my speculation that this might explain the recently discovered ever-increasing acceleration of the expansion of the cosmic system—as per Newton's Third Law. As ever more particles are constantly splitting into evermore smaller particles, a larger amount of energy is being released, thereby increasing the speed of the expansion of the system. Nessyahu died before this increasing acceleration was discovered.*

2. Most matter does not form organization, and most radiation diffuses. The result is the general expansion of the system and the occurrence of "interstellar matter" or "cosmic dust" within the system (*once again, "dark matter" perhaps being just an infinitesimally smaller form of cosmic dust*). This is the cosmic "stage" upon which the entire cosmic drama is played out.

3. Cosmic organization is produced by the reciprocal activity between a small proportion of matter and a small proportion of radiation—those particles of matter and radiation which happen to make contact. Upon contact with matter, particles of radiation lose their energy of movement at the speed of light and change into electric binding energy which maintains the organization of matter and radiation. The dissolution of that organization liberates the electric *binding energy* and changes it back into radiation energy.

4. Cosmic organization has two basic stages:

   a) The primary stage, with which we are not and cannot be conversant firsthand but can only speculate about mathematically and logically. This stage is characterized by compressed concentration in the large and small scale (the beginning; the singularity).

   b) This compressed concentration (or singularity) represents the natural resource out of which the second stage of the Cosmos, with which we are familiar, develops. This is the stage of atomic and sub-atomic elements in the small scale and of galaxies in the large scale. Both are created as a result of the dissolution of the primary stage. Dissolution is an inevitable result of the continuing fundamental process of matter transforming into radiation. Paradoxically, the organization process is, by its very character, one of dissolution—a supernova destroys the organization of a star, thus creating a reorganization of atoms into heavy elements. Even though the lifetime of the Cosmos is very great—as long as the cosmic process itself—cosmic organization is transitory because of the character of the fundamental process of ongoing dissolution (entropy).

5. We speculate that the singularity is a cluster formed by infinite Nature's fundamental process of the reciprocal activity between a small proportion of matter and a small proportion of radiation—those particles of matter and radiation which happen to make contact; a process copied, repeated, and mirrored in our finite Cosmos.

6. The concentration referred to in 4a) constitutes the principal organization of the Cosmos. This level of organization manifests itself in different degrees depending on the different places and times of the various concentrations within the expanding system. *I speculate that the ongoing fundamental process of the Cosmos continues to produce singularities, just as the ongoing fundamental process of infinite nature produced the original singularity that gave birth to our Cosmos. Thus, we may conclude that our Cosmos is a consequence of a multiplicity of big bangs that have produced a multiplicity of what we might call sub-cosmoses. These sub-cosmoses are of different ages and as such, might explain the incongruity of us being able to discern galactic systems that appear older than our "Cosmos" when what we are seeing are galactic systems created by an older sub-cosmos (our "Cosmos" being in actuality a very large neighborhood of a more extensive finite Cosmos).*

7. Whatever their present level of organization (or age), all the concentrations continuously expand as part of the fundamental continuous process of the division of particles and the expansion of the system. Once again, this conforms to Newton's Third Law of Thermodynamics ("For every action, there is an equal and opposite reaction"). The division of the particles is the action; the expansion of the system is the reaction (the so-called "dark energy").

8. It could be that primary stages of organization still exist and are organizing themselves in various places *within* our cosmic system. This would explain the different ages of different sub-cosmoses and lead us to conclude that there have been multiple big bangs. But the cosmic picture with which we are acquainted shows that an overwhelming number of these concentrations have already trans-

formed into the second stage of organization: that of atomic and sub-atomic elements and reactions on the small scale and star systems (galaxies and solar systems) on the large scale. This secondary stage of organization increases the diversity of the fundamental unity that characterizes the all-inclusive cosmic evolution without contradicting this unity. *My question is: are black holes representative of these primary organizations? Mini-singularities as it were?*

9. The second stage of organization is a result and a part of the process of the dissolution of the primary stage of organization. This process dismantles the concentrations into star systems; constructs atomic elements and liberates part of the binding energy which sustains the organization of the concentrations. This is the process revealed to us by our telescopes and microscopes.

10. The process of the transformation of hydrogen into helium, in the small scale, and the process of the creation of galaxies and stellar systems in the large scale, are what characterize this second stage of cosmic development. Preceding that observable process in cosmic history is the first stage of the primary organization and behind both stages is the basic process of infinite Nature: of matter transforming into radiation which created our Cosmos, which is but a product of the reciprocal activity between an insignificant proportion of infinite nature's matter and an insignificant proportion of infinite nature's radiation: i.e., those particles of matter and radiation which happened to make contact and created the particular singularity (or singularities) which evolved into our particular Cosmos. Indeed, it is this basic continuous process which creates the primary stage of organization, disintegrates it, and on the basis of this creates the secondary stage of organization. The "beginning" and the "end," and the "small" and the "large" are suffused within the quantitative process of the transformation of matter into radiation. **But all that occurs between the "beginning" and the "end" as well as the "small" and the "large"** *creates a new cosmic quality.* **This new "quality," amongst other things, eventually creates life, which eventually (obviously) has created self-reflecting consciousness.**

11. The underlying law of the Cosmos is the law of particles. The dividing of the particles, the differences between the particles, and the reciprocal activity of the particles is, in fact, what molds the

entire system. The system expands as a result of the sum total of the dividing particles. The large reflects the small. In the sub-systems of the Cosmos (galaxies, solar systems, etc.) the situation is different. Here there is a reciprocal influence between the large and the small. It is not only large-scale occurrence which reflects small-scale occurrence but also the opposite. It is not only the various particle combinations which mold the star systems, but also the star systems which create and mold the particle combinations (*eventually producing those complex elements that eventually enabled the emergence of life, which, in turn, eventually enabled the emergence of self-reflective consciousness*).

12. The difference between the system and its sub-systems is of decisive importance in regard to the next stage of cosmic organization; that of the complex molecular-cellular organization of life. Here the existence and development of the systems (the species) are primary while the particles (cells) and the parts (bodies) are provisional. But as we've said, it is the organization which is temporary vis-à-vis the Cosmos as a whole (every organization eventually "disorganizes"), while the process of the transformation of matter into radiation is *constant* within the cosmic domain.

13. There have been two competing cosmological theories that have tried to explain the Cosmos. The development theory (from the "Big Bang" to total expansion – now the accepted standard model) and the "Steady State" theory (the "continuous creation" of elements and galaxies within an inclusive stable structure—now rejected by scientific consensus). Both theories have lacked the four central elements of our conception:

a) Neither distinguishes between the *Cosmos*, as a *finite* domain-process which is an expanding system of dividing particles, and *infinite Nature*.

b) Neither identifies the basic process of the Cosmos—the transformation of matter into radiation—as a part of and as a result of this distinction between the finite and the infinite.

c) Neither distinguishes between two stages of organization: the *secondary organization* which is created out of the inevitable dissolution of the *primary organization*, as a result of the process of the transformation of matter into radiation.

d) Neither sufficiently explains the proliferation of concentrations of organization (galaxies) which eventually disintegrate as part and parcel of the fundamental domain-process described above.

There is no "continuous creation" of elements and galaxies, and there is no one "Big Bang." There is a "continuous creation" of radiation from matter and there are many "Big Bangs": the upheavals of the concentrations of primary organization (the dissolution of their organization which created the galaxies as we know them). There is one source and one framework for all the concentrations and all the expanding galaxies: that is the expanding system of particles of matter which radiate particles of radiation. *We might reasonably conclude, therefore, that infinite Nature is steady state (producing singularities ad infinitum) while our Cosmos is a product of one of these singularities which resulted in our Big Bang.* There are, of course, many phenomena in both the large and the small scale which are not directly explained by the broad cosmic approach presented here. But the fundamental facts and conceptions are incorporated and explained by this approach. This explanation's major liability is that it still does not yet have a mathematical expression. The new physics and cosmology are circumscribed by the mathematics which arose on the background of the conceptions of classical physics. This mathematics has been inadequate in explaining the qualitative change inherent in an evolutionary cosmos—it can only describe quantitative change. (*Re: "the Limits of Mathematics" described above*)

If there is a "cosmic formula" it is not "all is matter" as was thought in the nineteenth century, nor is it "all is field" as Einstein thought. It certainly isn't "all is water" as Thales thought. **"All"—within the finite domain of the Cosmos—is the process of matter transforming into radiation.** This definition corresponds in principle with the mathematical equation of Einstein concerning the relativity of Mass to Energy. It diverges, however, from classical mathematical concepts concerning the relativity of time-space continuity. It moves beyond them towards non-continuous physical relations that necessitate new mathematical concepts of matter and radiation. Mass and energy are mathematical concepts which reflect the conceptual system of classical physics. In the proposition presented here, matter and radiation are real entities that find only limited mathematical expression, within the statistical probabilities-framework of classical physical mathematical conceptions. Cosmological theories emerging from astrophysical experience require a new mathematical language. Cosmology must of necessity create its own mathematics, *or perhaps a distinctive explanatory language other than mathematics.* Until now, mathematics has only been able to describe quantitative change and movement. *But life and evolution are characterized by qualitative change and the evolutionary cosmic change described above is certainly qualitative. Thus, the language of mathematics might prove to be inherently inadequate to the task of describing cosmic evolution—that is unless it can create a new qualitative iteration of mathematical language.*

Chapter Sixteen: Society, Economy, and Science

There is no essential contradiction between working for the physical existence of humanity and working for the spiritual elevation of humanity. Indeed, working for the spiritual elevation of humanity might be the only way to guarantee the future physical existence of humanity. Economic Society has required humanity, throughout all of its history, to devote most of its time, strength, and effort towards assuring its very physical existence. With that, humanity's existence in general has never seriously been in question. During this period only a very small number of human beings have succeeded in devoting most of lives towards the spiritual elevation of the human race.

The dangers facing humanity today, however, threaten our continued existence. This survival challenge indicates the need for a solution dedicated to the elevation of the human race—an ascent to a new social and biological stage, *to a higher human or perhaps supra-human stage,* as a necessary prerequisite for our continued survival. Economic Society was a fundamental stage for the survival of the human animal. Now Scientific Society is becoming necessary (although insufficient in itself) to the ascent of the human race and thus to the very possibility of our survival. What are the differences between the existence of human beings in the Economic Society and the elevation of human beings in the Scientific Society?

a) In the Economic Society humans are enslaved to the geographical environment of the Earth's crust. In the Scientific society humanity will to a great extent become able to liberate itself from that narrow environment and become part of the cosmic environment.

b) In the Economic Society, humans sustain themselves on the limited resources of the external manifestations of organic and inorganic planetary nature which are produced by agriculture, craft, commerce, and industry. In the Scientific Society, humanity's sustenance will be assured by the almost limitless resources of the internal manifestations of the physical processes of the Cosmos which are revealed and exploited by the natural sciences in league with the most sophisticated technology.

c) In the Economic Society, humanity devotes itself mostly to assuring its physical existence; mainly by material means of production. In the Scientific Society, humanity will devote itself mostly to researching the Cosmos and life and in elevating itself by way of its active confrontation with the border between life and the material Cosmos.

The Economic Society is nothing more than the last stage of the physical development of the life system, the entire effort of which has been to assure its very physical existence within the limited framework of the Earth's crust within our solar system. The Economic Society has characterized most human development. *Humanity's spiritual product has either been in the service of physical wellbeing (science, technology, innovation, and entrepreneurship) or to a great extent dependent on an economic superstructure that enabled it to exist (art, literature, religion etc.).* We should perceive the Scientific Society as enabling the spiritual development of humanity becoming our predominant concern; with economic activity increasingly becoming the servant of this spiritual development. Human civilization's entire effort will come to be participation in the unconventional "race for life" which we postulate is already taking place throughout the Cosmos.

Human life differs from the life system in general because it has been active, and of late proactive, in changing its environment and developing productive and creative means to assure physical existence, while all other life on the planet passively makes do with what the environment provides. (*Science developed primarily as an instrument of economy. The Scientific Revolution was to a large extent a consequence of the requirements of commercial society. Gresham College, the forerunner of the Royal Society, was founded by the London merchant Sir Thomas Gresham, who realized that knowledge was power and power led to profit.*)

The transition from the Economic Society to the Scientific Society means converting the economy primarily into an instrument of science. Instead of science being the handmaiden of economic activity, economic activity will become the handmaiden of science. This transition will only be possible when science is able to ensure the physical existence of society, without society having to dedicate its principal labors to the ensuring of physical existence. *In other words, when all of humanity is liberated from drudge work and the need to "make a living," the vast preponderance of humanity's exertions will be dedicated to creative "work" in science, art, and technology. This creative work must include innovative, entrepreneurial activity in those economic aspects of life which must continue as long as we continue to be physical beings within organized societies dedicated to enhancing and uplifting our physical existence.* The transition from the Economic Society, in which a majority of people are simply ensuring their physical existence, to the Scientific Society, in which a majority of people are engaged in science and cultural-spiritual-entrepreneurial creativity (their physical existence having been guaranteed by science), is not only a question of choice or preference. While it is proper to choose and prefer that transition, since it emphasizes the elevation of humanity and the preeminence of the human spirit, the evolution from the concentration of human effort on economy to the concentration of human effort on science is a vital necessity for the most minimal possibility of the continued existence and development of our presently earthbound conscious life in the Cosmos. This would be a volitional, self-conceived, and self-directed evolution of the human race.

The current Scientific Revolution has developed in such a way that the dangers it currently presents are often greater than the solutions it offers. It might be the case that most of the quantitative investment in the conventional development of the Economic Society, which is beyond the minimum necessary for current sustenance, will be wasteful—similar to pouring money down a bottomless drain. Only a revolutionary qualitative investment in the unconventional advancement of the Scientific Revolution; only the rapid development of the Scientific Society parallel to, within, and in the course of time, instead of the Economic Society, may hasten the solutions before the actualization of the dangers. The path from the Economic Society to the Scientific Society may be long and difficult, due to vested interests and the habit of routine thinking in economic and scientific affairs and in human society in general. Because of these, the Scientific Society may be implemented too late. Nonetheless, the path can be made easier and shorter if led by a great vision; one which has the power to help humanity overcome its deficiencies. *We suggest that Cosmodeism can be that vision.*

Pragmatic Messianism

The process of transition from the Economic Society to the Scientific Society is difficult and complicated. But we have no choice. The implementation of this transition is the pragmatic-messianic challenge now facing humanity; that is if we really do desire life. It is a messianic challenge because it is utopianist, revolutionary, far-reaching, elevated, and profound—more than any other technological-scientific or socio-political challenge which humankind has known in history. The Manhattan and Space projects, in the scientific-technological domain, and the "New Deal" and "New Frontiers," in the socio-political domain (if we wish to use American examples), are inconsequential compared to the challenges of this new Scientific Revolution and the transition from the Economic Society to the Scientific Society. It is a pragmatic challenge because it does not entail the destructive power of weapons (themselves products of science) or the turmoil of social revolutions. It is a great practical challenge which requires vision and planning. It requires tremendous resources and great efforts. It requires cooperation and coordination between every scientific and social field and the inclusion of every nation and ethnic group on earth.

Historical experience shows that fanatic messianism, whether it be religious or secular, is appallingly dangerous. The dangers result from a lack of consideration for human weakness and human rights. On the other hand, pure pragmatism, which shies away from confrontation with fundamental, long range, problems, does not have the staying power to overcome the dangers and solve the fateful problems facing the human race as we move further into the 21st century. Only a combination of and a balance between messianism and pragmatism has the power to transport humankind over the chasm, to a new stage in the development of life in the Cosmos that will avert the danger of self-destruction—"the way of all flesh!" The transition from the Economic to the Scientific Society may be a fateful turning point. Not only in human society, but in the evolution of life itself: an evolution which will lead us from bodily life to spiritual life. *This evolution may integrate post-human (supra-human) life into the universal process of embedding conscious life into the very fabric of the entire Cosmos.*

Chapter Seventeen: The Transformation of the Object into Subject

The relationship between the "knower" and "what is known" is, in its various formulations, one of the most fundamental problems of philosophy. According to Spinoza "what is [to be] known" is infinite Nature which is identical to infinite God (the "substance"); Nature-God has an infinite number of adjectives. Only two—the adjective of expansion and the adjective of thought—are ascertainable by the "knower." According to Kant "what is [truly] known" is "[only] the thing in itself" (the ultimate reality of a thing); BUT this "thing in itself" can never be can never be truly known by the "knower." Only the "phenomena" (the external observable behaviors and *measurable* facts) of "the thing in itself" can be known by the "knower." The unity of one's experience does not derive from the unity of "what is known"—which cannot be ascertained; but rather from the unity of the mind of the "knower," by means of Kant's famous 12 categories: unity, plurality, and totality *for concept of quantity*; reality, negation, and limitation, *for the concept of quality*; inherence and subsistence, cause and effect, and community *for the concept of relation*; and the concepts possibility-impossibility, existence-nonexistence, necessity-contingency.

In other words, according to Kant (and others), "observable" unity is actually a subjective creation of our mind putting order on what we see in order to function in a rational way. This unity is in no way a unity of "the thing in itself" but rather a creation of the human mind—in postmodern terminology it is a construction (a construct) of our mind not wholly reflective of objective truth or facticity. Following are three additional conjectures based on this cosmological perspective:

a) The province of consciousness is to be found in finite domains. The largest of these *accessible* finite domains, in both the large and small scale, is the Cosmos. The limits of consciousness, however, are not to be found either in the "substance" or in "the thing in itself" but rather in the very infinitude of Nature; it is infinity itself which limits our ability to know. Within the *finite* domain of the Cosmos, however, there is no ultimate deterrent to the possible unity of the "knower" and "what is known." Understanding this enables a return to classical scientific thinking (let us call it neo-classical) in that the bounded finite domain is, indeed (in opposition to Kant), a knowable object to a thinking subject.

b) Expansion is a fundamental characteristic of the Cosmos. Thought is a fundamental characteristic of human life. But expansion and thought are not identical (just as there is no reason to suppose that Nature and God are identical or that the Cosmos and God are identical). Spinoza's pantheistic approach lacked the dynamic dimension of time and change. Thought is a recent development of cosmic evolution. If thought teaches itself how to survive (as probability indicates it can when speaking from a cosmic perspective) while faced with the continuing expansion of the Cosmos, and to impress its own likeness upon the Cosmos; and if "God" is understood to mean a universal, spiritual being—we may then say that the Cosmos is destined to transform itself into "God." And then the unity of the "knower" and "what is known" will finally be realized.

c) The unity of scientific experimentation does not derive from the unity of a knowing consciousness, but rather from the unity of reality itself—the basic unity of the Cosmos. Kant's categories of how we understand things are supposed to make unity of the consciousness possible but are themselves a clear proof of consciousness being dependent on experience which is really a *reflection* of reality, and not "reality itself." These are all derived from the concepts of classical science. But these classical concepts have been transformed by modern science. This transformation transpired on the heels of experimentation which broke through to a new domain in both the large and small scale and yet has not led to a new unity: the famous, as yet unperceived, "theory of everything" which will unite gravitation, quantum and relativity. The cosmological concepts which lead to the new unity will be fundamentally different from the classical concepts; they will derive from cosmic reality itself (as well as reflect it).

All the efforts of the various philosophical schools to present the Cosmos as reflecting a subjective (human) or objective (God) consciousness have failed to lead anywhere. There is no proof of a consciousness external to nature or the cosmic domain, and no proof of one which is independent of the Cosmos and its process of development (no transcendent, supernatural being or force). Consciousness reflects the Cosmos. But it also appears that consciousness has a stronger actual and potential hold on the Cosmos then was previously thought by any of the conventional materialist approaches. By means of subjective consciousness, the aggregate of conscious beings in the Cosmos, the Cosmos is destined to know itself and its environment; and to transform itself from a "dead" object—lacking awareness of itself; to a "live" subject—possessed of a universal consciousness; into what we might call "God."

The limits of conventional thought are manifest precisely in the two most universal minds which determined the shape of the 20th century: Karl Marx and Albert Einstein. The summits of their thought derived from the prevailing developments of 19th-century concepts. The limits of their thought were also rooted in 19th-century concepts, even as these concepts gave birth to the 20th century. We require concepts suitable to the 21st century and beyond. The concepts of Marxism are rooted fundamentally in the naturalistic conception of the perpetual motion of matter, the conception of life as a matter exchange system, the conception of human history as the development of material means of production, and the conception of society as an economic society. The solutions Marx offered did not go beyond that set of concepts, indeed they could not have gone beyond them. The tremendous revolutionary power of consciousness as a radiation exchange system within the life system, the special value of spiritual creativity in human history, and the possible transition from an economic society to a scientific society, are all beyond the limitations of Marxist thought. *It is rather pathetic that so many apparently intelligent people still adhere to this great thinker's intellectual frame of reference and are respected for it in academe. This is nothing more than a repetition of the university men attacking Galileo in defense of Aristotle and reflects, more than anything, the crisis of academe described in a previous chapter. Imagine if in the physics departments people still adhered to the subsequently revealed inadequate thinking of Newton, while ignoring the breakthroughs of Relativity and Quantum. Would anyone take them seriously?*

Einstein, more than anyone else, contributed towards the possibility of going beyond the limits of the physics he had inherited. He did not stray from the borders of mechanistic physics, but he stretched their limits to the greatest possible extent, making possible some of the greatest breakthroughs that followed. Achieving the unity of mass and energy and of space and time, and unsuccessfully aspiring to a unity between the electromagnetic field and the gravitational field ("all is field"), did not lead him beyond the mechanistic physical conception of continuous motion. He even opened the door to the discontinuous (the quantum) but did not discern the discontinuous processes of organization and disorganization of matter and radiation in the Cosmos, nor to their roots which is the process of the transformation of matter into radiation, which is simultaneously continuous and discontinuous.

Human society needs a "new Marx" and a "new Einstein," who will complement one another. This is because the productive-technological application of the process of the transformation of matter into radiation and the passage from the Economic Society to the Scientific Society are conditional on and condition one another. These interdependent processes—of the human exploitation of the cosmic transformation of matter into radiation, and of the transition from the Economic Society to the Scientific Society—may make possible a "new Darwin." Not as a discoverer of the origins of humankind, but as a guide for the future of humankind. *Darwin was a historian of nature; the "new Darwin" must be a futurist of nature.*

As long as there was no scientific, biochemical, or biophysical explanation for spiritual phenomenon, thinking on the matter tended towards various distinctions between "matter" and "spirit." On the other hand, all those who accepted a "material" basis for "spirit" related to "preservation of the soul" or to the idea of "God" (as a transcendent universal, all-inclusive entity) did so in opposition to supernatural explanations—i.e., argued for it on the basis of known natural law or speculations about future discoveries in natural law. *We envision a new cosmological/biological law, which will provide an opportunity for preserving the "spirit" of humanity, as immortal conscious life. In doing so, it will provide the scientific framework for the creation of "God" as a universal spiritual entity which will, in effect, be the sum total of conscious beings throughout the Cosmos; those that will have achieved immortal conscious life and which will have, together, impressed their image upon the Cosmos as a product of the natural selection of those selfsame planetary civilizations. This will not, of course, be a "spirit" which will be separate from "matter." It will occur as a result of the inexorable development of the Cosmos and life (life as represented by conscious life forms, hopefully including our own distant descendants). If our earthborn human race will succeed in ascending to immortal conscious life by adapting to the cosmic environment, it will, of necessity, be part of the same "race for life" which is occurring in many places in the Cosmos. It will be part of the universal process which is changing the cosmic object into a living subject, aware of and in control of itself. This will be the artificial-natural process of the Cosmos transforming into "God." Thus, "God" will be the aim and not the cause; in the future and not in the past; "in the end was created" and not "in the beginning created"; the creation of Man and not the creator of Man. It will not merely be a figment of human imagination, but will exist, in practice, as the crowning point of conscious life in the Cosmos.*

Physics and Metaphysics

This is not the pantheistic "God" of Spinoza. It is not a "God" which is identical to Nature, but a "God" which is created by Nature. It is not a Metaphysics which is identical to Physics, but a Physics which achieves a Metaphysical vision within a certain finite domain within infinite Nature. It is not a religion which is identical with science, but a science which realizes certain aspirations of religion (*realizing Sagan's dream*). Einstein was a follower of Spinoza's philosophical approach. This was not coincidental. Both Spinoza and Einstein believed in the basic unity of Nature and in the ability of consciousness to identify that unity. Einstein identified the unity of Space and Time, Mass and Energy, and Matter and Field. Geometry was his common language with Spinoza. We postulate not the identity of matter and radiation but the transformation of matter into radiation; and not the identity of expansion and thought, but expansion which transforms into thought.

"Spirit" is to be found *potentially* in "matter"; *a spiritual* $E=MC^2$ (*see references to panpsychism below*). The cosmic process not only leads from matter to radiation but also from "matter" (the flesh of life) to "spirit" (flesh eventually giving birth to consciousness). There is no reason to assume the preexistence of spirit, but there is the possibility of achieving the superiority of the spirit. Such an achievement will be the volitional choice of conscious life and will occur incrementally—in society, in life, and in the Cosmos. It will depend on our creating the Scientific Society, which will eventually create "immortal" conscious life, and eventually "God." "Spirit," in its various manifestations—mythological, religious, philosophical, scientific, ideological, and cultural—is nothing more than an inclusive, reflecting and creating expression of the subject relating to the object, to itself, and to the relationship between itself and the object, as a sum total of the extant material Cosmos in its various manifestations.

The objective cosmic process is the transformation of matter into radiation. But to the extent that the subjective "spirit" of all humankind, as manifested in all the scientific societies within the Cosmos, succeeds in impressing its subjective vision upon the Cosmos, it will transform into a transcendent, universal, all-inclusive spiritual entity: that is into "God." The cosmic object will transform into a "godly" subject. For if the cause of "everything," within the finite domain of the Cosmos, is the transformation of matter into radiation, then the aim of "everything," within the same finite domain, is the transformation of the Cosmos into "God."

Monotheism represents the highpoint of faith and religious thought that developed in the ancient world. Instead of a long list of gods with or without bodily forms, which were all identified with a specific part of nature or society, Monotheism postulated the one and only God, which was a universal spiritual being and which created both Cosmos and humanity. Instead of a material god, Monotheism postulated a spiritual God. Instead of the animistic approach, in which various objects were moved by various internal subjects, or the paganist approach, in which different objects were moved by different external subjects, Monotheism postulated that a general unified object—the Cosmos—was moved by an external general unified subject, i.e., by God. Monotheism incorporated three major visions:

a) The vision of God as a universal spiritual being, i.e., the superiority of the spirit within the framework of universal, cosmic, and human entities.

b) The vision of the "preservation of the soul," i.e., the possibility of eternalizing the spirit or, in other words, the sustaining of immortal conscious life.

c) The messianic vision of the universal redemption of humankind in the "end of days."

When viewed from the religious worldview of the ancient world, these three visions were bestowed with supernatural qualities. They were spiritual explanations which were seen as an alternative to material explanations or resulting from a lack of understanding of the material world which precluded material explanations. The scientific worldview of modern times offers us the possibility of achieving the visions of Monotheism, the dreams of religion (in a natural way), using the tools of science. Cosmodeism, as depicted by the cosmological model and the biological conjectures above, postulates the Cosmos transforming itself into "Godness" as the crowning point of its development—as the fulfillment of the subjective spiritual potential inherent in it through the medium of conscious life; that those aggregates of conscious lifeforms throughout the Cosmos, which will have succeeded in becoming scientific societies, enabling immortal conscious life, will create "God" in its own image. The Cosmos is destined to transform into a universal spiritual being. This will occur when the cosmic object changes into a living subject aware of itself and its environment. This will be the end result of the bodily and spiritual development of life affixing its image upon the Cosmos.

It is not to be assumed that all the finite cosmoses of infinite Nature will create "God." Just as not all solar systems create life, and not all life systems create human consciousness, and not all humanlike societies are capable of achieving that scientific society which would enable the possibility of immortal conscious life. But the immense dimensions of cosmic existence indicate a very high probability that this process is already taking place in our finite Cosmos and most assuredly somewhere in the infinite Universe. The three visions of Monotheism can be achieved, not as an alternative to "matter," but rather by discerning the hidden potential within "matter."

a) The realization of God not as the creator of the Cosmos and man, but as created by man (first in man's imagination, and then by man participating in an act of volitional "Genesis"). This will be achieved by implementing the spiritual potential inherent in the Cosmos in the form of conscious life.

b) The realization of the "preservation of the soul" by scientific-technological means enabling the preservation of the conscious part of the human brain independent of the body.

c) The realization of the messianic vision concerning the universal development of humankind. Such an achievement will prevent the total destruction of human society by raising it to a new stage of development made possible by the passage from the Economic Society to the Scientific Society.

The great dreams of religion, encapsulated in Monotheism, can be realized by Cosmodeism through the agency of science. There are two roads humankind must travel in order to redeem itself from destruction. The first leads to the physical source, to the process of matter transforming into radiation. The second leads to the spiritual apex, to the process of the Cosmos transforming into "God." The two cannot be separated. Only by traveling both paths at once can we succeed in redeeming humankind from destruction by way of participation in an act of "genesis." The process which creates the Cosmos is the same process which eventually creates "God."

Conclusion to Part IV: How Do Nessyahu's Conjectures Save the Phenomena?

The standard for judging a hypothesis is how well it coherently explains the *observed* phenomena, not how well it conforms to the logical grammar of mathematics or how well it explains away the anomalies of mathematical explanations of physical phenomena. Nessyahu's conjectures explain the clumpiness of the finite cosmos as it evolved out of an infinite universe. Since the process of matter into radiation and radiation colliding with matter and other radiation to create new radiation and new matter is an infinite process it creates an infinite number of aggregated finite clusters which when in proximity associate into a finite system (or order or cosmos—a system being a finite order by definition). The reaction to the action of the splitting particles reflects Newton's 3rd law of motion and provides an alternative means/explanation of enabling the clusters to hold together without the addition of "dark matter" to explain the necessary gravity to hold them together. Or, alternatively, the constant splitting of particles into ever infinitesimally smaller particles that are incapable of reflecting light (hence "dark") Perceiving the splitting particles as ongoing, continuing and *ever-increasing* explosions explains the expansion of the Cosmos without mysterious "dark energy."

These clusters not only interact with one another within the greater cosmic system, they have their own internal, autonomous existence. This is analogous to the autonomous internal life of the galaxies within these clusters, as it is with the sub-clusters (star systems) within the galaxies, as it is with the various solar systems. These clusters aggregate at different rates of time and thus some are relatively young and others are extremely old. Once these clusters reach a certain density (singularity) they explode (a big bang). Each cluster produces its own big bang. This is a reflection of Nessyahu's conjecture that there have been numerous big bangs that have created our Cosmos. Since these clusters have formed at different rates they exploded at different times and thus these sub-cosmoses are of radically different ages. This would explain the apparent contradiction between the "young" age of our sub-cosmos and the much greater age of many of the observed galaxies and galactic clusters within the greater Cosmos. In other words, our big bang occurred within a gigantic, preexisting cluster as a contributor to the expansion of that cluster which itself is a contributor to the expansion of the Cosmos. This would explain the apparent contradiction between the estimated age of our "sub-cosmos" (15–20 billion years) and galactic structures that must be 60–70 billion years of age in order to have formed which we see at the extreme borders of our observed physical Cosmos. In other words, current Big Bang theory is subsumed within the much grander theory of Nessyahu and satisfies the criticisms that the advocates of plasma physics cosmology have for Big Bang cosmology. Nessyahu's theory implies that even our "finite" Cosmos (within infinite nature) is much vaster, by several degrees of vastness, than has been previously conceived. It implies numerous (but not infinite) big bangs in the history of our finite macro-cosmos.

Our macro-cosmos is a product of this same process within infinite nature. The "birth" of our macro-cosmos was a consequence of various aggregates in infinite nature exploding and interacting with one another and forming ever greater aggregates, which like mega-black holes sucked in more of infinite nature's detritus until its mass and gravity began to turn it into a self-organizing autonomous finite system within infinite nature, which may have its own variations of general physical law. Nessyahu's theory reflects the observable phenomena of both plasma physics cosmology and Big Bang cosmology. If the universe is infinite in time and space, it is inevitable that "eventually" it would have produced a system with those evolutionary variations of general physical law and those physical structures that would have produced a cosmos, that created galaxies, that created solar systems, that created planets, that created life, that created conscious life. Infinity, by definition, must create infinite possibilities. This interpretation silences the statistical criticisms of evolution (those that say the Cosmos is not old enough to have created the building blocks of life, let alone complex life), as well as those who claim that all the delicate relationships that enable our Cosmos to exist are so statistically far-fetched as to have happened without planning. First of all, they are relating to the age of our sub-cosmos and not the Cosmos as such; secondly infinite nature—being infinite—is omnipotent and can do whatever it wants—such as create a cosmos like our own which has produced life. Being infinite in space and time, it is unavoidable that cosmoses like our own (capable of producing life) will have already been created.

Our Cosmos (formed by the infinite process of infinite nature) is just another bounded aggregate containing numerous sub-aggregates formed in the same way as galaxies. Our sub-cosmos is to the Cosmos what our solar system is to the galaxy (or clusters of solar systems), all with different ages. By judging the age of our cosmos by the age of our sub-cosmos, it is as if we are judging the age of our galaxy by the age of our solar system. The interdependence of all life on this planet is but a reflection of the interdependence of all the physical systems in the universe. In fact, evolution on this planet is not completely autonomous, but also a result of interaction with various aggregates and phenomena in the Cosmos. As Dyson advocates in *Infinite in All Directions*, there must eventually be a joining of biology to cosmology.

Other Challengers to the Standard Cosmological Model

Nessyahu and I are in no way eccentric outliers in perceiving the inadequacies of the current standard Big Bang Cosmos presented as absolute fact on scores of popular TV science channels. Not a few distinguished scientists have been pointing out its flaws both in mainstream peer-reviewed journals and in serious non-mainstream journals. We are not talking about wild-eyed quacks that propagate rubbish about ancient aliens on the History Channel; we are talking about serious people with serious careers that have themselves made predictions contradicting accepted cosmological tenets that eventually have proven to be accurate. Astrophysicist Tom Van Flandern concludes his trenchant critique of the Big Bang Cosmos entitled *The Top 30 Problems with the Big Bang Theory*[2] with:

> Perhaps never in the history of science has so much quality evidence accumulated against a model so widely accepted within a field. Even the most basic elements of the theory, the expansion of the universe and the fireball remnant radiation, remain interpretations with credible alternative explanations. One must wonder why, in this circumstance, that four good alternative models are not even being comparatively discussed by most astronomers.

The four models he is referring to are the:

1.   Quasi-Steady-State model[3]
2.   Plasma Cosmology model[4]
3.   Meta Cosmology model[5]
4.   Variable-Mass Cosmology model.[6]

Astronomer Fred Hoyle, astrophysicist Geoffrey Burbidge, and astrophysicist J.V. Narlikar—all giants in their fields—advocated for the *Quasi-Steady-State model.* Nobel Prize winning physicist Hannes Alfven proposed the *Plasma Cosmology model* (which was made known to the general public by Eric Lerner in his book *The Big Bang Never Happened.*) The *Meta Cosmology model* is Van Flandern's preferred model, and J.V. Narlikar (along with American astronomer Halton Arp) appears again in regard to the *Variable-Mass Cosmology model.* What all four of these alternatives have in common is their displeasure with the continuing addition of adjustable parameters (dark matter and energy) to make the Big Bang theory work. It reminds one of the never-ending additions of epicycles to make Ptolemy's model of the Universe work until it was finally destroyed by Copernicus and Galileo. For these thinkers, the Big Bang simply requires too many adjustable parameters to make it work, while the prediction successes of these alternative theories are equal or superior to the Big Bang theory. The non-empirical (until now completely unproven) concepts of "dark matter" and "dark energy" also disturb their sense of scientific rigor. In his paper "Alternatives to Dark Matter,"[7] Israeli physicist Mordechai Milgrom presents his concept of MOND (Modified Newtonian Dynamics), which all but eliminates the need for dark matter to explain what dark matter presumes to explain. In recent years, dozens, if not hundreds, of papers by reputable scientists in serious peer-reviewed journals have been challenging this or that aspect of the Big Bang Hypothesis. They all reflect my puzzlement at the Dark Matter Hypothesis and several reflect Nessyahu's conjectures about the infinity of existence. Indeed, Van Flandern claims that "we can now also show that the simplest cosmology, founded on *infinite eternal space* (italics mine), explains and solves these problems of cosmology relating to the Big Bang theory."[8]

Some critics of the Big Bang theory are more polemical than others. For example, according to Eric Lerner, Alfven had concluded that since it is without empirical support, "the Big Bang is a myth, a wonderful myth maybe, which deserves a place of honor in the columbarium which already contains the Indian myth of a cyclic Universe, the Chinese cosmic egg, the Biblical myth of creation in six days, the Ptolemaic cosmological myth, and many others."[9] Lerner's outlook is especially attractive to me as he rejects cosmic pessimism and perceives that human society is capable of resolving the energy/environment conundrum and sees no limits to the growth of life. He also hints at a neo-teleological view of the general direction of evolution towards ever growing complexity when he writes:

... the idea that the evolution of humankind is purely an accident, divinely engineered or otherwise, ignores the vast mass of evidence that there are long-term trends in biological evolution. Over these millions of years there has been an irregular but unmistakable tendency toward adaptability to a greater range of environments, culminating in human adaptation to virtually any environment. Over this period, the intelligence of the most developed animals on earth has risen with increasing speed, from trilobites, to fish, to amphibians, to the dinosaurs, to mammals, to primates, to the hominid apes and the direct ancestors of humankind.[10]

He concludes this line of thinking with his belief that our stage of the evolution of intelligence is but the latest phase, thus intimating that intelligence will continue to evolve since the general trend of evolution has increasingly become more specific (and not random) towards generating ever more intelligence at an ever-increasing rate of development. Needless to say, this kind of thinking would be most amenable to me. He will be referred to later in the chapter referring to scientific intimations.

These critics are not lonely contrarians. In 2004, Lerner wrote an open letter to the scientific community challenging its dogmatic hold on the research community and research budgets. It was signed by over 30 scientists, researchers, and academics.[11] Arguments against the Big Bang and for the Plasma Universe include:

1. Observed superclusters of galaxies 1,000,000,000 light years across which would have required 100 billion years to have formed, not the 14–16 billion years since the Big Bang.

2. "Over 99% of the matter in the universe is plasma—hot, electrically conducting gases,"[12] while according to the Big Bang theory, 90% of the universe is composed of dark matter and energy, which is something that has never been observed or measured or proven to exist. In other words, Plasma Cosmology is based on something that exists, is observable and measurable, while the Big Bang theory is based on mathematical inference.

Working empirically (that is to say inductively), plasma scientists extrapolate from empirical plasma evidence here on Earth—such as neon lights and microwave ovens—out to the Universe, much as Galileo did. Galileo did not assume that the Universe was composed of a 5th essence (the quintessence) not common to the earth, or that the heavenly bodies followed different laws than those of the Earth. He demystified the heavens, while Big Bang theorists, by positing creation out of nothing and the two "darks," have re-mystified the heavens. As we cannot create something from nothing on earth so we cannot do so for the Universe. Given the available evidence, we could easily say that dark matter is similar to the concept of a quintessence during Galileo's time and is an invented hypothesis, much like ether in the 19th century, to support a theory that is in fashion. Plasma cosmologists have arrived at "a universe that has always existed, is always evolving, and will always endure, *with no limits of any sort*"[13] (italics mine).

"No limits of any sort"—from inorganic to organic, from organic to life, from life to conscious life, from conscious life to spiritual life, from spiritual life to the ultimate Spirit—to God. Indeed, if the universe is infinite in time, we may conjecture that some cosmoses have already been created that are capable of giving birth to life and thus to us. I mention this, because advocates of intelligent design argue their case based on the fact that our Cosmos is so improbably delicately balanced in order to even have created life, let alone conscious life. Thus, according to a purely mechanistic point of view, it is self-evident that a greater supernatural intelligence had to design our Cosmos in order to enable us. But if the Universe is infinite in time and space, it is self-evidently true that it will have already created all possible worlds—to include the only possible world that could have enabled us to exist. Universal evolution has been experimenting for infinite time, until it has by evolutionary chance inevitably created our cosmos; suitable for us. Thus, the universal code has created our cosmic code, which has created the planet Earth, and us in order to further evolve until we have created godness. Existence is the infinite womb, slowly producing godness. Have the matriarchal religions of the past, worshipping female gods, intuited the "wombness" of existence?

Lerner marshals a great deal of empirical evidence to support plasma cosmology. Since the 17th century, we have known that the stars are suns like ours, not some mysterious quintessence. Almost 150 years ago galaxies with hundreds of billions of stars each were discovered. In the 1930s, observations showed that even galaxies are grouped together into classes, some containing 8,000 galaxies. In the 1970s, we discovered that these clusters are themselves but a part of superclusters containing dozens of these clusters—composing the "cosmic tapestry." Chaos theory predicts such self-organization, or what is called autopoiesis. The connection between chaos theory and plasma cosmology is intriguing, as both are based on rock solid empirical observation.

I believe that Lerner has demonstrated that Big Bang cosmology is nothing more than a temporary victory of speculative mathematics over empirical observation. The theoretical cosmologists have confused mathematics as the language of existence with mathematics as science—that what can be said mathematically must of necessity be empirically true. As already pointed out, the falseness of this assumption can best be described by the sentence "the Earth is flat." There is absolutely nothing grammatically wrong with this sentence. Its grammar is internally logical and coherent. Therefore, the earth must be flat. But we know the Earth is not flat, because we have actually *looked at it* rather than deduced it. Just as it is possible to say or write ridiculous things in spoken and written language that are grammatically correct in every aspect, so too can you present ridiculous things in mathematical language that are mathematically correct in every aspect. Lerner follows the path of his mentor Alfven and his mentor's mentor, Birkeland, who wrote "... the laboratory is a far better guide to the heavens than the authority of the most prestigious scientist." Similar to Galileo, they all extend their earthly experience to the skies and demystify cosmology.[14] In my opinion, the dispute between Plasma and Big Bang cosmology is really a philosophical dispute between apples and oranges. The big-bangers are dealing with their own sub-cosmic neighborhood, while Lerner is dealing with infinite existence as such.

Notes

1   Mills & Watson, p. 175.

2   Van Flandern, 2002.

3   Hoyle, Burbidge, & Narlikar, Chapter 9.

4   Lerner, 1991, pp. 23, 28.

5   Van Flandern, 1999.

6   Arp, 1998.

7   Milgrom, p. 215.

8   Von Flandern, 2002.

9   Lerner, 1991, p. 228.

10 Ibid., p. 401.

11 Lerner, 2004.

12 Lerner, 1991, p. 14.

13 Ibid.

14 Lerner, 1991, p. 180.

PART V

Non-Religious Intimations of the Cosmodeistic Hypothesis

Introduction

The Cosmodeistic Hypothesis, like other great ideas, was not a virgin birth. No human being is an intellectual island that floats in an ocean of ignorance. All thought is connected to that super-continent (that Pangaea) of thinking that gave birth to our intellectual ecology, which enables the evolution of all subsequent thinking, no matter how original. There is no Einstein without Maxwell, and a slew of others, just as there is no Nessyahu without Einstein, and a slew of others. The Cosmodeistic Hypothesis should be seen as a particular conclusion relating to humanity's innate longing to understand the meaning of its own existence since time immemorial. It relates to an all-inclusive perspective of the very meaning of the word "cosmology" which as defined by the *Mercer Dictionary of the Bible* is:

> ... a comprehensive view of all reality, attending to both the nature of the whole and also to the place *of all parts* within the whole. The origin, order, meaning, and *destiny* of *all that exists* are key issues in a cosmological system, as is also the question of what this "reality" in fact embraces.[1]

I am preoccupied with the italicized parts of this quote. For me the moral and spiritual insights of the conscious beings our Cosmos has created have equal claim to being considered existent factual parts of our Cosmos as much as black holes and electrons. As our finite Cosmos is a product of and part of the infinite nature that produced it, so too are "subjective" concepts, such as morality, beauty, and justice to be considered parts within the objective whole of the totality of existence. The scientific definition of cosmology as "the study of the origins and development of the universe over twelve to fifteen billion years"[2] strikes me as a trite and shallow reductionism in comparison.

I have already indicated in previous chapters some religious, philosophical, and scientific precursors. In this part of the book, I will go into a little more detail. I stress "little more" because the constraints of my own present knowledge joined to the constraints of the reasonable size of a readable book limit me to a general overview of all three areas. I will begin with a chapter on philosophy, then to science and finally to Part VI on religion.

Some repetitive overlap will be unavoidable, (as per my own argument against the non-overlapping magisteria thesis). The history of ideas, as with history in general, cannot really be separated into distinct chapters. Ideas and developments evolve over time. A chapter might be entitled "The Renaissance," but you cannot really understand the essence of the Renaissance without its roots and development throughout history. Complicating the issue even further is the undeniable fact that intellectual and spiritual instincts developed similar ideas about existence in radically different and separate cultural environments. Or perhaps, these cultures were not as distinct and separate from one another as we have thought—that perhaps deep in the mists of time, cultural contact and cross pollinations and cross fertilizations were more common than we might expect. For example, the ancient western classical world believed that the divine realm had numerous strata. This characterizes many eastern religions (especially Hinduism) —which might lead them to embrace the Cosmodeistic Hypothesis with greater openness. Likewise, process philosophy and process theology are inextricable intellectually, but must be discussed separately to accentuate their impact on the thinking of different institutional and spiritual entities. In general, I will be placing philosophers who discuss the essence of God in a nondenominational way such as Whitehead and Hartshorne in the chapter "Philosophical Intimations" while those, such as Teilhard deChardin, some Muslim thinkers and most of the Eastern philosophers (who, in their own time did not even know they were sages of that European invention the "Eastern Religions") in the three chapters on religion in Part VI.

I will be cherry picking various historical intimations to support my fundamental argument. I will leave it to the inevitable opponents of what is written here to cherry pick (from the same sources) criticisms of my argument. In point of fact, I believe that all philosophical and theological reasoning is by definition cherry picking, rationalizing as much as possible one's own predispositions. It was Nietzsche who wrote that philosophies say more about the philosophers than they do about objective reality; that reading philosophy is really a venture into the individual psychology of the philosopher. So yes, the Cosmodeistic Hypothesis reflects my psychological predispositions, and whenever I read something I am intuitively looking for external reinforcements to these predispositions. Yet I avow that everything written below is derived, in good conscience on my part, from all three areas and is as accurate and factual as is possible for a mortal human being to be.

Chapter Eighteen: Philosophic Intimations

Western philosophy has Cosmodeistic roots all the way back to the Greeks. Anaximander's concept of infinity opened the door to notions of multitudes of life bearing worlds and parallel universes. Epicurus propounded the *Doctrine of Innumerable Worlds* (our multiverse?). Lucretius and Anaxarchus also believed in infinities of worlds. Plato and Aristotle, on the other hand, argued that the Earth was unique (within an infinite existence) and since they were the philosophical basis of the scholastic thinking that subsequently impacted all three monotheistic religions, molding most subsequent philosophic and scientific thinking, plurality of worlds thinking was inhibited for millennia. For the Greeks, being human did not mean you weren't a beast; it meant not to be a god.[3] Yet the Greek myths that created superhuman heroes and panoplies of gods, were actually stories about humankind's potential to be godlike. For Plato, "godness" was the measure of all things, not man.

For the early Greeks, nature and divinity were intertwined. To make sense out of nature was to *know the gods*. Pythagoras formed a religion based on a creed of mathematics. Pindar felt that developing human abilities brought one closer to the gods. Thales believed that all material things are full of gods, i.e., that the material world is *inherently* divine. Aristotle viewed God as the *Final Cause* of what today we would call cosmic evolution, i.e., the very *idea* of God as drawing all existence to itself. Neoplatonists viewed reality as a succession of emanations in which intelligences are produced by God and lead down to earth—a divine *descending* ladder as it were (note the parallelism to Kabbalah). Cosmodeism would, of course, reverse the direction of the divine ladder: evolution emanating ever higher intelligences *ascending* to the divine.

The Renaissance Italian philosopher Tommaso Campanella (1568–1639) was close to the Cosmodeistic Hypothesis when he perceived reality as a hierarchy of matter that eventually led to life and then to God; in other words, what Cosmodeism would call cosmic evolution evolving into life, then conscious life, and eventually God. Friedrich Schelling (1775–1854) thought of all existence as being alive and all levels of nature striving towards consciousness. William James (1842–1910) viewed human reality as a continuous compounding of consciousness leading from the human to divine consciousness. Karl Krause (1781–1832) thought the entire universe was a divine organism; that the world was a finite creation within the infinite being of God. Gustav Fechnor (1801–1887) believed that every entity has at least the kernel of consciousness and that every entity is but a component of a more inclusive entity concluding with a divine being that includes all of reality (what is called Panpsychism). Alfred North Whitehead (1861–1947) held that humanity is immortal in the sense that the reality of its existence culminates in the very nature of God. Friedrich Nietzsche (1844–1900) saw humanity as an animal whose essence had not yet been clearly defined; an animal that portends the promise of a superior future being, a bridge to the future of a being (or essence) beyond its own present ability to even comprehend the significance of its own existence—a "Supraman" rather than an "Overman."

Samuel Alexander (1859–1938) posited that evolution possesses an internal striving towards ever higher entities. He perceived godness as encompassing the entire space/time of our Cosmos; that the evolution of space/time produces evermore emergents and that the final emergent of the endless process of evolution will be deity. I am particularly attracted to Alexander because he held that although mind emerges from body it also has a reality of its own; that while the self-conscious mind is *dependent* upon the organic brain, the emotions and thoughts it generates cannot be reduced to its biochemical components. I believe he might have been amenable to at least entertaining my speculation that consciousness and life have their own languages that cannot be reduced to mathematics, as well as to my claim that the division between materialism and spiritualism is artificial— that the Industrial Revolution and the Scientific Revolution were, in their civilizational effects, profound spiritual events. Alexander viewed space/time as the fundamental "thing" of the universe; the "thing" from which every other existing thing emerges. Matter emerges from space-time, life emerges from matter, mind emerges from life, and deity emerges from mind. Deity for him was space/time's never-ending evolutionary distinguishing characteristic to create ever more complex emergents. Since evolution is an infinite process the very concept of deity is always transcendent to any contemporary space-time; in other words, there is never going to be conclusiveness to the god concept. To rephrase the Biblical burning bush, God will *always* "be what it *will* be."

Spinoza's pantheistic philosophy is predicated (amongst other things) on the principle that human beings are an integral part of a nature which is coeval with God; that we are not entities separate from Nature (God) whose beliefs and activities are "unnatural." To put it in modern terms, we are conscious beings that are conscious of our own consciousness and this restless consciousness has been produced by the same evolutionary processes that has created our galaxy, our solar system, our planet, life on this planet and conscious life on this planet. Nature (God) has produced us and made us an integral part of itself. I deduce from this that a building is just as "'natural" as a beaver's lodge, or a bird's nest, or a bee's hive, or a termite's mound. If one accepts this aspect of Spinoza's thinking, contrary to modern nihilism, beauty and justice and honor and duty and human dignity are found in Nature everywhere human beings are found; just as cruelty, injustice, ugliness, indifference, and glorification of ignorance are also found in nature everywhere human beings are found. Purposeful genocide and irresponsible environmental destruction are just as natural as pediatric oncology and hyenas eating their prey alive. Humanity is evolution's greatest paradox; it can conceive of God yet conducts itself like a hyena.

Volition is an evolutionary development reserved exclusively for the human species. No other species can "decide" to act other than the way it acts in any significant way—a dog will always be a dog and bears will continue to shit in the woods. By creating volition, evolution itself has evolved and created a gateway to divinity (as well, as history has certainly taught us, to hell). *The human race on this planet must make a conscious volitional decision whether to continue to be an enhanced version of the hyena, eating the entire planet alive, or to consciously evolve into a supra-human race striving to realize its inherent divinity.*

Post-Enlightenment philosophy in the West has produced *Process Philosophy, Panpsychism* and *Panentheism* (all of which have historical roots going back millennia). All three, in one way or another, anticipated the centrality of consciousness and its inevitable emergence into ever higher levels of development. Today they might all be considered subsets of *Emergentism*—a philosophical way of thinking that posits that complex phenomena and characteristics emerge from simpler components in ways that could not have been deduced from the essential character of those simpler components (Holism being a version of Emergentism). Emergentism is especially germane to questions of the emergence of consciousness and the question of what "mind" really is (i.e., Philosophy of the Mind) —what "consciousness" and "thinking" are. This refers to the hoary *Mind-Body Problem*: does the "mind" derive solely from the body (the materialistic concept) or is "mind" something completely distinct from the body (Cartesian and Christian dualism), or by some other, as yet undefined, means. Neither explanation is satisfactory. The dualism of Descartes and Christianity is pure mysticism and no less an authority than Roger Penrose has all but proven that consciousness is non-computable, that it cannot be mathematized, thus completely debunking the assumption that AI will eventually become conscious. As I previously conjectured, while consciousness emerges from biology, it does so in conjunction with and dependent on, the emergence of a *separate* consciousness language; just as the organic emerges from the inorganic in conjunction with and dependent on a separate life language. In other words, I agree with the assumption of *Emergentism* that all these developments are naturalistic and not dependent on some mystic principle, but Cosmodeism widens the range of what might be considered naturalistic.

Process Philosophy deals with the ontology of becoming, which simply means that what we perceive as enduring physical objects, intellectual insights, or mental observations are ontologically dependent on the various natural processes of becoming, i.e., the "being" of anything is a transient event within the relentless "becoming" of its process context. To put it another way, the instant something "is," it "isn't" and becomes another "is." The "is" you "is" today, is not the "is" you were yesterday (or even ten minutes ago). The book you read last year is not the same book you want to reread this year. And the person you married ten years ago is certainly not the person you are married to today. Process is the ultimate "is"—the only *fundamental* reality. Alfred North Whitehead is recognized as its most prominent advocate. His writings, especially his book *Process and Reality,* are as foundational to the subject as Darwin's are to evolution. Some other well-known thinkers often identified with aspects of *Process Philosophy* include, Heraclitus, Nietzsche, Bergson, Heidegger, Peirce, James, and Merleau-Ponty, as well as a host of lesser known but no less important thinkers. Henri Bergson's *Creative Evolution* is perhaps the most imaginative and controversial version of process philosophy. It viewed intelligence as emerging naturally from the very processes of existence. It was neither mechanistic nor teleological; neither conditioned by existing forces nor by future aims. Bergson differentiated between matter and what he perceived as a life force (the *élan vital*) inherent to the evolutionary process itself. This life force imposes disorder on its material surroundings which results in free and unpredictable creativity, i.e., life and the complexification of life as we know it.

Panpsychism posits that all objects in the Universe "have an 'inner' or 'psychological' being."[4] This includes animals and plants and even inanimate objects. In a way, it is an advanced iteration of *Pantheism* and a natural companion to *Panentheism*. Using deductive logic, panpsychics assert that consciousness was not created whole cloth out of nothing; it did not have a virgin birth; it must be a *potential* emergent imbedded in every level of existence. Consequently, human consciousness evolved out of the emerging consciousness of the higher mammals, whose consciousness evolved out of the emerging consciousness of the lower animals, whose consciousness evolved out of the emerging consciousness of primitive life and so on and so forth. We now know, for example, that plants hear, remember, communicate, learn, compete, and cooperate, exhibit interspecies altruism and mutual aid, and have a very special relationship with the Fungi Kingdom which acts as a planetary communications system for the Plant Kingdom which of course has profound implications for the Animal Kingdom. Indeed, Jainism might be a view of existence that sensed this deep reality well before science. In other words, everything is connected to everything, and this includes various levels of consciousness as an evolutionary characteristic of existence as a whole, i.e., that every level of consciousness (and memory) has evolved out of a previous level down to the atoms and subatomic particles. (It occurs to me that this might be the unarticulated philosophical basis for homeopathy.)

James Cameron's Sci-Fi movie *Avatar* might be said to have had a panpsychic theme —the planet *Pandora,* being a protagonist in the film, seeming to possess *willful* self-defense mechanisms. In any case, the principle of the *Godding of the Cosmos* would not be foreign to any advocate of panpsychism, because if consciousness has been an emerging evolutionary development, why should its development have reached its pinnacle with us *Homo sapiens*? Why isn't our human consciousness an evolutionarily stage on the way to an even higher "supra" consciousness, and why won't it continue to develop again and again and again until it reaches a level that would have appeared to us as if it were a god? Panpsychics have railed against a mechanistic worldview that prevents people from noticing "and appreciating anything that cannot become the subject of measurement and calculation."[5] I am hopeful, therefore, that present-day panpsychics might also entertain my speculation that existence is, at a minimum, trilingual; that in addition to mathematics, there is another language for life and yet another for consciousness. Numerous thinkers throughout history were either self-declared panpsychics or inclined towards a panpsychic view of reality. These included, Thales, Bruno, Haeckel, Leibniz, Schelling, Peirce, Schiller,

Whitehead, Samuel Alexander, de Chardin and, once again, a host of lesser known but no less important thinkers.

As indicated in a previous chapter, Hegel also intuited the Godding process and was trying to summarize it using his rather turgid dialectical style (which only served to demonstrate how limited his intellectual ambitions were by the confines of human language). He also invited derision by the trivial nonsense he introduced into his system; for example, the place of the state, and his ultra-complex writing style that sometimes appeared to descend into gibberish (a writing style that became the conceit of many postmodernists and advocates of critical theory without any of the seriousness of Hegel). There is, of course, as we have pointed out, no mathematical language for this kind of theory of everything because the theory of everything is the "I/Thou" relationship between *every* existing thing with *every other* existing thing. For Bergson, for example, evolution was not something that is just happening; it is a consequence of the dialectic interaction between life and nonlife as well as various levels of conscious life. It is subject to and influenced by the infinite imagination of conscious life, or as Martin Buber might have put it by the "I/Thou" relationship between the brute fact of our own existence with the brute fact of existence itself. In truth, everything that exists whether it be a particle, a wave, a galaxy, or a cosmos is in an "I/Thou" relationship with every other existing thing. (Certain aspects of Hindu philosophy seem to have anticipated this particular Western intellectual development.) When you throw consciousness into the mix you make evolution a much livelier thing. This I believe is what religiousness without religion comes down to—recognizing, celebrating, and immersing oneself in the realization of the awesome reality that existence exists.

It seems to me that human beings, by their very nature, are teleological beings. Teleology by its very nature carries the nascent seed of the Cosmodeistic Hypothesis. The more sophisticated teleological worldviews may also be said to have had inklings of the Cosmodeistic Hypothesis. My late friend and fellow collaborator with Nessyahu, Zeev (Bill) Cohen, traced the evolution and future possibilities of the teleological idea in his unfinished book *Towards a Neo-Teleology*. (He passed away prematurely before being able to finish it.) Classical teleology turned human beings into spiritual slaves, compelled by a tyrannical God to fulfill a divine drama not of their choosing. The neo-teleology described by Cohen would reinforce human beings as autonomous subjects *dictating* the divine drama towards a freely created and freely chosen Godness. The teleology he refers to is not imposed on us from without—from our environment—but from within—our own volitional goalsetting. Every "to do" list is really a list of mini "final causes," directing and shaping much of our collateral activity; "to do" lists are intrinsically teleological. Organized societies can also have their "to do" lists. Kennedy wanted to put a man on the moon within a decade. Europe wants to be carbon neutral by 2045 (now moved up to 2035 by Putin's madness). These societal "to do" lists direct human society toward certain aims and values as well as certain types of social organizations which leads to certain types of research and development. This research and development changes the nature of human nature and human society and eventually (potentially) impacts the Cosmos.

In his book *Social Darwinism in American Thought*, Richard Hofstadter—referencing Lester Ward—wrote:

> ... if there is no cosmic purpose, there is at least human purpose, which has already given man a special place in nature and may yet, if he wills it, give organization and direction to his social life. Purposeful activity must henceforth be recognized as a proper function not only of the individual but of a whole society [*and I would add the entire cosmos*].[6]

Ward continued: "[our] collective Telesis (planned progress) alone could place society once more in the free current of natural law."[7] This seems to me to be anticipatory to the philosophy of de Chardin by indicating that human individuals *and civilizations* act purposefully and in doing so continually *create* ever greater final causes for existence as a whole. This is a part of their "human *nature*"; those propensities unique to any conscious species by virtue of their being conscious. Human activity influences the evolution of our entire planet as well *as the evolution of evolution itself.* The entire planet is now "purposeful" to the extent that almost every country, company, ethnic group, religion, and individual has plans and aims for the future.

The problem is that the first decades of the 21st century are revealing just how mundane our purposes are. There is a void in the soul of human civilization. The banality of our disputes and our obsessions in the face of the survival challenges at our doorstep reveals humanity to be at the development phase of irresponsible adolescence; the environmental challenge being already inside the door, occupying our living room and eating our sofa.

If humanity finally does achieve maturity and graduates from its infantile preoccupations and manages to adopt a shared human vision of our very existence, this vision would become the volitional teleology of human civilization at large. Designing a cosmic "to do" list that aims to master and fully know our solar system by let's say 2150 and perhaps even some neighboring solar systems by 2500 (leaving the entire galaxy to our supra-supra human descendants and the entire cosmos to the godness itself) would become the great justification and unifying vision of life on this planet, as represented by its present highest manifestation—US!

Panentheism, while related, is distinct from *Pantheism.* As the peer reviewed *Internet Encyclopedia of Philosophy* describes it: "In pantheism the distinction between God and nature is collapsed: God is a divine creative force immanent in all phenomena whatsoever. This is as *monopolar* a vision of divinity as monotheism, but one that renders all the changes and contingencies of nature illusory. For where everything is divine, nothing is genuinely other."[8] All (pan) *is* God (theism). When Spinoza applied the geometrical natural laws of his time, he made existence *per se* deterministic; mathematical language left no room for choice—it was an absolute. Every single event in the Universe was determined by these iron clad mathematical rules of nature and not subject to human volition. Spinoza's secular predestination turned humanity into a passive object that is subject to the rules of nature, just as Calvinist predestination had turned humanity into a passive object that is subject to the rules of God.

Panentheism, on the other hand, literally means "all (pan) *is in* (en) God (theism)." In other words, godness is embedded in the very fabric of natural existence, which is a living growing thing in constant interaction with all its particular components, including and especially with the consciousnesses that it itself has produced. This dialectical "I-Thou" relationship between existence and its "creations" (the products produced by the evolving complexity of existence) leaves tremendous room for freedom and development and change. Godness is embedded in existence and finds its expression in the transcendent strivings of the consciousnesses it has created. Existence is divine because the consciousnesses that compose it have the *potential* for divinity. As existence evolves, its godness is constantly emerging and becoming ever more aware of itself. Charles Hartshorne was a leading proponent of *Panentheism.* His book *Creative Synthesis and Philosophic Method* takes from Alfred North Whitehead and Henri Bergson, but also diverges from them in ways I find amenable to the Cosmodeistic Hypothesis. He advocated a *dipolar* god as opposed to the divine *monopolar* God of Monotheism or the natural *monopolar* god of Pantheism. For him, God is:

> ... a modulation between two poles or fundamental aspects: an eternal pole of *potentiality* and a temporal pole of actuality or manifestation. These two poles are the primordial divine nature and the consequent divine nature. The latter actualizes in the world the divine possibilities of the former ... material evolution necessarily implies a divine evolution [but] *limits the divine potential for infinitude, omniscience, and omnipotence* (italics mine).[9]

In other words, the godness we are creating will never be in control of everything and the free will of conscious beings will constantly be developing the ever being created godness—the "I will be what I will be"; that emerging godness that we are partners with in the ongoing act of creation. "Godness," therefore, is an ongoing *never-ending* process—God as process ("I will be what I will be"). There is much in this that reminds one of deChardin's *Alpha God* (primordial divine nature) and *Omega God* (subsequent divine nature as the ultimate "aim" of existence). Hartshorne's ontology is also strongly reminiscent of Nessyahu's. Note the following from the *Internet Encyclopedia of Philosophy*'s article on Hartshorne's Dipolar Deism:

> *If God is the greatest conceivable reality* (italics mine), then God must include all that is valuable in the universe. Otherwise, there would be a reality greater than God, namely, the universe-plus-God [the classic supernatural Monotheistic model] ... Each dynamic singular that comes to be is not simply an additional fact; it is, by virtue of Hartshorne's panexperientialist[10] psychicalism[11] also *a value-achievement* (italics mine), and that value-achievement is greater in more complex organisms [us conscious human beings] .... The sum total of value in the universe, which is inseparable from the dynamic singulars that comprise it, is ever increasing according to Hartshorne's process-relational metaphysic. It must therefore be included within God if *God is to be conceived as the reality than which none is greater* (italics mine).[12]

Panentheism views existence and all its existent components as being alive; "there is no such thing as dead matter." As with Panpsychism, there is nothing existent that is without some level of inherent consciousness. Godness has two poles, hence "Dipolar Theism" (I would have preferred Dipolar Deism as more in keeping with Hartshorne's panexperientialism, but why quibble?) An analogy often used is the human body. Let us say that our consciousness is the "godness" of our individual existence not only dictating to the organs and cells that compose us but also being affected *and effected* by our organs and cells—that our very being is *dipolar*: a dialectic relationship between the whole of our being and the various parts that make up that whole which is us (me and you). Rabbi Abraham Joshua Heschel proposed that our bodily functions offer an opportunity for spiritual experience. The first prayer an observant Jew says in the morning exemplifies this dialectic relationship between the banal temporal and the universal transcendent:

> Blessed are you our God, King of the Universe, Who formed man with wisdom *and created many openings and cavities within him* [refers to entire digestive and waste removal system from mouth to rectum and bladder]. It is obvious and known before your throne of glory that if any one of them were closed or if one of any one them were opened, it would be impossible to exist for even an hour.

This dialectic relationship is evident to all of us. When we are sick or suffering from chronic pain aren't we all subject to depressions and melancholy? Likewise when we are depressed or stressed aren't we at greater risk of getting physically ill? Even the most devout atheists exclaim THANK GOD when finally being successful after a prolonged bout of constipation. For panentheists, "God" is a meaningless abstraction unless we view it as *an extant that is extant because it is becoming; that its becoming is its extantness* (de Chardin's Alpha and Omega); the unknown and incomprehensible God: the *Ein Sof* [the endlessness] of the Kabbalists, the Brahma of the Vedantists. Eastern philosophy is also rife with intuitions of Cosmodeism, but since Eastern philosophical thought is inextricably linked with Eastern religious thought, most of these thinkers will be discussed in a subsequent chapter on religion.

Chapter Nineteen: Scientific Intimations

This chapter contains educated speculations and current theories about the nature of existence from recognized scientists, science writers and philosophers of science. I call this "speculative science"; that place where scientists have encountered the borders of present scientific knowledge and have begun to speculate, logically and empirically, about future possibilities, while conditioning their speculations on not gainsaying the known laws of nature and mathematics and descending into fantastical science fiction. This is the same principle/method that I use below in my "speculative theology." Both speculations are, as I have already indicated in "Debunking the Non-Overlapping Magisteria Thesis," not really mutually exclusive terms. I think Albert Einstein would have agreed when he wrote: "Everyone who is seriously involved in the pursuit of science becomes convinced that a spirit is manifest in the laws of the Universe—a spirit vastly superior to that of man, and one in the face of which we with our modest powers must feel humble."[13] I also harbor the conceit that science writer Heinz Pagels would have approved of my samples below when he wrote, "One cannot underestimate the role of intuition and imagination in the sciences."[14]

Thinking about a pluralism of worlds has had a long history in the West, and Aristotle's unique Earth viewpoint could not long survive Copernicus debunking Ptolemaic-Aristotelian cosmology. Galileo's telescope began to indicate the vastness of God's creation and thus it became not unreasonable that, being omnipotent, God might have created multitudes of worlds if it wished. Modern science has been no less fruitful in speculations that would leave space for the Cosmodeistic Hypothesis; some consciously articulated and some, as with George Cantor's *Set Theory's* "infinity of infinities," inferred from the very marrow of the theory. In his book *From Being to Becoming,* Nobel Prize winner physical chemist Ilya Prigogine describes a "physics of being" and a "physics of becoming." *Protobiology*—the study of the emergent pre-life stage of evolution when chemistry became biology— might be described as the chemistry of becoming. Evolution is certainly the biology of becoming. I suggest the proposition that consciousness is the godness of becoming. The zoologist W.E. Agar (member of the Royal Society), greatly influenced by Whitehead's Panpsychism, ridiculed the belief that "the mental factor ... made its appearance out of the blue at some date in the world's history."[15] He believed in the evolutionary development of consciousness from more primitive consciousnesses, thus making legitimate speculations about a supra-consciousness developing from our present, more primitive, consciousness. Even time is an evolutionary process according to Ilya Prigogine in his hypothesis about *The Arrow of Time*. Prigogine's views are somewhat in conflict with physicists like Einstein and Hawking in that he believes that the tenses of time are real entities, and that time is irreversible—constantly moving from a past into a future, even while being relative to both gravity and speed (slowing the greater the gravity and the greater the speed). Existence for him *is* directional; it is moving into an *always undetermined* future. This leads to fundamental questions such as: "Is all directionality purposeful to some extent or another?" or "Can we conceive of anything directional that is not being drawn to something or 'looking' for something?" I would suggest that anything directional is purposeful at some level.

According to the Internet magazine *Science the Wire*, Erwin Schrödinger (of "Cat Wanted Dead or Alive" fame), influenced by Schopenhauer and Spinoza, puzzled that:

> If the world is indeed created by our act of observation, there should be billions of such worlds; one for each of us [shades of Mormon Theology as we shall see]. How come your world and my world are the same? If something happens in my world, does it happen in your world, too? What causes all these worlds to synchronize with each other?

His answer, in conflict with the subsequent non-overlapping thesis, was: "There is obviously only one alternative, namely the unification of minds or consciousnesses. Their multiplicity is only apparent, in truth there is only one mind. This is the doctrine of the Upanishads (oops, Gould's non-overlapping thesis just winced again)."[16] Schrödinger said that "Consciousness cannot be accounted for in physical terms. For consciousness is absolutely fundamental. It cannot be accounted for in terms of anything else."[17] If it cannot be accounted for in physical terms, it cannot be described mathematically, so I believe he might also have found my speculation about a distinct consciousness language intriguing. For Schrödinger, individual consciousness was only a manifestation of a unitary consciousness pervading the entire Universe. Nobel Prize winner in physics, Eugene Wigner, was on the same train of thought when he wrote "It was not possible to formulate the laws of quantum mechanics in a fully consistent way without reference to consciousness."[18] I would claim that the views of both these giants of modern science anticipate various aspects of the Cosmodeistic Hypothesis. American philosopher and cognitive scientist, Jeffery Fodor, propounded the concept of LOT, or Language of Thought, which might have anticipated my speculation about a unique language of consciousness, but for the fact that he was a computationalist (someone who advocates the CTM—the Computational Theory of Mind). Penrose, in *The Emperor's New Mind*, disparagingly referred to this position as "people who believe that the brain is a computer made out of meat." In other words, consciousness is just another stage of computing, which, of course, is entirely mathematical—a view completely rejected by Penrose.

The philosopher of science, Ervin Laszlo, wrote in *Evolution: The Grand Synthesis*, that evolution "is subject to general laws that can be applied to physical, biological, ecological and social systems."[19] In other words, *all* of existence is constantly evolving and all its component parts are evolving in a mutually reciprocal relationship with themselves and with existence as a whole. In this context, cosmic evolution is driving the evolution of its component parts and the evolution of its component parts (in interaction with one another) are driving cosmic evolution (this is completely in line with Nessyahu's image of the Cosmos as described above). Being essentially a cosmic optimist who believes humanity is capable of solving its problems, Laszlo established *The Club of Budapest*, which could be seen as a corrective to the pessimism of *The Club of Rome* (while not denying their analysis of the severity of the problem), in order to "center attention on the evolution of human values and consciousness as the crucial factors in changing course—from a race towards environmental degradation, polarization and disaster to a rethinking of values and priorities so as to navigate today's transformation in the direction of humanism, ethics and global sustainability."[20] I would like to think he would support my arguments in the chapter "No Limits to Growth."

The nascent fields of epigenetics and stem cell research, separately and collaboratively, have given a second wind to Lamarck's thesis of the heritability of acquired characteristics. Both fields make use of the term *Neo-Lamarckism* to describe what they are finding. Stem cell research has revealed that stem cells can be directed to evolve into particular organs by how they are impacted by *external* environments. The subsequent cells of each organ replicate the cells of that organ and *never revert* to the primordial stem cells—thus the acquired characteristic is inherited from subsequent cells in the subsequent generations of the complex organisms in which they were originally implanted. Eliminate a genetic defect in living human beings and this repair will be passed onto their offspring. In stem cell research, human beings can now artificially manipulate stem cells to achieve desired results—to restore or regenerate damaged cells or organs. These are called "*induced* pluripotent stem cells," as opposed to "*natural* pluripotent stem cells." These changes are passed on to subsequent generations—thus the acquired characteristic is inherited by offspring. The genome is what is given by nature, but the DNA in that genome responds to how it is "packaged" by an epigenome ("epi" meaning over, above, or outer). These epigenomes can be produced by human beings (biologically *or socially*) and thus human beings can now begin to control the evolution of our own genes. It appears that genes are collaborative; they determine traits in association with the environment. They have an "I/Thou" relationship with the environment.

Epigenetics has even more revolutionary implications than stem cell research. It is now being demonstrated that one's social, cultural, economic, and *psychological* environment determines the *fluidity* of one's "natural" abilities. How genes are "expressed" (enhanced or subdued) by environmental experience also determines one's "natural" abilities, not only one's inherited genetic code. Perhaps the consistently lower IQ scores of American Blacks, Hispanics and Native Americans simply reflect the inferiority of America's social system rather than the inferiority of these ethnic groups. To demonstrate my point, I propose the following thought experiment:

> An African-American crack addict gives birth to identical twin boys in the South Bronx. One of the twins is adopted by an affluent Ashkenazi Jewish family on the upper west side of Manhattan. The wife is a physician and the husband a tax lawyer (why should I forgo stereotypes when I really need them). By the time the child is 14 he has been sent to the best nursery and private day schools in New York, has gone on numerous vacations (including abroad), been provided with the best computer equipment and educational games, and been privy to table conversation about politics, Broadway shows, and books. The other twin was raised by his addict mother, educated in inner city public schools, has never left the Bronx let alone been overseas, and has been privy to the street conversation of neighborhood gangs and wise guys. They are both given IQ tests at

14. Does one really expect that there will not be at least a 30-point difference in the results?

IQ tests, by the way, are similar to matriculation exams in that one can significantly improve one's score by intensive tutoring. The pretension that they judge inherent intellectual ability is utter nonsense. The only thing they prove is that some people are better at taking tests than others. Their predictive ability for future success is marginal at best. The predictive ability of one's social/economic/cultural background is much more reliable. I hereby predict that, statistically, people from a prosperous, culturally stimulating, background will do better in IQ tests. I hereby predict that, statistically, people from a prosperous, culturally stimulating, background will do better in matriculation tests. This seems to be as much a self-evident truth as "when a bird flies upside down it shits on its stomach."

The inherited *psychological* environment of Blacks and Native Americans might be even more pertinent than their present socio/economic environment. When Roy Wilkins, the iconic head of the NAACP at the height of the civil rights struggle, was once asked if it didn't bother him that whites thought Blacks are inferior, he answered (I will paraphrase): "No, it doesn't bother me that that whites think Blacks are inferior it bothers me that Blacks think Blacks are inferior." You cannot be told for generations that you are lesser than the other without internalizing some of that poison into your system. The war *Manifest Destiny* America conducted against Native American culture might have caused even greater transgenerational psychological dislocation as the institutional depressants to cultural self-esteem conducted as part of this war were being passed on to subsequent generations. We might be seeing a "pale" (pun intended) imitation of this process regarding the declining societal robustness of rural and small-town *white* America on the heels of postmodern economic dislocation. The opioid epidemic dulling the psychological hurt caused by the destruction of their socio-economic culture in the same way that alcoholism dulled the psychological hurt of Native Americans and crack and heroin that of inner-city Black America. Stem cell and epigenetic research, in tandem, are in the process of demystifying the "nature or nurture" argument by demonstrating the dialectic interaction between both. Hopefully this will be the final nail in the coffin of Social Darwinism.

We Jews have an empirical, not a speculative, example of what I am driving at, termed *Holocaust Psychology*. That the immediate survivors experienced profound psychological problems is self-evident. But the field deals with 2nd- 3rd- and 4th-generation effects of this trauma—passing delayed mourning and unresolved grief onto their children and grandchildren, thus molding their personalities and psychological health and the general vibe they give off. I cannot tell you the number of times I have met someone and guessed they were children of survivors by the haze of gloom that seemed to envelop them. How this has impacted the life achievement success (academic, career etc.) of the descendants of Holocaust survivors is not yet clear. The research data is conflicted, but anecdotal clinical evidence provided by working therapists indicates that the survivors' progenies tend to demonstrate predispositions "to PTSD, various difficulties in separation-individuation and a contradictory mix of resilience and vulnerability when coping with stress."[21]

What does any of this have to do with the Cosmodeistic Hypothesis? Well consider the effects on future generations if we solve the problem of poverty and the environment thus eliminating the guilt-ridden angst in which we are raising our children. Consider the psychological effects of a vision of a transcendent cosmic future: a civilizational epigenetics of cosmic optimism rather than the soul-eroding theories of alienation that have been franchised around the world like so many psychologicalist versions of McDonalds. Wouldn't this have an impact on the developmental propensities of our genetic code—individually and collectively? Wouldn't we then evolve "naturally" (whatever "naturally" means given our present stage of development) as a species into a supra-human stage of consciousness? If the evolution of consciousness to ever higher levels of complexity is a consequence of the dynamic, concurrent, reciprocal relationship between the Cosmos and all of its constituent parts, as well as consciousness as one of those constituent parts—which is always intra-relating with itself and relating in turn to the Cosmos—then isn't our own human will part of, and embedded within, our material environment? Can the "self-organization" (*autopoiesis*) and evolution of nature be influenced by the social, cultural, and *psychological* epigenetic impact of what conscious life does on this earth? Once consciousness appears, can there ever again be a "deterministic cosmic self-organization," or is willful consciousness now an integral part of a much higher cosmic concept of self-organization (or has it *always* been)?

The Evolutionary Impact of Consciousness

The fact is that complex consciousness increasingly drives its own evolutionary development to further complexify consciousness, which, in turn, complexifies the social systems which both sustain and, in turn, complexify it—in a never-ending loop of mutual complexifications. Consciousness reaches a point (on our planet it has already reached that point) at which it begins to impact on the evolution of an assortment of physical, biological, and ecological components. Human beings have already created new species, new materials, and new ecosystems on *this* planet. One must assume that other conscious civilizations throughout the Cosmos have done the same (some probably to an even greater extent than we have). In other words, consciousness's reciprocal interrelationship with its planetary environment has already impacted the evolution of that environment and thus of the entire Cosmos. Might we also speculate then, that the energy of consciousness (as a form of radiation) has a reciprocal interrelationship beyond the ecological limits of its own planet and has in some way begun to fill the great void of space, already impacting the evolution of the Cosmos at large? In other words, the Godding of the Cosmos might have already reached some intermediate embryonic stage and we conscious humans sense/intuit this aspect of existence and sense/intuit its inherent "divinity" and sense/intuit that it is accessible to us and affects us; and we have named this sense/intuition "God." Might this awareness be our first embryonic, albeit indirect, contact with other conscious civilizations throughout the Cosmos?

There is no logical reason to assume that as we move out into space, we will not retrofit suitable planets and moons to accommodate our living needs or utilize the asteroid and comet belts to accommodate our resource needs. There are already scientific speculations as to how we might modify Mars and some of the moons of other planets to make them amenable to life. This is called terraforming or planet molding. As Laszlo writes "Evolution … is not destiny; it is opportunity."[22] Evolution is potentially subject to human volition and human will based on an ever deepening understanding of the physical and biological processes of nature and the nature of cosmic evolution. Given the possibilities of modern genetics, following the applied advances made possible by the gene splicing technology of *CRISPR*, we might even create new kinds of human beings, more suitable to the physical challenges of outer space. Even today it is entirely logical to propose that people "suffering" from dwarfism are more suitable for space travel than typical size humans given that every extra pound we send into space costs a fortune. Perhaps dwarfism is an evolutionary preadaptation (much like the human brain) enabling us to cope more efficiently with the new human environment we are creating. We humans have already created dwarf varieties of grains and fruit trees in order to sustain yields with significantly less energy and resource inputs. Has evolution already performed this job for us by creating a "breed" of humanity most suited to survival in our new space-age environment; being able to perform all the specialized astronaut tasks of "typical" sized humans with significantly less energy and resource inputs? If we hadn't been infected by ablest prejudices about "little people" and sexist prejudices against women we would have realized that females with dwarfism were the ideal astronauts, and thus saved hundreds of millions of dollars.

Human beings are products of evolution, "in evolution," and driving evolution. As Laszlo puts it, we are a "product of the process [and] part of the process ... co-authors of the process."[23] Jewish tradition posits that human beings must be partners with the inherent divinity of existence in the ongoing, *never-ending* act of creation—thus including, by definition, the never-ending, ongoing creation of godness (the eternal "I will be what I will be"). Given the increased "rate of the rate of change" it is incumbent upon humanity to become proactive *in* rather than just reactive *to* the cosmic evolutionary drama. My interpretation of the implications of the Cosmodeistic Hypothesis is that without a transcendent future vision (creating "God"), acting as a final cause, proactively pulling us towards it, conscious civilization on this planet might collapse under the weight of its own existential confusion. When I say proactively, I mean acknowledging this "Godding" process as the "official policy" of conscious life and developing strategies for its implementation. We already know that cosmic evolution generates ever more complex chemical and physical properties and processes. These eventually produce life which evolves into ever more complex ecosystems. These ecosystems evolve into "social" systems (ants, etc.) and ever higher and more complex life forms which evolve into ever more complex social systems until they evolve into human consciousness. This higher human consciousness has already influenced and directed the evolution of the physical, the biological and the ecological and, as Nessyahu conjectured, must eventually begin to affect cosmic evolution itself. The more advanced manifestations of consciousness in various parts of the Cosmos may have already begun to do so; even, perhaps, already affecting us earthlings in an indirect manner.

It is Laszlo's thesis—as with Nessyahu—that all these evolutions are related, or better still interrelated, in a kind of cosmic dialectic. Laszlo marshals a huge amount of scientific evidence to support these claims, which Nessyahu intuited in his thought experiments. He writes about biophysics as an interface between physics and biology and sociobiology as an interface between biology and the social sciences. Nessyahu would also have claimed that there is also a biocosmology, wherein the life system, as represented by its highest manifestation (conscious life), is an interface between the evolution of life and the evolution of the Cosmos —i.e., not only the Cosmos giving birth to life and driving its evolution, but life itself being a major driving force in the cosmic evolutionary drama (and not just a passive product being dragged along by evolution). The evolutionary Cosmos has generated its own final causes—the ambitions of the conscious beings it has created. It is as if conscious life is the "final cause" of the evolutionary cosmic drama; that it is driving the Cosmos to become aware of itself, and fulfilling Arthur Clarke's prophecy described above, to become a cosmic consciousness by way of conscious life eventually evolving itself into a post-material being, becoming intertwined with the lattice framework of that quantum reality which is the foundational force driving cosmic evolution towards its omega point. This is an outlook that sees evolution as the "soul" of the universe; the very being of the universe; the "holy ghost" of the universe if you will. It is not *just* a process and it certainly is not an event. It is an outlook that actually advocates a dialectical "I/Thou" relationship between the evolution of consciousness and conscious evolution. Conscious evolution is not a deterministic process; it is a consequence of our own visions of the future. Our visions are the final causes of human society; our visions are pulling us towards their own fulfillment. If our vision is that God *will be* then that vision will be our final cause; it will be the very vision of God that ingratiates itself with the Cosmos, drawing us towards ultimate godness.

How does evolution itself reflect Nessyahu's radiation/collision thesis? Consider that the average human being has over 10,000 *known* species and an estimated 39 trillion individuals of microbes, archaea, and bacteria in and on his or her body (more than all the stars in the known Universe). Without these miniscule beasties we could not exist. They have evolved in order to adapt to our bodily environment but in order to do so had to provide various vital services to our bodily needs. In other words, the large scale of our bodies (and the larger scale of our species) has driven evolution in the small scale producing the miniscule beasties that make human life, hence human society, hence human culture even possible. No microbes, no Beethoven or Buddha! This is a perfect example of the unity between the large and small scale. Conversely, the evolution of these small-scale beasties drives the evolution of our large scale bodies (and thus our species). By being essential to our very lives, this dynamic interaction (ultimate unity) between the large and small scale has enabled the development of our consciousness and its ability to expand and to impact on ever larger complexifications of society and environment.

As our collective consciousness expands around the globe it will envelop the planet with a new layer of reality as objectively real as the layer we call the stratosphere. Teilhard de Chardin called it the *Noosphere. Noos* is Greek for mind; *Noosphere* therefore is a sphere of "mind" produced as much by the emergence of consciousness as the oxygenated air we breathe was produced by the emergence of photosynthesis. I would like to suggest that what we call *The Cloud* represents the first baby steps towards that eventuality and that this mind reality being generated by evolution will eventually expand into and possess our entire solar system. And in a future as distant from us as we are from the first Neanderthals it will expand into and possess the entire galaxy, along with other conscious life forms it will inevitably encounter. And in a future as distant from us as we are from the first Big Bang, it will expand into and eventually possess the entire Cosmos. This process will compel us to create new artificial environments which, in turn, will require that we "evolve" new microbial species (and even more complex species) to do our work for us. Synthetic life is in our future.

In his book *The Global Brain: Speculations on the Evolutionary Leap to Planetary Consciousness,* science writer Peter Russell traces how technological progress has increased the evolutionary rate of change and makes the extraordinary claim that this may enable us to make the kind of evolutionary leap that occurs once in a billion years. He writes:

> Just as ... life had emerged from matter ... from the physical level to the biological level, so it now has moved to a new level: consciousness. We could therefore hypothesize that the integration of society into a superorganism would occur through the evolution of consciousness rather than through physical of biological evolution. This implies a coming together of minds, which is why communication

is such an important aspect of evolution today; it is a mind linking process. Humanity is growing together mentally—however distant we might be physically.[24]

I would add political, ethnic, racial, and religious distance to physical distance and observe that the *Communications Revolution* is having a similar, even more extreme, impact on our so-called differences, than the *Commercial Revolution* in the past. Just as commerce eventually bent every human group it touched to the needs and vicissitudes of trade, so communications is doing with even greater intensity today. Rather than seeing this superorganism as similar to the Borg in *Star Trek*, Russell claims that it will actually "lead to greater freedom and self-expression on the part of the individual, and to an even greater diversity."[25] And while not using the terminology of "final cause," he certainly agrees with me about the need for optimistic visions of the future when he writes:

> ... the image a society has of itself can play a crucial role in the shaping of its future. If we fill our minds with images of gloom and destruction, then that is likely to be the way we are headed. Conversely, more optimistic attitudes can actually promote a better world. A positive vision is like the light at the end of the tunnel, which, even though dimly glimpsed, encourages us to step on in that direction.[26]

Now I must confess that nothing I have written so far is entirely original. What has been termed *The Epic of Evolution* has had a rich intellectual history over the past several decades. *The Encyclopedia of Religion and Nature* defines it as:

> "... the 14 billion year narrative of cosmic, planetary, life, *and cultural evolution* (italics mine)—told in sacred ways. Not only does it bridge mainstream science and a diversity of religious traditions; if skillfully told it makes the science story memorable and deeply meaningful, while enriching one's religious faith or secular outlook."[27]

Here we have a concise two-sentence debunking of the pretentious pseudo-sophistication of the *Non-Overlapping Magisteria* thesis. Prominent scientific advocates of the "Epic" view of existence include (amongst others) astrophysicist and Harvard professor Eric J. Chaisson. Professor Chaisson is a member of the Harvard-Smithsonian Center for Astrophysics, and elected

Fellow of the American Association for the Advancement of Science. Biologist Edward O. Wilson, known alternatively as "the modern Darwin" and "the father of biodiversity," is the winner of the Royal Swedish Academy of Sciences *Crafoord Prize* (the Nobel Prize for fields not covered by Nobel's original mandate) as well as a Pulitzer Prize-winning science writer. Many other scientists as well as scores of natural theologians and philosophers have also been advocates of *The Epic of Evolution*.

I have already mentioned physicist and science writer Eric Lerner above in connection to the Plasma Cosmology advocated by Nobel Prize winner Hannes Alfven. While challenging the current standard cosmological model, he allows that the Big Bang might have been a local event in an infinite universe. In this he is in accord with Nessyahu that the universe is infinite in time and space *and continually evolving*. In other words, existence is open ended and amenable to limitless possibilities; life without limits (and without guilt). If Lerner is right, as I suspect he mostly is, then Nessyahu's proposition that Godness *as a consequence* of this endlessly evolving universe must be inevitable. If Lerner is right (and both logic and the empirical evidence seems to support him) and he allows that the Big Bang might have been a local space-time event in an infinite space-time universe, then his analysis reinforces Nessyahu's thought experiment, i.e., that our Cosmos is but a local finite space-time organization within an infinite space-time Universe that contains an infinite number of local (finite) space-time *organizations* which are, by definition, organized self-contained cosmoses. Moreover, his entire critique of current cosmology agrees with Nessyahu's contention that mathematics is just a language which must *confirm* empirical observation. Mathematics is beholden to observation; observation is not beholden to mathematics. Mathematics does not dictate facts; facts tell us if the mathematics is right or wrong.

If the evolutionary process is infinite, as both Lerner and Nessyahu claim it is, then it is inevitable that consciousness is becoming an ever-larger constituent part of our cosmos; that our cosmos is becoming ever more self-aware. As Lerner writes: "Progress, the acceleration of evolution, is a long-term tendency of the universe ...."[28] This reflects the Greek concept of "entelechy" (defined as a vital force that directs an organism toward self-fulfillment); entelechy is that which realizes or makes actual what is otherwise merely potential. I believe, therefore, that our sacred duty to the Cosmos, as entities possessed of consciousness, is to make manifest the potential that is in ourselves and in this way (as a living cell of the cosmos) to make manifest the life potential of the Cosmos. Entelechy is the epistemological equivalent of the Godding process intimated in the Kabbala and demonstrates the universality of this intuition of the divine process of Godding.

The Big Bang theory implies that existence created itself out of nothing; that space-time created itself out of nothing. This is probably the most mystical, magical belief system in the history of human thought. At least Monotheism (and other belief systems) had a cause or a first mover. And if one reads the biblical creation story in its original Hebrew, one cannot but be struck with the thought that it strongly implies that God himself did not create existence out of nothing—he created order (cosmos) out of chaos; a chaos that preexisted cosmos! Indeed, Orthodox Jewish Professor of Philosophy (and my dear friend), the late Dr. Joe Levinson posited this very view; that God created the heaven and the earth of *this* planet Earth and *not* all of existence. Joe's perspective is especially convincing when one reads the second creation story of Genesis but can also be deduced from the first creation story.

The Big Bang theory, in its current iteration, has negative psychological and social and political consequences. It essentially says that the universe is doomed "to expand and decay into the nothingness of an eternal night."[29] This is a spectacularly pessimistic view of existence and could very well be the underlying background music to the current eco-pessimism which I have attempted to debunk above. As Lerner asks, in the same spirit as Pascal, "... what meaning can life have in a universe doomed to decay, unspeakably hostile and alien to human purposes?"[30] In other words, "What's the point?" This view of existence has been rich fodder for the postmodern nihilism I described in Part I. This is an attitude to life that that gives birth to mysticism and anti-rationalism. People are by nature hopeful. If rationalism is pessimistic, people reject it and tend to the supernatural: aliens, astrology, religion, and New Age. This is exactly what we are witnessing today. Nobel Prize winning physicist Steven Weinberg, in his book *The First Three Minutes*, celebrates the meaninglessness of existence. One must question why he bothered to write the book? Why didn't he just spend his life in libidinous self-indulgence instead of slaving away in the grind of endless scientific inquiry? Could it be that under his superficial shell of cynical nihilism he sensed that our ever-increasing knowledge of reality has intrinsic *objective* value? And doesn't the intrinsic value of the object imply that the various parts of that object, including our subjective lives, also have value and thus meaning after all? Could it be he sensed this in some unarticulated way, and this is what drove him to his extraordinary life accomplishments? I mean if you *really* believe in the meaningless of existence why get out of bed in the morning, let alone engage in the hard work of becoming a physicist?

Cosmic Codes and Cosmic Blueprints

The late American physicist (and former chief executive officer of the New York Academy of Sciences), Heinz R. Pagels (1939–1988) in *The Cosmic Code*, English physicist (and former chair of SETI) Paul Davies in *The Cosmic Blueprint*, and American geologist and noted science writer Louise B. Young (1919–2010) in *The Unfinished Universe*, as well as others, have presented certain scientific evidence upon which one might legitimately assume a purposeful universe—a neo-teleology based on science and not on philosophical wishful thinking. All three, however, use Cosmos and Universe interchangeably (as opposed to Nessyahu's assertion that they are distinct "entities"—that our finite Cosmos is but a component in an infinite Universe). I will not correct this confusion of terms in order to be faithful to the intentions of the authors. But I ask the reader to keep this distinction as background music to what follows.

Young especially reflects much of Nessyahu's basic arguments as well as my own deductions based on his arguments. In her book, she advocates that the continuously evolving universe does provide human existence with meaning and purpose. And like Nessyahu, she sees that entropy is only one side of the coin of the evolutionary cosmic process. The other side being that this very process is creating ever-more complex, organized, and efficient forms of existent systems, including life and ultimately consciousness. I have no idea if she had even heard of Samuel Alexander's *Space, Time, and Deity*, but her basic arguments are strikingly similar to his, as well as to Nessyahu's, "essential unity of the large and the small." She believes that the whole is immanent in all the parts, no matter how small," a sentiment agreeable with various aspects of Jain and Hindu worldviews.

Davies writes "It is clear that there exist *self-organizing* processes in every branch of science" because "cosmologists ... believe that immediately following the Big Bang the universe was in an essentially featureless state." There seem to be *inherent* physical processes that can turn a void into the complex constructs that characterize our cosmos—stars, crystals, people, etc.[31] Might this be a new explanation or rather meta-explanation for biological evolution? What, after all, are these physical processes? What is the evolutionary grand synthesis that keeps existence in a constant state of churning and producing ever more complex structures and numerous ever tinier particles? Why is the universe so "dissatisfied" with itself? Why can't it "leave" well enough alone? What is it "trying" to do? (Excuse my anthropomorphisms, but they seem unavoidable when honestly looking at the reality of existent nature.) Might it be that the cultural and scientific ambitions of human beings (along with the other conscious beings in the Cosmos) are a necessary cosmic component of a greater self-organizing process? Why can't we conclude that as humanity escapes the physical limitations of the crust of the planet Earth it would be logical that the evolution of our consciousness would continue apace and rise to ever higher levels of consciousness?

This would certainly be in keeping with Paolo Soleri's thesis in his book *Technology and Cosmogenesis* that our consciousness must ascend—that we must evolve both culturally and socially as a consequence of the complexity of the systems and technologies we ourselves are producing and that eventually this must impact on our biological evolution. Such an occurrence was anticipated by the science fiction writer Olaf Stapleton in *First Man, Last Man.* Given this, I would posit that the human race is still in the evolutionary "proof of concept" stage which has been undergoing numerous cultural iterations. The abundant variations of human cultures and sub-cultures are, in the Darwinian sense, "experiments" to determine which variations are most fit to survive in the Cosmic Age—what has been called in evolutionary theory "preadaptation." I personally find the very word "preadaptation" to be an oxymoron if one adheres to the strictures of neo-Darwinists. How can something evolve in order to adapt to an environment not yet in existence or a use not yet required for survival? However, if one adheres to the Laszlo/Nessyahu concept of evolution one has no problem with the concept whatsoever.

The fundamental question Davies asks is, are all the forms and structures of the Cosmos "accidental products of random forces, or ... the inevitable outcome of creative activity of nature?"[32] I would add: is this creativity activity the force that the ancients intuited and named God? Davies protests that the complexity, diversity, and organization of the Cosmos "cannot be accepted simply as brute fact."[33] Given the violence of nature, how do these complex structures not only survive but "prosper" and grow ever more complex and subtle as if in rebellion to the laws of entropy? According to Davies, the classic, essentially mechanistic Newtonian and thermodynamic scientific paradigms are being supplemented with a "new paradigm of the creative universe, which recognizes the progressive innovative character of physical processes."[34] Or as Ilya Prigogine metaphorically puts it: "God is no more an archivist unfolding an infinite sequence he had designed once and forever. He continues the labor of creation throughout time."[35] Prigogine's observation cannot but remind one of the Jewish dictate to "be partners [with God] in the [ongoing] act of creation." In this context, Davies' use of the word "blueprint" is less appropriate than Pagel's use of the word "code." A blueprint is an engineering term—this is the way you do something or the thing falls apart—a code provides access to a process that constantly changes over time with new inputs.

In his book *Infinity and the Mind: The Science and Philosophy of the Infinite* mathematician Rudy Rucker writes: "The study of infinity is much more than a dry academic game. The intellectual pursuit of the absolute infinite is, as George Cantor realized, a form of the soul's quest for God. Whether or not the goal is ever reached, an awareness of the process brings enlightenment."[36] This quote reflects the overlap between the truly scientific (as opposed to the technocratic) mentality and religiosity. The philosophical or religious questioning of an Einstein or a Sagan arises from their scientific inquiry. Einstein referred to "the mind of God" metaphorically, but Newton really meant it. He really wanted to know what God was thinking, and as already mentioned, Copernicus was concerned with protecting God's honor by explaining creation in a much more elegant and efficient manner, as befits the Supreme Being.

Sometimes I feel that Plato, Heisenberg, Gödel, and Sartre are all related somehow—that all four in their own way intuit the ultimate indefinability of existence itself. I am not referring to human existence, which is but a very recent manifestation of our planetary existence, but existence itself, existence qua existence. Here I might tend to agree with Sartre that humanity must invent its meaning—not as a self-deception to ease our own pain, but as an ontological categorical necessity to give the Cosmos itself meaning. Just as supernovas create heavy elements enabling the Cosmos to complexify, so we conscious beings create meaning enabling the Cosmos to have meaning. Since we are part of the Cosmos when we invent meaning we give meaning to the Cosmos. We are not separate from the Cosmos and the Cosmos is not separate from us; conscious life is in, within, and a driving force of the Cosmos, just as the Cosmos is in, within, and a driving force of conscious life. As Prof. Geoffrey Mure writes, assessing Hegel, "... man is an element in God's self-manifestation, his creative self-consciousness. As creator God is distinct from man, but as self-creating God *is* man."[37]

Implications of Modern Physics

The philosophical approaches and methodical strategies of modern physics (both Einsteinian and Quantum) lend credence to Nessyahu's grand thought experiment, and to the possibility of creating a science based neo-teleological worldview. The metaphysical implications of modern physics have had, and will continue to have, profound social, cultural, and psychological implications for humanity. Indeed, much of the angst and alienation worrying humanity today—first in Western cultures and now, with ever- increasing intensity, in non-Western cultures—derives from the profound intellectual dislocations implicit in modern physics.

The social/psychological dislocations we are witnessing in Japan, China, and Korea, have, at least to the external observer, become even more extreme than in the West. The still-developing world in Asia, Africa, and South America is only temporarily immune to these cultural ailments because of their present struggles to escape from material poverty. As previously indicated, it is difficult to be preoccupied with the ultimate meaning of life when you are only a few meals away from grinding hunger. What is clear for our purposes, however, is that modern physics has created the intellectual and spiritual space that enables those amongst us who are skeptical but not cynical to entertain Nessyahu's logical speculations with greater readiness (similar to how Aquinas's creation of secular space enabled the West to eventually assent to the scientific attitude). I will begin with discussing the movement from Newton's inductive methods, wherein theory supposedly derived from experiment in a direct causal pattern to Einstein's deductive methods, wherein experiments were used in an indirect way to verify or debunk the theory. I will then follow with the philosophical differences (and their consequences for civilization) between Einstein and Heisenberg (or Quantum mechanics in general).

Newton would boast that he made no hypotheses, but rather "deduced his basic concepts and laws from the explicit findings."[38] But as F.S.C. Northrop observed in his introduction to Heisenberg's *Physics and Philosophy: The Revolution in Modern Science,*

> Were this conception of the relation between the physicist's experimental observation and his theory correct, Newton's theory would never have required modification, nor could it ever have implied consequences which experiment does not confirm. Being implied by the facts, it would be as indubitable and final as they are.[39]

In other words, if this method was correct, Newtonian mechanics would have been true for all time and not only could never have been replaced by Einsteinian or Quantum mechanics but could not even have been modified on its own terms, because, by definition, it would have been impossible for contrary facts to have emerged.

Einstein, in apposition to Newton, claimed that "the physical scientist only arrives at his theory by speculative means"[40] (Einstein's famous thought experiments). This difference might have arisen because of an essential difference in temperament between the two. Isaac, after all, had all the signs of being anally obsessive, while Albert's endless, more cavalier, praise for informed intuition and imagination is well known. His thought experiments were simply letting his imagination run wild until he formulated a hypothesis which seemed to be logically coherent, even if contrary to current standards of empirical common sense. Like Plato, he was suspicious of our senses—feeling they provided us with a very incomplete concept of ultimate reality. Mathematics, therefore, was a much more dependable way to describe ultimate reality than our common-sense empirical observations and indeed expanded the intellectual range of empirical inquiry. Scientists began to do their empirical research on the basis of the predictions of newer more expansive mathematical formulations—actually educated guesses. If empirical research consistently confirmed the mathematical predications, the original hypothesis became an accepted theory and became foundational to the standard scientific model within which most scientists conducted their inquiries. This would continue until some maverick came up with a slightly different theory which subsumed the original theory within a much more comprehensive outlook. An imperfect example of this is how neo-Darwinism subsumed Darwinism—imperfect because, as previously noted, the biological sciences are incapable of mathematizing the fundamental construct of biology, i.e., life.

The General Theory of Relativity (1915) came to Einstein as a thought experiment, followed by relentless mathematical work (10-12 hours a day) until he formulated his final equation. It only became generally accepted theory *after* Eddington conducted his famous empirical experiment during a solar eclipse, which proved beyond a doubt that mass warps Space/Time and thus bends light (1919). Einstein's theoretical prediction had been proven, but in doing so, Eddington slightly modified the mathematical specifics of the prediction, because while Einstein predicted a deflection of 1.75 arcseconds, Eddington's experiment perceived a deflection of 1.6 arcseconds "plus or minus a standard error of 0.3 arcseconds."[41] The theory had been proved but the mathematical predictions had to be modified. This kind of modification would be impossible using Newton's supposed method of inquiry. His procedure would have been "observing" that mass bends light, deducing the existence of space-time, constructing mathematical formulas to describe this and as a consequence constructing his theory. The most obvious objection to Newton's inductive presumption is that he would have had to observe mass bending light in the first place. What would have motivated him to measure light as it approaches and passes mass if he had not been inspired to do so because of his own intuition about the nature of the Cosmos? This is not the kind of observation you make in passing; you have to really be looking for it in the first place to either prove or disprove a theory—science is intentional not accidental in method (not withstanding many accidental discoveries in the history of science). Moreover, Newton wouldn't have had the mathematics to even speculate about the phenomenon. Even Einstein's mathematical language was inadequate to explore his intuitions. He was forced to look for other mathematical language which he wouldn't have looked for or found but for his requisite need to logically explore his original intuition. His ideas came first, mathematical formulae next and empirical proof only at the end of the process.

Einstein's intuitive imagination and deductive logic have become the hallmarks of modern science. Quantum physicists like Heisenberg use exactly the same scientific strategy. The Cosmodeistic Hypothesis conforms to this intuitive/logical way of doing science and justifies the legitimacy of Nessyahu's thought experiment. Nessyahu's greatest weakness, of course, was not being able to translate his thought experiment into mathematical language, since he believed mathematics had been stretched to the very borders of its ability to describe the essence of existence and thus, his thought experiment. As to method, Einstein and Heisenberg are in agreement. It is the philosophical implications of modern science that are cause for polemics. As with Newton, Einstein assumed existence was omnicomplete. But as Northrop notes, "quantum mechanics has brought the concept of potentiality back into physical science."[42]

Potentiality, as an inherent and integral part of the physical universe, implies that the speculations of conscious beings (as products of the evolution of the physical universe) are also an integral and potentially dynamic part of the future evolution of the universe. In other words, our ideas are just as much a part of objective reality as the earth circling the sun and our solar system circling the galaxy. As Northrop puts it, "quantum theory [is] as important for ontology (i.e., the very being of existence) as it is for epistemology (i.e., the limitations of the human intellect in thinking about and describing the phenomena of existence)."[43] For Einstein, the ultimate being of existence is ontologically omnicomplete, and any ambiguity is a product of the epistemological limitations of human understanding. For Heisenberg, quantum mechanics demonstrates the ontological ambiguity of existence itself. And thus, new energies/information (such as consciousness) can affect and effect the ultimate fate of the Cosmos.

In other words, things are not indeterminate because of the limits of human intellect and language but because the very essence of existence is indeterminate; existence per se, existence qua existence, existence as such is fluid, pliable and malleable in and of itself—it is not "just is." Its "isness" is subject to the will and intent of that cosmic wildcard we call consciousness—its "isness" is a never-ending "becoming"; a "becoming" influenced, and eventually driven, by the future visions of its conscious entities. It is consciousness itself that is ultimately the creative God. *Que sera, que sera* (whatever will be, will be) is no longer the case—what will be is what we conscious entities (in aggregate) *decide* what will be. The implication being that even an all-powerful, omniscient, supernatural God cannot know everything that is going to happen because "everything" is never an omnicomplete reality—there can never be an "everything" at any particular point in space/time because "everything" is in a constant state of creating itself. Appalled by the philosophical implications of this, the determinist Einstein, in protest, uttered his famous objection that "God doesn't play dice" (to which one of his colleagues replied, "Yes he does, and stop telling God what to do"). The question I have is if the ontological implications of quantum mechanics are true, is it even logically possible to formulate a theory of that so-called "everything" which is never omnicomplete (thus can never be everything). I suggest that the civilizational thought revolution introduced by quantum mechanics enables us to relate to existence in ways that would give Sartre's subjective "creating your own meaning" objective weight, as well as providing a scientific base for a neo-teleology.

The Eternal Intelligence

I will conclude this chapter with the fascinating scientific personality— Freeman Dyson. In 1979, he proposed the concept of "eternal intelligence" (popularly called the Dyson Scenario), in which he envisaged an immortal intelligence being able to transcend the inevitable heat death of the universe (Cosmos) by extending subjective time *ad infinitum* while only expending finite amounts of energy at any given time. His speculation relied on something called *Bremermann's Limit* named after mathematician and biophysicist Hans-Joachim Bremermann (1926–1996). According to the Wikipedia entry on the subject, this describes the "limit on the maximum rate of computation that can be achieved in a self-contained system in the material universe [and] is derived from Einstein's mass-energy equivalency and the Heisenberg uncertainty principle."[44] I confess that I have no idea what this even implies in justifying Dyson's speculation about the possibility of an "eternal intelligence." I only know that Dyson based his idea on the solid scientific evidence of the time and not as a result of some "whoopdy-doo" mystical experience. He suggested that some future supra-supra intelligent beings would be able to store finite amounts of energy and use fractions of this energy, *ad infinitum*, to power their thought. The fractions of energy would get smaller and smaller and thus the thoughts smaller and smaller but in an infinite universe there would still be an infinite number of them (a reflection both of Cantor's "infinity of infinities" and Nessyahu's observation that there can be nothing so small that there cannot be something smaller). Given the discovery of the increasing acceleration of the expansion of the Cosmos, Dyson withdrew this idea, evidently for purely scientific reasons which, as with *Bremermann's Limit*, I cannot even pretend to understand. I include it here to demonstrate that a general propensity to deduce such conclusions is not limited to Nessyahu or me, and that serious scientists, such as Dyson, have let their logical imaginations speculate, scientifically, about such possibilities. Moreover, critics of his notion, including, subsequently, himself, ignore the possibility that a consciousness so advanced would have deduced much more complicated scientific truths about cosmic reality that would enable it to overcome the limitations of *present* scientific knowledge. I simply see the Cosmodeistic Hypothesis as the ontological necessity of existence per se.

Chapter Twenty: Some Convergent Thinking

In this chapter I will discuss some contemporary thinking that closely resembles the Cosmodeistic Hypothesis in various aspects. And while some use religious idiom to describe their thinking, they are more the musings of philosophies of cosmology than of clearly defined religious thinkers. For example, in *Space, Time, and Aliens*, former Chief Historian for NASA, Steven J. Dick[45] describes *Cosmotheology* as a theology that "takes into account what we know about the universe based on science … a naturalistic theology in the tradition of religious naturalism." His definition of religious naturalism "denies that an ontologically distinct and superior realm including God, soul, and heaven is required to give meaning to the world."[46] If I interpret him correctly, experiences of wonder, mystery and transcendence do not depend on the supernatural but are inherent in the simple fact that existence exists. He lists several foundational assumptions that intersect with the Cosmodeistic Hypothesis to an extraordinary degree:

1. The supernatural does not exist.

2. We are not physically, biologically, cognitively, or morally central in the universe.

3. Any concept of God must be grounded in naturalistic cosmic evolution.

4. An expansive moral dimension, an *astroethics* extending to all life in the universe.

5. While a human destiny linked to cosmic evolution rather than supernaturalism is a radical departure from the past, it is, in the end. beneficial and liberating.

6. Such a worldview resolves many ancient theological problems such as bad things happen to good people because the universe is hostile rather than loving.

7. The prospect of contact with life beyond earth leaves open the possibility of interacting with that life, and the idea of a loving and compassionate "God."

8. The concept of God can be expressed naturally in the way we treat our fellow humans and other creatures in the universe without resorting to supernaturalism.

9. Stripped of supernaturalism and other accoutrements, compassion is at the core of all religions, even if the ideal is not always met.

10. Universal compassion is at the core of cosmotheology.

Dr. Dick has written extensively on the evolutionary argument for the Cosmos being embedded not only with life, but also with intelligent life, and by implication with supra-intelligent life. In his essay "Cultural Evolution, the Postbiological Universe and SETI," he posits *The Intelligence Principle,* which suggests that once life becomes intelligent (i.e., conscious of its own consciousness) that intentional, cultural evolution replaces accidental, biological evolution. This generates an emergent unifying tendency of all intelligent societies (terrestrial and extra-terrestrial), in which "The maintenance, improvement and perpetuation of knowledge and intelligence is the central driving force of cultural evolution, and that to the extent intelligence can be improved, it will be improved."[47] In other words, when cosmic evolution eventually produces life, it will inevitably produce self-reflective intelligence (i.e., consciousness) which, by the very nature of the curiosity that is inherent in consciousness, will produce a cultural paradigm dedicated to an ever-increasing social and cultural tendency to expand intelligence. If Dr. Dick is right (and every bone in my body says he is) and evolution is becoming ever more dominated by the intelligence it birthed, then cosmic existence *per se* is becoming ever more teleological; existence *per se* is becoming ever more purposeful; its final "end" being to create intelligences that would appear to the infant consciousness of the human species to be "gods." He writes:

Cosmotheology must be open to radically new conceptions of God, not necessarily the God of the ancient near East, nor the God of the human imagination, but a God grounded in cosmic evolution. It is entirely possible that beings have evolved in the natural course of the universe with many of the traits we attribute to God, including omnipotence, omniscience, and so on. It is even possible such beings have meddled in human affairs ... Whether one wishes to call such a superior being "God" is also open to discussion, but an expansive theology might do so.[48]

His "astroethics" doesn't have much truck with the view that morality stems from a belief in a supernatural God. His "astroethical principles stem from [a] reverence for life in all its manifestations, the product of the creativity of cosmic evolution, whether terrestrial or extraterrestrial." Dick posits a human destiny that is not supernatural but a result of:

... the endpoint of cosmic evolution. If cosmic evolution ends with humans and we are alone in the universe, our destiny involves stewardship of our pale blue dot and perhaps spreading, nurturing or even creating life in the universe—all pathways filled with ethical considerations. If cosmic evolution results in a biological universe—one in which life and intelligence is common, our destiny is to interact with this life in all its myriad possibilities, involving a quite different set of ethical considerations ...[49]

Dr. Dick's writing introduced me to a myriad of intellectual "fellow travelers," whose writings, in turn, led me to become acquainted with other intellectual "fellow travelers," some of whom I will now reference. (Thank you, Dr. Dick.) These communities of Space Age spiritual seekers are not composed of new age shamans but rather disciplined scientific and philosophic thinkers who adhere stringently to empirical data and deductive logic based on that data. Nessyahu would have been overjoyed to discover their existence. He had come to his preliminary conclusions regarding the Cosmodeistic Hypothesis as a young man in 1951 and then neglected them for over 20 years until he subsequently shared them with me soon after we first met and, recognizing my intellectual confusions and my own intellectual propensities, reckoned I was a harmless enough interlocutor. When I asked him why he had neglected this work for so long he answered, "When you come to certain conclusions that are so radical and you are completely alone with these conclusions you begin to think that maybe you are crazy." He would have been delighted to know that if he was crazy that at least he was in very good company. But I digress.

In *Reinventing the Sacred: A New View of Science, Reason, and Religion,*[50] physician, theoretical biologist, and complex systems researcher Stuart Kauffman proposed "a natural divinity that draws its sacred quality from the creativity of the universe itself,"[51] which we can call God (Carl Sagan would have loved this sentence.) He also doesn't believe that biology is reducible to physics and cannot be defined mathematically. He avers that biology deals with functions while physics describes happenings:

> The concept of "function" lifts biology irreducibly above physics, for as we shall see, we cannot prestate [provide the conditions for] the ever-new biological functions that arise and constitute the very phase space of evolution.

> Hence, *we cannot mathematize the detailed becoming of the biosphere* (italics mine; reflecting my instinct for a different language for life), nor write differential equations for functional variables we do not know ahead of time, nor integrate those equations, so no [physical] laws "entail" [i.e., resolve the inheritance of characteristics over a number of generations of] evolution.[52]

When he writes "functional variables we do not know ahead of time," he intersects with the ontological indeterminacy of Heisenberg cited in a previous chapter—the selfsame indeterminacy that exasperated Einstein. He also seems to agree that evolution creates its own final causes which drive the future course of evolution, creating ever more final causes—the emergence and evolution of consciousness putting this process on steroids. He writes, "Evolution creates the very possibilities into which it becomes."[53] This reflects my own observations that evolution is constantly producing its own, more sophisticated 'final causes' and is in keeping with the concept of *potentiality* that quantum physics introduced into the conversation. Moreover, *natural* selection takes no part in achieving "the very adjacent possible opportunities into which it becomes" because when human beings generate "economic evolution, we co-create the possibilities, often unknowingly, into which we are sucked." In other words, we conscious beings inadvertently create our own final causes by way of our own socio-economic creativity. Every thinker discussed in this chapter advocates creating our final causes intentionally rather than inadvertently, even though they do not use this kind of language.

In a *Scientific American* essay, science writer John Horgan writes approvingly about philosopher Thomas Nagel's book *Mind and Cosmos: Why the Materialist Neo-Darwinian Conception of Nature Is Almost Certainly False*:

> Nagel contends that current scientific theories and methods can't account for the emergence of life in general and one bipedal, big-brained species in particular. To solve these problems, Nagel asserts, science needs "a major conceptual revolution," as radical as those precipitated by heliocentrism, evolution and relativity.... A genuine theory of everything should make sense of the extraordinary fact that the universe "is waking up and becoming aware of itself." In other words, the theory should show that life, mind, moral-

ity, and reason were not only possible but even inevitable, latent in the cosmos from its explosive inception.[54]

Both Kauffmann and Nagel are in essence stressing the limitations of mathematical science to describe either life or consciousness, so I am certainly not an outlier in this contention. Continuing in this non-reductionist vein, philosopher David Chalmers, conjectures "that information, which emerges from certain physical configurations and processes and entails consciousness, is *a fundamental component of reality* (italics mine), as much as time, space, matter and energy." In other words, consciousness is as much *a fundamental component* of the cosmos as all the other cosmic stuff (matter and energy) and not just an epigenetic consequence of the other cosmic stuff. Evolutionary biologist, ethics philosopher and NASA exploration systems projects team member, Dr. Mark Lupisella envisions "a morally creative cultural cosmos—a post-intelligent, post technological universe that enters the realm of conscious evolution driven largely by moral and creative pursuits." Dr. Dick views this as "a worldview in which meaning and value may be bootstrapped from the universe,"[55] which I interpret to imply that a teleological universe has been being created by the very evolutionary character of the universe. Or perhaps our very existence as a consequence of cosmic evolution is the Cosmos reflecting on its own existence—perhaps consciousness is the Cosmos daydreaming about itself.

Australian-based evolutionary theorist John E. Stewart, of the *Evolution, Complexity and Cognition Group* of the Free University of Brussels has written extensively about the implications of the *future* evolution of consciousness for our planetary civilization and for the Cosmos in general. For my purposes I will rely on his book *EVOLUTION'S ARROW The Direction of Evolution and the Future of Humanity* as well as two of his most seminal essays, "The Future Evolution of Consciousness" (FEC) and "The Trajectory of Evolution and Its Implications for Humanity". Dr. Stewart's worldview is neatly summed up in the opening sentences of *EVOLUTION'S ARROW*:

> The emergence of organisms who are conscious of the direction of evolution is one of the most important steps in the evolution of life on any planet. Once organisms discover the direction of evolution, they can use it to guide their own evolution. If they know where evolution is going, they can work out what will produce success in the

future and use this to plan how they will evolve.[56]

I would have slightly modified "where evolution is going" to "the potentialities of where evolution can go" because the entire point in all of his writings is that once evolution produces consciousnesses, it inevitably masters evolutionary progression, thus becoming less deterministic and more volitional. Or, as he puts it, "can we [conscious humanity] play a significant role in the future evolution of life in the universe?"[57] His answer is most definitely yes—not only can we, but we unequivocally should. Like me, he believes it is imperative for humanity to implement societal policies and adopt individual ethics that will enable us to survive in the short-term as we begin to realize the very long term cosmic destiny we should choose for ourselves. As with the Cosmodeistic Hypothesis, he perceives "large-scale patterns in the evolution of life"[58] that are leading to certain inevitable consequences; that we conscious beings must comply with if we are to survive in the future. In opposition to most current evolutionary thought (exemplified by the late Stephen Jay Gould), Stewart asserts "that evolution has direction and that *the direction is progressive* (italics mine)."[59] Whether inevitability and progressive directionality indicate a teleological cosmos or not he is somewhat ambiguous about (as befits a member of the scientific community at this point in time). As we have seen, I am less coy on this subject. I really don't see any real difference between directional, inevitable, and purposeful. I will concede the working scientist's dogma opposing teleology, but if something is logically and empirically inevitable what's the difference? Isn't this a semantic problem; a modern iteration of how many angels can dance on the head of a pin? It is my view that the inevitable becomes teleological when the consciousness that evolution has inevitably produced becomes cognizant of the very process that created it and begins to take charge of its own future evolution—not as inevitability but as volitional choice. It seems to me that this is Stewart's main argument, whether you call it teleology or not (and he doesn't). Yes, evolution is random, but in the end it becomes purposeful by way of us.

Consider the lowly photon. It takes about 2 million years for it to make its way from the center to the surface of the sun, bouncing randomly like a pinball back and forth. Yet it is statistically *inevitable* that an infinitesimal percentage of photons will reach the surface where they will become *directional* light. An infinitesimal percentage of these directional photons will land on planet Earth becoming the fundamental food source of life on earth in the form of photosynthesis, whereupon they will have become in-sentiently *purposeful*. Now imagine if a photon had achieved consciousness and not only had become aware of its own evolutionary trajectory but had achieved the knowledge of how to control that trajectory and volitionally directed itself to the green leaves of Gaia, because it had become aware of *its* purpose in the ongoing spread and evolution of life in the Cosmos—wouldn't that be a volitional teleology that would have increased the speed of the evolution of life immeasurably. Now compare that to humanoid consciousness *deciding* that the evolutionary trajectory of consciousness is its expansion throughout the Cosmos and achieving the knowledge to control that trajectory makes it its civilizational mission to do so—volitional teleology eventually conquering the entire Cosmos.

In support of his fundamental argument, Stewart alludes to the self-evident *scientific* FACT (as opposed to philosophical deduction) of ever-increasing evolutionary cooperation between simpler organisms creating evermore complex organisms. I have previously described how our individual human existences are dependent on the trillions of microbial beasties that inhab-it our bodies, which in turn are dependent on us for their own existence; this cooperation being an evolutionary development for both us and the beasties. The emergence of consciousness has constantly created evermore complex and cooperative societies in the course of human history; "it is not only through increases in cooperation that evolution progresses. It also progresses through increases in the ability of living processes to adapt and evolve." Gould claimed there are no apparent mechanisms that would justi-fy progressivism in evolution; Stewart claims that ever-increasing coopera-tion that enhances ever faster adaptability is one of those mechanisms. He intersects the worldview of the Cosmodeistic Hypothesis when he writes:

> ... evolution exploits the benefits of cooperation amongst living entities through the formation of complex organi-zations of those entities. The organizations are structured so that cooperation is supported within the organization. On this planet, evolution has produced cooperative orga-nizations of molecular processes to form cells, cooperative organizations of cells to form multicellular organisms such as insects, frogs and ourselves, and cooperative organiza-tions of humans to form human societies .... Continued repetitions of this process forms cooperative organizations of larger and larger scale, each containing the smaller-scale

organizations that have evolved previously. As a result, human social systems include humans which include cells which include molecular processes. This evolution of organizations of larger and larger scale extends the scale over which living processes are organized cooperatively but leaves unexhausted the potential for cooperation between organizations of the largest scale. The potential for further beneficial cooperation will not be finally exhausted until all living processes are permanently organized into a single entity that is of the largest possible scale. The potential for increases in the scale of cooperation in this universe will end only when the entire universe is subsumed in a single, unified cooperative organization of living processes. *It will end only when the matter, energy and living processes of the universe are managed into a super organism on the scale of the universe* (italics mine).[60]

The primary evolutionary advantage of self-reflective consciousness (and to my mind the mechanism that should interest us most) is that it can now direct its own changes purposely. Volitional teleology has been let loose on the Cosmos. As Stewart puts it, conscious beings "will not just become aware of the direction of evolution. They will also become aware that their increasing awareness of the direction of evolution is itself a significant step in evolution."[61] Stewart's ultimate vision corresponds wholly with the Cosmodeistic Hypothesis and seems to me he has expanded the logic of Gaia theory to include the entire Cosmos.

Modern human societies are obviously not an endpoint of evolution. The organisms that play a significant role in the evolution of life in the universe will not be those that stop evolving when they reach the position we have. Guided by awareness of evolution's arrow, they will go on to form cooperative organizations of larger and larger scale and of greater and greater evolvability. First, they will form a unified planetary organization that manages the matter, energy and living processes of the planet. Then this organization will be progressively expanded to form still larger-scale societies of increasing evolvability. Matter, energy and life will be managed on the scale of the organism's solar system and, eventually, its galaxy. The greater the scale of the resources the organism is able to manage, the more likely it will be able to adapt to whatever challenges it faces in its conscious pursuit of future evolutionary success.[62]

Stewart, by implication, is friendly to my assertion that there is really no such thing as "natural" and "unnatural"; that conscious volitional humanity is as much a part of nature as a lake or a waterfall and thus technology and human infrastructure is a "natural" (and now primary) part of evolution on this planet. In his essay "The Future Evolution of Consciousness," he mobilizes a mass of research showing that consciousness in effect constructs its very own epigenetic modifiers that drive its own evolution—that humanity consistently and constantly creates ever more complex and ambitious societal and technological final causes modifying its own evolution. Human innovation is the very mechanism justifying the concept of progressive evolution that Gould claims does not exist. Gould's position is really the last gasp of a philosophical view that completely separated the researcher subject from the researched object. Quantum mechanics shattered this philosophical artifice in physics long ago. Stewart's (and others') worldview is undermining this artifice in evolutionary theory today; the absolutist pretensions of evolutionary *scientism* are being increasingly undermined.

It occurs to me that consciousness might be the ultimate evolutionary survival mechanism. The more developed the consciousness the better chance to survive in a constantly changing cosmic environment—consciousness being the ultimate survival of the fittest. Expanding this idea to infinite nature we might conclude that those cosmoses that have become conscious of themselves—i.e., become a supplementary "god" to the ever expanding "I will be what I will be" (infinite nature's) "Elohim," will have achieved infinite survivability. Cosmoses that haven't will perish and their detritus will be recycled by infinite nature to create new cosmoses; an eternal reincarnation process (a concept that various Hindu worldviews would not find strange). To know, really truly KNOW that you are part of this eternal process and that the star dust that has made you the totally unique you that you are—a unique you that has never existed before and will never exist again, but will forever be creating new existents, is truly thrilling and is what gives ultimate meaning to our individual and collective existences. We are all part of the everlasting and eternal Godding of the Universe and it might even be that the undifferentiated energy/information of our individual consciousnesses will also survive forever; that the stardust and the energy/information that has been us has always existed and will always exist; our very being as an inextricable part of and contributor to the eternity of existence.

Chapter Twenty One: Some Other Intimations

Literature, including essays and fiction, has also provided hints congruent with the CH. The most lasting literary triumph of Islam's Golden Age was the *Thousand and One Nights*, which contained stories depicting a multitude of worlds each with its own conscious beings. Walt Whitman believed that the human soul was in a state of progressive development. In *Walden*, the transcendentalist Thoreau writes "What distant and different beings in the various mansions of the universe are contemplating the same [stars] at the same moment [as we] .... Nature and human life are as various as our several constitutions." Transcendentalism is rife with such thinking. Ralph Waldo Emerson's poetic essay *The Over-Soul* describes the dichotomy between the phenomenological multiplicity of individual souls and the transcendental unity of the Over-soul; that collective "I am" indivisible soul of existence, incorporating those individual souls which are prevented from perceiving their essential unity with the very being of existence because of the inhibiting overlay of their individual experiences. Emerson describes it thus:

> We live in succession, in division, in parts, in particles. Meantime within man is the soul of the whole; the wise silence; the universal beauty, to which every part and particle is equally related, the eternal ONE. And this deep power in which we exist and whose beatitude is all accessible to us, is not only self-sufficing and perfect in every hour, but the act of seeing and the thing seen, the seer and the spectacle, the subject and the object, are one. We see the world piece by piece, as the sun, the moon, the animal, the tree; but the whole, of which these are shining parts, is the soul.[63]

In his book *Eureka*, Edgar Allan Poe anticipated modern science and cosmology. *Eureka* describes"

> ... a process that is now popularly known as the 'Big Bang' and the expanding universe. But it also contains ideas about the unity of space and time, the mathematical equality of matter and energy, the velocity of light and a rudimentary concept of relativity, black holes (including one at the center of our Milky Way), a "pulsating" universe that renews itself eternally, and other universes in other dimensions with different laws of nature. Contrary to the 19th-century

belief in a static and clockwork universe, *Eureka* describes
a dynamic universe that is continually evolving, *including
evolution and succession of species on earth, even the human
one* (italics mine).[64]

Science fiction is also rampant with such speculations. Arthur Clarke, in
2001 A Space Odyssey, referring to human aspirations to transcendence,
writes:

> A few mystically inclined biologists went still further. They
> speculated, *taking their cues from the beliefs of many religions*
> (italics mine), that mind would eventually free itself from
> matter. The robot body, like the flesh-and-blood one,
> would be no more than a stepping-stone to something
> which, long ago, men had called "spirit." And if there was
> anything beyond that, its name could only be God.

In *Childhood's End*, Clarke introduced the concept of the *Overmind* as a
cosmic collective of supra-conscious species under the direction of a supra-supra consciousness to determine if and when conscious species were
ready to graduate out of childhood and advance towards integrating with
the supra-supra consciousness. Nietzsche, with his concept of the *Overman*
(Supraman) certainly would have been sympathetic to Clarke's rendering.
More significant, for the purposes of this book, Clarke speculated that "*It
may be that our role on this planet is not to worship God but to create him.*"[65] In
similar fashion, the magnificently unique science fiction writer, Olaf Stapledon, spoke about the *emergence* of God in a talk at the British Interplanetary Society entitled "Interplanetary Man":

> Perhaps the final result of the cosmical process is the at-
> tainment of full cosmical consciousness, and yet (in some
> very queer way) what is attained in the end is also, from
> another point of view, the origin of all things. So to speak,
> God, who created all things in the beginning, is himself
> created by all things in the end.

One sees parallels to Teilhard's Alpha and Omega God in this pronounce-
ment. During the same talk, Stapledon expressed fears—similar to those of
James and Thoreau—about a civilization based entirely on experts that are
inherently prejudiced against the more expansive intellects and specula-

tions contained in science fiction, philosophy, and religion.

> Modern civilization cannot get along without experts .... But just because this is preeminently an age of experts, we have to face the serious danger that the human race may come to consist wholly of experts none of whom understands what his fellows are doing, or why they are doing it, and all of whom are ignorant of the pattern of human life as a whole. *Knowledge has become so vast that no single mind can speak with authority save in relation to his own particular corner of it ...* scientists are apt to make far-reaching pronouncements about matters beyond their special competence [such as] politics, ethics, religion, and philosophy.

Stapledon went on to chastise the lack of humility of these experts intruding into areas they are unfit for. (I am trying to imagine a debate between Stapledon and Gould regarding the "Non-overlapping Magisteria" hypothesis.)

Another slap in the face to this doubtful hypothesis would be the philosophical/theological implications of George Cantor's set theory. As Rudy Rucker observes in his book *Infinity and Mind*, "the intellectual pursuit of the absolute infinite is, as George Cantor realized, a form of the soul's quest for God."[66] Cantor's "infinity of infinities" upset many legacy theologians and he found himself in correspondence with Christian philosophers, Catholic Bishops and even the Pope in connection to the theological implications of his theories. In *The History of God*, Karen Armstrong writes that God "has been one of the greatest human *ideas* of all time";[67] that it represents humanity living up to its *divine potential*. Is this not reminiscent of Nietzsche's view that humanity is but a link to the future *Overman* (Supraman), which will be but a link to the Supra-Supraman and so on until divine potential becomes divinity realized? Or, in other words, humanity (conscious life) is Godness in the cosmic birth canal; Godness being born. Philosopher Benedikt Göcke has written: "the history of the world is the one infinite life of God, and we are part of the one infinite *divine being* (italics mine). We ... are therefore responsible for the future development of the life of the divine being"[68]; or, as we Jews would put it "being a partner in the ongoing act of creation." From Fraser Cain's web blog *Universe Today*, I learned that the famous Russian rocket scientist Konstantin Tsiolkovsky wrote an essay entitled "Is there a God?" in which he theorized "that a state of 'perfect intelligence' lay in humanity's future" and that other life forms in the Universe had *already* achieved this state of what I call supra-supra-intelligence. Cain quotes the great man:

> Millions of milliards of planets have existed for a long time, and therefore their animals have reached a maturity which we will reach in millions of years of our future on Earth. This maturity is manifest by perfect intelligence, by a deep understanding of nature, and by technical power which makes other heavenly bodies accessible to the inhabitants of the cosmos.

The Transhumanism movement is another mental attitude that mirrors the general logic of Cosmodeism. It seems to me that the desire to create Godness is the fundamental (volitional or subliminal) impulse of Transhumanism. I do not consider Transhumanism to mean going beyond humanism, thus negating the great humanist project of post Enlightenment humanity, as many critics claim it does. On the contrary, I believe it means that it is our *humanist* duty is to strive towards a *Transcendent* humanism; to volitionally evolve our species into supra-humans. It is our duty to overcome our present mediocre selves; to realize humanity's divine potential (as Armstrong would have it) or to become one with the divine being (as Benedikt Göcke would have it); not to disaffirm humanism, but to become transcendent humans: supra-humans; godlike humans. A fundamental Transhumanist task would most properly be to reunify humankind's various spiritual predispositions (religious, scientific, philosophical, literary) in order to realize Carl Sagan's vision that: "A religion, old or new, that stressed the magnificence of the Universe as revealed by modern science might be able to draw forth reserves of reverence and awe hardly tapped by the conventional faiths." To do this, we must recognize the emergence of self-reflective consciousness as the very essence of the cosmic drama. I believe *Cosmodeism* can become the foundation for a *Transhumanist Theology* that can inspire human beings to strive to become part of the *Divine Drama* (the *Godding* of the Cosmos); a theology that emphasizes that every one of us is part of the *Divine Drama* by virtue of our individual existence; that every one of us affects the development of the *Divine Drama* by our planetary actions (a cosmic butterfly effect); that our individual existence is inherently meaningful but it is up to us to make it actively purposeful by volitionally striving to transcend the limitations of humanness—to become transcendent humans; a bridge across time towards an end called "God."

Notes

1   Mercer's *Dictionary of the Bible*, p. 175.

2   Stuckey, 2000.

3   Snell, p. 246.

4   *Encyclopedia of Philosophy* Vol. 6, p. 22.

5   Ibid.

6   Hofstadter, p. 81.

7   Ibid., p. 84.

8   Viney.

9   Ibid.

10   Panexperientialism (literally, all [pan] of experience) is the view that evolution goes all the way down to subatomic particles. Consequently, human experience must have originated at the subatomic level, which implies that not just humans but individual cells, molecules, atoms, and particles, such as photons or electrons, incorporate a degree of subjective interiority.

11   A view that all reality is composed of minds or experience.

12   Ibid.

13   Einstein, 1936.

14   Pagels, p. 304.

15   Edwards, Vol.6, p. 23.

16   Schrodinger, 1956, pp. 84-88.

17   Schrodinger, 1984, p. 334

18   Wigner, Mehra, & Wightman, p. 14.

19   Laszlo, 1987, p. xi.

20   Laszlo, 2004, p.176

21   Kellerman.

22   Laszlo, p. xii.

23   Ibid., p. xv.

24 Russell, p. 98.

25 Ibid., p. 97.

26 Ibid., p. 10.

27 Teylor, pp. 612-615.

28 Lerner,1991, p. 8.

29 Ibid., pg. 12.

30 Ibid.

31 Davis, p. 1.

32 Ibid., p. 1.

33 Ibid., p. 3.

34 Ibid., p. 2.

35 Quoted in Davis, p. 3.

36 Rucker, p. xi.

37 Mure, p. 2.

38 Heisenberg, p. 3.

39 Ibid.

40 Ibid.

41 Aczel, p. 135.

42 Heisenberg, p. 4.

43 Ibid.

44 Wikipedia, *Bremermann's Limit*.

45 Dick, 2020, pp. 191-206.

46 Ibid.

47 Dick, 2003, pp. 65-74.

48 Dick, 2020, pp. 195-196.

49 Ibid., p. 196.

50 Kauffman, 2008.

51 Ibid., p.197.

52 Kauffman, 2014, pp. 3-8.

53 Horgan, 2015.

54 Horgan, 2013.

55 Dick, 2020, p. 199.

56 Stewart, 2000, p. 5.

57 Ibid., p. 6.

58 Ibid.

59 Ibid.

60 Ibid., pp. 19-20.

61 Ibid., p. 9.

62 Ibid., p. 11.

63 Emerson, 1841.

64 Van Slooten.

65 The quotation was provided by many sources.

66 Rucker, p. ix.

67 Ibid., p. 10.

68 Benedikt.

PART VI

Religious Intimations of the Cosmodeistic Hypothesis

Introduction

I believe our legacy faith traditions (what I have, heretofore, disparagingly referred to as "the Religion Business") have already intuited the Cosmodeistic Hypothesis in one way or another, or can accommodate the Cosmodeistic Hypothesis, to one degree or another, without significant damage to their self-perceived role in the divine drama. Every historical faith system, whether Monotheistic or non-Monotheistic, has evolved and changed beyond the recognition of its originators. There is an ironic Talmudic story about Moses coming back to life and sitting in on a Bible class given by Rabbi Akiva and admitting he had no idea what the good Rabbi was talking about. When he complained about it, he was told to shush and just listen to the wisdom of the Rabbis lesson. Erich Fromm's *You Shall Be as Gods* posits that the entire theme of the Old Testament—when examined as a historical whole—is not only that the very concept of God evolves but implies that the ambition of humankind is to become godlike. In justifying his conclusions, Fromm writes "a history that ascribes the same importance to all facts is nothing but an enumeration of events; it fails to make sense of the events."[1] I would add that any religious tradition that is not constantly evolving (i.e., continually *reinterpreting* its "holy" scriptures) eventually fails to seem sensible to growing numbers of its adherents and becomes either boring rote, or mystical mumbo-jumbo, alienating ever-growing numbers of its adherents.

Before gods or human beings existed, the raw material for divinity had existed for eternity. Chaos is a sloppy jumble where everything lacks boundary, definition, and identity, where everything is just undifferentiated stuff. Babylonian myth talks about divine evolution, whereby every subsequent reality gained ever-greater definition—this was the inspiration for the biblical creation story. Babylonian laws of reality compel the gods also: this is a premonition of natural law. The Babylonian god Marduk who created humans out of God anticipates the Hebrew belief that humans were made "in the image of God." It is now our task to create God out of humans. In her book *A History of God*, Karen Armstrong writes:

"... human beings are spiritual animals .... Homo sapiens are also homo religious ... [that] started to worship Gods as soon as they became recognizably human; they created religions at the same time as they created works of art ... like art, religion has been attempts to find meaning and value in life ... our current secularism is an entirely new experience, unprecedented in human history."[2]

Armstrong also asserts that the most profound religious thinkers have viewed the very concept of God as a product of the creative imagination and that even some medieval mystics claimed that "ultimate reality—mistakenly called God—was not even mentioned in the Bible."[3] This is because the idea of God is beyond banal concepts such as "existence." The very phrase "I believe in God" is pregnant with epistemological difficulties: what is belief *for you*; what is God *for you*? Armstrong stresses that every generation creates its own image of God according to the spiritual needs of the particular historical period they live in. If so, then religion might be the most pragmatic utilitarian construct of civilization.

If it is the *Idea of God* that is important, then surely people can accept the concept of a future God, or a God as an integral part of a never-ending evolutionary process. Armstrong's book is an outstanding survey of the evolutionary character of religion. I recommend reading the last chapter, "Has God a Future?" First, it is an excellent summation of the intellectual experimentation taking place amongst modern and postmodern theologians and serves as an excellent underpinning for my purposes in this book. Using this last chapter as a literary final cause for what precedes it, go and read the entire book for its educational and intellectual value. Reza Aslan's *God: A Human History of Religion* is another excellent read (with interesting speculations as to the future of religion in the "Conclusion"). Bart Ehrman's *How Jesus Became God* is also recommended. If after you have read any one of the three you are not convinced as to the evolutionary character of our legacy religions, you have probably have not even have gotten this far in this book.

The Scholastic period in particular (c.1100 to the Renaissance) highlights how syncretic accretions stimulated the evolution of western faith traditions. During this period, neo-Platonic, neo-Pythagorean and Aristotelian thinking profoundly impacted Judaism, Christianity, and Islam, leading to neo-Platonic and neo-Aristotelian syncretisms that radically transformed the philosophical *and theological* foundations of Catholicism, Orthodoxy and Protestantism. St. Augustine was influenced by Plato, and St. Thomas Aquinas was influenced by Aristotle. Maimonides (Rabbi Moses ben Maimon—the Rambam), of whom it has been said by the most orthodox of Jews, "not since Moses has there been one like Moses," venerated Aristotle. His teachings upset so many Rabbis of his time it is rumored that some tried to assassinate him (his greatness *universally* acknowledged by Jews only after his death). His intellectual authority was so great that even the Catholic Saint Aquinas referred to him several times when that great doctor of the Medieval Church was making his Aristotelian arguments in the *Summa Theologica*. Maimonides, for his part, had been significantly influenced by several great Aristotelian and neo-Platonic Islamic thinkers such as Al-Farabi, Avicenna, and Averroes.

Viewed historically, every religion has responded to political power, technological innovation, changing cultural and social values, and new intellectual perceptions in order to guarantee their institutional survival. Any social, cultural, or national entity that has survived until today has evolved, because what does not evolve perishes. Since every legacy religion in the world is now struggling to maintain and pass on its accumulated wisdom about how to live a truly human life ("in the image of God?!") when their Bronze and Iron Age belief systems and practices have become increasingly repugnant to ever-growing numbers of well-educated people looking for meaning in their lives, I believe Cosmodeism provides a lifeline by offering a Space Age metaphysics which by definition will be anti-dogmatic, on the one hand, and an inspiration to a revised human ethics, on the other. This is not only a strategic maneuver on my part (to advance the Cosmodeistic Hypothesis by all means possible); it also substantive. I see no benefit in throwing out the baby of wisdom and practiced social interaction accumulated over centuries and expounded in traditional religious practices with the dirty dogmatic bathwater of the organized Religion Business.

I also have more utilitarian reasons for trying to access the organized religion avenue, despite my loathing for the hypocrisies, cruelties, and barbarities of the organized Religion Business throughout history (and continuing even today). Because, as Armstrong has noted, even more than *Homo sapiens* (so-called "intelligent" humankind), human beings have been *Homo religiosus*. This is not simply a psychological/philosophical speculation; it is an objective empirical fact. Let's face it, intelligent human beings are but a tiny minority of the planet's population, whereas religious human beings still seem to be the vast majority (perhaps there is an inverse proportional relationship: the more religious we are the stupider we seem to become). This weak attempt at witticism aside, *Homo religiosus* refers to the notion that human existence is inherently religious. Even the most dogmatic atheists—if they be honest observers of history and culture—must admit to the objective fact that the religious propensity of humankind is one of the most persistent facts of human history and human nature. Proponents of this notion have included Hegel, Kierkegaard, William James, Karl Jaspers, Paul Tillich, Erich Fromm, Viktor Frankl, Abraham Maslow, Erik Erikson, and a myriad of lesser known but no less important thinkers. As philosopher, psychologist and theologian Todd DuBose puts it:

> The inherent religiosity these and other theorists refer to, is not a person's creedal beliefs or institutional commitments per se (in my words the organized Religion Business) but refer to *our existential drive toward transcendence, freedom, and meaning-making, no matter the differences of religion, or religious backgrounds or, convictions* (italics mine).[4]

The Cosmodeistic attitude to traditional religious texts and traditions is utilitarian, i.e., their usefulness to the fundamental Cosmodeistic premise—that godness is an inherent, ongoing, evolutionary process of existence as such. Such an attitude influences the history of all religious traditions. The Talmud is a prime example. It bends biblical texts to the commonplace needs of a living people interacting with a complex, ever-changing, often hostile environment. This utilitarianism was not only practical it was intellectual. Amongst the Jews, Philo interpreted the tradition in the spirit of Plato, the Rambam (Maimonides) in the spirit of Aristotle and Herman Cohen in the spirit of Kant. Muslim and Christian theology is as much Platonic and Aristotelian as it is Koranic or New Testament. Thought evolves, and, as Erich Fromm suggested, the way we think about thought also evolves "... ideas .... have their roots in the real life of society."[5]

The point is that even atheists are religious in the sense that we yearn for transcendence and meaning—as in: WHAT THE HELL DOES IT ALL MEAN! And here I must differentiate between faith and meaning. If religion were to deal exclusively with meaning rather than faith (faith being belief in something *without* evidence) it would have something to say to the modern human being. Today, of course, the fundamentalist denominations of our legacy religions seem to demand faith *against* evidence, which, given their political power, is leading to numerous damaging social phenomena and policy decisions around the planet. Alain de Botton, in his book *Religion for Atheists,*[6] sketches a secular need for religion that gives meaning to our communal and individual selves. While first affirming his credentials as an atheist, he avers that human beings have invented religions to solve certain problems that secular societies have not dealt with successfully; namely, how to create harmonious communities despite our selfishness and inherent violence, and how to cope with the angst of being human beings aware of our own inevitable erasure from existence as well as the daily frustrations, losses, and defeats of life. I disagree with his first claim. It seems to me that secular *Constitutionalism* has done a better job than religions in creating civilized societies out of a mixed multitude of peoples who hold radically different religious views.

Indeed, it was the European *Wars of Religion* (killing as many people as the Black Death in some areas of Europe) that was one of the main stimuli to the development of modern Constitutionalism. His second point is better taken and a major incentive of mine in writing this book. He, like me, does not want to discard the accumulated wisdom and structured rituals and ceremonies that have evolved naturally over time and have enabled us to deal with the absurdities of our existence. I am referring to the familiar folkways, celebrations and traditions of various religious legacies which can, and perhaps should, be preserved even when their metaphysical foundations have become absurd—especially in a world where the increased rate of the rate of change is so intense, we begin to feel we are in the midst of a terrible cultural storm without any anchor to secure us. Traditional practices can be that anchor, connecting us to our past as we venture into an unsure future at the speed of light, while keeping us firmly moored in our essential humanity.

For example, as a Jew, I believe the tradition of becoming "Bar Mitzvah" (beginning to accept the responsibilities of becoming an adult human being) can be a serious antidote to the airheaded, irresponsible preoccupation with trivialities characteristic of the *TikTok* generation. According to Jewish law, parents are responsible for their child's actions until a certain age (13 for boys, 12 for girls), after which children begin to be held accountable for their own actions. In other words, becoming "Bar Mitzvah" is a "this is your life" moment. You are now beginning a lifelong task of taking increasing responsibility for your life; increasingly prohibited from blaming your parents, society, teachers, friends, colleagues, and social status at birth for what you do with your life. The Universe really could not care less about your whining, so begin to grow up. I don't have to believe in talking snakes, or miracles, or a vengeful old man in the sky who will be annoyed if I eat shrimp, to celebrate this as a valuable ritual in the ongoing development of the planetary citizens of the future. Ironically, my atheistic repurposing of Bar Mitzvah might have much more spiritual significance than the ostentatious show it has become in which the child declaims a portion of the Torah the meaning of which, the historical context of which, and the ethical implications of which he doesn't even understand—all in order to have a big expensive party afterwards enabling parents to strut with pride and show off.

Jewish mourning practices are another example of what I would like to see preserved. To my mind, they are an example of psychological genius. The first seven days after the funeral (the *Shiva* means seven) is devoted to dealing with the immediate shock and trauma. Traditionally you are enveloped in support from extended family, friends and neighbors who come to visit and reminiscence about the deceased as well as discuss other mundane things of the day in order to distract and help alleviate the pain. After the seven days you are required to return to your regular life, because in Judaism life always trumps death. Judaism is not a death cult that celebrates suffering as spiritually enlightening or brings you closer to God. Following the *Shiva*, Judaism recognizes that you are still spiritually burdened with a terrible sense of loss, so thirty days after the burial (the *Shloshim* literally means thirty) family and friends get together at the grave for another ceremony and after a year (*Yom Ha'Shana*) yet again. In other words, you are gradually brought out of your pain in a systematic way and returned to normal life without ever forgetting the deceased. You are not permitted to make a fetish out of visiting the grave, on the one hand (not a death cult), nor are you permitted to forget, on the other hand ("never forget"). Every year you light a candle and perhaps visit the grave. But this is more a celebration of our memories of the person rather than as an obsession with mourning. Many times, this yearly visit to the grave becomes occasion for jokes and pleasant memories about the deceased as well as joining with friends and family in an enjoyable meal afterwards. I put it to the reader that if you combined the insights of Freud, Jung, Adler, Rank, Frankl, and Maslow, you could not have come up with a more psychologically astute process. And you don't have to believe in a supernatural God who created the entire universe and then chose the Jews ("how odd of God to choose

272

the Jews") in order to take spiritual advantage of this practice.

Cosmodeistic "Catholics" might do something equally transformative with Confession and Communion if they demystify both, making them intellectually and psychologically accessible to an educated human being in the 21st century. The Catholic sacrament of Confession might be as psychologically astute as Jewish mourning practices. Getting one's accumulated guilt off of one's chest can be as therapeutic, if not more so, than paying good money to go to a psychiatrist. But, with one caveat: getting absolved of one's sins and transgressions by another human being who is God's so-called representative on earth and walking out of the Confessional feeling truly cleansed would only work for modern human beings who have sociopathic propensities to begin with. As far as Communion goes, I can see it being repurposed to commune with the Godding of the Cosmos rather than with Jesus as the incarnate God by drinking his blood and eating his flesh. If it were communion with Jesus as a mortal human being, who in the course of human civilization has been one of the primary human links in "The Great Chain of Godding" (endowed with a Kabbalistic "spark" of divinity), I could envision it as an act as profound as the Bar Mitzvah (de Chardin talked about communion with existence itself). Even today, does any modern Catholic seriously view Communion as other than a metaphor and not a cannibalistic reality: the wafer magically turning into the actual flesh of Jesus and the wine into the actual blood of Jesus? I suggest that if they really believed this, most Catholics would have trouble not gagging with nausea when they took Communion. More important, as a Jew, I wouldn't want any Christian to stop celebrating Christmas. It's many Jews' favorite time of the year—the only time we sense that Christians actually seem to behave as Christians say they should behave all the time.

What we must keep in mind at all times is that our legacy religions have developed their traditions based upon, and as a reaction to, vast historical and social experience. These traditions are often as not commonsensical and nuanced, reflecting long epochs of human experience and understanding of the subtleties of the human condition. They are like the variegated layers of the great cities of history, with their ancient, medieval, modern, and postmodern architecture existing side by side and interacting, each with the other, in the daily lives of the populace, acting as a kind of physical background music framing the psyche and sense of aesthetic of its citizens. They are interesting, unlike the sterile, one-dimensional cities of America's

Sunbelt. One does not have to believe in literal transubstantiation in order to be stunned to the depths of your soul by the spiritual ambitions of the people who built the great Gothic cathedrals. Likewise, one does not have to believe in talking snakes to be struck by the awesome personalities and stories of the Old Testament. One can be a complete atheist and still be moved to tears by Church and Synagogue music. One can reject completely the theological underpinnings and arguments of Maimonides and Aquinas and still be thrilled by the power of their minds. Just as urban renewal has moved from tearing down everything old in order to create an ultra-rational "newness," towards keeping what is valuable from the old and allowing a new aesthetic ecosystem to evolve out of what was, so might our spiritual reformers do the same—enabling a new psychic ecosystem to evolve out of what has been.

Following are some general observations as to how traditional religions might accommodate Cosmodeism. I will begin with the religious possibilities of my people—the Jewish People—and devote disproportionate space for the simple reason that despite being completely non-observant it is the tradition I am most familiar with. Also, I am more in tune with the postdenominational Rabbi Zalman Schacter-Shlomi, who saw himself as "a Jewish practitioner of a generic religion"[7] and looked for truth in every spiritual tradition. He praised Buddhist, Hindu, and Sufi meditative practices, especially *vipassana*. In this he was a practitioner of the "Perennial Philosophy"—the view that all religions and philosophies can be traced back to the same fundamental (perennial) questions.

Chapter Twenty-Two: Jewish Intimations

Jewish literature over the millennia is pregnant with raw material amenable to the Cosmodeistic Hypothesis—the Kabbala especially. I refer, of course, to the prodigious intellectual thought experiments conducted by the giants of the Kabbala, not the magical mumbo jumbo of counter-culture Kabbala that excites the "great thinkers" of the entertainment industry and pop culture fashion setters. For Kabbalists, existence has existed forever (the *Ein Sof*—the eternal "without end"), yet nothing accessible to human understanding—whether physical *or spiritual*—had yet been created. The *Ein Sof* was not a "thing," it was "no thing"; it was "nothing." It encompassed infinitudes and latent finitudes, out of which appeared the creative force; "spirit" which became the creator of our world—the fountainhead of all subsequent creation: *our* "God" who created "the heavens and the earth." Or, in the language of the Cosmodeistic Hypothesis, infinite existence (the Universe) enabled the creation our finite world (our Cosmos). Godness itself—the creative force ("may the force be with you")—was itself created by the "no thing" infinitude of existence. Kabbalistic thinking also did not have a virgin birth; it was implied in numerous preexistent sources. A *Midrash* posits that God created many worlds but was not satisfied until he created the world he *was* satisfied with—this world. Other Midrashim conclude that the "first week" of Creation lasted for extremely lengthy periods of time.[8]

The Ramban (Nachmanides) (1194–1270), portending evolutionary thinking as well as process philosophy and theology, highlighted the limitations of human language in describing the existence of existence when he wrote:

> The Holy One, blessed be He, created all things from absolute non-existence. Now we have no expression in the sacred language for bringing forth something from nothing other than the word 'bara' (created). Everything that exists under the sun or above *was not made from non-existence* (italics mine) at the outset. Instead He brought forth from total and absolute nothing a very thin substance devoid of corporeality but *having a power of potency*, fit to assume form and to proceed from [quantum] *potentiality* into reality.[9]

The first verse in the Torah reads, "In the beginning, *Elohim* created the heavens and the earth"—*Elohim* being a pluralized title meaning "Master over all forces" The Ramban interpreted this to mean that "*Elohim* is the Master over all forces of creation; the word being a compound construction alluding to all the forces God uses to run His universe." For Kabbalists, *Elohim* expresses the *phenomena* of the creator. *YHWH*, on the other hand, indicates a concept of God that moderns might call the *noumenon* of the creator (What C.S. Lewis called the Tao—the abyss before creation.)

Other sages calculated that the world was billions of years old. Maimonides taught not only that Judaism must adapt its teachings to the discoveries of science, but also that the Bible was not to be taken literally, especially the story of creation from the beginning to the 6th day of so-called creation. I have a mental image of him adapting the *Halacha* (the code of Jewish behavior) to Paul Davies's quote above and repeated here that "It is clear that there exist *self-organizing* processes in every branch of science" because "cosmologists ... believe that immediately following the Big Bang the universe was in an essentially featureless state."[10] Davies's depiction of existence is compatible with the opening lines of Genesis: "In the beginning God created the heaven and the earth. Now the earth was unformed (chaotic) and void (which can mean empty but also invalid or worthless or an undifferentiated mass of raw stuff or in a featureless state) ..." and then the spirit of God (evolution) created order (cosmos) out of chaos (order being something of value). Substitute the term God (Elohim: meaning powers) for self-organizing process and we have set the table for the Godding (*YHWH*—the "I will be what I will be") of the universe, or as Davies says, "the universe has never ceased to be creative." I would have added that the Universe (infinite space/time) has never ceased to be *created*. Substitute Big Bang for *Elohim* and our own phenomenological cosmic space-time (the heavens) was created but was without form (featureless) and the spirit of God (evolution) moved upon this featureless state (Thales' waters) and created order (featureness).

The negative theology of Maimonides (what God is not), joined to the evolutionary concept of God implicit in the Kabbalah, framed by the very language of the Bible, could enable various constituents of the Jewish community to adopt Cosmodeism as their underlying ideological foundation. *Apophatic theology* is the technical term for negative theology. It has impacted, to one degree or another, the speculative musings of every great religion on the planet. Since God is beyond description, *apophatic theology* rejects all positive statements of God; statements that describe what God is. To attribute qualities to God is to limit it because descriptions and definitions limit the illimitable. The Hebrew word for "to define" is "lehagdeer" from the word "gadair," or fence—literally meaning to fence in or put a border around. To use the language of this book, it means to define a finite order (cosmos) that can be precisely described, thus distinguishing it from the limitlessness "chaos" (*tohu vevohu*) of infinite existence. Dictionary definitions of "define" include: "to mark out the boundary or limits of; to show or describe (someone or something) clearly and completely; to show the shape, outline, or edge of [something] very clearly." Dictionary definitions of "describe" include: "give an account in words of [someone or something]; including all the relevant characteristics, qualities, or events [such as] the man was described as a short white guy in shorts and really ugly legs." God cannot be described or defined; it is not a "tall black man with freckles"—it is not Morgan Freeman, despite what Hollywood would have us believe. God is not a thing; God is no thing; *God is nothing.* God is, using C.S. Lewis's words once again, the Tao, "[the]... reality before all predicates; the abyss [infinite nature; *tohu vevohu*] *before* the Creator Himself (the Big Bang creating our cosmic space/time)."

The fact is, in contradiction to that rather infantile and misleading concept "the Judeo-Christian Tradition," there really is no Jewish theology—literally knowledge of God. One cannot know what one cannot describe. This is precisely why it is forbidden for Jews to actually phonate the tetragrammaton (YHWH), as by phonating it they would be limiting it. Jews substitute Adonoi (Lord), or Hashem (the name). The second alternative is an epistemological paradox: what cannot be named is *the* Name; the unnamable being, the very identity *and name* of existence per se. Karen Armstrong describes how this inability to actually talk about God has been the uniting thread of the greatest thinkers of *every* religion: Monotheistic, Eastern and Pagan.

I have already noted the evolutionary concept of God implicit in the fact that the so-called names of God in the Bible are verbs, not nouns, that the proper translation would be "Godding," rather than God. The proper translation of Yehovah, (YHWH as it is pronounced with vowels added—since Hebrew has no vowels), in Modern Hebrew could be *"will be* constituted"—a futurist, never-ending process. In Biblical Hebrew it is in the imperfect form. Consider the irony of that; the so-called perfect entity described in the imperfect form. It is suggested by some scholars that the other name for God (Elohim) refers to the plural "gods"— a generic term for all the pagan gods, which, unlike YHWH, are nouns, i.e., *defined* entities. The commandment "Thou shalt have no other gods before me" is essentially a *henotheistic*[11] statement, which recognizes the existence of other gods but commands the Israelites to worship their god exclusively, or preeminently. As we know, in Canaan, the Israelites also worshipped other gods—hence the grouchiness of the prophets. Given this interpretation, *Baruch Ata Adonai Eloheinu Melech Ha'Olam* could be construed as, "Blessed art thou, *our* Lord, who is the *actual King* of the Universe, over the other gods." An even more accurate reflection of its intent might be "Blessed art thou *my* God, the true King of the Universe over all the other inferior gods." A Cosmodeistic Judaism could easily revise that to "blessed art thou, the foundational evolutionary force of the universe that directs all other forces in the universe." Or as they said in *Star Wars* "may the force be with you." (My late friend and former collaborator Rabbi Moshe Dror thought *Star Wars* was a theologically intriguing movie.)

But it is the Kabbalah that offers the Jewish tradition the opportunity to adopt the Cosmodeistic Hypothesis more than any other. The *Zohar*[12] is a major constituent of the Kabbalah. It translates the first line of the Torah—*BeResheet Bara Elohim*—differently than the standard translation: not *"In the beginning God created,"* but rather it was *"the beginning* [that] created God"; infinity being the force (the *Tao*) that created the Big Bang (our God) which created our evolutionary space/time (the heavens and the earth).[13] The Cosmodeistic principle of an infinite nature creating our finite Cosmos was anticipated almost 500 years ago by Isaac Luria (known as the Ari) (1534–1572). Lurianic Kabbalah became the prevailing method of interpreting the Kabbalah until this very day. He wrote:

> *Prior to Creation (italics mine)*, there was only the *infinite* light filling all existence. When it arose in God's Will to create worlds and emanate the emanated ... He contracted (in Hebrew "tzimtzum") Himself in the point at the center, in the very center of His light [the singularity?]. He restricted that light, distancing it to the sides surrounding the central point [thus creating a bounded finiteness, or cosmos], so that there remained a void, a hollow empty

space [the unbounded space/time of infinite existence], away from the central point .... In the space of that void He emanated, created, formed and made *all the worlds* [the Big Bang and our evolutionary, cosmic space/time, as well as others].[14]

In Kabbalistic literature, the world of the Edomite kings that *predated Adam*, is known as *Olam HaTohu*; literally, "world of emptiness," which is referred to at the beginning of the Bible, in Genesis 1:2: "... when the earth was empty ..." (The word "chaos" has also been taken as being a direct translation of *Tohu*.)

The thinking of Rabbi Abraham Isaac Kook (1865–1935), considered by many to be one of the greatest rabbinic figures of the 20th century, could also accommodate the Cosmodeistic Hypothesis. Consider the following poem (*The Song of Existence*) which contains his entire philosophy of life, and hence by implication how a good Jew should perceive and conduct his or her own existence:

> "There is the one who reaches higher—*uniting with all existence* (**italics mine**), with all creatures and *all worlds* (**the multiverse**). They sing a song with all of these."
>
> An individual locates himself in himself. (***If I am not for myself who will be***)
> Then he locates himself in the world that surrounds him, his society, community, and nation. (***If I am only for myself what am I***)
> The community locates itself in itself *and then locates itself in all humankind.* (***If WE are only for ourselves what are WE***)
> Humankind at first locates itself in itself and *then in the world.* (***From the earth's crust to the entire Cosmos***)
> The world locates itself in itself and then locates itself in *all the worlds that surround them.* (***The eventual joining with other conscious life forms***)
> The whole universe locates itself in itself, and then locates itself in the elevated inclusiveness of all existence. (***Finite cosmos within infinite existence***)
> Existence locates itself in itself and then locates itself in the full treasure of the supernal light, in the multitudinousness

of life and its oceanic source in the Divine Light.

And all these recognitions unite together and return
to become one unit that in its entirety is great beyond
measure. It is powerful, whole, complete, and outstanding
beyond limit and purpose. (*The Cosmodeistic Godding*)
and the flow of life flows forth, and holy light grows.
Notebook 8:46[15]

Consider, also, the words of the *Amora* Rabbi Hoshayah (circa 200 CE) in
the *Midrash* Bereishit Rabbah 9:2: "Anything created in the first six days,
needs further actions (i.e., are incomplete), for example mustard seeds
need sweetening, peas needs sweetening, wheat needs grinding, even humans need fixing." One may deduce from Hoshayah's words that the major
task of humanity is to actively improve God's creation (to be his partner in
the *ongoing* never-ending act of creation). In the same portion we also find
the following:

> Rabbi Levi began: (Proverbs 25:2) "It is the glory of
> "God" (**infinite nature**) to conceal a matter, and the glory
> of a king (**conscious life**) to explicate a matter." Rabbi Levi
> said in the name of Rabbi Chama bar Chanina: From the
> beginning of the book to this point is Divine glory, a con-
> cealed matter. From this point on is kings' glory, explicated
> matters. The glory of the words of Torah, which are com-
> pared to kings, as it says, (Proverbs 8:15) "Through me
> [Wisdom] kings reign," are explicated matters.

How might a modern Jew interpret these words? Well, first of all that human beings have no idea why existence exists, because the creative force
of existence is forever concealed from us: the "Divine glory [is] concealed
from us." And if, according to the great Zionist leader and thinker, Zeev Jabotinsky, "every man is a king" and according to Rabbi Levy it is the "king's
glory [to] explicate matters" it is the task of every human being to be a partner with the Divine Glory of existence (the "I am that I am," the "suchness"
of existence), which in achieving wisdom and explicating matters, including, and perhaps especially, the matter of our cosmic future. It most certainly does not mean we must consult with an ignorant Rabbinate that builds
and maintains its power by declaring education in science, math, and computers as being fundamentally opposed to the Torah. As the *Amora* Gamliel

said (further repeated by the Rambam 1,000 years later), "love work and hate the Rabbinate"—"work" meaning the effort to understand and "hate" meaning to despise the presumption of a self-appointed elite to know what the "suchness" of existence truly is, let alone wants. And perhaps to speculate that conscious life as a product of and an integral part of the "I am that I am" (which by the way is translated in the Greek language bible as "I am being [itself]"), must, as its ultimate existential project, *create* the meaning of existence *per se* and thus the meaning of its own existence. The present level of consciousness is of course incapable of doing this and thus it is our intermediate task to take control of our own evolution and strive to achieve a supraconsciousness that will continue our path to divine glory. Allow me to continue from the same Midrash:

> "And God saw all that He had made, and behold it was very good." Rabbi Tanchuma began: (Eccl. 3:11) "He brings everything to pass precisely at its time." Rabbi Tanchuma said: The world was created at its time; the world was not appropriate for creation before this. Rabbi Abahu said: From this we learn that the Holy Blessed One *was creating worlds and destroying them, creating worlds and destroying them, until he created these.* (italics mine; an analog to Hindu cosmology!) He said, "This is good for me; those are not good for me." Rabbi Pinchas explained Rabbi Abahu's reasoning: "And God saw all (pl.) that He had made and behold it (sing.) was very good." THIS [**world**] is good for me; THOSE [**worlds**] were not good for me.

I interpret this to mean that *this* world is good for Him because in this world (this Cosmos) the creative mechanism of evolution can be that Holy Spirit "hovering over the waters."

In his book *Sefer HaBrit* (Book of the Covenant), the Kabbalist Rabbi Pinchas Eliyahu Horowitz of Vilna (1765–1821), in reference to Judges 5:23, contended that *Meroz* is an inhabited planet and that God created an infinite number of worlds, of physical, spiritual, and inter-dimensional nature. He also had some very harsh criticisms for Jews who did not educate their children for secular professions and the sciences. In this he was like Maimonides and the Vilna Gaon (literally, the "Genius of Vilna"—universally recognized as the greatest Rabbi of his era). Relying on his interpretations of many Talmudic sources, Rabbi Horowitz made reference to something like 10^{18} stars in the observable universe, a figure that is very close to the accepted number that can now be seen. He was of the opinion that many planets are inhabited and that just as sea creatures differ from land creatures, because of their different environments, so too will natives of other worlds differ from human beings. The Ari (Rabbi Yitzchak Luria), also spoke of an "infinite number of spiritual worlds." The Kabbalist Rabbi Yitzchak of Akko (1250–?) contradicted the popular fundamentalist interpretation of the six days of creation and a 6,000-year-old Earth. Referring to the work of Rabbi Nehunya Ben haKanah (1st/2nd centuries?), who believed there were 42,000 years prior to the biblical Adam and depending on Psalm 90:4 that for God a 1,000 years is as one day and thus a divine year equals, 365,250 earth years, as well as on the Talmud portion that claims the world will exist for seven 7,000 year "Sabbatical" or *Shemita* cycles, calculates the age of the universe as being 15,340,500,000 years old—similar to that which Big Bang cosmologists attribute to our Cosmos.

The belief that many human civilizations existed before Adam was common amongst early Talmudic Sages. They would refer to Psalms (105:8) which read: "He remembered His covenant forever—the Word he commanded for *a thousand generations* ..." Talmud commentary infers from this that that God's Law, the Torah, was given at Mount Sinai *after* the elapse of 1,000 human generations. Since Moses was of the 26th generation following Adam, this implies that *974 generations existed before Adam*. They would support this view by referencing Genesis 36: 31-39 which gives the names of the kings who "... reigned in the land of Edom *before* a king reigned over the Children of Israel." Since the sages considered Adam, to be the first "King of Israel," it becomes self-evident that generations upon generations existed before the story of Genesis. The Kabbalah teaches that the actions of an individual human being, even minor actions can have significant consequences and even impact the entire Universe. There is certainly an ethical anticipation of the butterfly effect of Chaos Theory in the following from Isaac Luria: "There is no sphere of existence, including organic and *inorganic* (italics mine) nature, that is not full of holy sparks which are mixed in with husks (i.e., divinity as part and parcel of material manifestations) and need to be separated from them and lifted up."[16] This is certainly a panpsychic intuition which also anticipates Kant's differentiation between the external phenomenon (husks) and the noumenon of a thing (the essential spark of its very being), as well as Einstein's ultra-Realism when he expressed his reservations about quantum theory describing ultimate reality rather than just a mathematical technique that simply describes the behavior of reality, and gives us the means to manipulate that behavior (much like behaviorism in psychology) rather than really understanding reality as such.

Abraham Abulafia (c.1240–c.1290), the founder of the school of *Prophetic Kabbalah*, wrote: "now we are no longer separated from our source, and behold we are the source and the source is us .... We are so intimately united with It, we cannot ... be separated from It, for we are It."[17] I interpret this as follows: to know yourself is to know God; to know God is to know yourself —the "yourself" being the I/Thou relationship described by Martin Buber (1878–1965). This is reminiscent of Emerson; not the lonely individual alone in creation but the essential internal unity of the divine "It" which by definition contains the divine potentiality of every conscious being. I suggest that this observation can serve as a foundation for a new Jewish ethics in which all of us are charged with contemplating the possibility that we might potentially be *a* "messiah" (a factor in introducing the messianic age) and thus to act accordingly, in the spirit of Tikkun Olam (literally—"repairing the world" —something that Jews are expected to engage in), and eventually to achieve the cosmic godness that the Cosmodeistic Hypothesis suggests. Rebbe Nachman of Breslov (1772–1810) wrote "There are many levels of universes beyond this ... level above level ..."[18] and believed that a tsaddik (a righteous man) can attain a "cosmic consciousness." Mordechai Kaplan (1881–1983), founder of the Jewish Reconstructionist movement, perceived God as the sum of natural processes. Rabbi Norman Lamm, former chancellor of Yeshiva University, in the intellectual tradition of the Rambam (i.e., it is incumbent on every generation to reinterpret the Torah), asserted that if the existence of extraterrestrial life should be confirmed, religious scholars must revise their teachings and didn't rule out this possibility from an Orthodox Jewish point of view.[19] Rabbi Joseph Soloveitchik, considered by many to be the one of paramount American Orthodox Rabbis of all time, remarked that life on other planets would only reflect God's greatness, and would not contradict the role of the Jewish people to perform God's will here on Earth.[20]

From all this legacy Rabbinic elucidation to the possibility that the Jews will accept a concept of the multiverse and an infinite number of cosmoses which have been created by the infinite "I am," the infinite "suchness," the infinite "itness," requires no great stretch of the imagination. The unique, finely tuned precise laws of our Cosmos, without which life could not have possibly arisen, is often cited by the more enlightened Rabbis (such as the late, great Chief Rabbi of Great Britain, Jonathan Sachs) as proof of the existence of a conscious *purposeful* God. But our precisely-tuned Cosmos can be logically explained in another way. If the Universe is infinite in time and space, then it is inevitable that infinities of worlds have been created (Cantor's "infinity of infinities"). This makes the creation of the finely-tuned precise laws of our Cosmos inevitable. The manner of infinite nature creating and destroying these worlds is beyond science's ability to explain (and even the Rabbis did not deign to inquire about God's *how and why* regarding the 7,000 divine year cycles). But, being infinite in time and space, it is inescapable that infinite nature has created other cosmoses like ours. The fact is, *we* are here, "Kings" of our domain "commanded" by our own internal teleological predispositions and propensities to explicate *our* world and, being an integral part of the Godding process, "perfect" it.

Nessyahu envisioned a special place for the Jews and the Jewish outlook on life in "influencing" the rest of humanity to join what he called this "cosmic race for survival and significance." He justified his Jewish ambition by referring to the historic role the Jews had played in the development of human civilization and felt that the Zionist project would be essentially meaningless unless it strove to give concrete expression to this historic role within the unique circumstances of the 20th and 21st centuries. The Jews had not clawed their way through the muck of history to finally achieve independence only to be satisfied with producing good fighter pilots, farmers, and hi-tech entrepreneurs. The Jews for him were an "Am Olam"; a universal people; a people of the entire world; a people whose very "peoplehood" was dependent on and a reflection of its ongoing interaction with and contribution to the other peoples of the planet Earth. This concept of the Jewish People as an "Am Olam" is deeply rooted in the Jewish tradition and must serve as a foundation rock of any Jewish identity in the Space Age, whether one accepts the Cosmodeistic Hypothesis or not.

Nessyahu had a deep-rooted belief that because of their special historical travail, the Jewish People had been particularly endowed with certain cultural and psychological characteristics, capabilities and temperamental propensities that would enable them to play a pioneering role in establishing the Cosmodeistic project on this planet. He felt that the character and needs of modern Israel and world Jewry made them the most suitable objectively and the most needful subjectively to engage in a heroic project of this type. He agreed with Ben Gurion that unless modern Jewry strove to be a "Light Unto the Nations" vis-à-vis the all-human challenges of the 20th and 21st centuries, they would not become a light unto the Jews and would not be able to generate the energy to survive as a people. He was fearful of the Zionism of mediocrity, advocated by the early Zionist thinker Jacob Klatzkin, which encouraged the Jews to be satisfied with the banal attributes of "normalcy." He would have agreed with Rabbi Moshe Dror who viewed "*Tsionut*" (Zionism) and "*Hitstainut*" (excellence), as derived from the same lexical root, as synonyms—and hence mediocrity was by definition anti-Zionist and thus, in the end, anti-Jewish.

Nessyahu based his views on an historical analogy. He believed that the modern Jewish situation of a national center (Israel) inter-relating with a universal Diaspora was analogous to that era of a national center (Jerusalem) interacting with a universal Diaspora (primarily Babylon) that created both the Jerusalem and Babylonian Talmuds and codified Monotheism. This was the worldview that united the far-flung parts of Jewry into a cohesive culture and also changed the course of all of world history. He believed that Cosmodeism (like Monotheism in the past) would create a new Jewish cultural energy and once again change the course of all of world history. Nessyahu rejected "The Nation That Dwells Alone" concept. He knew that both ancient and modern Jewish cultures were built with the raw materials of non-Jewish civilizations and cultures. Monotheism was clearly formulated by the Jews but it built on the raw materials taken from other peoples and it came to world cultural predominance by way of other religions (Christianity and Islam).

So it would be with Cosmodeism. The raw materials will have come from other peoples (as well as totally unrelated disciplines such as cosmology and physics) and its success will depend on other peoples, cultures, and religions adopting its basic principles and adapting them to their own cultural traditions. But the Jews could be those people that "choose" themselves to become the progenitors and propagators of this project as well as to be a living example of it. Thus, we would have to invent a new Space Age interpretation of the concept of the "Chosen People" and of being a "Light unto the Nations." He believed that just the ambition to implement the Cosmodeistic Project would recharge and rejuvenate human civilization and rescue it from the malaise characterized by postmodernism. He certainly believed that it would rejuvenate Jewish identity and provide added value to the young university educated non-orthodox modern Jew. One can ascribe to the notion that we must cultivate ambitions to create Space Age versions of Judaism without subscribing to the Cosmodeistic Hypothesis. But we all must recognize the need to proffer alternative Jewish visions of a depth and a breadth that at least approaches that of the Cosmodeistic Hypothesis if we are to generate and sustain Jewish ambitions in the 21st century.

In this regard, it might behoove the post-Enlightenment Jewish world to recognize and incorporate into our Jewish tradition some Jewish prophets of modernity. Reclaiming Spinoza and revoking his excommunication *ex post facto* would be a good start. Can there be any doubt that he reached his pantheistic conclusions based, amongst other factors, on a deep study of the Jewish sources, and an understanding of the epistemological subtleties of the Hebrew Language? The Rabbis of Amsterdam considered him a Talmudic prodigy before he went his own intellectual way, and it is clear he was excommunicated more out of fear of the reactions of the Calvinist majority and the Calvinist Dutch State which had given the Jews refuge from the Spanish Inquisition. Prominent Reform Rabbi, Emil G. Hirsch (1851–1923) wrote that "Judaism rightly apprehended posits God not ... as an absolutely transcendental One. Our God is the *soul* of the Universe. ... *Spinozism and Judaism are by no means at opposite poles.*"[21] Might I not claim that evolution is "the soul of the Universe"; that autopoiesis is "the soul of the Universe" and thus that the Cosmodeistic Hypothesis might also be conceived as "Judaism rightly apprehended." The French Jewish *Process Philosopher*, Henri Bergson, is another prophet of modernity. His thinking influenced Teilhard de Chardin in ways that remind us of the effect that Maimonides had on Aquinas. His *Theory of Creative Evolution* can be interpreted as a modern iteration of partnering with God in the act of creation (as an endless ongoing process called evolution) as well as *élan vital* (or life force) which anticipates my speculation about multi-lingual existence. Another modern Jewish prophet would be Samuel Alexander, whose evolutionary philosophy of Space/Time evolving into Deity anticipates Nessyahu. Albert Einstein is, to my mind, the most religious (small 'r') Jew of the 20th century in terms of his transcendent reactions to the very mysteries of existence. Erich Fromm's *You Shall be as Gods* is a precursor to Armstrong's *A History of God* in that it traces the development of the identity of God from tyrant to constitutional monarch and claims that the ultimate message of the Torah (if properly understood in the light of modern reason) is that human beings should themselves strive to become gods. I might also add Ernest Becker as a minor prophet, given his honest attempts to explore the religious instinct scientifically, and, of course, both Frankl and Maslow—not only ethnic Jews, but quintessentially Jewish in the way they thought. The Jewish people have produced some of the most spiritually impactful individuals in the last 400 years, but we do not celebrate them as our own. Our so-called religious leaders, in their self-congratulatory ignorance, often treat them with disdain, while humanity at large rejoices in their intellectual and moral contributions. "We have seen the enemy and it is us." We 21st-century Jews must extricate our evolutionary identity from the fossilized embrace of this spiritually constipated Rabbinate.

The Evolution of the Jews

For just as the concept of God has been evolving, so has Jewish Identity. In historical perspective, there is really no such thing as authentic Judaism, let alone normative Jewish identity. I differentiate between Judaism (the *present* religion of the Jewish people) and Jewish peoplehood—the Jews as an ethnic composite evolving over historical time. Keep in mind that the words Judaism and religion do not appear even once in the Bible and the word Jew only four times—three times in the Book of Esther (in which God is not even mentioned). Before the advent of Christianity, the appellation "Jew" referred to a person from Judea, not someone who practiced the religion of Judaism—just as American refers to someone from America or Russian to someone from Russia. It was a geographical reference not a faith reference. According to the Oxford English Dictionary the English language word *Judaism* (to describe the specific life practices of the Jews) first appeared in 1511, interestingly enough as an 'ism' (what in modern times would be considered an ideology). Historically it has been used (as with the word Hebraism) in counter distinction to Hellenism—another 'ism,' which is a cultural identity rather than a religious identity, an attitude to or philosophy of life. Orthodox Prof. Joseph Levinson, in private conversation with me, has suggested that Judaism is not a religion in the Western sense of that word, but rather a life system much like the other "-ism religions" such as Buddhism, Hinduism, Taoism, and Confucianism—none of which worship or even believe in God as the West comprehends that concept and all of which advocate a way of life (a *Halacha*), a philosophy of life, an *ideology* of life (hence 'ism').

Identity is evolutionary for every vigorous, historically enduring, people. To be English today, for example, is different from being English in the time of Queen Victoria, Elizabeth I, or Alfred the Great. A case could even be made that modern English identity was invented by an Italian Jew (Disraeli) glorifying a German Queen (Victoria) in the name of *"our* ancient English traditions rooted in the mists of time." We could also make a case that modern Jewish identity was created, to a large extent, by the Christian Belgian printer Danial Bomberg, who designed the printed Talmud page in Renaissance Venice—the page that enables the "tradition" of *daf yomi* (the daily page of study) and stimulates the associative thinking identified with creativity, which my late friend and colleague Rabbi Dr. Moshe Dror felt was greatly responsible for the tremendous outburst of Jewish creativity over the past three hundred years. Likewise, being Jewish in the 21st century is different from being Jewish a hundred years ago, five hundred years ago, or two thousand years ago. Even the various sects of ultra-Orthodox Judaism are only 200 years old. As with Moses not recognizing the teachings of Akiva, so too, Saadia Gaon, the Rambam, Ibn Ezra and the Vilna Gaon would have difficulty in indulging the incoherencies of the present day ultra-Orthodox. Maimonides especially would be disgusted by their purposeful ignorance, contempt for science and making a living from religion. In the *Mishnah Torah*, he wrote:

> Anyone who occupies oneself with Torah and not working, but supporting oneself with charity, desecrates the Divine name, dishonors the Torah, extinguishes the light of faith, brings evil to oneself and forfeits life in the world to come because it is forbidden to benefit from the words of Torah in this world. Our sages say, "All who benefit [materially] from the words of Torah forfeit life in the world."
> ... And they also commanded, "Love work and hate the Rabbinate and all Torah that is not accompanied by work in the end will be negated and will lead to sin. The end of such a person will be that he steals from others."

Traditions do not mystically emerge out of the mists of time; they are human inventions responding to certain social, political, cultural, *and technological* developments in historical time (vis. the printed Talmud which facilitated the *daf yomi*; the study of one page of Talmud daily as a routine Jewish practice). Recognizing this, the great Sephardi Rabbi Bahya Ibn Paquda (1050–1120) wrote in *Duties of the Heart* that "To accept tradition without examining it with intelligence and judgement is like the blind

blindly following others." He felt that blind belief is plain wrong. "The Torah ... appeals to reason and knowledge ... It is therefore a duty incumbent
upon everyone to make God an object of speculative reason and knowledge, in order to arrive at true faith."[22]

Positive attitudes towards worldly wisdom and the requirement of Jewish
thinking to adapt to this wisdom have been expressed by all the greatest
Jewish thinkers throughout the ages; most prominently Saadia Gaon and
the Rambam up to the Vilna Gaon who is reported to have held the view
that "If a person is deficient in worldly wisdom, he will inescapably be deficient in one hundred measures in Torah wisdom." The Rambam felt it was
incumbent upon every generation to reinterpret the Torah and renew it
based on knowledge gained, not only from Jewish sages, but from the other
nations of the world. To his mind, Halachic thinking must adapt to objective knowledge, not ignore it or dismiss it as being against Halacha because
the source of this knowledge came from non-Jews or contradicts "traditional" interpretations of the Torah. A good example of this kind of thinking
is the Jewish "tradition" of matrilineal lineage. This was instituted in the
exilic period when Jews were enveloped in Gentile societies and subject to
rape and interethnic extramarital affairs and thus one could never really be
sure of the identity of the father. Patrilineal lineage had been the tradition
of our forefathers for over 1,000 years prior. When the Reform Movement
recognized both matrilineal and patrilineal lineage, they were more in accordance with Jewish "tradition" than the Orthodox—especially since now
DNA testing can absolutely identify the father of the child.

Identity as an ongoing evolutionary/reinvention process is especially ap-
plicable to the Jews. Modern Jewish identity is a consequence of thousands
of years of cultural progression from *The Fathers* (Abraham, Isaac, and Jacob) to the *Judges*, to the *Kings*, to the *Prophets*, to the *Sadducees*, to the
Pharisees, to Rabbinic Judaism, to post-Enlightenment Judaism. After the
Scientific Revolution and the European Enlightenment (which enabled the
Emancipation of the Jews, thus creating modern Jewish distinctiveness)
Jewish identity became pluralistic. Reform and Conservative Judaism undermined the faith monopoly of Orthodoxy and eventually spun off Reconstructionist and Humanist Judaism. Bundism, Territorialism and oth-
er "secular" Jewish identities stirred 19th century European and American
Jewry. Israel-centered Zionism has been the most recent iteration of the
ever-changing character of Jewish identity. Given this, I would like to sug-

gest a more rational up to date definition of "Who is a Jew" more suitable to the needs and realities of contemporary Jewry.

1. Anybody whose mother *or father* is recognized by the community at large to be a Jew and wants to be considered a part of the Jewish People.

2. Anybody whom Hitler would have killed if he had had access to DNA testing (20% or over Jewish ancestry) and wants to be considered a part of the Jewish People.

3. Anybody who is accepted as Jewish by Orthodox, Conservative, Reconstructionist or Humanist (or other) denominations.

4. Anybody who wishes to be considered a part of the Jewish People and undergoes some kind of formal initiation (religious or otherwise) by Orthodox, Conservative, Reform, Reconstructionist or Humanist (or other) denominations. The Humanist denomination probably being the default procedure for completely secular people who wish to remain within or join the Jewish tribe.

Paradoxically, if Orthodox, *halachic*, standards of Jewish identity had been applied in biblical times King David would not be considered today a member of the Jewish People (his ancestor Ruth not having undergone a halachic conversion; *simply declaring* her wish and intention of joining our tribe). A normative, restricted definition of what it means to be Jewish is entirely self-defeating. What would be the number of Jews in the world given the above definition? What would be the potential for Aliya to Israel, for peace with the Palestinians and indeed the entire Arab and Muslim worlds given that 40 million Jews in the world might more readily disabuse the remaining radicals amongst them from believing they could really destroy Israel? Would not such a Jewish condition provide my persistently paranoid people with a renewed self-confidence, which injected into the peace process, would at least provide hope for more successful results?

Jewish *religious* identity includes ultra-Orthodox and modern Orthodox, Conservative, Reform, Reconstructionist, Humanist and Postdenominational Judaism. Jewish *ethnic* identity also includes secular atheists and agnostics, including the greatest Jews of modern times: Einstein, Freud, Herzl, Ben Gurion, Weizmann, and Jabotinsky. Even prior to the Enlightenment, Jewish identity had been modified geographically and culturally by the non-Jewish cultures the Jews had lived in. These Jewish identities included Ashkenazi, Sephardi and Middle Eastern which further subdivided into German, Yemenite, Russian, Iraqi, Moroccan, American, and so on and so on. The only consistent universal norms of Jewish identity have been the prohibition against idolatry and the requirement of unqualified individual responsibility. Judaism is an 'ism'—an ideology about life that *contains* a religious tradition. It is a tradition and a worldview dependent on individual behavior. It has little place for the vicarious "salvation" inherent in the principle of grace or "right belief," prescribed by Christianity.

This difference alone completely debunks that silly and false concept, *The Judeo-Christian Tradition*. There is not now, and never has been such a tradition; there is a Jewish way of thinking about individual responsibility and a Christian way of thinking about individual responsibility. Jews are instructed to be "partners with God" in the ongoing act of creation; it is an active, not a passive belief system—you have to *do* things, not just pray (something ultra-Orthodox Jews seem to have completely disremembered). Given this, could not "partners with God" evolve into "partnering with the Godding?" If, as the Kabbalah avers, the Cosmos is pregnant with divine consciousness (Jewish *Panentheism?*) then our purpose in life must be to act as a midwife trying to birth it. This is empirical not mystical. We must first repair our individual selves, then the societies we live in (socially and environmentally) and in this way we can help repair the world, thus creating a healthy foundation upon which we can pursue our cosmic destiny. Ben Gurion's vision of Zionism was that Israel must be a "Light unto the Nations" if it is to survive let alone justify the Zionist project. Vladimir Zeev Jabotinsky, Ben Gurion's ideological polar opposite, envisaged three stages to Zionism: creation of state, ingathering of the exiles, and creating a model society as the proper ambition for every great civilization. Both would have been appalled at the cultural and intellectual mediocrity of the political parties that presently presume to speak in their name.

In a way, the Jewish pre-Enlightenment "partners with God" attitude anticipated the Enlightenment human-agency mindset that rewards human energy and might explain the tremendous achievements of individual Jews in the 19th and 20th centuries. It might also be an explanation for disproportionate Jewish involvement in the great reformist political and social movements of the 19th and 20th centuries; changing society for the better found a natural home in a mindset conditioned by a culture that advocated "being a partner with God in the act of creation." The way one behaves

(*Derech Eretz*) has always been more fundamental to Jewishness than one's religious fastidiousness. The recent hijacking of Jewish tradition by a politicized right-wing Orthodox religious establishment dedicated to land idolatry on the one hand and Rebbe idolatry on the other hand, presenting itself as "authentic" Judaism has alienated many Israelis and Diaspora Jews from Jewish religious tradition and ultimately from its quintessential secular expression—Zionism. This has caused an ongoing devitalization of Jewish identity both in Israel and in the Diaspora (weakening Jewish communal life as well as support for Israel).

The test for Jewish survival had always been empirical. If a form of Judaism endured, it was because it had contributed something of value to a critical mass of Jewish individuals, not because it had some inherent abstract theoretical value, granted authenticity by some supernatural "whatever" or some self-important rabbinical "papacy." It was the spiritual equivalent of the survival of the fittest. What survived did so because it answered a need and gave value to real human beings. Culture, after all, is not a museum dedicated to preserving artifacts from the past, nor is it a cemetery dedicated to eulogizing the dead heroes of the past. It is a dynamic, future-oriented creative process; it is a living thing that evolves as a consequence of its dynamic interaction with other cultures and other cultural environments. What does not interact does not evolve; what does not evolve dies. I believe the Cosmodeistic principle can be most attractive, in descending order, to Humanist, Reform, Reconstructionist, Postdenominational and Conservative Jews—and of course to secular Jews who wish to preserve their ethnic identity (for whom Humanist Judaism might be their default framework). I have no illusions regarding its appeal to the various idolatrous iterations of present-day Orthodoxy—although I would be happy to be proven wrong.

Some thinkers have advanced the notion that the Jews actually invented the very idea of the future as a divine drama that is playing out and leading to a future Messianic age, and that the *Idea of the Future* is the greatest contribution the Jews have made to human civilization —greater even than Monotheism from which it derives. This argument posits that every civilization up to the Jews was cyclical—events and trends repeating themselves throughout eternity. The arrow of historical time was invented, according to these thinkers, by the Jews: there was a beginning ("in the beginning"), a middle (the story of human history) and an end (the messianic age), i.e., a progression leading to a better future. In other words, *The Idea of Progress* that has been driving Western civilization (and now all humanity) since the Scientific Revolution derives from the *Idea of the Future* and is thus significantly indebted to the annoying Jewish habit of complaining about the present and advocating for a better future. Maimonides viewed the messianic age (or "World to Come") not as supernatural (spending eternity at the right hand of God) but as simply a better future *in this material* existence, thus enabling humanity to spend its time in study and prayer—engaged in obtaining wisdom rather than drudge work to keep body and soul together. In this he was a precursor to Keynes' view of the future cited above. I am smiling as I write this; as an atheist Jew I am less minimalistic about the messianic age than the greatest Rabbi in history. At least, I believe we Jews are capable of helping to create an entirely new *divine* reality.

The Bible

This chapter would be incomplete without at least some mention of the most celebrated and most maligned book in human history. I am referring, of course, to what self-important Christians, who claim to have a "personal relationship with God" (consider the arrogance of that claim) call the Old Testament, not the so-called New Testament. My own ethnocentric inclinations find the views of that doyen of radical atheism, Friedrich Wilhelm Nietzsche, most amenable regarding comparisons between the two. In the *Genealogy of Morals*, he writes,

> I do not like the New Testament, that should be plain;
> I find it almost disturbing that my taste in regard to this
> most highly esteemed and overestimated work should be
> so singular (I have the taste of two millennia against me):
> but there it is! "Here I stand, I cannot do otherwise"— I
> have the courage of my bad taste. The Old Testament—
> that is something else again: all honor to the Old Testament! I find in it great human beings, a heroic landscape,
> and something of the very rarest quality in the world, the
> incomparable naïveté of the strong heart; what is more, *I
> find a people* (italics mine). In the New one, on the other hand, I find nothing but petty sectarianism, mere rococo of the soul .... How can one make such a fuss about
> one's little lapses as these pious little men do! Who gives a
> damn? Certainly not God.[23]

"I find a people" is core insight of the above quote. The Bible is "divine" not because it was bestowed on us by the supernatural creator of the world, but rather because it unabashedly tells the *honest* story of how one rather primitive tribe (my tribe) evolved civilizationally out of the primeval slime of antiquity. It does this without apology, warts, and all. And when I say warts, I really mean warts. Father Abraham, in essence, pimps off Sarah twice to gain leverage in material arrangements beneficial to him. And the way he treats Hagar and his second son Ishmael would have him "canceled" and his career ruined if he were living today. Lot's daughters get him drunk so that they might have sex with him, but only after he sanctioned their being gang raped by a mob in order to save his own honor. Jacob robs his elder brother (Esau) of his birthright by lying to his own father, after which he "struggles" with God and becomes Israel (which literally means struggling with God or as a modern Jew might put it "struggling with the god concept").

In other words, *my* entire tribe is named after a lying thief. The Book of Joshua is the story of the first *recorded* incident of genocide (there were certainly numerous prior unrecorded incidences); men, women and children slaughtered as if they were lab rats. Various biblical calls to exterminate the Amalekites are noted with the same tonal indifference as a modern human being might use when facing an infestation of cockroaches. David sends his good friend to get killed in battle so that he might rape his wife and force her to marry him. And while the Evangelicals cite biblical sanction when pontificating that a godly marriage is between one man and one woman, one wonders how they get around King Solomon's 1,000 wives and concubines. It seems to me that Hugh Hefner would be better served citing the Bible as justification for his lifestyle than the God-fearing folk of Middle America. I would even argue that the *Song of Songs* is the most erotic poem ever written. Moreover, read the Prophets; they weren't cranky for no reason. My forbearers were a real piece of work. My ancient ancestors certainly would have identified more with those modern members of my tribe so central to creating that modern Sodom and Gomorrah, Las Vegas, than with the "pious little men" that constitute the so-called *Moral Majority*. The Bible doesn't even leave God off the hook. In the *Book of Job*, God tortures his most loving and faithful servant with the cruelest physical and emotional agonies one could conceive of in order to win a bet with Satan. Whenever I read this portion, I think of God as some sadistic, willful, spoiled little brat pulling the wings and legs off a grasshopper.

The "heroes" of the Bible are living, flesh and blood, human beings with tremendous flaws but still capable of tremendous actions and intellectual breakthroughs that have advanced all of human civilization. As an aside, I suggest teaching about the Founding Fathers of the United States in the same manner—as if they were greatly flawed Old Testament figures who still did great things rather than the holier than thou, walk on water New Testament like figures we have been marketing to our children. This would not only contextualize the present controversies over their sins against Blacks and Native Americans (which were unquestionably appalling) but also highlight the good they did in ways that later enabled the mitigation of these crimes and, hence, would be more educationally beneficial. Why more educationally beneficial? Because children know they are flawed, and this would enable them to cultivate great moral and ethical ambitions despite their flaws. This is the real moral lesson of the Bible —not to be a goody two-shoes, but to try to do at least something good in your life given that you most probably will be a moral weakling during much of your life. Abraham might have been a disgusting husband and father but according to the Talmud, God presented him with the covenant and not Noah because he argued with God to save innocent people in Sodom and Gomorrah, while Noah, upon hearing about God's plan to exterminate the entire human race, except his own family, didn't let out a peep and went and built a boat. The Bible tells us stories about right and wrong so that we might decide between right and wrong *in this life*; it is a paean to human volition. The New Testament recognizes this in First Corinthians 10:11 where it is written: "These things happened to them *as examples* and were written down as warnings for us, on whom *the culmination of the ages* has come." Here we see the fundamental difference between the two "faith" traditions. Corinthians admonishes in order to prepare for the "end times"—"*the culmination of the ages*" while for the Jews these are lessons for how to live in and improve human society in the here and now; the "these times." For Judaism (as properly understood) the spiritual derives from the material and consequently is not separate from it. We are, to be *partners* with (not slaves to) God in the ongoing act of creation, on this earth in this Cosmos. We are to be "godly" in our behavior, *as well as in our cosmic ambitions.* I suggest that Cosmodeism become a central cosmic ambition of the Jewish people.

Chapter Twenty-Three: Christian Intimations

Despite its image, the Catholic Church has been characterized by more doctrinal fluidity than most people imagine. Doctrinal variability, and thus flexibility, appeared at the very outset. As contrarian theologian Bart Ehrman writes:

> In Matthew, Jesus comes into being when he is conceived, or born, of a virgin; in John, Jesus is the incarnate Word of God who was with God in the beginning and through whom the universe was made. In Matthew, there is not a word about Jesus being God; in John, that's precisely who he is. In Matthew, Jesus teaches about the coming kingdom of God and almost never about himself (and never that he is divine); in John, Jesus teaches almost exclusively about himself, especially his divinity. In Matthew, Jesus refuses to perform miracles in order to prove his identity; in John, that is practically the only reason he does miracles.[24]

The concept of the Trinity (Father, Son, and Holy Ghost) only became doctrinal creed at the Council of Nicaea in 325 CE; over three hundred years after Jesus died and over 200 years after the New Testament was written. According to the *Stanford Encyclopedia of Philosophy* the "New Testament contains no explicit Trinitarian doctrine .... It was only in response to the controversy sparked by the Alexandrian presbyter Arius (256–336) that a critical mass of bishops rallied around what eventually became standard language about the Trinity."[25] In other words, it was essentially a consequence of a political power struggle between various trends in primitive Christianity. Catholic doctrine regarding newborn babies being blemished by original sin (that has to be washed away by Baptism) derives substantially from St. Augustine of Hippo in 5th century Africa – there is absolutely nothing in the New Testament even implying such an ignominy. Later, from the *Cluniac Reforms* (910 plus) to the *Council of Trent* (1545–1563) to the *Second Vatican Council* (1962–1965), the Church has revised its business plan according to perceived challenges and needs. Priestly celibacy is a good example. Saint Peter himself, as well as various popes, bishops, and priests during the church's first 270 years were married men, and fathers of children. The practice (not the obligation) of celibacy, and not marrying *after* ordination, stems from the Council of Elvira (305–306). Clerical celibacy as a universal practice can be traced to the 11th century, but only became a formal part of canon law in 1917. Confession only became a sacrament in the 13th century. Since the Church changes so slowly it is difficult to see. After all, do we really see glaciers moving? I wouldn't be surprised, for example, if we see female priests by the end of this century.

The teachings of Thomas Aquinas are a prime example of radical change within the Church. His teachings were initially proscribed by the Church before Thomism eventually became the ideological backbone of the Church, and, as Pope Pius X (1835–1914) ruled, the very philosophical underpinning of Church theology. Aquinas had distinguished between things that can be understood by reason and things that must be taken on faith, thus creating the secular space that eventually enabled the emergence of modern science in the West. His Aristotelian model initially offended Church sensibilities, but in historical perspective, Aquinas enabled the Church to accommodate itself to certain aspects of secular knowledge without damaging its institutional preeminence, or its self-perceived role in the divine drama. Unfortunately, the same Pope Pius X conducted a battle against the modernists of the Church who wanted to "correct" Church dogma based on the insights and discoveries of the Enlightenment and the Scientific Revolution. This Pope's reactionary stance (i.e., in reaction to modernism and progress, the true meaning of reactionary) gave a second life to certain attitudes which had characterized the medieval Church. This led to the moral turpitude of the Church becoming the social/cultural backbone of fascism in the 20th century. Notwithstanding this dreary history, the internal logic of Thomism has enabled the Church to make doctrinal changes when these become absolutely necessary to maintain its political/social/cultural power in the post-Enlightenment secular world.

As we see, the Church has *always* been changing certain previously defined "infallible" doctrines in order to make the institution itself more marketable to changing societal predispositions. I put the word "infallible" in inverted commas because papal infallibility was only defined as *official* doctrine in the 19th century at the *First Vatican Council* (1869–1870) during the papacy of Pope Pius IX (1792–1878), the same Pope that in 1854 ruled that Mary was conceived without original sin (the *Immaculate Conception*). Yet even the doctrine of infallibility has subsequently been declared fallible by many prominent Catholic thinkers. The reformist priest Hans Küng (1928–2021), a central intellectual figure of the *Second Vatican Council* (1962–1965), rejected the concept outright. For Kung, papal infallibility is a political tool, an instrument of power, rather than a theological reality which would be an instrument of truth for the Church.[26] He believed the New Testament was self-contradictory and contained many false statements. His obituary in *The New York Times* noted that,

> As a liberal, he criticized church policy on governance, liturgy, papal infallibility, birth control, priestly celibacy, the ordination of women, mixed marriages, homosexuality, abortion, the meaning of hell and much else. On some issues, Dr. Küng admitted, Buddhism and Judaism were more constructive than Catholicism.

Catholic historian and Pulitzer Prize winner Garry Wills (b.1934), sometimes called the "most distinguished Catholic intellectual in America," also declined to accept papal infallibility as a requisite of Catholic devotion. Brian Tierney, former President of the *American Catholic Historical Association*, has written in *The Origins of Papal Infallibility* that,

> There is no convincing evidence that papal infallibility formed any part of the theological or canonical tradition of the Church before the thirteenth century; the doctrine was invented in the first place by a few dissident Franciscans because it suited their convenience to invent it; eventually, but only after much initial reluctance, it was accepted by the papacy because it suited the convenience of the popes to accept it.[27]

Hans Küng and Garry Wills probably would have been burned at the stake 400 years ago, so at least in this regard we see significant, albeit glacial, progress in the Church.

There is also the sociological reality of individual Catholics living in post-Enlightenment constitutional democracies which is impacting Church thinking more and more. I often wonder how many self-declared Catholics actually continue to be Catholic *despite* the dogmas they routinely ignore in order to continue experiencing a certain kind of spirituality. I have often joked that if I were a politician in North America or Europe and every Catholic that used birth control, had premarital sex, and accepted abortion as a regrettable but legitimate option voted for me and every Catholic who lived according to the letter of Church dogma on these issues voted against me, I would win in a landslide greater than any in political history. The actual historical and social reality of the Church has made the very word "dogma" somewhat undogmatic. Ironically, today it is the most conservative and retrograde Catholics that reject the authority of the Pope—not the so-called modernists. Küng might be more representative, *de facto*, of practicing Catholics today than the traditional *Religion Business* of the Church with its self-serving institutional interests. He combined a belief in the spiritual substance of Catholicism with a healthy skepticism regarding its traditional dogmas and institutions.

The revolt of Boston's Catholic laity against the Church's response to priestly child molestation might just be an historical foreshadowing of what is to come. This democratic lack of deference to authoritarian Church power and vested interests by Boston's Catholic laity might be viewed by future historians to have been as revolutionary as the *Council of Trent* in the ongoing evolution of the Church; it being perhaps the first time in history that the laity dictated morality to the Church instead of the other way around. One has to wonder what is in the air or water of Boston that gives birth to this stubborn lack of deference to authority. It happened once before when the sober Protestant burghers of Boston began throwing tea overboard to show their contempt for another, quite different, self-serving authoritarian.

Since the death of Pope Pius XII (1876–1958), the Church, perhaps a bit embarrassed about its de-facto support for Fascist regimes in the 1930s, has modified its anti-Enlightenment anti-Modernism. I refer, specifically, to its newfound support for certain Enlightenment values and constructs. Miraculously, they have discovered numerous biblical and canon law justifications in support of equality, tolerance, democracy, and constitutionalism; concepts that had been dismissed, as recently as the 1930s as secular perversions of the natural order (natural order being the supremacy of the Church in every aspect of social and political life—hence their support for Fascism). Extraordinarily, since WWII, the Church has invalidated two teachings that had characterized it for 2,000 years—the role of the Jews in the divine drama and the very existence of *Limbo* for unbaptized infants. In 2007, the Church ruled that *Limbo* is only a theory and not a requisite of Catholic faith—you can believe in it or not without doing offense to the teachings of the Church. This astounding ruling, with a wave of the hand, eliminated a belief that, for millennia, had been a source of unremitting despair for parents who had lost their children at birth and would, for eternity, not be allowed into Heaven but frozen in *Limbo*, because they had not been baptized and washed of original sin before they died. Previously, and even more astounding, *The Second Vatican Council* (1962–1965) repudiated the belief in collective Jewish guilt for the Crucifixion of Jesus, and in 2015 the *Vatican specified that Jews do not need to be converted to find salvation*. Amazing! Just think of all that wood wasted on burning Jews and copies of the Talmud throughout the ages—a real ecological scandal!

Historical Background

There is no *spiritually* historic reason preventing the Church from eventually accommodating a Catholic version of Cosmodeism the same way it has accommodated Aristotelian *Thomism*. The previously condemned writings of the contrarian priest Teilhard de Chardin (*Teilhardism*) might even eventually replace *Thomism* as the backbone of Catholic teaching and endorsed by some future Pope as the very philosophical underpinning of Church theology. I will return to Teilhard in a moment, but first a look at previous church intellectual innovators. The profound insights of Dominican friar, Giordano Bruno (1548–1600) as to the very essence of existence achieved by a pre-Einsteinian thought experiment combined with deductive logic, earned him the death penalty—to the eternal shame of the Church. Perhaps the Church should reclaim him just as the Jews should reclaim Spinoza. His crime was suggesting the material Universe is infinite (thus putting into question *Creatio ex nihilo*—God creating the material universe out of nothing) and that this infinite universe contained a multitude of other inhabited worlds. His arguments (like Ockham's) were theological, not scientific. If God is God, and infinite in his being and in his power, then he can create an infinite number of finite worlds with an infinite number of beings like us. As he put it in *De l'infinito universo et mondi* (1584), "innumerable celestial bodies, stars, globes, suns and earths may be sensibly perceived therein by us and an infinite number of them may be inferred by our own reason." This implies, of course, that the Israelites might not have been God's only chosen people (in an infinite Universe), and, more importantly, that Jesus might not be his only son and thus Mary not the only vessel for his cosmic sperm (could God have been a polygamist—perhaps, heaven forfend, even a Mormon?). Could anything undermine the preeminence of accepted (and acceptable) theology more than this? Consequently, Bruno was tried by the Inquisition and burned at the stake.

Cardinal Nicholas of Cusa (1401–1464) preceded Bruno by over a century in speculating about an infinite universe, a plurality of worlds and alien life.

In *On Learned Ignorance* (1440), he talks about the human mind *becoming* divine and in this way "knowing" God because God not only enfolds creation and but also unfolds itself within the ongoing process of creation. There is a similarity here to Kabbalistic and Neoplatonic concepts of God and a portent of Teilhard's concept of the *Alpha* creator God evolving into the *Omega* God when the collective consciousnesses of the Cosmos merge with the *Alpha* God (as an ongoing process). The human mind becoming divine is certainly a view that could accommodate Cosmodeism with little discomfort. Similar to many medieval Rabbis, Cusa was a polymath interested in math, astronomy, and medicine. And as he was the first to initiate the practice of calculating and evaluating pulse as a diagnostic tool, we have yet another example of the barrenness of the Non-overlapping Magisteria thesis. The Catholic Encyclopedia writes that:

> The astronomical views of the cardinal are scattered through his philosophical treatises. *They evince complete independence of traditional doctrines* (italics mine), though they are based on symbolism of numbers, on combinations of letters, and on abstract speculations rather than observation (very Kabbalistic). The earth is a star like other stars, is not the center of the universe, is not at rest, nor its poles fixed. The celestial bodies are not strictly spherical, nor are their orbits circular. The difference between theory and appearance is explained by relative motion (wow, did Einstein read him?). Had Copernicus been aware of these assertions, he would probably have been encouraged by them to publish his own monumental work.

Why wasn't Cusa burned at the stake as was Bruno 150 years later or afraid to publish his views as was Copernicus? I reckon because the Church was completely confident in its monopolistic preeminence and while looking askance at contrarian views it felt secure enough to let them pass. The Church's "tolerance" of Cusa was a consequence of indifference, not enlightenment. Cusa was writing well before the Reformation, the discovery of the Americas, and the subversive influence of the newly invented printing press. In contrast, when Bruno wrote, the Church was faced with serious Reformation competition gaining strength by way of the printing press and America was, in a way, a new planet containing human beings, animals and plants not even mentioned in the Bible. The Americas provided Bruno's speculations about numberless alien worlds with some logical validity. Not only was the Church's spiritual market share shrinking (those pesky Protestants), but along comes Bruno and undermines certain key features of its very business model. When any Religion Business is thus threatened, it reacts with vicious ruthlessness—conveniently ignoring its own PR about love and compassion. Nevertheless, in order to hold on to its present, ever more educated, consumers as we move deeper into the 21st century, the Church will have to undergo an internal reformation similar to and perhaps greater than the *Cluniac* and *Council of Trent* reformations centuries earlier.

Teilhardism

The thinking of Pierre Teilhard de Chardin (1881–1955), as previously indicated, would be the perfect candidate to replace *Thomism* as the ideological backbone of the Church, which by implication will have meant a certain acceptance of the Cosmodeistic Hypothesis. What is really interesting, as already mentioned, is that de Chardin was greatly influenced by the atheist Jew Henri Bergson's book *Creative Evolution,* which became a major stimulus to his unorthodox theology (e.g., no Adam and Eve, no original sin, no creation *ex nihilo),* which began to emerge even *before* he took his final vows as a Jesuit. *Teilhardism* has already penetrated Catholic (as well as Protestant) thinking. The *Center for Christogenesis* is one example of this intellectual and spiritual penetration of Teilhardism into the mainstream of Catholic discourse. They describe themselves thusly:

> If evolution is the story of the cosmos, that is, the order of physical reality, then evolution is essential to our understanding of God and God's relationship to the world. Evolution marks the break from a closed, static, world of law and order to an open world of change and play. Evolution tells us that nature is not a closed, causal system of events but a complex series of fluid, dynamic, interlocking, and communicative relationships. While scientists continue to understand how evolution works for physical systems, the Center for Christogenesis seeks to understand how evolution works for religious systems, *as physical reality and spiritual reality are intertwined* (**italics mine: support for my view that the scientific and industrial revolutions are the two most spiritual events in history**). As a process

of evolution, the universe is incomplete, and we humans are incomplete. We can change, grow, and become something new. We have the power to do so, but do we have the will? The Center for Christogenesis seeks to create a new religious imagination that ignites our energies to move beyond mediocrity and fear, one that anticipates a new future of planet life. *We are an unfinished species, corporately and personally*, grounded in an infinite depth of Love; thus, openness to love and what this means in terms of creatively reinventing ourselves as persons in evolution is the challenge ahead of us. The divisive fragmentation of our age reflects a need for a new holistic synergy of science and spirituality to heal our divisions, deepen our compassion, and ignite the human spirit toward greater unity and flourishing. The Teilhardian concept of "Omega"—upon which our Center's vision and work is based—is understood not as destination, but as deepening toward a more unified future. Omega is the revelation of God as the fullness of love, the dynamic center at the heart of all Creation.

Other predominately Catholic organizations dedicated to Teilhardism include:

1. The American Teilhard Association,
2. The British Teilhard Network,
3. Association des Amis Pierre Teilhard de Chardin,
4. Centre de Teilhard de Chardin,
5. Fondation Teilhard de Chardin,
6. Deutsche Gesellschaft Teilhard de Chardin,
7. Associazione degli amici di Teilhard de Chardin (Italy),
8. Associação dos Amigos de Teilhard de Chardin em Portugal,
9. Asociación de Amigos de Teilhard de Chardin (sección española),

In his book, *The Prayer of the Universe*, de Chardin acknowledges what he calls "The Holiness of Evolution," that "The world is still being created ...,"[28] that our "participation in the work of creation"[29] is an obligation, that "man has the duty to consciously and deliberately advance the progress of evolution."[30] Teilhard's youthful optimism about the titanic potential of our species is also magnetically attractive to non-Christians, even when put off by his absolutist Christology. It is a refreshing antidote to the intellectual and moral laziness of the pessimist and the cynic. Not for him the weary sigh of pseudo-sophisticates impatient with the naiveté of the optimist who just doesn't know the true reality of the power structure and the meaningless-ness of existence. For de Chardin, existence consists, in its entire totality, of the ongoing, consistent, and immediate interaction between space/time and all its constituent particulars: the interaction between organic and in-organic, the interaction between life and nonlife, between incipient con-sciousness and the non-consciousness and nonlife from which it sprang, between the endless stages of consciousness and their interaction with and between the rubrics aforementioned. For him, existence is the sum total of these ever more numerous and ever more complex interactions. In this cos-mic drama, the emergence of self-aware and self-reflective consciousness creates a new cosmic reality and a new cosmic responsibility, and most of all, a new cosmic potentiality.

Humanity's ability to analyze and break down and reorganize both itself and its external environment (which it itself is constantly changing) creates a kind of incipient "godness"—the ability at once to create cosmos out of chaos and chaos out of cosmos; then again reorganize the chaos it has cre-ated into a new cosmos. This constitutes the beating heart of cosmic evolu-tion. Just as the human heart and human consciousness are the products of primeval evolution, so is human consciousness now the molder and driver of future evolution. The very future of the Cosmos is now dependent on us. As human beings, we must plunge boldly into the current of things. In other words, we must live the life of this world, the life and times, and place and family, and language and identity we were dealt by the very evolution of our species. We must embrace our material and social world if we are to discover a door to the absolute, not desert hermits, or performative utopia-nist communitarians, or survivalist escapees from the vulgarities of modern consumerist society. The universal is to be found in the particular. The door to transcendence exists within the reality of our *present* everyday world not outside it. Those that isolate themselves in annoyed disapproval of human life as it is lived are embracing a demonstrative and false self-effacement that is artificial and inauthentic in the extreme. It is either cowardice (fear of the trials and tribulations of everyday life), or self-deception, or an arro-gant ambition to set oneself up as morally superior to one's fellows. Being proud of one's humility cannot be a virtue. Uriah Heep cannot be a model for the ambitions of humanity. Teilhard puts it thus: "... dissociation from everything that makes up the noblest charm and interest of our natural life cannot be the basis of supernatural growth."[31] For Teilhard, human beings have "to learn to appreciate the value of sacred evolution as an instrument of beatification and the eternal hopes it contains."[32] "If man is to come up to his full measure, he must become conscious of the infinite capacity for carrying himself still further—he must realize the duties it involves, and he must feel its intoxicating wonder."[33] De Chardin reflects a Kabbalistic view that the progress towards the Godhead, towards the godness of nature, is firmly rooted in our material social reality—that Godness (or divinization as he puts it) cannot be achieved by a petulant denial of the value of our material world. The success of our participation in a Godding of the cosmos is totally dependent on our solving our mundane problems, while the vision of that Godding might inspire us more to solve these mundane problems. The self-indulgent, and annoyingly demonstrative "spiritualism" of morally lazy "dropouts" who adopt the pose of "look at me I am so sensitive I cannot demean myself to deal with the vulgarities of real life" has, as with Uriah Heep's prideful humility, no social value whatsoever.

Before I continue, I must acknowledge certain negative opinions regarding not only the thinker but also the human being Teilhard de Chardin. First of all, in response to the various brutal criticisms of him by scientists such as the great biologist Peter Medawar that Teilhard "uses in metaphor words like energy, tension, force, impetus, and dimension as if they retained the weight and thrust of their special scientific usages,"[34] I simply do not agree that these words are the sole possession of a scientific monopoly. These words are also legitimately used in a more spacious, less scientifically precise, way of thinking about the world that is no less legitimate and often more informative about the mystery of why existence exists than science (which, given the precise parameters of scientific discipline, *justifiably* refuses to entertain such metaphysical thoughts). Now I cannot disagree with Medawar regarding the silly pretentiousness of Teilhard's style of writing, which seems to characterize many French thinkers. Bergson's flights of stylistic fancy are just as tiring as Teilhard's. I personally think that Teilhard did his fundamental thesis a great disservice by trying to be a poet when discussing scientific subjects; his style sometimes reminds one of the inane gibberish of postmodernism and critical theory. However, as for his central great idea regarding the evolution of consciousness until it reaches a godhood, various other scientists such as evolutionary biologist David Sloan

Wilson, have praised Teilhard's work as being "scientifically prophetic in many ways ... modern evolutionary theory shows that what Teilhard *meant* by the Omega Point is achievable in the foreseeable future."[35] Previously, the evolutionary biologist Julian Huxley, while also expressing some reservations about his scientific pretensions, praised Teilhard for perceiving human development through a more spacious integrated universal sense of evolution.[36] Geneticist and evolutionary biologist, Theodosius Dobzhansky, felt that Teilhard's view of evolution was relevant to humanity's understanding its place in existence. He called him "one of the great thinkers of our age."[37] THINKER—not scientist, not philosopher, not theologian but THINKER—someone whose thinking cannot be reduced to the research constraints of a specific university department, or the reductionist mechanistic view of life and intelligence still prevalent (and perhaps methodologically necessary) in the thinking of working scientists.

A more serious criticism of Teilhard would be how his thinking might have led him into some of the darker corners of eugenics that many have labeled racist. I tend to think that a more thoughtful reading of his remarks about non-Europeans would be culturist and not racist. Not that some races are inherently (i.e., genetically) inferior but rather that some cultures are—that some cultures enhance the chances for humanity to survive and prosper while some cultures worsen the chances for humanity to survive and prosper. I will quote the words of one of his intellectual interpreters, Max H. Begounen, to validate my own understanding of his views. Begounen wrote that Teilhard held that a "social or ethnic group which can find no better answer to the tragic circumstances of life today than to increase its own selfish demands shows by that very fact its own moral bankruptcy." In contradiction to the accusations of racism, Teilhard called the various peoples of the earth "the *natural* units of humanity" and instructed them to: "Remain true to yourselves, BUT on condition that they "move ever upward toward greater consciousness and greater love! At the summit you will find yourselves united with all those who, from every direction, have made the same ascent. *For everything that rises must converge.*"[38]

On this particular issue, we need serious and more general discussion about the differences between *multiculturalism* as an ideology that promotes the notion that all cultures are equal and *multicultural* as an adjective simply describing a certain social reality celebrating diversity. I am unfashionable in that I endorse value hierarchies regarding cultures, and do not believe that makes me a racist. Cultures that actively promote the equality of women in *all* things (especially agency over their own bodies) are *superior* to cultures that discriminate against women and deny them agency. Cultures that recognize the rights and worth of gay people are *superior* to cultures that throw gay people off buildings or behead them. Cultures that endorse the constitutionalist protections of *formal* democracy are *superior* to cultures that promote the notion that the state or religion (or majority) decide the rights of individuals. Cultures that recognize that formal democracy becomes a useless abstraction without some degree of *social* democracy enabling access to the institutions and benefits of formal democracy are *superior* to cultures that deny that such social rights even exist. I confess, I might be giving Teilhard an easy pass here, but if so, I assert that the essential legitimacy of his thinking about the evolution of existence is in no way diminished by any evil inclinations he might have in other areas. Similarly, I would claim that the wickedness of Thomas Jefferson's overweening hypocrisy regarding slavery does not diminish the essential truth of the sentiments expressed in the *Declaration of Independence* or *The Virginia Statute for Religious Freedom*. As previously indicated, I have an Old Testament view of great human beings rather than a New Testament view. Old Testament heroes are often *more* deeply flawed than the average human being. Just as King David sent Uriah to die in battle so he could sleep with his wife Bathsheba, so did Gandhi sleep with prepubescent girls in order to demonstrate he could resist his sexual attraction to them (shades of Michael Jackson). And are we to reject Martin Luther King because of his retrograde views of homosexuals and his sordid behavior towards women? Bertrand Russell reportedly seduced his own daughter-in-law. How would that, if true, damage the greatness of The *Principia Mathematica* or the relevance of his advocacy for a universal basic income? Rousseau disowned all five of the children he fathered, sending them immediately after birth, to an orphanage because he just couldn't be bothered to take care of them. Einstein's treatment of his first wife and their children is anything but admirable. I remember how relieved I was when J. Edgar Hoover revealed Martin Luther King's sexual peccadillos (hoping to neutralize his moral standing in the eyes of the public). You mean I could still be a relatively good human being and achieve great things even though in certain areas of life I was just as sleazy as Dr. King? And after all, who was the cross-dresser and closet homosexual Hoover to moralize about the sexual peccadillos of other people? In any case, this is the lens through which I believe we should consider Teilhard's intellectual/spiritual offerings.

Modern Christian Thinking

Teilhardism is but one example of how modernity itself has generated turmoil within Christianity, subverting established Christine dogmas and doctrines. *Christian Modernism,* also known as *Liberal Theology,* has influenced various Christian denominations and offshoots, with significant theological implications. These developments reinterpret Christian teaching in the light of science and *modern* concepts of ethics. For their adherents, reason and empirical evidence *supplant* inherited doctrine (shades of Maimonides and Bahya Ibn Paquda). They accept the evidence of evolution and modern biblical criticism (a development that might be seen as analogous to the Reform Movement in Judaism). They see reverence for the literal word of the Bible *as a form of idolatry,* and relying on the stringent scholarship of Biblical Criticism have concluded, in the words of the American Protestant theologian Schubert Ogden (1928–2019), that *"none of the New Testament writings can be said to be apostolic in the sense in which it has been traditionally held to be so."*[39] In other words the Bible is a book of instruction that uses stories of both actual and fictional characters to teach us how to act and how not to act—it is *not* the divine word of God and it is presumptuous to claim so and arrogant to lecture people in the name of God's word. The Bible's divinity lies in its ability to empower human beings to behave in a more godlike way, not because it is the written word of some supernatural whatever.

Liberal Christians of the 19th century believed in the idea of progress in *this* world and were optimistic about the future of humanity in *this* world. They believed humanity could build the kingdom of God in *this* world and not in the world to come (a view very similar to the Rambam's concept of the messianic era, Keynes vision of the future, and my views in the chapter "No Limits to Growth"). Similar to the great Dutch Catholic theologian and humanist philosopher Erasmus (1466–1536), they believed that there is a dialectic synergy between human volition and a divine plan; that human beings are not impotent automatons dictated to by a deterministic divine plan, but rather the divine plan is a consequence of how we human beings behave; or to paraphrase the great thinker Pogo, "we have seen destiny and it is us." This view is nothing more than a revisitation of the underlying worldview of the prophets—behave justly and this will happen; behave unjustly and that will happen. The German philosopher and Protestant theologian Friedrich Schleiermacher (1768–1834) has often been called the "Father of Liberal Theology" because of his attempts to reconcile Protestant theology with the civilizational consequences of the Scientific Revolution and the Enlightenment. He was certainly an advocate of small 'r' religiosity as against the dogmas of the big 'R' Religion Business when, in his *Addresses on Religion* (1799), he wrote:

> Religion is the outcome neither of the fear of death, nor of the fear of God. It answers a deep need in man. It is neither a metaphysic, nor a morality, but above all and essentially an intuition and a feeling .... Dogmas are not, properly speaking, part of religion: rather it is that they are derived from it. Religion is the miracle of *direct* relationship with the infinite (italics mine) .... Similarly belief in God, and in personal immortality, are not necessarily a part of religion; one can conceive of a religion without God, and it would be pure contemplation of the universe; the desire for personal immortality seems rather to show a lack of religion, since religion assumes a desire to lose oneself in the infinite, rather than to preserve one's own finite self. (This last phrase reminds me of the concept of Nirvana).

Progressive Christianity, which grew out of *Liberal Christianity*, tended toward panentheism rather than supernatural theism. It also advocated *salvation in this world* instead of in heaven; that one is saved *for* a robust and abundant life rather than saved *from* hell. Right actions are more important than right beliefs. Exercising one's reason is more important than blind allegiance to rigid doctrines and dogmas. It does not believe that Christianity is the only valid or viable way to connect to God. Episcopalian Bishop John Shelby Spong (1931–2021) in a Tweet he made public in 2015 wrote "God is not a noun that demands to be defined; God is a verb that invites us to live, to love and to be" (shades of Rabbi Cooper). Spong's "Twelve Points for [Christian] Reform" could serve as foundational thinking for an Episcopalian iteration of Cosmodeism—especially the first: "Theism, as a way of defining God, is dead. So most theological God-talk is today meaningless. A new way to speak of God must be found." Similarly ordained minister in the United Church of Canada, Bruce Sanguin (b.1955) writes: "It's time for the Christian church to get with the cosmological program ... We now know, for instance, that we live in an evolving or evolutionary universe. Evolution is the way that the Holy creates in space and in time, in every sphere: material, biological, social, cultural, psychological, and spiritual. This new cosmology simply cannot be contained by old models and images of God, or by old ways of being the church.[40]

The project of this part of the book—finding intimations of the Cosmo-deistic Hypothesis in our legacy religions—can find its justification from Spong's internet article, "A New Christianity for a New World":

> As I look at the history of religion, I observe that new re-ligious insights always and only emerge from the old tra-ditions as they begin to die. It is not by pitching the old insights out but by journeying deeply through them into new visions that we are able to change religion's direction. The creeds were 3rd and 4th-century love songs that people composed to sing to their understanding of God. We do not have to literalize their words to perceive their mean-ing or their intention to join in the singing of their creedal song. I think religion in general and Christianity in partic-ular must always be evolving. Forcing the evolution is the dialog between yesterday's words and today's knowledge. The sin of Christianity is that any of us ever claimed that we had somehow captured eternal truth in the forms we had created.[41]

In his magnum opus *Systematic Theology*, the Lutheran Protestant theolo-gian Paul Tillich (1886–1965) makes the astonishing declaration that, "God does not exist. He is being itself beyond essence and existence. Therefore, to argue that God exists is to deny him."[42] (I am trying to imagine a conver-sation been Tillich and Maimonides.) Tillich coined the word *Transtheism*, which is really an iteration of the negative theology that characterized the thinking of Maimonides and is neither theistic nor atheistic but beyond trite attempts to even define the God concept. It is a view reminiscent of C. S. Lewis's use of the *Tao*, cited several times above, and actually places him closer to the insights of the various Eastern religions. Tillich's ontology sees God as being beyond scholastic concepts such as essence and existence. This includes rejection of pantheistic conceptions of God as a universal es-sence. In other words, God is the *itness* of existence; God is the existence that exists—not the essence of existence nor the highest manifestation of existence or the creator of existence or something that exists in and of itself but existence as such; existence *qua* existence. As previously noted, the Greek translation of "I am that I am" is "I *am* being [existence itself]." Attaching this concept to the view that the evolution of this existence is the ultimate ontological and metaphysical fact, there is no barrier to considering the possibility of the inherent Godness of *Ein Sof* existence and the future, albeit contingent, Godness of our home Cosmos. The *"living* God," in Tillich's notion of the "living God" is the itness of evolution, evolution as the holy spirit of infinite existence. He does not think of God as a being that exists in time and space, because that constrains God, and makes God finite. If all beings are finite, and God is the Creator of all beings, then logically God cannot be finite since a finite itness cannot be the sustainer of an infinite variety of finite things. Thus, God is considered beyond being, beyond finitude and limitation; God is the abyss, the *Tohu Vevohu*, the *Tao* underlying *everything.*

Religious Naturalism

Religious Naturalism, as articulated by Christian thinkers, is a complement to the above. It "is a perspective that finds religious meaning in the natural world and rejects the notion of a supernatural realm."[43] Religious naturalists use the term *religious* as I have used it; as small 'r' religiosity, in numinous awe before the facticity of existence rather than as an adherent to particular dogmas and doctrines. Schleiermacher was a forerunner of *Religious Naturalism* in his attempts to reconcile science and religion. Gordon D. Kaufman (1925–2011), an ordained Mennonite Minister and Professor of Divinity at Harvard Divinity School, who identified with *Religious Naturalism,* suggested, in his *Prairie View Lectures* that:

> ... we should no longer think of God as The Creator (a kind of super-person) but rather as the *creativity* manifest throughout the universe from its beginning in the Big Bang, through the cosmic and biological evolutionary developments ... today [what we] should regard as God is the ongoing creativity in the universe—the bringing (or coming) into being of what is genuinely new, something transformative; ... In some respects and some degrees this creativity is apparently happening continuously, in and through the processes or activities or events around us and within us ... [the] God!—to which we should be responsive is not the private possession of any of the many partic-

ular religious faiths or systems .... This profound mystery of creativity is manifest in and through the overall human bio-historical evolution and development everywhere on the planet; and it continues to show itself throughout the entire human project, no matter what may be the particular religious and or cultural beliefs.[44]

In further anticipation of the Cosmodeistic Hypothesis, and somewhat similar to Rabbi Cooper, Kaufman wrote in *A Religious Interpretation of Emergence: Creativity as God* that:

> Thinking of God today as *creativity* (instead of as The Creator) enables us to bring theological values and meanings into significant connection with modern cosmological and evolutionary thinking. This conception connects our understanding of God with today's ideas of the Big Bang; cosmic and biological evolution; the evolutionary emergence of novel complex realities from simpler realities, and the irreducibility of these complex realities to their simpler origins; and so on ... This mystery of creativity—God—manifest throughout the universe is quite awe-inspiring, calling forth ... a sense of the profound meaningfulness of human existence in the world .... It is appropriate, therefore, to think of God today as precisely this magnificent panorama of creativity with which our universe and our lives confront us.[45]

Theologian Henry Wieman (1884–1975), ordained as a Presbyterian Minister and subsequently becoming a Unitarian, believed it was:

> ... impossible to gain knowledge of the total cosmos or to have any understanding of the infinity transcending the cosmos. Consequently, beliefs about these matters are illusions, cherished for their *utility* in producing desired states of mind .... *Nothing can transform man unless it operates in human life* (italics mine). Therefore, in human life, in the actual processes of human existence, must be found the saving and transforming power which religious inquiry seeks and which faith must apprehend.[46]

As with the Cosmodeistic Hypothesis, Wieman's religious naturalism led him to redefine God as a natural process rather than a supernatural entity:

> How can we interpret what operates in human existence to create, sustain, save, and transform toward the greatest good, so that scientific research and scientific technology can be applied to searching out and providing the conditions—physical, biological, psychological, and social—which must be present for its most effective operation? *This operative presence in human existence can be called God.* (Italics mine)

Unitarian theologian Jerome A. Stone has been prominent in the development of Religious Naturalism. His book *Religious Naturalism Today: The Rebirth of a Forgotten Alternative* encourages spirituality without dependence on a supernatural entity. In an article in *The American Journal of Theology & Philosophy* he wrote:

> ... let's get religious for a minute. What if the earth and its creatures were sacred? The sacred we treat with overriding care. What if the earth and our sibling creatures were sacred, either inherently sacred, or because they have a derivative sacredness as creatures of God ... I would say that my enlightenment involves finding out that I am of the earth, earthly. The continuing task is to find out what this means and to live by it.[47]

Loyal D. Rue (1944), who received his Master of Divinity at an Evangelical Lutheran Divinity School, authored a book entitled *Religion Is Not About God*. Ordained Catholic Priest, religion historian, and eventually president of the American Teilhard Association, Thomas Berry (1914–2009) believed that "the universe, the solar system, and planet Earth in themselves and in their evolutionary emergence constitute for the human community the primary revelation of that ultimate mystery whence all things emerge into being."[48] Michael Dowd is a former fundamentalist pastor who has developed a *Gospel According to Evolution* or "sacred evolution." It denies the reductionist scientific view that evolution is mindless, purposeless, and without direction and asserts that Creationism and Intelligent Design are both trivializations of the god concept. Inspired by John Stewart's "Evolution's Arrow" he proposes the intrinsic progressive directionality of evolution. He sees the whole "universe story" as "God's revelation." "God" is the sacred name for the whole of reality, measurable and immeasurable. He and his science writer wife, Connie Barlow, coined a new word "creatheist" suggesting that the whole of reality is creativity in a vested, directional sense. It means realizing religious ideals. There are other serious groups and thinkers who identify with concepts such as *Christian atheism, Death of God theology, and Secular theology,* including a group of *Nontheistic Quakers* who believe you can be a good Quaker without believing in a supernatural God.

It was Protestantism that carried Aquinas's creation of secular space to its logical conclusion. It was Protestantism that sanctified the secular, infusing our everyday way of making a living with divinity: what we did was a "calling" (by God). This democratized society. The trader and the farmer were just as sacred in what they did as the priest or the king. In regard to the Protestant concept of "calling," if Cosmodeism is correct then everything positive we do contributes to the ongoing sanctification of the universe. What we do radiates out into the cosmos (a kind of spiritual 2nd law of thermodynamics). All of us are serving the Godding of universe by contributing to the constant and ongoing process of creation—and, as a Jew might put it, partnering with God in its own ongoing creation.

The Mormons are an especially interesting iteration of Protestantism. As weird as some aspects of their theology appear to the outsider, much of their fundamental belief system accords with modern cosmology, enabling the eventual emergence of a *Reformed Mormonism* that reflects the Cosmodeistic Hypothesis. For example, they believe that existence was not created *ex nihilo* (literally out of nothing), but rather out of existing matter and that Earth is only one of many other inhabited worlds. In his essay *Eternal Progression in a Multiverse: An Explorative Mormon Cosmology,* Professor of Mechanical Engineering (specialties thermodynamics, fluid mechanics and heat transfer) Mormon Elder Kirk D. Hagen provides a wonderful condensation of Mormon belief that coincides with many aspects of the Cosmodeistic Hypothesis. For example:

> ... the ultimate human potential is to become like God himself ... *man is a god in embryo* (italics mine) ... and as his eternal growth is continued, he will approach more nearly the point which to us is Godhood, and which is everlasting in its power over the elements of the universe ... the ultimate future status of the children of God is godhood itself. [49]

Hagen concludes his essay with a provocative paragraph that would certainly drive Evangelicals and mainstream Catholics crazy (not to mention devout atheists).

> Are there communication and movement of the gods and other premortal and post mortal beings between universes? When a universe experiences a big crunch or big freeze, does the god of that universe generate a new universe or "relocate" to another universe fit for carrying out the "great plan of happiness" for a new household of spirit children? Did God, our Father in Heaven, achieve godhood in this universe or a prior one? If God was exalted in a prior universe, how many universes has he governed? Jesus Christ is the redeemer for this universe, but is he the redeemer for others? Are some universes "stillborn" in the sense that they do not have the required values of the physical constants for a universe capable of sustaining life? Because the multiverse is infinite, are there replicas of us in other universes as postulated by the replication paradox? Cosmologists speculate whether the physical laws are the same across the ensemble of universes, but what about the spiritual laws? Are the spiritual laws "multiversal" or just "universal?" As multiverse cosmologies develop scientifically, these questions and others will stimulate much discussion.[50]

Anticipating Hagan's speculation about multiple redeemers in a multiplicity of universes, C.S. Lewis considered the possibility of other *Sons of God* (Christ's cosmic siblings) incarnating in other worlds, or, alternatively, that God might have an assortment of salvation plans distinct for each world. The Swedish mystic, Emanuel Swedenborg, wrote that:

> Anyone with a sound intellect can know from many considerations that there are numerous worlds with people on them. Rational thought leads to the conclusion that massive bodies such as the planets, some of which are larger than our own earth, are not empty masses created merely to wander aimlessly around the sun and shine with their feeble light on one planet. No, they must have a much greater purpose than that .... What would one planet be

to God, who is infinite, and for whom thousands, or even tens of thousands of planets, all full of inhabitants, would be such a trifling matter as to be almost nothing?[51]

I could go on with this inventory of thinking derived from the Christian experience by individuals whose thinking would enable people to accept a "Theology" derived from the Cosmodeistic Hypothesis, but that would be tiresome and never ending. For the purposes of this book this is sufficient.

Chapter Twenty-Four: Islamic Intimations

I confess that this chapter is a bit of a stretch in regard to drawing analogies to the Cosmodeistic Hypothesis. One of the problems is that there is little translated literature coming out of the Muslim world that would enable a non-Muslim to access thinking similar to what is cited above in Jewish and Christian contexts. There are several reasons for this: some objective and some subjective. While it has become a commonplace judgement of historians that neither the Renaissance nor the Scientific Revolution could have occurred without the intellectual and mathematical contributions of the *Golden Age Caliphate* (8ᵗʰ to 14ᵗʰ century), it is clear that Muslim countries in general and Arab countries in particular have not successfully confronted the modernist consequences of the Scientific and Industrial Revolutions for which their own thinking built the foundations. Consider, for example, that in 1960 Egypt had a higher per capita standard of living than war ravaged South Korea and compare the development of both countries today. Malaysia has been the only predominately Muslim country that has been modernizing successfully. Indonesia, the world's largest Muslim country, has also been showing positive signs of modernizing but still not comparable to Malaysia. Iran has the human and cultural potential to emerge, but for the fact that it is ruled by a cult of primitive Islamists. The Arab countries range from failed states (Libya, Somalia) to basket cases (Syria and now Lebanon), to seemingly having made peace with corrupt governments and sluggish cultural lives (Egypt), to being in a constant state of revolutionary chaos (Sudan), to narcissistic medieval monarchies (Saudi Arabia), to pretentious upstarts with only the patina of modernity enabled by fabulous oil wealth (the Gulf States). This is ironic to the extreme because, to a very great degree, the *Golden Age* laid the groundwork for modernity. In fact, I would claim that the historical contribution of Islam to the "Making of Europe" is as great, if not greater, than that of the Church. The incompatibility between *historical* Islam and the West is a narrative fabricated by European orientalists on the one hand and political Islamists on the other hand. *Islam is a western not an eastern* religion: its theology is monotheistic not polytheistic, and its philosophical foundations are Greek, not Chinese or Indian.

I want to suggest, therefore, that Islam, despite its current situation, also has the ability to evolve its theological thinking into a Cosmodeistic framework. This is because the concept of an infinite existence containing a multitude of worlds and other conscious beings is not foreign to historical Islam from its very beginnings. The Shiite Imam Muhammed al-Baqir (676–733) wrote "Maybe you see that God created only this single world and that God did not create humans besides you. Well, I swear by God that God created thousands and thousands of worlds and thousands and thousands of humankinds."[52] Abu Nasr Al-Farabi (c. 872–950) came perilously close to a pantheistic Islam by preaching that God is eternal—that he is both essence *and existence* (i.e., the entire material world). Consequently, if God is both eternal and existence as such, then one must conclude that existence has always existed; that God rearranged its own existence in order to create a chaos that would enable a cosmos to emanate from that chaos (a view that seems to anticipate the Kabbalistic concept of "Tzimtzum"). Al-Farabi influenced both Avicenna and Maimonides with his negative theology — that it is simply impossible to make any positive claims about the attributes of God; that it is a concept beyond description. According to Al-Farabi, the world (our Cosmos) emanated from this concept beyond description (C.S. Lewis's *Tao*) and *the supreme goal of humanity is to become one with its existence.* Not only does this remind one of de Chardin in that it is the job of humanity to become one with the Alpha God (existence as such) thus creating the Omega God (existence as such), but as with de Chardin, the Cosmodeistic Hypothesis can turn this progression on its head and posit that the supreme goal of humanity is to become one with existence, thus creating the Omega God, which will have *emanated* from existence as such.

Fakhr al-Dīn al-Rāzī (1150–1210), recognized by the Sunnis as the *Sultan of Theologians*, also anticipated the concept of a multiverse. He proposed *infinite* space that God has the power to fill with an infinite number of universes. Basing himself completely on Quranic verses he wrote:

> It is established by evidence that there exists beyond the world a void without a terminal limit and it is established as well by evidence that God Most High has power over all contingent beings. Therefore, *He has the power to create a thousand-thousand worlds* beyond this world such that each one of those worlds be bigger and more massive than this world as well as having the like of what this world has ...

Al-Razi was particularly reliant on the Qur'anic verse "All praise belongs to God, Lord of the *Worlds*" (stress on the plural *worlds*). For him existence was infinite and God had the power to fill it with infinite universes—a portent of Cantor's "infinity of infinities." Al-Razi was not some eccentric Islamic contrarian, but wholly part of Islam's mainstream. He identified with the dominant orthodox Ash'ari school of Sunni theology founded by the atomist Abu al-Hassan al-Ash'ri (874–936) who believed that existence is composed of infinitely small particles ("atoms" in the language of the times) in constant interaction with one another and responsible for all of what we see and experience in reality. He would have no trouble relating to Nessyahu's cosmology.

Subsequent Ash'arite thinkers such as Said al-Din al-Taftazani (1322–1390) argued that Islam, "must be proven to be true by rational arguments [in order to be] accepted as the basis of the religion. [Muslims] must be convinced on the basis of rational arguments [that Islam is true]."[53] This line of thinking is reminiscent of Maimonides. As with Maimonides being "proscribed" (*Herem* in Hebrew), as Spinoza later was, by Jewish anti-rationalists, so too these Islamic scholars were also attacked for introducing Greek thought (i.e., rationalism) into the Islamic theological debate. Interestingly, Maimonides' was also influenced by the thinking of the Ash'arite theologian Imam Muhammad-al Ghazali (1058–1111) as was Aquinas. Modern Islamic intellectuals such as Abdullah Yusuf Ali (1872–1953) have also depended on the Quran to argue for life on other planets.

As far as adapting to the intellectual, moral, and ethical strictures of modernity, Islamic modernists would do well to cite the example of the great Andalusian Islamic polymath Averroes (1126–1198). Europeans called him the *Father of Rationalism* because of his commentaries on Aristotle. Like Maimonides, he believed theology should adapt to science and philosophy and not the reverse. Along with Aquinas, he is considered one of the creators of secular space. Millennia ahead of his time, he believed women should be equal with men; that they should have a full share in the activities of society, including serving as soldiers, philosophers and rulers; that limiting their potential contributions to society weakens the state's well-being. Averroes was a radical intellectual democrat. He believed that every human being shared the same intellect and had access to the same universal knowledge. This notion was rejected by Aquinas and not appreciated by current philosophers, although it reminds me a bit of Emerson's *Over-Soul*. Yet, I believe the concept might be reborn in a reverse iteration; that *becoming* a universal intellect should be a future aim of conscious life rather than its present reality. By standing Averroes' speculation on its head, it would conform to the Cosmodeistic Hypothesis while being firmly within Muslim intellectual tradition. Averroes has already become a symbol of Islamic modernists such as the Moroccan philosopher Mohammed Abed Al Jabri (1935–2010). The very titles of Al Jabri's books (*Democracy, Human Rights and Law in Islamic Thought* and *The Formation of Arab Reason: Text, Tradition, and the Construction of Modernity in the Arab World*) reveal visions of future Arab societies that are achievable if not for the stifling overlay of corrupt, incompetent governance in tandem with the most obscurantist and ignorant religious establishment.

The failure of most of the Muslim World to assimilate into modernity is quite ironic given the dominate impact Islam's intellectual and material civilization has had on creating the very foundations of modernity. A brief sketch of this contribution is in order to demonstrate the historic legacy that present and future Islamic modernists might draw upon to enable their people to, once again, become a prominent force in cocreating our common human future. Muslim philosophical thinking, as well as scientific and mathematical imagination and mercantile resourcefulness, were absolutely vital for the 12th-century and 15th-century European Renaissances, which birthed the subsequent Scientific Revolution, and have impacted the course of human history until this very day. The introduction of classical Greek thought into Europe by the Arabs, first in Spain (providing the intellectual foundations for the 12th-century Renaissance), and then in Italy (providing the intellectual foundations for the 15th-century Renaissance) has been so well documented that it has become a commonplace. It is generally agreed amongst historians that neither Renaissance would have occurred without the Arab contributions revolutionizing how Europeans thought.

The introduction of what Europeans call Arabic numerals transformed Europe. Hindu-Arabic or Indo-Arabic numerals were invented by Indian mathematicians (Ironically, Muslims actually call them Hindu numerals not Arab numbers). They were first introduced into 10th-century Europe by way of the Arab merchants in Spain because they made keeping business records so much easier. It took several centuries for them to be universally adopted across Europe. The great medieval mathematician, Leonardo Fibonacci, (1170–1240) first learned about Arabic numerals primarily through his contact with Arab merchants across the Mediterranean basin. Merchants were the first to replace Roman Numerals with the Arabic because the ten number system and positional notation[54] allowed for easy calculation and manipulation of numbers. Fibonacci introduced these numbers as an *accounting* innovation (and is thus considered one of the fathers of modern accounting). In his book the *Liber Abaci* (1202), he demonstrated how practical Arabic numerals were for commercial bookkeeping. Following Fibonacci, Florentine merchants developed double-entry bookkeeping (impossible without Arabic numbers) in the late 13th and early 14th centuries. This was codified into a coherent system by the Franciscan Friar Luca Pacioli in 1494 (considered another founder of modern accounting). This was as radical an advance in making business calculations and storing data in the medieval period as the computer has been in the modern era. And, as another rebuff to the non-overlapping magisteria thesis, I should note that pre-modern Europe viewed double-entry bookkeeping as having theological and cosmological connotations by reminding one of the symmetry of God's world (God's balance sheet as it were); a concept that contributed to a scientific mental attitude: God's symmetrical creation implying God's codex of laws that governed the natural world. This attitude of mind molded Copernicus and Newton. Who would have thought accountants were such revolutionaries? They put Lenin and Mao in the shade when it comes to influencing the course of human history.

We could justifiably claim that the introduction of Arabic numbers into Europe was as profound a development as the conversion of Europe to Christianity, because it abetted the development of European banking and accounting which facilitated the *Commercial Revolution*; a revolution which quickly led to both the Age of Exploration and the Renaissance. How so? Because the rapid development of commerce required new markets and new supplies (the stimulus for the Age of Exploration) as well as a framework of commercial and banking law which the Catholic Church, with its initial hostility to banking, could not provide. The solution was to study ancient Roman commercial law, primarily at the University of Bologna, in order to produce lawyers and judges who could adjudicate commercial disputes. A lawyer from the University of Bologna plays a central role in *The Merchant of Venice* in resolving the "commercial dispute" between Shylock and Antonio. And here we run into one of the great unintended consequences in history. The study of Roman commercial law led to some of the more curious law students to start reading some of the non-commercial aspects of Roman thinking (Cicero, etc.) and helped midwife the concept of humanism in the Church (re. Erasmus). This is known as the Latin Renaissance, quickly followed by the Greek Renaissance, because as scholarship deepened, the Greek sources of Roman thinking became apparent. This Greek Renaissance was reinforced when the Turks conquered Constantinople and Byzantium's Greek-speaking scholars escaped to Italy. The reader must forgive me for this lengthy digression, but I feel it necessary to back up my claim that without the Islamic contribution to the West there would be no modern Europe and hence no America, and to demonstrate that Islam has its own historical raw materials not only to embrace modernity but to become once again one of the intellectual leaders of human civilization.

I continue with these developmental connections because the historical thigh bone is indeed connected to the historical hip bone and one must understand this not only to make sense of human progress until this point, but also to give us an idea of the future possibilities of Islamic progress. The critical thinking of classical civilization reborn in the Renaissance (literally meaning "rebirth") met the emergence of an expanding literate middle class (a product of the Commercial Revolution) which combined with the invention of the printing press and the subsequent availability of inexpensive Bibles, to enable the Protestant Reformation. One must remember that before printing, an actual physical Bible written by a scribe was only affordable to the super wealthy of the time and to the Church. As a comparison, today the cost of a scribe-written Torah scroll is estimated at $30,000 to $100,000. Not too many people are going to have that on their night table to peruse before they go to sleep! The vast majority of the population had never even physically touched a Bible, let alone owned one. Indeed, they may not have even seen one close up. And since the vast majority of the population was illiterate anyway, people only knew of the Bible what semi-literate village priests read to them, which being in Latin even the priest didn't really understand. When John Wycliffe (1320?–1384) translated the Bible into vernacular English and then sent out his minions to teach the peasants how to read, all the while sermonizing against the temporal power of the Church, it really pissed off religious vested interests. So much so that he was put on trial *after he died*. Found guilty of heresy he was excommunicated retroactively, his corpse exhumed and burned, and the ashes cast into a river. Being able to actually read the Bible was dangerous to the business model of the Church. Reading the Bible critically, one found no mention of Popes and Cardinals or the various opulent doodads of the Church. Certain mental attitudes were emerging, reinforced by the new technology of the printing press mass producing cheap Bibles that could be owned by anyone, that laid the groundwork for the Reformation. The communications revolution introduced by the printing press was the most profound in history until the advent of the computer and the Internet.

Critical thinking as well as the kind of technical knowledge useful for commerce also contributed to the Scientific Revolution. The merchant class couldn't care less if Galileo's telescopes revealed that the moon isn't absolutely smooth or that Saturn has moons (to the dismay of the Church and the Aristotelian pedants of the academies) but only that it was extremely useful in making shipping more secure, and thus more profitable. It also enabled speculators to see ships approaching from a distance (and not lost at sea) who then hurried to the bourse in order to invest in the ship before it docked. Businessmen loved this invention and purchasing them provided Galileo with a very comfortable living. The Scientific Revolution, as is well known, birthed Enlightenment thinking when scientific and critical thinking began to be applied to human society and economic activity in the attempt to make it more efficient and more just. And, of course, there is no Industrial Revolution without science or the Constitutionalism that derived from the Enlightenment. There is a direct evolutionary line between Islam's contribution to civilization and all these, as it were, European developments.

The Arab impact on the Scientific Revolution, and on culture in general, is revealed in the Arabic words that are now commonplace in our scientific vocabulary: alchemy (from which derives chemistry), alcohol, algebra named after the book *AL-JABR wa'l muqabalah* by the Baghdadi mathematician Al-Khwārizmī in 820 A.D. (algorithm is a corruption of the name Al-Khwārizmī), alkaline, almanac, average, azimuth, cipher, elixir, nadir, soda, zenith, zero, and so on. Our general vocabulary also contains many words of Arabic roots: admiral, adobe, alcove, amber, arsenal, assassin, caliber, candy, check, cork, coffee, cotton, gauze (derived from Gaza where it was originally woven), guitar (also lute), hazard, lazuli, mascara, mattress, monsoon, mummy, racquet, ream, safari, sash, satin, sofa, talcum, Swahili, zircon, and tariff. Even the infamous word, Mafia, is said to have entered Sicilian Italian during the period of the Arab Emirate of Sicily (831 to 1091). Some linguists even claim the expression "so-long" entered English as a corruption of the Arabic word *Salaam* (good-bye).

Why did the most cosmopolitan, tolerant, and intellectually curious civilization in human history, up until that point, decline into the obscurantist, backward looking reactionary entity it has become? I believe it can be attributed to two major historical events—both of which together caused Islam in general and the Arabs in particular to close their cultural gates which had previously been open to every culture in the world. From Byzantium (the eastern Roman Empire) they took Greek philosophy, from India numerals, from Persia and China they also took without embarrassment, false modesty, obsequiousness, or haughty arrogance but as proud and self-confident students of civilization who quickly became teachers of civilization. In the Golden Age, Islam had become the greatest cultural entrepôt in the history of the human race. Baghdad was its intellectual and cultural capital, a combination of Paris and New York. But in 1258, the Mongols conquered Baghdad, slaughtered 800,000 inhabitants, including its entire intellectual and cultural class, and burned all its books. Imagine if you will if Paris had been totally destroyed at the beginning of the 19th century with its entire cultural and intellectual class slaughtered, leaving only ignorant, narrow minded village priests as the teachers of the French people. Would we be speaking of French civilization today or would France more closely resemble communist Albania?

The other event was, of course, the Crusades, in which the Arabs were finally "triumphant" in 1291. I use inverted commas for "triumphant" because given subsequent historical developments, Europe came out the winner. The Crusades and the Mongol sack of Baghdad were such profound traumas that Islam withdrew within itself, while the "defeated" Europeans profited immensely by an increase in international trade and exchange of ideas and technology which, as noted above, evolved into the Commercial Revolution, the Renaissance and all that followed. I have digressed into so much historical detail simply to show that Islamic modernists striving to become a leading cultural historical force once again have a rich history to hold up as a model to the Muslim peoples of the world.

Chapter Twenty-Five: Asian Intimations

The belief systems covered in this portion reflect a typical Western conceit in that I relate to these diverse religious traditions as if they were a single overarching civilization. They actually have less in common than the three Monotheistic religions have with one another. So please be assured that this is done more out of convenience (and my own limited anecdotal knowledge) than out of disrespect. It might be analogous to America's current political sociology speaking of "Asian Americans," which includes Chinese, Indians, Japanese, Koreans, and Filipinos, as a voting bloc. The appellation "Asian Americans" is really as silly as calling Italians and Jews from Brooklyn, Scots-Irish from the Appalachians, Poles from Chicago, and Scandinavians from Minneapolis "European Americans." This being said, I believe the worldviews of what the Europeans have called the Eastern "religions" (Hinduism, Buddhism, Taoism, Confucianism, and Jainism) —none of which even knew they were "religions" until the European's told them they were—might be more amenable to the Cosmodeistic Hypothesis than any of the Monotheistic religions. Their cosmologies are so sophisticated and congruent with the discoveries of modern science that they make a literal Biblical worldview of a 6,000-year-old universe seem infantile by comparison. Moreover, the religious philosophies of India are intrinsically non-doctrinaire. Hinduism, for instance, is a repository of accretions, additions and modifications constantly changing and complexifying through the ages; it might even be called a universe of religious instincts, intuitions, and intimations. The space/time immensity of Hindu cosmology (311 trillion and 44 billion years) enables it to accommodate the Nessyahu Conjectures about the nature of existence more than any other legacy faith system. There is certainly nothing in Cosmodeism that would offend any of the radically dissimilar views of the various schools of Hindu metaphysics. Buddhism and Shintoism also have evolved and created numerous sects without causing much mischief to their underlying attitudes to life. Buddhism and Confucianism are actually a-theistic (no gods) or non-theistic (no need for Gods) and not even religions in the Western sense of the world.

Intellectual convergence between the more sophisticated Hindu, Buddhist and Taoist philosophies with modern cosmology and quantum physics have been well documented in a slew of well written bestsellers such as: *The Tao of Physics* by Fritjof Capra, *Mysticism and the New Physics* by Michael Talbot, and *The Dancing Wu Li Masters* by Gary Zukav. Less so regarding the Monotheistic religions, which have been perceived by the cultural fashion-setters to be less cool, but also because the ideological and cultural control mechanisms of the monotheistic Religion Businesses are much more robust than those of the Eastern religions. My comments and observations about these Eastern traditions will, by the necessity of my own ignorance, be less detailed. I apologize in advance for all lacunae; this chapter is more a suggestive theme rather than comprehensive research.

Hinduism has many gods and is actually not a distinct faith tradition but a catchphrase for numerous diverse religious practices. that are neither Muslim nor Christian and was, some claim, invented by British orientalist imperialists to facilitate their control of India, although this perspective has also been fiercely criticized. Actually, what is true is that Hindus have thought of themselves as a peoplehood (much like the Jews) rather than a distinct clearly delineated faith system. Indeed, the Hindu attitude towards life is not particularly amenable to a single, indubitable truth. The Hindus perceive time and space as infinite; generating infinite numbers of [finite] universes that preceded our [finite] universe and will continue to produce infinite numbers of [finite] universes following the expiration of ours. In other words, they have been teaching the Cosmodeistic principle of infinite space/time having produced our own finite Cosmos for over 4,000 years. Brahma is the ultimate creator "god" of all the universes and exists for 311 trillion forty-four billion years (okay, not really infinity, but since scientists reckon that our particular Cosmos is only 14 billion years old, why be petty?). The cosmological intuition of Hinduism is the most profound and sophisticated of all the religious traditions. The ultra-vastness of the cosmological imagination of Hinduism is unmatched and more amenable to the Cosmodeistic conjecture than any other spiritual tradition.

Similarly to Hinduism, the Buddha viewed the duration of existence as equivalent to the time taken to erode a huge rock measuring 1x1x1 mile by lightly brushing it with a silk cloth, once every century. Both views are congruent with Nessyahu's observation that there is no beginning of which we cannot conceive something before and no end of which we cannot conceive of something after—no smallness of which we cannot conceive something smaller and no largeness of which we cannot conceive something larger. Cosmodeism continues in this line of thought: there is no level of consciousness of which we cannot conceive something higher and greater until our Cosmos creates a consciousness that can interrelate with the infinite consciousness of infinity—the Brahma. We might envisage a reinterpretation of the concept of Nirvana in which Nirvana is perceived as achieving ultimate peace in the no-thingness of the cosmic Godding by becoming one with the Cosmos—ending all strife with objective existence by *becoming* objective existence. The descriptions of reality of both traditions as they pertain to dimensions of existence and levels of consciousness are as intricate, subtle and sophisticated as quantum physics, eleven-dimension space and string theory. Unlike the Monotheistic religions, there is nothing in modern physics and cosmology (and one might even say biology and evolution) that would require any of these religions to suffer doctrinal angst. They could even say, with a bit of smugness at the presumptions of the West, "So, what's new? We came to many of these conclusions thousands of years ago just by thinking logically about the problematics of existence, without benefit of science!"

Jainism also does not believe in a creator deity. The 12th-century Sanskrit text, the *Yogasastra*, declares: "The universe is not created nor sustained by anything; it is self-sustaining, without any base or support." In other words, existence, and everything associated with it (matter, space, time, and principles of motion), has always existed. "Gods" for them are the souls of individual human beings that have achieved higher stages of consciousness. Jains believe that godliness, defined as being the very process of achieving higher consciousness, is inherent *in every living organism* (thus their devoted avoidance of killing or causing harm to *any* living thing). Jain ethics requires conscious life to consciously strive to achieve this higher consciousness. Enlightenment comes from one's own efforts not from some supernatural being. Godliness, therefore, has nothing to do with God. The 9th-century Jain monk *Jinasena*, simply using deductive logic, mocked the idea of a creator deity in his Sanskrit poem *Mahapurana*:

> If God created the world, where was he before the creation? If you say he was transcendent then and needed no support, where is he now? How could God have made this world without any raw material? If you say that he made this first, and then the world, you are faced with an endless regression.

> If you declare that this raw material arose naturally you fall into another fallacy, for the whole universe might thus have been its own creator and have arisen quite naturally.

If God created the world by an act of his own will, without any raw material, then it is just his will and nothing else—and who will believe this silly nonsense?

If he is ever perfect and complete, how could the will to create have arisen in him? If, on the other hand, he is not perfect, he could no more create the universe than a potter could.

If he is form-less, action-less, and all-embracing, how could he have created the world? Such a soul, devoid of all modality, would have no desire to create anything.

If he is perfect, he does not strive for the three aims of man, so what advantage would he gain by creating the universe?

If you say that he created to no purpose because it was his nature to do so, then God is pointless. If he created in some kind of sport, it was the sport of a foolish child, leading to trouble.

If he created because of the karma of embodied beings (acquired in a previous creation), then he is not the Almighty Lord, but subordinate to something else.

If out of love for living beings and need of them he made the world, why did he not make creation wholly blissful free from misfortune?

If he were transcendent he would not create, for he would be free: Nor if involved in transmigration, for then he would not be almighty. Thus the doctrine that the world was created by God makes no sense at all.

And God commits great sin in slaying the children whom he himself created. If you say that he slays only to destroy evil beings, why did he create such beings in the first place?

Good men should combat the believer in divine creation, maddened by an evil doctrine. Know that the world is uncreated, as time itself is, without beginning or end, and is based on the principles, life, and rest. Uncreated and indestructible, it endures under the compulsion of its own nature.

328

The Chinese have similar views: "... the foundation of Chinese thought is the belief in a single cosmic universe, a oneness with no beginning or end"[55] and thus it is a belief system that can certainly accommodate the concept of an infinite nature unified in the large and small. Concepts of the *Yin* and *Yang* interacting to create reality out of the endless void, which was the beginning, would have no trouble functioning as a metaphor for Nessyahu's concept of the various particles interacting to create the cosmic reality with which we are familiar. The Chinese concept of the *Tao* (or *Dao*) is very similar to the Jewish concept of God. It is the unformed, unnamable guiding principle of existence: "... in the beginning the world was an endless void ..." [infinite nature?]. Moreover, as with the Jews, the Taoists believe that there is human correspondence and participation with the Tao, and, as with Cosmodeism, that the aim of life is to ultimately become joined with the absolute. Laozi put it thus: "It is something formlessly fashioned, that existed before heaven and earth .... Its name we do not know; Tao is the byname that we give it ..." The Tao concept of the Yin and Yang is somewhat similar to Buber's "I/Thou" as it relates to existence as such: "opposites [that] ... weave together and interrelate to create an infinite world of possibilities."[56] This is a concept that can certainly accommodate the postulate of an infinite nature creating an infinite number of cosmoses advanced by Cosmodeism.

Taoism influenced and was influenced by Buddhism and Confucianism. The Chinese "religious" attitude is a combination of all three. I put religious in inverted commas because, as already pointed out several times, by Western standards it is difficult to call any of them a religion. Confucianism is more a life-system than a religion and Buddhism purports no God and has no theology, while classical Taoism is more philosophy than religion. Even so, all three, in their popularized (and vulgarized) expressions, take on the form of the same superstitious and gullible religious practices that characterize Western Religious Businesses. As philosopher of comparative religions, Huston Smith, put it:

> Popular Taoism is not a pretty sight ... the original doctrine of Tao ... was a concept too subtle to be grasped by the average mind or spirit. It was perhaps inevitable that when the concept was translated to make contact with the average villager and *institutionalized* around this translation it would be rendered in cruder and eventually perverted

terms. To pass from the lofty heights of the *Tao Te Ching* to the priest craft of Popular Taoism is like passing from a crystal mountain spring to the thick, fetid waters of a stagnant canal. Mysticism becomes mystification and religion is perverted into necromancy and sorcery. There have been long epochs in China's history when Taoism in its popular form could be characterized as little more than a funeral racket.

This, of course, is a criticism that could be made of any religion in the world; none of them are a very "pretty sight." I would even say that today's popular Kabbalah being peddled by spiritual oafs reflects Huston Smith's observations about Taoism. The original sublime and ineffable insights of profoundly intuitive individuals have always been institutionalized into various branches of the Religion Business, profiting from the fears, insecurities and superstitions of human beings trying to come to terms with the meaning of their own existence in confrontation with ultimate reality. But as to the specifics of *Taoism* and its potential relationship with Cosmodeism, I would describe it as follows. Tao denotes "the primordial essence or fundamental nature of the universe." Tao is not a "name" for a "thing" but the underlying natural order of the universe whose ultimate essence is difficult to circumscribe. Tao is thus "eternally nameless" (like the Hebrew God of the Burning Bush) and distinguished from the countless "named" things which are considered to be its manifestations. It is ultimate reality (infinite nature) that cannot be circumscribed as a finite order (cosmos) but only apprehended instinctively from within the finite order in which humans find themselves. But it still is to be celebrated and venerated as the infinite potential of existence and of finite life within that existence in order to feel at home in the universe. Philosophical Taoism (as distinguished from Popular Taoism) stresses "the interrelationship of natural processes"[57] and thus can relate to Bergson and Teilhard as well as to the concept of evolution as the grand synthesis.

Cogley writes: "In intellectual Hinduism, pantheism is a more dominant theme than polytheism. The idea that there is only *one reality* (italics mine), called Brahman runs throughout."[58] The point being that at the higher levels of the non-monotheistic religions, the theological *Law of Parsimony* also dominates. But with the Hindus there is no hint of a personal God that takes an interest in our pitiable little existence. "All that can be said of Brahman is that it is the Ground of all Being, the —unchangeable, in-definable, *ultimately unknowable, and totally impersonal* (italics mine). One does not pray *to* Brahman, one meditates *on* 'it.'"[59] This would be a close approximation to Cosmodeism but for its unchangeable aspect. If evolution is the grand narrative of all being and chaos theory demonstrates that every action changes ultimate reality, then the *Ground for all Being* is the very *process* of constant evolution or constant change and not a "fixed for eternity" truth. But the Hindu view that the *Ground for all Being* is ultimately unknowable, indefinable, *and wholly impersonal* is a view totally in accordance with Cosmodeism. Hindus believe that "... [humans] bear their own subjective relationship to the Principle of All Being, about which nothing can be said except that it is *not* this, *not* that, *not* the other thing."[60]

Cogley goes on: "The idea of the divine personality is regarded by the intellectual Hindu as *merely a useful way* (italics mine) to look upon the ultimate. That the *Ground of Being* is apprehended as a person is due not to the nature of the Ultimate Reality itself but to the weakness of the human intellect."[61] This weakness has been resolved by science but as mentioned above, science has not yet been able to make its wondrous insights accessible to the mass of humanity. It is my hope that Cosmodeism will be able to correct this deficiency and help make intellectual Hinduism more accessible to the masses and especially to the modern, well-educated Hindu. "Loving God" in the intellectual Hindu sense might be interpreted to mean to love the very facticity of the unknowable "Ultimate Reality."[62] As with the Kabbalah, Hinduism has interpretations that do not in any way contradict the general principle of "Evolution as the Grand Synthesis." These are interpretations that construe Hinduism itself as an evolutionary process. Cogley quotes Sarvepalli Radhakrishnan who wrote in *The Hindu View of Life* "Hinduism is a movement, not a position; a process, not a result; a growing tradition, not a fixed revelation."[63] His views placed him in opposition to big 'R' Religion (and by implication in favor of small 'r' religiosity) when, criticizing the Hindu Religion Business, he said, "It is not God that is worshipped but the group or authority that claims to speak in His name. Sin becomes disobedience to authority not violation of integrity." He anticipated the volitional teleology of Cosmodeism when he asserted that "Man is not a detached spectator of a progress immanent (deterministic) in human history, but an *active* agent remolding the world nearer to his ideals." When the Jews say that man must be a partner with God in the ongoing act of creation, they essentially mean the same thing.

Buddhism anticipated modern alienation theory by 2,500 years. For the Buddha, "the patient was humankind and the illness the human condition itself."[64] His diagnosis was correct, as I pointed out in Part I; it is "the human condition itself" that disturbs us. But his prescription was wrong because it was impossible and "unhuman." We cannot reach Nirvana "by annihilating the "unreality" of the ego and conquering human desires."[65] What makes us human is our ego—our consciousness of our own consciousness; this is the reality of human being—one cannot be human without ego. Self-lessness (self-naughting), taken literally, means to be without self—not to be conscious of our own consciousness, of our own individuality, of our own uniqueness within nature, within life and within the human species. A selfless person cannot be moral, as a fearless person cannot be heroic. You can only be a hero if you are terrified and still manage to function with competence and dignity in doing your duty; you can only be moral as an active self-conscious, *self-interested* ego functioning in interaction with other egos. Only Buber's "I/Thou" defines us as human. When teaching or lecturing I would often ask my listeners to consider if Robinson Crusoe was truly human before he met Friday. To be in relation with the "thou," to behave morally to the "thou" you must first have an "I," according to Hillel's two famous dictums:

1. "If I am not for myself, who will be for me? But if I am only for myself, who am I? And if not now, when?"

2. "That which is hateful to *you*, do not do to others. That is the whole Torah; the rest is the explanation; go and learn."

The only way we can transcend the human condition is not to *avoid* the vicissitudes of life but to *embrace* them and overcome them. Not to detach from the life of society and live in meditative monasticism, but to engorge oneself with the living of life—not to be a Buddha but rather a Zorba—living the physical life to its full is the highest form of spirituality. Not to deny the body but rather to satiate the body is the way to spirituality. We must first solve the material problems facing the human race, which, for the first time in history we can do in this century. We will then be able to face the spiritual challenge of coming to terms with ultimate reality. Here the Cosmodeistic Hypothesis can help point the way by helping us to embrace the Cosmos rather than fearing it; to acknowledge the Godding process inherent in every human being and to nurture it; to acknowledge the devil in every human being and to fight it; to raise our individual and social being to a state of being that is "Beyond Good and Evil," to become Nietzsche's *Zarathustra*. Material suffering cannot be overcome simply by ignoring it and striving to reach a spiritual state which enables us to ignore it; it can only be overcome by ameliorating it which will then enable us to achieve a superior spiritual state. Mother Teresa's sadomasochistic celebration of suffering can never be a model for an enlightened society.

I offer the "popularity of Buddhism" amongst "humble" celebrities like Steven Seagal, Brad Pitt, Sharon Stone, Richard Gere, Oliver Stone, and a dozen others (including the "modest" Steve Jobs) as empirical proof of my critique of this particular aspect of Buddhism. Have these "stars" really annihilated the unreality of their own egos or are they the quintessential examples of ego? Isn't it the case that they use Buddhist *techniques* to help them achieve a state of mind that enables them to advance their careers and achieve their egoistic ambitions? The very term "popularity of Buddhism" is really an oxymoron if one truly believes in a philosophy of ego annihilation. That popular Buddhism has become just another self-promoting religion racket (similar to the popular Kabbalah racket and conmen televangelists) is particularly apparent in regard to the Steven Seagal case. The Lama Penor Rinpoche declared that Seagal was a *Tulku*, a reincarnated guardian of Tibetan Buddhism—i.e., a spiritual status comparable to that of the Dalai Lama, if you can actually digest that absurdity. Next, we will have the Catholics declaring Joe Peschi a saint, and the Jews declaring Lewis Black the reincarnation of the Baal Shem Tov. Needless to say, envious competitor Buddhists, quite credibly, accused Seagal of buying his "Buddhahood" with donations to Penor's organization. AND YET, I would aver that a neo-Buddhism that modified the fundamental principle from individual goal of annihilation of the individual ego into a civilizational goal in which the rather silly pretensions of finite human consciousnesses (silly in respect to the space/time vastness of existence expressed in Pascal's despair) were subsumed within cosmic evolution, then the Cosmodeistic Hypothesis would have resonance within this faith tradition also.

Confucianism is essentially a social ethos and not a religion, a life system rather than a faith tradition. Yet because of this, Confucian countries might be the most amenable to Cosmodeism, especially given their attitude to the very concept of veneration. The duty to venerate one's ancestors was carried to an extreme of ancestor worship which hindered China's development for centuries, because it celebrated the past rather than the possibilities of the future. Yet the principle is sound: venerate what has given you birth, what has given you being, what has brought you into being and made you a human being—your ancestors. Veneration for the Cosmos itself, for that ultimate ancestor of us all would also include a veneration of our future, a responsibility to the future and not only to the past.

During the Sung dynasty (960–1279), a Confucian revival made Confucian scholarship preeminent again displacing what had, for centuries, been dominated by popular Buddhism. The revival produced two schools of thought: the *School of Mind or Intuition*, and the *School of Principle*. Both embraced the principle of the Great Ultimate. The *School of Mind* emphasized that the human mind is perfectly identical with the Universal Mind or the Ultimate Principle—that studying the human mind will lead one to understand all objective reality. The *School of Principle* believed that the mind of humanity is essentially the same as the mind of the Universe and can be perfected to reflect that higher mind. They were empiricists who believed that studying the material world would enable them to understand the human mind. One school studied the mind to understand the world; the other school studied the world to understand the mind. It occurs to me that emerging schools of thought in the field of Artificial Intelligence reflecting underlying philosophies about intelligence and consciousness tend to bridge these two schools of thought.

Japan is an interesting—and in many ways special—case. On the one hand it is one of the most atheistic countries in the world; on the other hand, it might be the most religious country in the world. There is no real contradiction here. Eastern religions, especially Buddhism, Confucianism and Shintoism, really do not seem to need the God Hypothesis. Consequently, according to Japanese census numbers, there are actually more religion adherents in Japan than there are people in Japan. Most Japanese consider themselves both Buddhist and Shinto at the same time while actually living according to a Confucian ethos. There are also a multitude of new cults and folk religions—the new cults perhaps reflecting a great spiritual hunger. It seems that the Japanese treat religion as a great buffet—picking and tasting at various times of their lives. They might be married by a Shinto priest and buried by a Buddhist priest while celebrating the holidays of the various folk religions. Ironically, this might make them the most amenable, intellectually, to the Cosmodeistic Hypothesis.

Notes

1 Fromm, 1969, p. 13.

2 Armstrong, p. 3.

3 Ibid., p. 6.

4 DuBose, p. 8.

5 Rosenfeld.

6 De Botton.

7 Cooper, p. 14.

8 Sefer Ikkarim 2:18; Midrash Bereshit Rabbah, p. 9.

9 Ramban, p. 23.

10 Davis, p. 1.

11 Henotheism means devotion to a single primary god while accepting the existence or possible existence of other deities.

12 Wikipedia, Zohar.

13 Ibid.

14 Miller.

15 Kook.

16 Cooper, p. 28.

17 Ibid., p. xi.

18 Cooper, p. 1.

19 Lamm, p. 107.

20 Holzer.

21 Hirsch, pp. 25-46.

22 Kohler & Broyde.

23 Nietzsche, 1994, Third Essay, Section 22.

24 Ehrman, Chapter Four.

25 Zalta & Nodelman.

26 Smeeton.

27 Tierney, p. 281.

28 De Chardin, 1973, p. 92.

29 Ibid., p. 185.

30 Ibid., p. 178.

31 Ibid., p. 45.

32 Ibid., p. 45.

33 Ibid., p. 43.

34 Medawar, *pp. 99-106.*

35 Wilson, David Sloan.

36 Huxley.

37 Dobzhansky.

38 Teilhard, *Building the Earth*, Foreword.

39 Ogden, pp. 403-416.

40 Sanguin.

41 Spong.

42 Tillich, p.205.

43 Murry.

44 Kaufman, Gordon D.

45 Ibid.

46 Bretall & Wieman, p. 4.

47 Stone, pp. 252-267.

48 Lonergan & Richards, p. 112.

49 Hagen.

50 Ibid.

51 Swedenborg.

52 Weintraub, pp. 161-168.

53 Heer, pp. 10-11.

54 Simply means the position of the numbers moving from right to left (the direction of both Arabic and Hebrew) indicates their multiples of value determined by the position of each digit in the number. For example, the number 444 represents four hundred and forty-four. The first number from the right is a multiple of one, the second number a multiple of ten, and the third number a multiple of a hundred, and so on.

55 Ibid., p. 5.

56 Simpkins, p. ix.

57 Cogley, p. 49.

58 Cogley, p. 41.

59 Cogley, p. 41.

60 Cogley, p. 42.

61 Ibid.

62 Ibid.

63 Cogley, p. 43.

64 Cogley. p. 44.

65 Ibid.

Conclusion: SO WHAT!

How does any of this solve MY fundamental problem of the meaning of MY life, you may ask? This of course is a really good question to which I cannot even presume to provide a satisfactory answer. *YOUR LIFE* is yours, not mine. This book, to be honest, is really a product of my own subjective (selfish?) question regarding the meaning of my own life, rather than a product of any messianic delusions about saving the entire human race. All I can say is that this intellectual journey of mine has given *me* a degree of peace regarding the ultimate existential question of WHY at all. It has also made me a little more tolerant of academic pedants who sometimes have insights that can salve the soul. Schelling, for example, wrote, "Evolution has always been a fundamentally spiritual concept [and] History as a whole is a progressive, gradually self-disclosing revelation of the Absolute." Can one read these words without feeling at least a little bit better? The real question everyone must ask themselves is "Shall I embrace the absurd irony of my finite existence with joy, or should I let it weigh me down?" In any case, I hope that to some degree I have mitigated the sense of irremediable impotence—what our professors of despair call alienation—which is felt by so many modern human beings; even those who pretend to have found relief in the legacy Religion Business.

As for embracing the absurd irony of my own finite existence, and at the risk of sounding flippant, I would like to make the case for laughter as a religious sacrament or mitzvah. Laughter, with greater efficiency than meditation, puts one immediately into the absolute present, devoid of the inherited angst of the past and the anticipated angst of the future. Laughter purifies the soul in a way that formal prayer can never hope to do. Is God a standup comedian and Robin Williams, Dave Chapelle, and Lewis Black his prophets? What is the evolutionary function of humor and laughter? I am fairly sure that we are the only species that tells jokes (imagine a chimpanzee comic beginning his act with "two baboons walk into a bar"). Let us dwell on the nature of humor and more specifically on jokes for a minute. Is it not a truism that most humor and jokes result in us laughing at the absurdity of particular events or human behaviors, helping us to deal with those absurdities? Are not self-deprecatory jokes and jokes about one's own ethnic group often sometimes the funniest? Isn't humor in general more effective in bringing home the absurdity of our own existence than tragedy or serious drama? When we laugh not only do we release pent-up negative energy, but we open ourselves up to the very joy of existing. An over-whelming amount of evidence has proven scientifically that having a good laugh is actually physically healthy and not just mentally healthy. The only thing that can compete with a good laugh is really good sex and, in fact, I have heard that the Eskimos actually call sex "laughing"; that they have the same word for sex and laughing, that to laugh means to have sex. In the Hebrew Bible, there are numerous commands by God for us to take delight in things (including *in* our spouse). We Jews even have a holiday (Purim) where it is obligatory to act silly, perhaps to remind us to "lighten up" and not take ourselves so seriously.

Would I be accused of racialist culturalism if I claimed that cultures that can laugh at themselves and their leaders are *superior* to cultures that are humorless? Telling a joke about Hitler could get you sentenced to death; a joke about Stalin and "hello Gulag"; American Presidents (until Trump) participated in their own roasts in which they were parodied and pilloried. Looking at the face of the Ayatollah Khomeini could you even imagine him laughing even once in his life? The Egyptians tell endless jokes about themselves and their leaders but try to imagine a Wahhabi joke book ("We beheaded 10 Shiites last week; it was hilarious"). We Jews ceaselessly tell jokes about Moses; try telling a joke about Mohammed and live to see the sun come up the following day. Israel even has a television program called "The Jews are Coming" which amongst other things has parodied Abra-ham willing to kill his own son and the contradiction between circumcision and the command to go forth and multiply ("It's really difficult to multiply when you have bandages on your wee-wee daddy"). The program once de-picted Joseph (of coat of many colors fame) as a conceited, over the top, flaming gay narcissist, constantly insulting his brothers by strutting around in his gay flag coat and telling them how beautiful he was and how ugly they were (as the reason they sold him into captivity). Is this Jewish penchant for not considering anything *completely* sacred related to our creativity and innovation and inherent contempt for authority? It occurs to me that Pas-cal's despair derived in part from a lack of a sense of humor; he could have looked at the heavens, smiled and said "seriously, are you kidding me," and then gone and had a drink and told a few jokes. This would have been more useful to his peace of mind than his intense metaphysical *Oi Vey*!

In any case, and despite any *individual* reservations about the specifics of the Nessyahu Conjectures, the concept of conscious life creating God is an idea whose *civilizational* time has come—a civilizational turning point.

Consider what kind of art, music, architecture, would result from a widespread infatuation with Cosmodeism? How would it affect mental health: those kinds of mental disabilities rooted in sincere confusion about the meaning of it all? As our knowledge of the never-ending vastness and complexity of existence grows at an ever-increasing rate, the great existential "why" becomes even more oppressive to our mental and moral wellbeing. It must at least dawn on us as a species that the great purpose, aim, final cause of human existence and civilization is to invent or construct the why of our own existence; to stop asking the question and start answering it in a substantive way. The individual ethical implications would be that everyone should act as if he or she is the Messiah. I suggest this is the real, between the lines, message of the Hebrew Bible (as Fromm hinted at in his book *You Shall be as Gods*).

It may be the case that future historians of science will view Nessyahu as they have Descartes—while wrong in the specifics of his scientific assumptions, to a great degree correct in regard to his general attitude towards reality. Descartes's total mechanization of existence being a rather adolescent oversimplification, serving to demystify, while stimulating the search for generalized laws of existence that could be methodically used to expand knowledge. This would be the same regarding Bacon's corpuscular view of the universe—perhaps not accurate, but certainly useful in conveying the subtlety of the universe to future thinkers, thus stimulating them to search for ever greater accuracy.

Let us agree at least that, despite scientific and philosophical objections and reservations towards teleological thinking, human beings essentially are teleological beings and that this will always give human existence a religious tinge. The neo-teleology I advocate is not imposed from without—from objective existence—but from within, from our own volitional goalsetting. As I have pointed out, every "to do list" is really a list of final causes, pulling and molding all collateral activity. In doing so it directs human society toward certain aims and values as well as certain types of social organizations which leads to certain types of research and development. This research and development changes the very nature of our immediate environment, and thus the very nature of our own consciousness, and thus, eventually, the entire Cosmos. What this really means is that as human beings create their own purpose and act purposefully—they constantly create ever greater final causes. This influences the evolution of our entire planet as well is the evolution of evolution itself. The entire planet is now purposeful to one degree or another. If we finally come to our own maturity, and adopt a common human vision, our existence would become a volitional teleology. To the extent that we begin to conquer our solar system, it too, will become a volitional teleology, and so on to the galaxy and so on, eventually, to the entire Cosmos. Classical teleology turns human beings into slave-like objects, compelled to fulfill a divine drama not of their choosing according to the dictates of an autocratic God. Neo-teleology provides direction to the potentiality of quantum physics, reinforcing human beings as autonomous subjects dictating the divine drama towards a freely created, freely chosen Godness.

What is clear is that our era needs a new worldview, one powerful enough to create its own Zeitgeist, just as the Scientific Revolution and the Enlightenment did. What is needed is a cosmic natural theology—creating a futurist mythology upon which our reasoning volitional mind can turn the mythology into reality. We have to find a vision capable of being shared by the entire human mosaic. Cosmodeism is a logical candidate for such a worldview. It may be seen as a late axial age development in which individuals experience the sacred immanence of the godding of the Universe. Cosmodeism, while based on science and logic, is replete with a tendency towards transcendence which can be integrated into all the axial traditions, enrich them and replug them into their original spiritual insights, which have been stunted over time by overlays of the big 'R' Religion business. Super-hero pop culture is, in my opinion, a comic book substitute for the perennial philosophy and a fundamentally healthy reaction to the nihilism of a certain intellectual "elite" whose devotion to analytic thought has explained away everything that people know in their gut and in their heart makes them human. The current worldwide returning to big 'R' Religion (which is really an impoverished reflection of the *Axial Age* impulse) actually reflects a healthy instinct for the transcendent. Culture, like nature, does not tolerate a vacuum. If you kill the gods, then pop star gods will fill the firmament. The 15 minutes of fame syndrome is really a reflection of the internal drive to be Godlike. The *Axial Age* has degenerated into organized Religion. *The Age of Enlightenment* has degenerated into a one-dimensional secularism. The Cosmodeistic Hypothesis can be viewed as the possibility to be a synthesis of the axial age and the Enlightenment Age.

I have no desire to create a new religion or to dispel any other variety of religious or nonreligious identity. Indeed, I believe that all of the great diversity of religions is a consequence of an original divine deduction that anticipates the insights of the Nessyahu conjectures; what we call the *Perennial Philosophy*. I believe that Cosmodeism can be a unifying factor within the great diversity of religious imaginations—much like the growth of Monotheism and the move to one God in the non-monotheistic religions, or the great scholastic synthesis of the European Middle Ages, which enabled the three monotheistic religions to enter into discourse using the same language. Pursuing the Cosmodeistic vision in many diverse culturally familiar ways will enrich the quest and make that quest less uneasy and unfamiliar. As John Cogley writes in *Religion in a Secular Age*, "... finding a vocabulary that will mean the same to everyone at this point in history may be impossible. Words like "God" or "faith" simply do not seem to mean the same to all." But, perhaps, the Cosmodeistic Hypothesis might be one way to overcome this epistemological dilemma since it does not require religious terminology to "...mean the same to all." It is the reason I affirm the necessity of plurality in pursuing the search for ultimate meaning. But there is a more substantive reason for a plurality of pursuit; that in trying to comprehend the infinite variety of ultimate reality, we need nuanced variations of various interpretations. The one-dimensional theological strategy of our legacy religions in trying to perceive ultimate reality is (and has been) a recipe for the spiritual impoverishment of our culture, as well as brutal persecutions and atrocities. Nothing in history has been more vicious than the adherents of various faith traditions operating in the name of God or some other absolutist religious or secular truth (I include *applied* Marxism in this absolutist religious category). Needless to say, solving our material dilemmas is a necessary prerequisite for engaging in this great all-human quest.

Another reason I do not want it to become a religion is that—as with many 20th-century cults—it might become a new idolatry. If expressed within the ancient traditions, this tendency will most likely have been ameliorated over time (the rough peaks of the theological Rockies having been eroded down by the horrors of history into the rolling ecumenical hills of modern social reality). With all their diseased crimes over the millennia, our legacy religions have been the means by which we humans have dealt with the history of existence, ultimate reality, and final meaning. It is the only human enterprise designed to do this. Human beings created religions and dogmas as a psychological defense mechanism against the insufferable anxiety of our own existence. The hostility towards the professional debunkers of religion stems from the fact that the awe-inspiring wonder of science is still not accessible to the vast majority of the human race and thus, resentment towards those who would tear down the emotional defense mechanisms of religion. Disbelief has become for some just as much an intolerant dogma as belief. If we are to suspend belief in order to gain enlightenment, we must also suspend disbelief for the same reason. The imperious attitude of "enlightened" atheists can be just as irritating as the smug self-righteousness of the theists. We have to look into the abyss until the abyss looks into us; that abyss, which, like a Black Hole, contains the information of our past, and since information cannot be destroyed it also contains belief.

My wish is that Cosmodeism be assimilated by the legacy religions as Aristotelianism was assimilated by the medieval scholastics of Judaism, Islam and Christianity—enabling them to speak god-talk in a civilized manner, while preserving the integrity of their own social and cultural traditions. The rational debunking of a supernatural God was a necessary cleansing of humanity's intellectual digestive system (a theological colonoscopy if you will) in order to envision an even greater transcendence; the concept of existence *per se* evolving into God with the active participation of conscious life. Monotheism will be seen by future historians of ideas as having been analogous to Ice Age humans being the necessary prelude to modern humans—extinct but a necessary prelude to this higher concept of God. For those who do not and cannot believe in a supernatural God there are two choices: to simply deny the existence of God (as with the professional atheists) or to strive to give meaning to the concept of God within the framework of the natural laws of the Cosmos. The first choice will lead to nihilism and the meaninglessness of life (with suicide becoming a rational option *à la* Camus). The second has the possibility of developing into a rich cultural texture. We can build a mental construct that satisfies the intuitive constructs of legacy religions and integrates them in an eclectic manner— an option that reflects the cosmology of the Hindu, the theosophy of the Kabbalah, and the end of days of the Christian.

Yet if Cosmodeism *were* to become a religion my wish would be that it would instruct each and every individual to:

1. contemplate your connection to both your past and your future and your responsibility to both your ancestors and descendants to live the most fulsome life you can.

2. contemplate that what you are made of (the atoms and subatomic particles) has existed forever and will exist forever.

3. contemplate that every time you take a breath be aware that you are breathing at least one atom that every other human being (as well as every other living thing) has ever breathed; that Moses, Jesus, Buddha, and Mohammed breathed that atom—that Einstein, Newton, and Beethoven (as well as Hitler and Stalin) breathed that atom. So be attentive to what you do with those breaths and live your life fully until your final days.

4. In other words, contemplate that every act you do is affected by and affects the entire finite Cosmos (and perhaps all of infinite existence); that all life and especially conscious life has been a fundamental part of the infinite evolutionary process of existence per se.

I have renamed *Cosmotheism* as *Cosmodeism* for assorted reasons. Foremost among them is that *theism* conjures up an image of a supernatural god (outside of nature and natural laws) while *deism* places the concept within the limitations of natural theology—a theology not in contradiction to science or rigorous logic, but rather dependent on both. Equally important is the disturbing fact that the term *Cosmotheism* has been co-opted by a neo-Nazi group that has registered it as a church and irony of ironies and chutzpah of chutzpahs, has no reservations about reprinting (and thus misrepresenting) some of my writings on their website, without attribution of course (how embarrassing if they were caught publishing a JEW [OMG]).

Appendix

A. Some Second Thoughts about Organized Religion

Despite my reservations about the organized Religion Business, I have to allow that certain logical deductions from the Cosmodeistic Hypothesis might actually give credence to some of the intuitions of the legacy religions. For example, if consciousness is a unique, as yet undefined, form of energy (as I suspect it is), and the laws of thermodynamics pertain to it as much as they do for other forms of energy, then it cannot be destroyed and must also endure, even after we die, albeit in a different form. Alternatively, if consciousness is a coherent information system and according to the laws of quantum mechanics information cannot be destroyed, then it also survives in a different form. This includes the incipient consciousness of the lower animals. When I say in a different form, I mean we humans would not retain our individual identities after death as ghosts annoying Whoopi Goldberg, and Fido would not go to canine heaven where he would spend eternity happily humping the legs of 72 virgin angels. The aggregates of these transformed energy/information consciousnesses would be filling the Cosmos with an as a yet undefined element (perhaps a "dark consciousness?") thus becoming a progressively integral part of cosmic evolution. The belief in reincarnation of many religions reflects this concept of consciousness as an indestructible energy/information entity and might be called panpsychism comes of age, or, alternatively, legacy religious intimations about the "soul" coming of age but revealed as a dialectical *two-way process* instead of the linear one-way progression previously expounded. Indeed, this might already be part of the Godding process.

Consider how Einstein's $E=MC^2$, proving the essential unity of matter and energy, might translate into biological thinking in support of the above. I refer to the corresponding essential unity of body and mind. This is why I contend that the energy of individual consciousness transforms into a different form when the matter of the individual's body dies and disintegrates into its component elements. If consciousness is an integral component of the physical body, then what do our material bodies have to do with the *individuation* of our consciousness. This has to do with the entirety of our very being as conscious human beings; that aspect of consciousness that makes me a differentiated me, and you a differentiated you. I refer to the fact that the human gut contains 500 million nerve cells and 100 million neurons (about the size of a cat's brain), compared to 100 billion neurons in the human brain. These are connected to and communicate with the brain, primarily via the Vagus nerve. Research has shown that the gut "talks" to the brain as much, if not more, than the brain talks to the gut. Similarly, the human heart contains 40,000 neurons and also "talks" to the brain as much, if not more, than the brain talks to the heart, again by way of the Vagus nerve. So, the question becomes "where does our individuated consciousness reside," solely in our brains or in our entire objective material being? When we say "trust your gut" or "trust your heart" are we plugging into some as yet unarticulated wisdom, or are we simply mumbling irrational gibberish? The fact is that there is serious "neurological evidence for a three-factor model of head, heart, and gut aspects of embodied cognition in decision making."[1]

In other words, the me that is me and the you that is you is an *entirety* of what is me and what is you, i.e., mind and body, or to be more precise, the parts of the body that is mind. This is a view of human *being* more in tune with the holistic Jewish outlook as exemplified in the morning prayer of observant Jews (noted above) and in counter distinction to both Cartesian and Christian dualism that expound the complete dissimilarity between soul and body—a complete human being *is* body and soul *together*.

Moreover, the infinity of reality is a double-edged polemical sword, in that it somewhat neutralizes my own polemics against the legacy Religion Business. Because at the same time it rebuts the statistical arguments for the existence of God made by religious fundamentalists regarding the improbability of a Cosmos evolving by chance that would enable the existence of us, it also confutes the atheist argument against the existence of God, since, if nature is infinite in space and time, it is impossible that a god has not already been created in some other very ancient Cosmos. The question then becomes, is this an active God "taking interest" in other subsequent (younger?) cosmoses and molding them in its own image—planting planets that can support life which can then evolve into conscious beings capable of conceiving God and eventually developing an instinct to take active part in the Godding of all of reality by way of the Cosmodeistic ambition. Are these already extant cosmic gods lonely; do they *need* evermore cosmic gods (the collective Elohim) to emerge to join the Godding of the Universe? Of course, this would not be a supernatural God—a God beyond nature but a natural God; a God that nature/existence has created. It would be supra-natural "Godness" not a supernatural God. To carry this argument even further I cannot rule out the possibility that a godness in the form of a supra-supra consciousness already exists in our particular Cosmos. Arthur Clarke played with this notion of an existing godness overlooking evolution on Earth in his Sci-Fi classics *Childhood's End* and *Space Odyssey: 2001*. Furthermore, could the contrarian religious thinkers I have cited even existed but for the actuality of the institutional frameworks of the legacy religions they have rebelled against, and would we have access to their thinking without these institutional frameworks?

I maintain that the implications of Cosmodeism for legacy religions are great. It could become to be seen as the new iteration of the perennial philosophy, which recognizes the fundamental divinity of ultimate reality that lies at the base of all legacy religions and spiritual traditions. This is at the metaphysical level. At the psychological and social level, by recognizing that every individual and every society is an integral and *essential* part of endlessly evolving ultimate reality, we might mitigate the angst of the human condition and finally understand what unifies all humanity. Just as the velocity of the constitutionalist tendency in Western civilization greatly increased in the 14th-century English Peasants Rebellion with reference to the fact that we are all descendants of Adam and Eve and thus are all brothers and sisters, so too might a universal recognition that each and every one of us are products of and part and parcel of the ongoing, endless Godding of existence and thus inherently divine; foreshadow the end of angst and the rebirth of heroic education enlightening us that the "purpose" of our lives is to take intentional and conscious part in the Godding of the Universe. In the history book of the Planet Earth, the entire history of life is but a preface; the emergence of conscious life is but a paragraph in that preface. Conquering the solar system would only be chapter one in a book with an infinity of chapters. Subsequent chapters are beyond our science-based imaginations. But we may assume that the "final cause" of our Cosmodeistic vision will cause them to be written by "us" consciousnesses over the course of infinite time—*The Never Ending Story.*

B. Debunking the Fermi Paradox

The *Fermi Paradox,* simply stated, is the gulf between the various enormous estimates regarding the ubiquity of conscious life in the cosmos and the absence, so far, of any empirical evidence that there is even primitive life anywhere else, let alone conscious life. The most famous support for the

ubiquity of sentient life is the Drake equation which advocates the probability of up to 100,000,000 conscious civilizations in our Milky Way galaxy
alone. Astronomer Philip Plait claims "there could be as few as hundreds of
millions of planets, or as many as maybe hundreds of *billions* in our galaxy
alone that we could live on!" David Kipping, an astronomer based at the
Harvard-Smithsonian Center for Astrophysics, estimates there are 50 million habitable planets and 25 million habitable moons in our galaxy alone
(based on 300 billion stars in our galaxy). None of this, of course, presumes
to claim that conscious life and sophisticated technological civilizations are
anywhere near as ubiquitous as life systems *per se*, but the probabilistic implications are clear.

Minimalistic objections to the pervasiveness of conscious life allow that
there is, on average, probably only one conscious civilization per galaxy.
But even this minimalist estimation allows for hundreds of billions if not
trillions of conscious civilizations in our Cosmos alone and in no way ne-
gates the Cosmodeistic Hypothesis. Even if there were, on average only one
conscious civilization per 10 galaxies our Cosmos would be swarming with
conscious life. Moreover, if indeed, we are the only conscious civilization
in our galaxy, it would make our moral and ethical responsibility to survive and expand even more profound. Yet I cannot help but believe that
we do have galactic neighbors. So, "Where are they?" as Enrico Fermi so
succinctly put it, jokingly, over a beer with friends. (It should be noted that
Fermi was not agnostic about alien life—he did believe there were other
conscious civilizations)

One of the doubters' most prominent arguments is based on an analogy to
human life on this planet—that if it took several tens of thousands of years
for humans to occupy every livable niche on the planet it would have taken
an advanced cosmic civilization 20 to 50 million years to occupy every livable niche in our galaxy. I believe this is a very silly analogy. Every corner of
this planet is capable of supporting life. There are no lifeless spaces on planet
Earth. The space of our galaxy, on the other hand, is 99.9999% completely
barren of anything let alone areas that can sustain complex life. Humanity
expanded gradually into life supporting spaces on Earth that were contiguous to the life supporting space from which they were coming. But if the pre-
historic life supporting space on this planet which enabled the evolution of
humankind was as far from another as planet Earth is from *Proxima Centauri*
(the closest star to our sun—four light years away), we would not assume
that life should have spread. This is the proper equivalence.

The problem is that the vastness of our galaxy has no equivalence to our common-sense earthbound space/time perceptions. We cannot even picture in our minds what four light years really means in terms of distance, let alone the 80,000 light years diameter or the 300,000 light years circumference of our galaxy. Even if life systems were limited to a 1,000 light year band at the very outer limits of our galaxy's diameter (highly likely given the violence of the galaxy as it becomes ever denser as we move towards its center), and on average every 100 light years from us in all directions a conscious civilization had arisen, there would be tens of thousands of such civilizations. The question then becomes: how many of these civilizations developed before us and are thus more advanced than us? They could still be at their Neanderthal or Old Testament stage of development. We might be one our galaxy's first and thus most advanced life systems.

But even if some are much more advanced than us, they still cannot communicate faster than the speed of light. We have been broadcasting radio signals for just over a century, so our presence could only be detected within a radius of about 100 light years around the Earth. This means that they would only have detected us several decades ago, at best, and even if they decided *immediately* to respond (highly unlikely) we would still have to wait another century to hear from them. If they had achieved space travel at half the speed of light, we would have to wait another two centuries to actually meet them. That is if they had decided to make the stupendous economic investment and found individuals prepared to live their entire lives in space and perhaps reproduce in space in order that their children would meet us (once again, highly unlikely). There is of course the so-called "zoo hypothesis," that other intelligent creatures observe us without revealing their presence, we being to them like animals in a nature reserve, [this] was examined in 1977 by Thomas Kuiper and Mark Morris, who argued that aliens keep us in quarantine until we can offer something usable. This, of course, is entirely possible (although not very complimentary to Homo Sapiens hubris) and might explain a certain reality of the UFO phenomenon, but of course actually debunks the Fermi Paradox.

What we do know is that existence has NEVER created only one of anything: one person, one species, one planet, one star, one solar system, one galaxy, or even one Cosmos. How likely is it that existence has only created one self-reflective, conscious civilization. Before Columbus "discovered" America was there no America because we had not yet "discovered" it. No, we certainly have "neighbors," and maybe even close cousins—we just have not "discovered" them yet, although they might certainly have already discovered us, and since they haven't done to us what we did to the American Indians we must assume they are a rather compassionate and affable bunch. They most certainly can take a joke, given the giggles they must be having at humanity's rather pathetic pretentions compared to their abilities as a supra-conscious civilization waiting for us to grow up and become their active partners in the spiritual development of our Cosmos.

Note

1 Soosalu, Henwood, Deo'Head.

References

Abrams, Nancy Ellen & Primack, Joel R. *The New Universe and the Human Future: How a Shared Cosmology Could Transform the World.* New Haven: Yale University Press, 2011.

Aczel, Amir D. *God's Equation: Einstein, Relativity and the Expanding Universe.* New York: Delta,1999.

Adams, Henry. *The Education of Henry Adams;* New York: Modern Library (3rd ed.), 1999.

Alexander, S. *Space, Time, and Deity: The Gifford Lectures at Glasgow, 1916-1918.* Miami, FL: HardPress Publishing, 2013.

Anders Juul Nielsen. "European freelancers in numbers: Why the trend will continue". *FREELANCER WORLDWIDE.* London, 23 May 2016.

An-Na'im, Abdullan Ahmed. "Islam and the Secular State is a Framework for Constant Contestation, not Claim of Categorical Resolution". *Emory University School of Law,* 1 March 2015.

Armstrong, Karen. *A History of God.* Great Britain: Mandarin Paperbacks, 1994.

Armstrong, Karen. *The Great Transformation: The Beginning of our Religious Traditions.* New York: Anchor Books, 2007.

Arp, H.C. *Seeing Red.* Montreal: Apeiron,1998.

Aslan, Reza. *God: A Human History of Religion.* London: Corgi, 2018.

Astyk, Sharon. "Who Will Grow Your Food? Part I: The Coming Demographic Crisis in Agriculture". *Scienceblogs.com.* (based on National Agricultural Statistics Service U.S. Department of Agriculture), 4 January 2010.

Augstein, Rudolf. *Jesus, Son of Man.* New York: Urizen Books, 1977.

Bacon, Francis *Novum Organum*

Barrett, William. *Irrational Man.* New York: Doubleday, 1962.

Barrow, John D. & Tipler, Frank J. *The Anthropic Cosmological Principle.* New York: Oxford University Press, 1988.

Barzun, J. *Darwin, Marx, Wagner: Critique of a Heritage*. New York: Double-day Anchor Books, (2ⁿᵈ edition), 1958.

Becker, Ernest. *The Structure of Evil*; New York: The Free Press, 1968.

Becker, Ernest. *The Birth and Death of Meaning* (2nd ed.). New York: The Free Press, 1971.

Becker, Ernest. *The Denial of Death*. New York: The Free Press, 1973.

Becker, Ernest. *Escape From Evil*. New York: The Free Press, 1975.

Becker, Carl. *The Heavenly City of the 18ᵗʰ Century Philosophers*. Yale Univ. Press, 1966.

Behe, Michael J. *Darwin's Black Box*. New York: Touchstone, 1998.

Behlau, Lothar & Bullinger, Hans-Jörg (eds.). *Technology Guide: Principles, Applications, Trends*. New York: Springer, 2009.

Ben-Dasan, Isaiah. *The Japanese and the Jews*. New York: Weatherhill, 1984.

Benedikt, Paul Göcke. "Panentheism, Transhumanism, and the Problem of Evil: From Metaphysics to Ethics"; *European Journal for Philosophy of Religion*, vol. 11, 20 June 2019.

Bergson, Henri. *The Creative Mind: A Study in Metaphysics*. New York: The Wisdom Library, 1946.

Bergson, Henri. *The Two Sources of Morality and Religion*. New York: Anchor, 1954.

Biao Xiang, "Emigration Trends and Policies in China: Movement of the Wealthy and Highly Skilled.", *Migration Policy Institute*, 2016.

Bloom, Howard. *The God Problem*. Amherst New York: Prometheus Press, 2012.

Boulding, Kenneth. "Towards an Evolutionary Theology" in *Science and Creationism*, ed. Ashley Montagu. Oxford University Press, 1984.

Bretall, Robert. *The Empirical Theology of Henry Nelson Wieman*. NY: Macmillan, 1964.

Buber, Martin. *I And Thou*. New York: Charles Scribner's Sons, 1958.

Bury, J.B. *The Idea of Progress*, New York, Dover, 1987.

Butterfield, H. *The Origins of Modern Science*. New York: Free Press, 1965.

Camus, A. *The Myth of Sisyphus & Other Essays*. Trans. by Justin O'Brien. New York: Vintage, 1991.

Caplan, Lincoln. Article on op-ed page of N.Y. Times, 1981.

Capra, Fritjof. *The Tao of Physics*. New York: Bantam, New Age, 1980.

Capra, Fritjof. *The Turning Point*. New York: Bantam, New Age, 1983.

Capra, Fritjof. *The Web of Life*. New York: Anchor Books, 1997.

Chu, Ted. *Human Purpose and Transhuman Potential: A Cosmic Vision of Our Future Evolution*. San Rafael, CA: Origin Press, 2014.

Clark, Arthur. *2001 A Space Odyssey*. New York: New American Library, 2000.

Coase, Ronald, "Saving Economics from Economists". *Harvard Business Review*, Dec. 2012.

Cogley, John. *Religion in a Secular Age*. New York, Mentor Books, 1969.

Cooper, David A. *God is a Verb*. New York: Riverhead Books, 1997.

Cornish, Edward. (ed.) *Careers Tomorrow*. Bethesda MD: World Future Society, 1983.

Cox, Harvey. *The Secular City*, New York, MacMillan, 1967.

Cox, Harvey. *Religion in the Secular City: Towards a Postmodern Theology*. New York: Touchstone (Simon and Schuster), 1984.

Davies, Paul. *God and the New Physics*. New York: Simon and Schuster, 1983.

Davies, Paul. *Superforce*. New York: Simon and Schuster, 1984.

Davies, Paul. *The Cosmic Blueprint*. New York: Touchstone, 1989.

Davies, Paul. *The Mind of God: The Scientific Basis for a Rational World*. New York: Touchstone, 1993.

Davies, Paul. *The Fifth Miracle: The Search for the Origin of Life*. New York: Penguin, 1999.

De Botton, Alain. *Religion for Atheists*. New York, Vintage Books, 2013.

De Chardin, Teilhard. *The Phenomenon of Man*. New York: Harper, 1965.

De Chardin, Teilhard. *Building The Earth*. University of Michigan: Dimension Books, 1965.

De Chardin, Teilhard. *The Prayer of the Universe*, New York: Perennial Library, 1973.

Despommier, Dickson. *The Vertical Farm: Feeding the World in the 21ˢᵗ Century*. New York: Picador, 2011.

Dexter-Smith, R. (ed.) *Civil Engineering in the Nuclear Industry*. London: Thomas Telford, 1991

Dick, Steven J. "Cultural Evolution, the Postbiological Universe and SETI". *International Journal of Astrobiology*: Cambridge University Press, 2003.

Dick, Steven J., "Toward a Constructive Naturalistic Cosmotheology". *Space, Time, & Aliens*. Switzerland: Springer, 2020.

Dobzhansky, Theodosius. "Nothing in Biology Makes Sense Except in the Light of Evolution". *The American Biology Teacher*. University of California Press, March 1973.

DuBose Todd. "Homo Religiosus". *Encyclopedia of Psychology & Religion*. Boston: Springer, 2014.

Durkheim, Emile. *Suicide: A Study in Sociology*. New York: Free Press 1997.

Dyson, Freeman. *Disturbing the Universe*. New York: Harper Colophon, 1981.

Dyson, Freeman. *Infinite in all Directions*. New York: Perennial Library Edition, 1989.

Edelheit, Hershel & Abraham, J. *The Jews: Race, Nation, or Religion?* Philadelphia: Dropsie College Press, 1936.

Edelman, Gerald M. *Wider than the Sky: The Phenomenal Gift of Consciousness*. Yale University Press: Note Bene edition, 2005.

Edwards, Paul. "Panpsychism", *Encyclopedia of Philosophy*. New York: Macmillan, 1972

Ehrman. Bart D. *Jesus Interrupted: Revealing Hidden Contradictions In The Bible.* New York: HarperOne, 2010.

Ehrman. Bart D. *How Jesus Became God.* New York: HarperOne, 2015.

Einstein, Albert. "The Meaning of Life." In *Living Philosophies,* edited by Henry Goddard Leach, New York: Simon & Schuster, 1931.

Einstein, Albert. Letter of 24 January 1936 to a schoolgirl, Phyllis Wright.

Feynman, Richard. *The Character of Physical Law.* Cambridge, Mass.: The M.I.T. Press, 2017.

Frankl, Viktor E. *The Unconscious God.* New York: Touchstone (Simon & Schuster), 1975.

Frankl, Viktor E. *Man's Search for Meaning.* New York, Pocket Books, (Simon & Schuster), 1977.

Frankl, Viktor E. *The Will to Meaning.* New York: Meridian/Plume, 1988.

Frankl, Viktor E. *The Unheard Cry for Meaning.* New York: Washington Square Press, 1985.

Frankl, Viktor E. *Man's Search for Ultimate Meaning.* London: Ebury Publishing, 2011.

Friedman, Maurice S. *Buber: The Life of Dialogue.* New York: Harper Torchbooks, 1960.

Fritze, J.G., Blashki, G.A., Burke, S. & Wiseman, J." Hope, Despair and Transformation: Climate Change and the Promotion of Mental Health and Wellbeing". *International Journal of Mental Health Systems,* 17 September 2008 (and dozens of others; one that attributes the rise in suicides in Italy to global warming anxiety)

Fromm, Erich. *Escape from Freedom.* New York: Avon, 1967.

Fromm, Erich. *You Shall Be as Gods.* New York: Fawcett World Library, 1969.

Frye, Herman Northrop. *The Educated Imagination.* Bloomington: Indiana Univ. Press, 1964.

Gay, Peter. *The Enlightenment, Volume II.* New York: Norton Paperback, 1977.

Ghai, Anita. *Rethinking Disability in India.* New Delhi: Routledge, 2017.

Göcke, Benedikt Paul. "Panentheism, Transhumanism, and the Problem of Evil - from Metaphysics to Ethics". *European Journal for Philosophy of Religion,* 2019.

Goodell, Jeff. "The Prophet of Climate Change: James Lovelock"; Rolling Stone, Oct. 2007.

Gould, Stephen Jay." Humbled by the Genome's Mysteries". N.Y. Times, February 19, 2001.

Grassie, William. *Politics by Other Means: Science and Religion in the 21st Century.* Bryn Mawr, PA: Metanexus Institute, 2010.

Grassie, William. *The New Sciences of Religion.* New York: Palgrave, Macmillan, 2010.

Grassie, William & Hansell, Gregory R. *Transhumanism and its Critics..* Bryn Mawr, PA: Metanexus Institute, 2011.

Gribbin, John. *In Search of the Big Bang.* Great Britain: Corgi, 1987.

Gribbin, John. *The Reason Why: The Miracle of Life on Earth.* New York: Penguin, 2012.

Hagen, Kirk D., "Eternal Progression in a Multiverse: An Explorative Mormon Cosmology". *Dialogue: A Journal of Mormon Thought.* University of Illinois Press, July 2006.

Hallam, Anthony & Wignall, Paul, B. *Mass Extinctions and Their Aftermath.* Oxford University Press, 1997.

Harari, Yuval. N. *Homo Deus: A Brief History of Tomorrow.* London: Vintage, 2017.

Harrison, Edward. *Masks of the Universe.* New York: Collier Books, 1985.

Harrison, Peter. *The Territories of Science & Religion.* University of Chicago Press, 2015.

Hazony, Yoram. *The Philosophy of Hebrew Scripture,* Cambridge University Press, 2012

Heer, Nicholas. L. "A Lecture on Islamic Theology", *Semantic Scholar,* 10 August 2009.

Heinberg, Richard. "Peak coal: Sooner than you think: Energy Bulletin, May 21, 2007.

Heisenberg, Werner. *Physics and Philosophy: The Revolution in Modern Science*. New York: Harper Torchbooks, 1962.

Hirsch, Emil G. "The Doctrine of Evolution and Judaism", *Some Modern Problems and their Bearing on Judaism*. Chicago: Reform Advocate Library, 1903.

Hofstadter, Richard. *Social Darwinism in American Thought*. Boston: Beacon Press, 1955.

Horan, Martin. *The Little Book of Jewish Wisdom*. Rockport, Mass: Element, 1995.

Horgan, John. "Scientific Seeker Stuart Kauffman on Free Will, God, ESP and Other Mysteries". *Scientific American*. New York, 14 February 2015.

Horgan, John. "Is Scientific Materialism Almost Certainly False?" *Scientific American*. New York, 30 Jan. 2013.

Hori Ichiro (et al.). *Japanese Religion*. Tokyo: Kodansha International, 1984.

Hoyle, C.F., Burbidge, G., & Narlikar J.V. "The Origin of the Light Elements". *A Different Approach to Cosmology*. Cambridge University Press, Chapter 9, 2000.

Hume, David. *An Enquiry Concerning Human Understanding*, 1748.

Huxley, Julian. "Introduction". *The Phenomenon of Man*. (de Chardin), NY: Harper, 1965.

Internet Encyclopedia of Philosophy

Iso-Ahola, Seppo E., & Crowley, Edward D. "Adolescent Substance Abuse and Leisure Boredom", *Journal of Leisure Research*; Arlington, Va., Vol. 23, Jan 1, 1991.

James, William. *The Varieties of Religious Experience*. University of Toronto Press, 2011.

James, William. *The Will to Believe: and Other Essays in Popular Philosophy*. Mineola New York: Dover Books, 1956.

Jastrow, Robert. *God and the Astronomers*. New York: Norton, 1978.

Jaynes, Julian *The Origin of Consciousness in the Breakdown of the Bicameral Mind*, Boston: Houghton Mifflin, 1982.

Jeffreys, William H. & Berger, James O. *"Ockham's Razor and Bayesian Statistics"*. New Haven, CT: *American Scientist, 1991* 64–72.

Josephson, Eric, & Jsephson Mary. *Man Alone: Alienation in Modern Society*, New York: Dell, 1962.

Jung, C.G. "Psychology & Alchemy". *Collected Works. Vol.12;* Princeton Univ. Press, 1980.

Jung, C.G. "Alchemical Studies". *Collected Works Vol.13;* Princeton University Press, 1983.

Kant, Immanuel. *The Critique of Pure Reason. Norman Kemp-Smith (trans. ed.).* London: Macmillan, 1929.

Kaplan, Mordechai M. *The Religion of Ethical Nationhood*. New York: Macmillan, 1970.

Kuhn, Thomas S. *The Structure of Scientific Revolutions*. University of Chicago Press, 1970.

Kaufman, Gordon D., " Prairie View Lectures: Some Concluding Remarks". Bethel College, Kansas: Mennonite Life, Dec. 2005.

Kauffman, Stuart. *Reinventing the Sacred: A New View of Science, Reason, & Religion.* New York: Basic Books, 2008.

Kauffman, Stuart. "Prolegomenon to patterns in evolution". *ScienceDirect.* Elsevier, 2014.

Kaufmann, Walter. *The Faith of a Heretic.* New York: Anchor Books, 1963.

Kaufmann, Walter. *The Portable Nietzsche.* New York: Penguin, 1968.

Kellermann, Natan "Psychopathology in children of Holocaust survivors", *The Israel Journal of Psychiatry and Related Sciences.* (February 2001).

Kennedy, E. "Thomas Aquinas's Christian Secularism." In *Secularism and its Opponents from Augustine to Solzhenitsyn,* New York: Palgrave Macmillan, 2006.

Keynes, John Maynard. *Essays on Persuasion*. Classic House Books, 2009.

Lichtenhaler, Gerhard. "Mahmud Muhammed Taha: Sudanese Martyr, Mystic & Muslim Reformer". *Institute of Islamic Studies*, 30 July 2014.

Kook, Rabbi Avraham Yitzhak HaCohen, *Existence*.

Kraft, Christopher C. Jr. & Spencer, Scott. "Our economy needs a robust space program." *Houston Chronicle*, August 22, 2010.

Kuhn, Thomas & Hacking, Ian.; *The Structure of Scientific Revolutions* (2nd Edition). University of Chicago Press, 1962.

Lamm, Norman, "A Jewish Exotheology," *Faith & Doubt: Studies in Traditional Jewish Thought*, New York: Ktav Pub. House, 1971.

Laszlo, Ervin. *Evolution: The Grand Synthesis*. Boston: New Science Library, 1987.

Laszlo, Ervin. *Science and the Akashic Field: An Integral Theory of Everything*. Rochester Vermont: Inner Traditions, 2004.

Layzer, David. *Cosmogenesis*. Oxford: Oxford University Press, 1990.

Lerner, Eric J. *The Big Bang Never Happened*; New York: Random House, 1991.

Lerner, Eric J. "An Open Letter to the Scientific Community". *New Scientist*, May 22, 2004.

Lewis, C. S. *The Abolition of Man*. Oxford: Oxford University Press. 1982.

Logsdon, Tom. *The Robot Revolution*. New York: Simon and Schuster, 1984.

Lonergan, Anne & Richards, Caroline. *Thomas Berry and the New Cosmology*. Waterford, CT: Twenty-Third Publications, 1987.

Lovejoy, Arthur O. *The Great Chain of Being*. Harvard University Press, 1964.

Lukacs, John. *Historical Consciousness*; New York: Schocken Press, 1985.

Macdougall, Doug. *Frozen Earth: The Once & Future Story of Ice Ages*. University of California Press, 2006.

Margulis, Lynn. *Symbiotic Planet: A New Look at Evolution*. New York: Basic Books, 1998.

Matson, Floyd W. *The Broken Image: Man, Science & Society.* New York: Anchor, 1966.

Medawar, P. B. "Critical Notice" *Mind.* Oxford University Press, 1961.

Meera, SP, Anusha, Sreeshan, & Anu, Augustine. "Functional Screening & Genetic Engineering of Mangrove Salt Responsive Genes". *Bioscholar* Vol. 2, No. 12, 2013.

Macarov, David. *Quitting Time: The End of Work,* International Journal of Sociology & Social Policy, 1989.

Menger, Karl. "A Counterpart of Ockham's Razor in Pure and Applied Mathematics: Ontological Uses". *Synthese* 12: 415 in *Logic and Language: Studies dedicated to Professor Rudolf Carnap on the Occasion of his Seventieth Birthday,* Springer, 1962.

Milgrom, Mordechai. "Comments on Astrophysics". Springer Link: *The Astronomy and Astrophysics Review* Vol. 13, Issue 4, 1989.

Miller, Rabbi Moshe. "The Great Constriction". *KabbalaOnline.org.,* 24 Jan 2005.

Mills, C. Wright. *The Sociological Imagination.* New York: Oxford University Press, 1959.

Mills, Watson. ed. *Mercer's Dictionary of the Bible,* Mercer University Press, 1990.

Monbiot, George. *Heat: How to Stop the Planet from Burning.* London: Allen Lane, 2006,

Moore, Alan. *The Watchman.* New York: DC Comics Illustrated Edition, (May 20, 2019).

Morris, Richard. *The Edges of Science.* New York: Prentice Hall Press, 1990.

Mure, G.R.G. *The Philosophy of Hegel,* London, Oxford University Press, 1965.

Murry, William R. *Reason and Reverence: Religious Humanism for the 21st Century.* Boston: Skinner House Books, 2007.

Naam, Ramez. *The Infinite Resource.* University Press of New England, 2013

Nagel, Thomas. *Mind and Cosmos: Why the Materialist Neo-Darwinian Con-*

ception of Nature is Almost Certainly False. Oxford University Press, 2012

Naím, Moisés, "Can the World Afford a Middle Class?" *Foreign Policy,* February 19, 2008.

Needleman, Jacob. *The Heart of Philosophy.* New York: Bantam New Age, 1984.

Nessyahu M. 1997. *Cosmotheism,* Tel Aviv: Poetica Press (Hebrew)

Nietzsche, Friedrich. *Beyond Good & Evil;* Mineola, New York: Dover Thrift Editions, 1997.

Nietzsche, Friedrich, *The Genealogy of Morals,* Third Essay, Section 22, 1994

Novak, Michael. Thomas Aquinas, the First Whig: What Our Liberties Owe to a Neapolitan Mendicant, *Crisis Magazine,* October 1, 1990.

Ogden, Schubert M. . "Sources of Religious Authority in Liberal Protestantism", *Journal of the American Academy of Religion.* Oxford University Press, 1976.

Packer, George. "The Moderate Martyr." *The New Yorker,* September 3, 2006.

Pagels, Heinz. R. *The Cosmic Code.* New York: Bantam Books, 1983.

Pagels, Heinz. R. *The Dreams of Reason.* New York: Bantam Books, 1989.

Pascal, B. *Pensées.* Translated by A. J. Krailsheimer. London: Penguin Classics, 1995.

Pearce, Fred. *The Coming Population Crash.* Boston: Beacon Press, 2010.

Penrose, Roger. *A Brief History of Time* (movie). Burbank, CA, Paramount Pictures, 1992.

Penrose, Roger. *The Emperor's New Mind.* New York: Vintage, 1990.

Peterson, D.J. *Troubled Lands: The Legacy of Soviet Environmental Destruction.* Boulder COL: Westview Press, 1993.

Pink, Daniel, H. *Free Agent Nation.* New York: Warner Business Books, 2001.

Polmear, I.J. *Light alloys from traditional alloys to nanocrystals.* Oxford: Elsevier/Butterworth-Heinemann, 2006.

Pofeldt, Elaine. "Are We Ready for a Workforce that is 50% Freelance?" Forbes, (Oct. 2017).

Prigogine, Ilya & Stengers, Isabelle. *Order out of Chaos: Man's New Dialogue With Nature.* New York: Bantam Books, 1984.

Rajvanshi, Anil. "How Three Minds of the Body – Brain, Heart and Gut, Work Together for Producing Happiness". *Thrive*, 7 February, 2020.

Ramban (Nachmanides). Commentary on the Torah. (trans. Dr. Charles B. Chavel). New York: Shilo Publishing House, 1971.

Random House Dictionary of the English Language: College Edition, 1968.

Rank, Otto. *Beyond Psychology.* New York: Dover Books, 1958.

Ratner, Sidney. "Evolution & the Scientific Spirit in America" in *Science and Creationism* (ed. Ashley Montagu) Oxford University Press, 1984.

Reinecke, Ian. *Electronic Illusions;* New York: Penguin Books, 1982.

Ridley, Mark. *The Problems of Evolution.* New York: Oxford University Press, 1985.

Ridley, Matt. *The Rational Optimist.* London: Fourth Estate, 2011.

Roll, Eric. *A History of Economic Thought.* London: Faber & Faber, 1992.

Rose, Steven. *From Brains to Consciousness?* New York: Penguin, 1999.

Rucker, Rudy. *Infinity and the Mind;* Boston: Bantam Books, 1983.

Russell, Peter. *The Global Brain;* Los Angeles; J.P. Tarcher, 1983.

Sagan, Carl. *The Dragons of Eden.* New York: Ballantine, 1977.

Sagan, Carl. *Pale Blue Dot: A Vision of the Human Future in Space.* N. Y. Ballantine, 1994.

Sagan, Carl. *Billions & Billions: Thoughts on Life and Death.* New York: Ballantine, 1998.

Sands, Ronald & Westcott, Paul. Impacts of Higher Energy Prices on Agriculture & Rural Economies. USDA Economic Research Report, 2011.

Sanguin, Bruce. Darwin, Divinity and the Dance of the Cosmos. Kelowna, BC: Woodlake Publishing, 2007.

Scheffler, Israel. *Science and Subjectivity.* New York: Bobbs Merrill, 1967.

Scholem, Gershom G. *On the Kabbalah and its Symbolism.* New York: Schocken, 1973.

Schrodinger, Erwin. *What is Life?* New York: Doubleday, 1956.

Schrodinger, Erwin. "General Scientific and Popular Papers" in Collected Papers, Vol. 4. Wiesbaden: Vieweg & Sohn, 1984.

Seife, Charles. *Decoding the Universe.* New York: Penguin Books, 2007.

Senor, Dan & Singer, Saul. *Start-Up Nation.* New York: Twelve, (Hachette Books) 2009.

Shapiro, Robert. Origins: A Skeptics Guide to the Creation of Life on Earth. New York: Bantam New Age, 1987.

Sinicki, Adam, "An Examination of Jung and Frankl's Views on Man's Search for Meaning", *HealthGuidance.Org.,* (February 13, 2020).

Simpkins, Alexander C. & Simpkins, Annellen. *Simple Taoism.* Tuttle Publishing, 1999.

Smeeton, Donald Dean, "Hans Kung: Architect of Radical Catholicism" *Melios,* Vol.7, 2.

Smolin, Lee. *The Life of the Cosmos.* London: Phoenix, 1998.

Snell, Bruno. *The Discovery of the Mind in Greek Philosophy & Literature,* NY: Dover, 1982.

Soleri, P. 1985. *Technology and Cosmogenesis.* New York: Paragon House, 1985.

Soosalu, Grant, Henwood Suzanne, & Deo Arun. *Head, Heart, & Gut in Decision Making: Development of a Multiple Brain Preference.* Thousand Oaks, CA: Sage Open, March 2019.

Spong, John Shelby. "A New Christianity for a New World". Gig Harbor, WA: Progressing Spirit, 15 April, 2011.

Steiner, Christopher. *$20 Per Gallon.* New York: Grand Central Publishing, 2009.

Stewart, John E. *Evolution's Arrow: The Direction of Evolution and the Future of Humanity*. Orange, CA; Chapman Press, 2000.

Stewart, John E. "The Future Evolution of Consciousness". *The Journal of Consciousness Studies*. Exeter UK: Academic Imprint, 2007.

Stewart, John. E. "The Meaning of Life in a Developing Universe" in *Foundations of Science*. New York: Springer, 2010.

Stewart, John E. "The Trajectory of Evolution & Its Implications for Humanity". *Journal of Big History*. Villanova, Pennsylvania: Online, 2019.

Stiernotte, Alfred O. & Wieman, Henry Nelson. *God and Space-Time: Deity in the Philosophy of Samuel Alexander*. New York: Philosophical Library, 1954.

Stone, Jerome A. "Itinerarium Mentis ad Naturam". *American Journal of Theology & Philosophy*, Sept. 2002.

Stuckey, Mark. Metanexus Essay (February 13, 2000) reviewing Paul Brockelman's *Cosmology & Creation: The Spiritual Significance of Contemporary Cosmology*. Oxford University Press, 1999

Swedenborg, Emmanuel. *Earths in the Universe: Their Spirits and Inhabitants (Life on Other Worlds)*, 1758. Square Circles Publishing, 2014.

Sullivan, J.W.N. *The Limitations of Science*. New York: Mentor, 1952.

Taha, Mahmoud. *The Second Message of Islam*. Syracuse University Press: 1987.

Talbot, Michael. *Mysticism & the New Physics*. New York: Bantam New Age, 1980.

Talmon, J.L. *The Origins of Totalitarian Democracy*, London: Secker & Warburg, 1952.

Tarnas, Richard, *Passion of the Western Mind: Understanding the Ideas That Have Shaped Our World View*. New York: Random House, 1993.

Taylor, Bron. (ed.) *Encyclopedia of Religion & Nature*. New York: Continuum, 2005.

Tierney, Brian. *The Origins of Papal Infallibility 1150-1350*. Leiden (Netherlands): Brill, 1988.

Tillich, Paul. *Systematic Theology* Vol.1. University of Chicago Press, 1951.

Toulmin, Stephen. *The Return to Cosmology. Postmodern Science and the Theology of Nature.* Los Angeles: University of California Press, 1982.

Tucker, R. C. *Philosophy and Myth in Karl Marx.* New York: Routledge, 1964.

US Department of Labor: Bureau of Labor Statistics "Employment by major industry sector". (October 24, 2017).

Van Flandern, Tom. *Dark Matter, Missing Planets & New Comets.* Berkeley: North Atlantic Books, 1999.

Van Flandern, Tom. "The Top 30 Problems with Big Bang Theory". *Meta Research Bulletin,* 2002.

Van Slooten, René. "Edgar Allan Poe--Cosmologist?", *Scientific American,* February 1, 2017.

Vernon, Mark. "Carl Jung, part 8: Religion and the search for meaning". *The Guardian.* Intl. Edition, 18 Jul 2011.

Vernon, Mark. *God.* London: Hodder Education, 2012.

Viney, Donald Wayne. Charles Hartshorne, "Dipolar Theism", *Internet Encyclopedia of Philosophy,* 1995.

Weintraub, David A. "Islam" in *Religions and Extraterrestrial Life.* New York: Springer International, 2014.

West, Darrell M. & Lansang, Christian. "Global Manufacturing Scorecard: How the US Compares to 18 other Nations". *Brookings Institute,* Center for Technology Innovation, July 10, 2018.

Whisenand, Thomas. "Oil from algae? Scientists seek green gold". The Assoc. Press, 2007.

Whitehead, Alfred North. *The Concept of Nature.* MASS: Courier Corporation, 2004.

Wigner, Eugene Paul, Mehra, Jagdish & Wightman, A. S. *Philosophical Reflections and Syntheses. Volume 7, Part B.* Berlin: Springer, 1995.

Willett, Walter C. "Balancing Lifestyle and Genomics Research for Disease Prevention". *Science* vol. 296, 26 Apr 2002.

Williams, Pete. "Looking for Meaning in all the Wrong Places". Jung Society of Atlanta, 2004.

Wilson, David S. *This View of Life: Completing the Darwinian Revolution.* New York: Random House, 2020.

Wilson, Edward O. *Consilience: The Unity of Knowledge.* New York: Vintage Press, 1999.

Wine, Sherwin T. *Judaism Beyond God: A Radical New Way to be Jewish.* Farmington Hills, Michigan: Society for Humanistic Judaism, 1985.

World Energy Outlook. International Energy Agency OECD/IEA, 2014, p.2.

World Petroleum Council: "The Oil & Gas Industry on the Edge of a Demographic Cliff". Deloitte Research, 2005.

Young, Louise R. *The Unfinished Universe.* New York: Simon and Schuster, 1986.

Zalta, Edward N. & Nodelman, Uri. (eds.) *Stanford Encyclopedia of Philosophy* (internet). "History of Trinitarian Doctrines". (no date)

Zaretsky, Adam. "Bioart In Question" (with Shannon Bell, Sam Bower, Dmitry Bulatov, George Gessert, Kathy High, Ellen K. Levy, Oron Catts, Ionat Zurr and Jennifer Willet). Discussion in *Digicult Web Magazine,* Fall 2005.

Zukav, Gary. *The Dancing Wu Li Masters: An Overview of the New Physics.* Bantam, 1980.

Index

Related Titles from Westphalia Press

The Limits of Moderation: Jimmy Carter and the Ironies of American Liberalism by Leo P. Ribuffo

The Limits of Moderation: Jimmy Carter and the Ironies of American Liberalism is not a finished product. And yet, even in this unfinished stage, this book is a close and careful history of a short yet transformative period in American political history, when big changes were afoot.

The Role of Values in Sustainability Transition: The Case of Chinese Ecological Agriculture by Yingjie Wu

In sustainability discourse, economic, social, and ecological values are frequently mentioned, with economic ones often taking precedence. This book focuses on ecological agriculture in China through the lens of values, examining the underlying motivations for practicing such agriculture.

Sinking into the Honey Trap: The Case of the Israeli-Palestinian Conflict
by Daniel Bar-Tal, Barbara Doron, Translator

Sinking into the Honey Trap by Daniel Bar-Tal discusses how politics led Israel to advancing the occupation, and of the deterioration of democracy and morality that accelerates the growth of an authoritarian regime with nationalism and religiosity.

Notes From Flyover Country: An Atypical Life & CareeS by Max J. Skidmore

In this remarkable book, Skidmore discusses his "atypical life and career," and includes work from his long life in academe. Essays deal with the principles and creation of constitutions, anti-government attitudes, the influence of language usage on politics, and church-state relations.

Stratagems of Land Warfare in the Ancient World: A Collection of Essays
by Mary Jo Davies

This collection of essays investigate warfare from the late Bronze Age of Egypt and the Near East, through the historiographic period of ancient Greece and Rome. These essays reveal the changes that took place in warfare within these eras, and illustrates the changes that took place in warfare over the course of ancient history.

Siddhartha: Life of the Buddha
by David L. Phillips,
contributions by Venerable Sitagu Sayadaw

Siddhartha: Life of the Buddha is an illustrated story for adults and children about the Buddha's birth, enlightenment and work for social justice. It includes illustrations from Pagan, Burma which are provided by Rev. Sitagu Sayadaw.

Queer Diplomacy: A Transgender Journey in the Foreign Service by Robyn McCutcheon

Join Robyn McCutcheon, an out and proud transgender woman, on her journey as a diplomat with the U.S. Department of State. Follow her on travels that took her through the Soviet Union as a historian, to the stars as an engineer in the Hubble Space Telescope project, and onward to Russia, Romania, Uzbekistan, and Kazakhstan as a Foreign Service Officer

Issues in Maritime Cyber Security
Edited by Dr. Joe DiRenzo III, Dr. Nicole K. Drumhiller, and Dr. Fred S. Roberts

The complexity of making MTS safe from cyber attack is daunting and the need for all stakeholders in both government (at all levels) and private industry to be involved in cyber security is more significant than ever as the use of the MTS continues to grow.

The French Rite: Enlightenment Culture
by Cecile Révauger

This book, focused on the French Rite, covers the founding principles of the Enlightenment and their influence on the birth of modern Freemasonry as we know it today. The authors revisit the fundamental values of the Enlightenment, from a rational approach to religious tolerance and cosmopolitanism.

Bunker Diplomacy: An Arab-American in the U.S. Foreign Service
by Nabeel Khoury

After twenty-five years in the Foreign Service, Dr. Nabeel A. Khoury retired from the U.S. Department of State in 2013 with the rank of Minister Counselor. In his last overseas posting, Khoury served as deputy chief of mission at the U.S. embassy in Yemen (2004-2007).

Managing Challenges for the Flint Water Crisis
Edited by Toyna E. Thornton, Andrew D. Williams, Katherine M. Simon, Jennifer F. Sklarew

This edited volume examines several public management and intergovernmental failures, with particular attention on social, political, and financial impacts. Understanding disaster meaning, even causality, is essential to the problem-solving process.

User-Centric Design
by Dr. Diane Stottlemyer

User-centric strategy can improve by using tools to manage performance using specific techniques. User-centric design is based on and centered around the users. They are an essential part of the design process and should have a say in what they want and need from the application based on behavior and performance.

Masonic Myths and Legends
by Pierre Mollier

Freemasonry is one of the few organizations whose teaching method is still based on symbols. It presents these symbols by inserting them into legends that are told to its members in initiation ceremonies. But its history itself has also given rise to a whole mythology.

How the Rampant Proliferation of Disinformation has Become the New Pandemic by Max Joseph Skidmore Jr.

This work examines the causes of the overwhelming tidal wave of fake news, misinformation, disinformation, and propaganda, and the increase in information illiteracy and mistrust in higher education and traditional, vetted news outlets that make fact-checking a priority

Thirst: A Story of a German ISIS Member & Her Yazidi Victim by Suzan Khairi

Through its unflinching portrayal of the Yazidi genocide and the heinous acts perpetrated by ISIS, this novel serves as a powerful reminder of the ongoing struggle for justice and the resilience of those who refuse to be silenced in the face of evil.

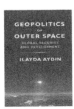

Geopolitics of Outer Space: Global Security and Development by Ilayda Aydin

A desire for increased security and rapid development is driving nation-states to engage in an intensifying competition for the unique assets of space. This book analyses the Chinese-American space discourse from the lenses of international relations theory, history and political psychology to explore these questions.

Contests of Initiative: Countering China's Gray Zone Strategy in the East and South China Seas by Dr. Raymond Kuo

China is engaged in a widespread assertion of sovereignty in the South and East China Seas. It employs a "gray zone" strategy: using coercive but sub-conventional military power to drive off challengers and prevent escalation, while simultaneously seizing territory and asserting maritime control.

Discourse of the Inquisitive Editors: Jaclyn Maria Fowler and Bjorn Mercer

Good communication skills are necessary for articulating learning, especially in online classrooms. It is often through writing that learners demonstrate their ability to analyze and synthesize the new concepts presented in the classroom.

westphaliapress.org

Policy Studies Organization Resources

The Policy Studies Organization (PSO) is a publisher of academic journals and books, sponsor of conferences, and producer of programs. There are numerous resources available for scholars, including:

Journals
Policy Studies Organization publishes dozens of journals on a range of topics:

Arts & International Affairs
Asian Politics & Policy
China Policy Journal
Digest of Middle East Studies
European Policy Analysis
Latin American Policy
Military History Chronicles
Popular Culture Review
Poverty & Public Policy
Proceedings of the PSO
Review of Policy Research
Risks, Hazards & Crisis in Public Policy
Ritual, Secrecy, & Civil Society
Saber & Scroll Historical Journal
Sculpture, Monuments, and Open Space (formerly Sculpture Review)
Sexuality, Gender & Policy
Security & Intelligence (formerly Global Security & Intelligence Studies)
Space Education and Strategic Applications
International Journal of Criminology
International Journal of Open Educational Resources
Journal on AI Policy and Complex Systems
Journal of Critical Infrastructure Policy
Journal of Indigenous Ways of Being, Knowing, and Doing
Journal of Online Learning Research and Practice

Indian Politics & Polity
Journal of Elder Studies
Policy & Internet
Policy Studies Journal
Policy Studies Yearbook
Politics & Policy
World Affairs
World Food Policy
World Medical & Health Policy
World Water Policy

Conferences

Policy Studies Organization hosts numerous conferences, including the Middle East Dialogue, Space Education and Strategic Applications, International Criminology Conference, Dupont Summit on Science, Technology and Environmental Policy, World Conference on Fraternalism, Freemasonry and History, AI – The Future of Education: Disruptive Teaching and Learning Models, Sport Management and Esport Conference, and the Internet Policy & Politics Conference. Recordings of these talks are available in the PSO Video Library.

Yearbook

The Policy Yearbook contains a detailed international listing of policy scholars with contact information, fields of specialization, research references, and an individual scholar's statements of research interests.

Curriculum Project

The Policy Studies Organization aims to provide resources for educators, policy makers, and community members, to promote the discussion and study of the various policies that affect our local and global society. Our curriculum project organizes PSO articles and other media by easily serachable themes.

For more information on these projects, access videos of past talks, and upcoming events, please visit us at:

ipsonet.org

Made in the USA
Middletown, DE
10 September 2024

60055107R00235